THE EFFECTIVE NURSE
Leader and Manager

The Effective Nurse
Leader and Manager

Laura Mae Douglass
R.N., B.A., M.S., Ph.D.

Consultant of Nursing Leadership and Management;
former Chairman, Department of Nursing,
Point Loma College, San Diego, California;
former President, California Board
of Registered Nursing;
former Nursing Education Instructor
and founder and director of RN refresher programs,
Good Samaritan Hospital, San Jose, California

FOURTH EDITION
with 65 illustrations

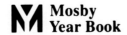
Mosby
Year Book

St. Louis   Baltimore   Boston   Chicago   London   Philadelphia   Sydney   Toronto

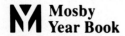

Mosby Year Book

Dedicated to Publishing Excellence

Executive Editor: N. Darlene Como
Associate Developmental Editor: Brigitte Pocta
Project Manager: Linda J. Daly
Designer: Susan Lane

FOURTH EDITION

Mosby–Year Book, Inc.
11830 Westline Industrial Drive
St. Louis, Missouri 63146

Library of Congress Cataloging-in-Publication Data

Douglass, Laura Mae.
    The effective nurse : leader, manager / Laura Mae Douglass.—4th ed.
      p. cm.
    Includes bibliographical references and index.
    ISBN 0-8016-6320-2
    1. Nursing services—Administration. 2. Leadership. I. Title.
    [DNLM: 1. Leadership. 2. Nursing, Supervisory. WY 105 D737e]
  RT89.D667 1992
  362.1′73′068--dc20
  DNLM/DLC   91-16828
  for Library of Congress   CIP

92 93 94 95 96 GW/DC/DC 9 8 7 6 5 4 3 2 1

To
My daughter **Linda** for her unconditional
love, encouragement, and help

My son **Wade** for his utmost confidence
in my ability and for the many things he has taught me

And my son-in-law **Errol** for his diligent
and expert assistance in the preparation
of the manuscript

Preface

In writing this and earlier editions of *The Effective Nurse: Leader and Manager,* I have tried to respond to two major influences. One is the continuing input from students, educators, nursing staff and nurse administrators. The other is the burgeoning volume of research, new ideas, and techniques—particularly from nursing, business administration, and the behavioral sciences—that is now being applied to leadership and management. The primary goal of this fourth edition is to present the leader and manager roles as challenging and rewarding and to provide the reader with contemporary information and tools that enable one to develop effective leadership and management skills.

The chapters have been updated, reflecting the latest in management thinking and practice in all types of health care settings, while avoiding fads. All references and bibliographies have been carefully reviewed and updated to provide guidance for further information about specific topics covered. Many examples and vignettes have been added to assist the reader in applying theory to real-life situations.

Survival as a leader and manager depends on the nurse's ability to adapt personal resources to the job situation as quickly and as effectively as possible. Some nurses are able to satisfactorily make the necessary transition from directing individual work load to directing group activities and feel good about themselves. Others are not so fortunate. Those who fail to cope with the demands of a complex situation irreparably damage their self-concepts. As a result of the frightful experience, both nurse and profession suffer loss of whatever leadership potential might have been generated.

How much better it would be if nurses were to receive preparation for the leadership position *prior to their appointment!* Nurses should be introduced to the concept of leadership and management as one of challenge and excitement, with opportunity to see what needs to be done in the interest of the consumer. They should know how to spark a group of workers into getting the job done, while understanding the theory underlying the action taken.

The effective nurse is portrayed as able to lead and to manage. Leadership and management are presented as a learned process that can become habitual with practice. To be successful a leader must have followers. The nurse leader earns the right to direct others within formal or informal situations. Managers, on the other hand, are appointed to their positions and may or may not possess leadership qualities. Effective nurses acquire skill as leaders and managers, thereby becoming able to function in the health care delivery system with assurance, knowing they are well equipped for their roles.

The book is designed to provide a practical, purposeful means of instruction. Each chapter contains (1) behavioral objectives for the major concepts included, (2) presentation of theory, (3) a summary of major ideas at the end of each chapter, (4) questions for study and discussion, (5) references cited in the chapter, and (6) suggested readings that may be used for further study. The glossary provides ready references to terms used throughout the book.

The instructor may program student activities in the classroom or learning laboratory, or students may be in command of their own learning experiences, moving at their own pace and evaluating their own progress. A further advantage to this book is that the student may complete the course of instruction at a time when the clinical assignment is not in a setting where the concepts of leadership and management can be applied. This manual allows the practitioner to reinforce learning through a systematic review of important concepts. It also provides ready reference for leaders and managers who need resource material for their practice.

Chapter 1 introduces the concepts of leadership and management at first-line, middle, and top levels, indicating similarities and differences in the roles, with emphasis on need for an effective nurse to be both a leader *and* a manager. A behavioral science approach is continued as an effective method for increasing the nurse manager's ability to provide quality care to patients and clients.

Chapter 2 reviews the styles of leadership and management used by people in authority positions. A leadership and followership test helps students to assess their own individual style. A flexible approach is taken whereby effective nurses lead and manage according to their individual style of leadership, followers' characteristics, and expectations and conditions present in the work situation.

Chapter 3 presents an overview of organizational structure in health care agencies, with focus on the decentralized approach. Discussion of magnet hospitals, and community health and home health care nursing has been added. The bureaucratic and human relations approaches to management are compared, with rationale offered for selection of an appropriate organizational structure for a health agency.

Chapter 4 examines nursing personnel and their varied roles. A discussion of role theory follows. The functional roles of nurse managers are examined. A survey of nurse population, nursing educational programs, and nurse licensure practices in the United States is given. Contemporary and expanding roles for nurses are presented including the emerging role of the nurse case manager, along with controversial issues regarding differing educational preparation.

Chapter 5 focuses on the nursing staffing process and factors that influence nurse staffing delivery systems. Staff projection, data collection, and patient classification are presented with examples of how to compute staffing needs, including use of the computer for patient classification. Systems used for the delivery of patient care are reviewed.

Also included are recruitment, selection, and placement of nursing personnel and criteria important to the staffing process. Total care, functional, team, primary, modular and nurse case management delivery systems are presented along with the advantages and disadvantages of each.

Chapter 6 discusses the planning and decision making processes and their importance for nursing managers at the top, middle, and lower or first levels. Patient care planning with standard care plans is emphasized. Included is material concerning assessment of the work situation, need identification and priority setting, management by objectives, implementation of the plan, and evaluation or control. The scientific, pragmatic and intuitive approaches to decision making are introduced along with a discussion of group decision making.

Chapter 7 concentrates on the direction-giving process utilized by the nurse manager at the lower or first level. The significance of the delegation process is considered as well as barriers to effective delegation. Numbers of nursing personnel necessary for provision of care and mix of the work group are considered, with reference to criteria and responsibilities for assurance of quality care. Detailed guides are presented for preparing assignments and worksheets and for supervising ongoing nursing activities.

Chapter 8 studies the communication process, differentiating between interpersonal and organizational communication. Guidelines for effective communication are given. An effective communication model for the nurse manager is set forth, and barriers to the communication process are identified. The informal or "grapevine" channel of communication is reviewed, identifying positive and negative features of the system. Content regarding information systems including the use of the computer has been added.

Chapter 9 recognizes the existence of conflict in all organizational settings and the importance of nurse managers developing skill in conflict resolution. The chapter considers attitudes toward conflict, kinds of conflict, consequences of conflict, the process of conflict resolution, and passive, aggressive, and assertive behaviors.

Chapter 10 considers the control process from two aspects: financial and nursing services with emphasis on the impact of third party control upon nursing. The financial control is presented under a decentralized plan, with examples of how to prepare and administer a budget. The discussion of control of nursing services provides steps necessary for task analysis and for quality control of nursing care. A section is included on performance review and controlling the problem employee.

Chapter 11 develops the logic of staff development for first-level leadership and management: management skills needed by staff nurses, how these skills are acquired, and the nurse population in need of training and development; specifically the new employee, the new graduate, and staff nurses who need preparation for the preceptor role. Knowledge important to the success of all training and development programs is reviewed—role clarification, the adult learner, the teaching-learning process, theory of group dynamics (with application to the small work group), and forces that influence change and the change process. Situations are given for individuals or groups to identify the problem and develop a plan for change. Three staff development programs are presented: orientation of the new employee, new graduate internship, and the preceptor training program. A section is included on self-learning programs, discussing methods both small and large agencies can utilize to improve and upgrade employee performance.

Chapter 12 contains two significant topics: legal and ethical issues. Legal terms important to nursing are defined, the nurse practice act is explored, and disciplinary procedure explained. The value of malpractice insurance carried by both the employer and the individual is emphasized, as well as protective measures the nurse can take to prevent personal lawsuit. The roles of a nurse as a witness in court are outlined, along with directions as to how best to defend oneself if sued. Ethical issues are presented, with case studies for consideration.

I have attempted to avoid labeling the nurse as he or she; however, when necessary, the nurse is referred to as she, recognizing that far more women than men are involved in the nursing profession.

I am especially grateful to my colleagues and the many students who have enrolled in my nursing leadership and management classes, whose probing questions, comments, and suggestions have helped me maintain interest and currency in the field of leadership and management.

I wish also to thank the nursing personnel in the clinical settings where I have taught and practiced for their generous sharing of knowledge and expertise and for being models of what an effective nurse leader and manager should be.

I want to extend a sincere thank you to Brigitte Pocta and to Darlene Como for their excellent editorial assistance throughout the preparation of this manuscript.

Laura Mae Douglass

Contents

1 Nursing Leadership and Management 1

Behavioral objectives, 1
Effective nurse leaders and managers, 2
　Leadership, 2
　Leadership process, 2
　Informal and formal leadership, 3
Influence, 3
Managerial influence, 4
Authority and power, 4
　The basis of power, 5
Management, 6
　Similarities and differences between leaders and managers, 6
　The nurse as leader and manager, 6
　Definitions of management, 6
　Management process, 6
　Organizational structure and management functions, 7
　Levels and types of managers, 8
　The nurse management process, 8
Interpersonal relationships, 9
　Behavioral science approach to management, 9
　Behavioral science approach applied to nursing management, 9
　Interdependent relationships in the management role, 11
Summary, 12
Questions for study and discussion, 13
References, 14
Suggested readings, 14

2 Styles of Leadership and Management 16

Behavioral objectives, 16
Characteristics of a leader, 17
　Trait theory, 17
　Characteristic theory, 17

Leadership style theory, 18
　Behavioral styles, 18
　Learned behavior, 20
Authoritarian, permissive, and democratic styles of leadership and management, 20
　Authoritarian style of leadership/management, 20
　Permissive, ultraliberal, or laissez-faire style of leadership, 21
　Democratic, participative, or consultive style of leadership, 22
　Comparison of styles of leadership, 23
Leadership and management by situation, 24
　Management by situation, 24
　Manager's style of leadership and expectations, 28
　Followers' characteristics and expectations, 29
　The work situation, 30
　Flexibility of managers to use various leadership styles, 31
Summary, 31
Questions for study and discussion, 32
References, 32
Suggested readings, 33

3 Organizational Structure and Mahagement Systems 34

Behavioral objectives, 34
Formal and informal structure, 35
Health care institutions and the hospital, 35
　Government-owned health agencies, 35
　Voluntary health agencies, 36
　Proprietary health agencies, 36

Community hospital mergers, 37
  Merger and the nurse manager, 37
  Health care reimbursement systems, 37
  Retrospective payment systems, 38
  Prospective payment system (PPS) di-
    agnosis-related groups (DRGs), 38
  Preferred provider organizations
    (PPOs), 39
  The Omnibus Budget Reconciliation
    Act (OBRA), 39
  Adaptations to reimbursement sys-
    tems, 39
Magnet hospitals, 39
Public health services, 40
Community health nursing, 40
Public health organizational structure, 40
Home health care/visiting nurse services,
  41
  Origin, 41
  Services provided, 41
  Organization, 42
Accreditation, 42
Organization and organizational struc-
  ture, 43
  Organization, 43
  Organizational structure, 43
Centralization, decentralization, and ma-
  trix systems, 45
  Significance of organizational charts, 46
Organizational designs, 48
  Bureaucratic approach to management,
    48
Human relations or participatory ap-
  proach to management, 50
  Human relations, 50
Adoption of an appropriate organizational
  structure and management system, 54
Summary, 55
Questions for study and discussion, 57
References, 57
Suggested readings, 58

**4 Nursing Personnel and Their Roles
60**

Behavioral objectives, 60
Roles of nursing practice, 60
  Role characteristics, 61
  The nurse's role, 61
  The nurse manager's role, 61
Nurse licensure, 61
Nurse population, 62
Foreign nurse licensure, 63
Nursing education, 63

Nursing schools: number and types, 63
  Enrollment upswing in basic nursing
    education, 65
  Enrollment upswing in RNs returning
    to BSN programs and to graduate
    education, 65
Technical versus professional nursing
  practice (AD versus BN), 65
  Arenas, not levels, of practice, 66
Certification programs, 66
Scope of RN practice, 66
  Staff nurse, 67
  Critical care nurse (CCN), 67
  Clinical nurse specialist/nurse clinician
    (CNS/NC), 67
  Operating room nurse (ORN), 68
  Community health nurse, 68
  Community health/public health nurse
    (PHN), 69
  Home health care nurse/visiting nurse,
    69
  Nurse practitioner (NP), 70
  Nurse midwife, 70
  Occupational health nurse (OHN), 71
  School nurse, 71
  Professional nurse case manager
    (PNCM), 71
  Licensed practical nurses/licensed vo-
    cational nurses and other categories
    of nurse caregivers, 72
  Assistive nursing personnel, 72
  Need for the nurse assistant (NA), 72
Summary, 73
Questions for study and discussion, 75
References, 75
Suggested readings, 76

**5 Staffing Process and Nursing Care
Delivery Systems 78**

Behavioral objectives, 78
Nurse supply, 78
Nurse turnover, 79
RN work priorities, 79
Graduating seniors' priorities, 79
Salaries for experienced nurses, 79
Salaries for new graduates, 80
Employment procedures, 80
  Recruitment, 80
  Employers' recruitment strategies, 80
  Experienced nurses, 80
  Registry nurses, 81
  Responsibility for selection of nursing
    personnel, 81

Induction and orientation, 82
Criteria important to the staffing process, 83
    Typical performance responsibilities for a primary care nurse, 83
    Typical performance responsibilities for a clinical nurse specialist in a middle management role, 84
Staffing process, 84
    Data collection, 84
    Patient classification systems, 85
    Staff mix, 86
    Staff scheduling, 86
Nursing care delivery systems, 88
    Need for an effective contemporary nursing care delivery system, 88
    Total care nursing, 91
    Functional nursing, 91
    Team nursing, 92
    Primary nursing, 94
    Modular nursing, 96
    Nursing case management, 96
Summary, 98
Questions for study and discussion, 100
References, 100
Suggested readings, 101

6 Planning and Decision Making: Fundamental Processes 103

Behavioral objectives, 103
Scope of planning, 104
    Top-level managers, 105
    Middle-level managers, 105
    Lower- or first-level managers, 105
Decision-making process, 107
    Variables present in decision making, 107
    Decision-making styles, 110
    Group decision making, 115
Management by objectives, 116
    Goals and objectives, 116
    Process of management by objectives, 116
    Guidelines for management by objectives, 116
    Management by objectives in nursing management, 117
Implementation of the plan, 119
    Developing alternative courses of action, 119
    Nursing care planning, 119

Evaluation or controlling the plan, 121
    Results of evaluation or control process, 121
Summary, 121
Questions for study and discussion, 123
References, 123
Suggested readings, 124

7 Direction 125

Behavioral objectives, 125
Size and mix of the work group: span of management, 126
    Factors influencing number of workers and span of control, 126
    Criteria for assurance of quality care, 127
    Physical support system, 128
Significance of the delegation process, 128
    Barriers to delegation, 128
Responsibilities of direction giving, 129
    Guidelines for implementation of responsibility, 129
Summary, 147
Questions for study and discussion, 149
References, 149
Suggested readings, 150

8 Communication Process 151

Behavioral objectives, 151
Importance of the communication process, 152
Guidelines for effective communication, 153
    Communication model, 153
Barriers to effective communication, 157
    Physical barriers, 157
    Social-psychologic barriers, 158
    Semantics, 159
Informal communication—the grapevine, 161
    Process, 161
    Utilization of the grapevine, 161
Management functions and communications, 162
    Downward communication, 162
    Upward communication, 162
    Horizontal communication, 162
Assessing organizational communication, 163

Information management, 164
   Nurse utilization of computers, 164
   Introducing nurses to computers, 165
   Computers and the future, 165
Summary, 166
Questions for study and discussion, 167
References, 168
Suggested readings, 168

9 Conflict Resolution 169

Behavioral objectives, 169
Attitudes toward conflict, 170
Kinds of conflict, 170
   Conflict within an individual, 170
   Conflict between health organizations, 171
   Conflict within health organizations—interpersonal and intergroup, 171
Consequences of conflict, 172
Conflict resolution, 173
   Competition/power, 174
   Smoothing, 175
   Avoidance, 175
   Compromise, 175
   Collaboration, 176
Passive, aggressive, and assertive behaviors, 177
   Passive behavior, 178
   Aggressive behavior, 178
   Assertive behavior, 178
Summary, 179
Questions for study and discussion, 180
References, 180
Suggested readings, 181

10 Control 182

Behavioral objectives, 182
The impact of third-party control on nursing, 183
Control process, 183
   Financial control system; 184
Centralized budgeting, 184
Decentralized budgeting, 184
Types of budgets, 184
   Operating budget, 185
   Capital expenditure budget, 185

   Personnel budget, 185
Preparation of the budget, 186
   Participants review agency policies, standards, and objectives, 186
   Top-level projections and guidelines, 186
   Preparation of budget by middle-level managers, 187
   Review of budget by administrator of nursing services and controller, 189
   Acceptance or modification, 189
   Implementation with biweekly, monthly, and annual review, with modification and changes as necessary, 189
Nursing services control system, 189
   Establishing standards for measuring performance, 189
   Establishing methods for measuring performance, 191
   Measuring actual performance, 191
   Comparing results of performance with standards and objectives, 192
   Reinforcing strengths or successes and taking corrective action as necessary, 192
Task analysis and quality control of nursing care, 192
   Task analysis, 192
   Quality control, 192
Performance appraisal, 196
   Nurse manager's responsibility, 196
   Historical events in the development of performance appraisal, 196
   Components of an effective nursing performance appraisal system, 200
   Methods of measuring performance, 201
Performance review session, 203
   Purpose, 203
   Process, 203
Controlling the problem employee, 204
   Progressive discipline policy and procedure, 205
Summary, 206
Questions for study and discussion, 208
References, 208
Suggested readings, 209

11 Staff Training and Development 210

Behavioral objectives, 210
Importance of training and development, 210
Training and development function, 211
Management skills needed by staff nurses, 211
   Technical skill, 211
   Human skill, 212
   Conceptual skill, 212
   Diagnostic skill, 212
   Coach and mentor skill, 213
How management skills are acquired, 213
   Education, 213
   Experience, 213
   Mentor or preceptor relationships, 214
Nurse population in need of training and development, 214
   The new graduate, 214
   The new employee, 215
   Staff nurses, 215
Concepts important to the success of all training and development programs, 215
   Role clarification, 215
   Teaching and learning process, 217
   Group dynamics, 221
Change process, 223
   Forces that influence change, 223
   Change process: a planned procedure, 224
   Steps in change process, 224
Examples of orientation and staff development programs, 229
   General orientation program, 229
   Nurse internship for the new graduate, 230
   Preceptor workshop, 232
   Self-learning programs, 233
Summary, 234
Questions for study and discussion, 235
References, 235
Suggested readings, 236

12 Legal and Ethical Issues 238

Behavioral objectives, 238
Legal issues, 238
   Importance of law to the nurse, 238
Law in the practice of nursing, 239
Nurse licensure, 240
The nurse practice act, 240
Board of nurse examiners, 242
Nursing risk management, 243
Nurse liability for short-staffing situations, 244
Malpractice insurance for nurses, 244
   Employer coverage, 244
   Nurse coverage, 244
   Statute of limitations, 244
   Avoiding lawsuits, 245
   Accountability, 245
   Proper documentation, 245
   Transcribing orders, 245
   Physician's orders: in person or over the phone, 246
   When an order is questionable, 246
   Honest mistakes, 246
   Documentation for someone else, 246
   Falsifying records, 246
The nurse as a witness, 247
   The nurse as an expert witness, 247
Good Samaritan laws, 248
Nurses' responsibility in an emergency, 248
   Breach of duty, 248
Guidelines for nurses who are sued, 248
Doctrine of sovereign immunity, 249
Contracts for nurses, 249
   Types of contracts, 249
   Breach of contract, 250
Ethical issues, 250
   Patients' rights, 250
   Ethics committees, 250
   Wills: the nurse's responsibility, 251
   Policy considerations related to AIDS, 253
   Protection of civil rights: defamation of character, 253
   Ethical dilemmas in nursing practice, 253
Summary, 254
Questions for study and discussion, 256
References, 256
Suggested readings, 257

Glossary, 259

THE EFFECTIVE NURSE
Leader and Manager

1

Nursing Leadership and Management

_____ **BEHAVIORAL OBJECTIVES** _____
On completion of this chapter the student will be prepared to:

☐ Define the leadership process and differentiate between formal and informal leadership.
☐ Explain the significance of managerial influence and identify ways of application.
☐ Identify the relationship among authority, power, and ability and relate it to leadership and management.
☐ Differentiate between the terms *leadership* and *management*.
☐ Define the management process.
☐ State the primary purpose of organizational structure.
☐ Apply the behavioral science approach to nursing management.

Most of the readers of this book will spend a good part of their lives working in health care organizations, either as staff nurses or in other positions of responsibility. Whatever the role, all nurses lead and manage to some degree. In the business world the first task of employees is usually to learn to be successful subordinates. Before they are promoted to the role of leaders/managers, they must first prove they are capable of subjecting themselves to the will and direction of others. The very nature of the role of nurse, however, requires leadership/management from the first day of employment. Nursing is a decision-making process in which the nurse helps the patient/client to reach a state of optimal health. In the process the nurse assesses a need or problem, formulates plans for nursing action, implements the plans, and evaluates the procedure. Further, nurses accomplish goals for nursing care through the help of others, in agencies of every size and type, and using whatever system for delivery of quality nursing care is in effect. To accomplish these demanding tasks, nurses must be leaders and managers.

Regrettably, too few nurses have the preparation necessary to meet the challenge of leadership and management, thus hindering the provision of quality care. Inexperienced nurses who expect themselves to be able to function competently in the leadership/management role without further education or practice may discover that they are not able to do so.

This book is based on the belief that an understanding of the leadership and management process will help nurses to value themselves as leaders and managers and to acquire the knowledge and skills necessary to be responsible leaders and managers in all nursing settings.

EFFECTIVE NURSE LEADERS AND MANAGERS

Many nurses believe that to be effective, a leader needs to be superhuman. Nurses and other health care professionals have many realistic and unrealistic expectations of the nurse who aspires to this role. Important concepts to remember are that leadership can be an exciting experience and that leadership/management is a *learned* process. To be successful, potential nurse leaders/managers begin their preparation for the role with the expectation that they are capable of becoming effective leaders/managers.

To perform well as a leader/manager, the nurse must identify individual strengths, weaknesses, and potential (or capacities); acquire knowledge of the theory and practice of leadership and management; and use self systematically to get the right things done at the right time (see formula below).

Some leaders/managers fail because they fear responsibility. Others fail for lack of preparation to cope with the complexities of the role. By gaining understanding of the leadership/management process, nurses can function in the health care setting with assurance, knowing they have equipped themselves for the role. This chapter introduces the concepts of leadership and management, differentiating between them, with application of merging concepts to nursing practice in any setting.

Leadership

The word *leadership* is an intriguing one, conjuring up images of all kinds of people. Immediately, certain names come to mind— Confucius, Plato, Abraham Lincoln, John F. Kennedy, Martin Luther King. One may think of a relative or teacher who had a noticeable effect on one's life. In nursing, who would not name Florence Nightingale if asked for a single example of a leader in the profession? There is something special about a leader that distinguishes that person from all others.

Leadership is present in any group of people, regardless of age or setting, in normal times or in times of crisis. Watch children play; a leader soon emerges. The same pattern occurs in all life situations—in games, clubs, committees, political parties, religious bodies, and all social and work groups. Some persons rise to the position of leader, whereas others want to follow their direction.

Leadership Process

Leadership is "the use of one's skills to influence others to perform to the best of their ability."[1,p.210] Leadership, or the exercise of power and influence, involves one individual trying to change the behavior of other individuals.[1,p.211]

Nursing leadership is the process whereby a nurse influences one or more persons to achieve specific goals in the provision of nursing care for one or more patients/clients. Successful nursing leadership depends on a relationship that is mutually stimulating for leader and followers. To be a leader, one *must have followers.* Leadership requires one or more persons willing to be led. The leader's behavior is crucial, since the degree to which group objectives are understood and accepted strongly affects the quality and quantity of work performance. Keith Davis, noted management expert, comments: "Leadership transforms the potential of machines and people into reality of organization."[2] An effective leader, then, has the ability and the power to guide one or more persons toward achieving single or multiple goals.

A leader is able to command the trust, commitment, and loyalty of followers. Most work is done by ordinary people. Many of these people are leaders who take responsibility for reaching group goals. A leader is the person who communicates ideas to others and influences their behavior to achieve an objective. The dy-

| Understanding of individual strengths, weaknesses, and potential | + | Knowledge of basic ingredients for leadership and management | + | Systematic use of self to get the right things done at the right time | = | Effective leadership and management |

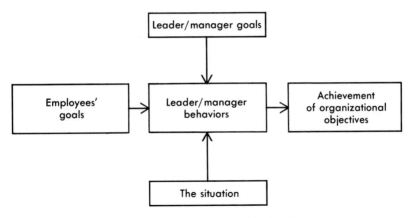

Figure 1-1. The dynamics of leadership.

namics of leadership include the leader, the follower(s), and the specific situation (Figure 1-1).

Informal and Formal Leadership

There are two types of leaders: formal and informal. The *formal* or appointed leader is chosen by administration and given official or legitimate authority to act. Formal power has its greatest impact when the followers accept the leader and the members work positively toward goal accomplishment. An *informal* leader does not have official sanction to direct the activities of others. Informal leaders can play a valuable role in organizations if their behavior and influence are congruent with the goals of the organization. If the informal leader influences the other workers to perform their work more efficiently and effectively, then he or she is acting in support of the organization's purposes. An informal leader is chosen by the group itself, as in a social group, church organization, political party, or work group. Leaders of informal groups usually become leaders because of age, seniority, special competencies, or an inviting personality. Informal leaders can extend their influence over several groups, or they may be looked to for guidance on matters pertaining to only one specific competency. Some informal leaders are recognized for their ability to communicate with and counsel others.[2]

There are positive and negative ramifications of informal leadership in work situations. In hospitals, for example, a nursing group may go through the motions of accepting the leadership of the formally appointed team leader and look for sanction to act from another, thus creating conflict and confusion. Or this same group may accept orders from the team leader and have these orders reinforced by a team member who is highly supportive of the team leader. The ideal situation is for the person who has been appointed formal leader to function in such a way that all members of the work group will want to be influenced by that person.

Nursing leadership most commonly occurs in formal, organized settings, such as in hospitals, public health departments, and clinics, where the nurse is officially sanctioned to practice.

INFLUENCE

Influence is any attempt by an individual to change the behavior of others; influence is not inherently good or bad. Researchers have identified specific kinds of influence. Eight different influence actions have been delineated[3]:

1. *Assertiveness.* Sending direct messages to others; standing up for oneself and one's rights without violating the rights of others.
2. *Ingratiation.* Making an individual feel important or good before making a request; acting humble or friendly before making a request.
3. *Rationality.* Trying to convince someone by relying on a detailed plan, supporting information, reasoning, or logic.
4. *Sanctions.* Giving or preventing pay increases or promotions; promising extra benefits.
5. *Exchange.* Offering an exchange of favors; reminding a worker of a past favor; offering to make a personal sacrifice.

6. *Upward appeal*. Obtaining formal or informal support of a higher-up; sending someone to see the next person in authority.
7. *Blocking*. Backing up a request with a threat to damage an individual's opportunity for advancement; threatening to stop working with someone; ignoring or not being friendly with a person until he or she gives in to a request.
8. *Coalitions*. Getting co-workers to back up a request; having someone attend a conference at which a request is made.

Researchers have found that there is no difference between the tactics used by male and female employees. Influence tactics vary according to different leadership styles. Employees wishing to influence authorization managers generally rely on ingratiation, upward appeal, and blocking. Rationality is used most often to sway participative managers.

MANAGERIAL INFLUENCE

The term *managerial influence* implies a host of managerial actions, such as motivation, power, leadership, and behavior modification. Although the results may be the same, each of these various influence processes works in a different way. Consider the actions of Teresa Beckers, newly appointed nurse manager, who was given the administrative position with the expectation that she "turn things around." The nursing unit had recently been operating haphazardly, with people coming and going pretty much as they desired. As a result, more nurses' auxilliary staff than usual were required to provide even minimal care.

EXAMPLE: Teresa made a concerted effort to become acquainted with every staff member, indicating she was interested in each as an individual. She met with all members in small groups, letting them know that she was the new manager and as such expected certain consistencies and behaviors (showing deference to the manager, reporting for work on time, taking breaks according to schedule, working for the provision of quality care, and so on). She explained the importance of compliance (to achieve efficiency and effectiveness), indicating that positive results would lead to job satisfaction and possible advancement, whereas failure to comply would lead to disciplinary action, even dismissal.[4,pp.505-506]

In terms of the eight influence tactics just discussed, nurse manager Teresa relied on ingratiation (showing concern for workers), assertiveness (outlining expectations), rationality (explaining the importance of changes), and sanctions (describing the results of choices). In all probability, most of the influence tactics will come into play, to some degree, before a nursing unit runs smoothly. Because influence is such a fundamental part of effective management, leaders and managers need as many techniques as possible at their command. In nurse manager Teresa's case, she must continue the process of influencing for some time before optimum functioning of the unit is achieved.

AUTHORITY AND POWER

Leadership and management in an organization inevitably require authority and power to influence the thoughts and actions of other people. *Authority* is the legitimate right to give commands, to act in the interest of an organization. Authority is an officially sanctioned responsibility. *Power* is the ability to organize human informational and material resources to accomplish a task. Power is central to the leadership process in the development of a manager's self-confidence and willingness to support staff members.[5,p.468] From this vantage, power should be accepted as a natural part of any organization. Power is not evenly distributed among individuals or groups; however, every individual has some degree of power. Nurse managers have a responsibility to recognize and develop their own power to coordinate and uphold the work of staff members. Nurse managers who understand power, its bases, and its responsibilities are in an advantageous position for getting things done through others.

Power affects organizations in the following ways:

Decisions.

EXAMPLE: A primary nurse decides to sign up to care for more critical patients after hearing her nurse manager's suggestion that she extend herself.

It influences behavior.

EXAMPLE: An LPN achieves a month of perfect attendance after receiving verbal and written warnings about absenteeism from his nurse manager.

It changes situations.

EXAMPLE: The productivity of a nursing station increases dramatically following the installation of computerized work stations.

Note the word *ability* in the definition of *power.* Authority is the right to direct the activities of others. Authority, although an officially sanctioned privilege, may or may not get results. Power, on the other hand, is the demonstrated ability to get results. As illustrated in Figure 1-2, a nurse may at one time possess authority but have no power, or possess both authority and power. The first situation—having authority but no power—occurred in one hospital where staff nurses refused to follow the nurse manager's example in caring for AIDS patients. Power without authority can occur, for example, when a staff member responds to the wishes of a visitor to bring in pets, a practice not condoned by the agency. Finally, a nurse manager who gets her staff to work dilligently on a special research project has both authority and power.

The Basis of Power

It is important for the nurse manager to understand that power to influence can originate from a variety of sources. One of the most widely used descriptions of organizational power was proposed by French and Raven[6] who list five different forms of power a leader / manager may possess:

1. *Legitimate power* is given to the manager by the organization because of the manager's position in the hierarchy. The organization usually sanctions this form of power by titles such as director of nurses, supervisor, clinical coordinator, head nurse, or team leader.
2. *Reward power* is based on the ability of the manager to control and administer rewards to others (such as promotions and praise) for compliance with the leader's orders or requests.
3. *Coercive power* is founded on fear, depending on the manager's ability to use punishment of others (such as reprimands, isolation, and blaming) for noncompliance with the manager's orders.
4. *Expert power* is derived from some special ability, skill, or knowledge demonstrated by the individual. For example, the only nurse who knows how to operate the kidney dialysis machine may use that expertise to influence the schedules of others.
5. *Referent power* can be shown in at least two forms in an organization. First, it can be based on a certain attractiveness or appeal of one person to another. *Charisma* is a term frequently used in conjunction with referent power. The nurse who is consistently supportive, helpful, and empathetic of others, for example, may be able to influence others easily to agree with her views. Referent power may also be based on a person's connection or relationship with another powerful individual. For example, the assistant to the director of nurses may be seen by an aspiring nurse to have much influence with the director, and therefore the assistant's referent position has great power over that nurse.

Legitimate, reward, and coercive power are given to the manager by the organization and are based on the control of important organi-

Authority but no power	Authority plus power	Power but no authority
The nurse has the right but not the ability to get the job done.	The nurse has the right and the ability to get the job done.	The nurse has the ability but not the right to get the job done.

Figure 1-2. The relationships among authority, power, and ability.

zational resources. Expert and to some extent referent power are based on the characteristics of the individual and may or may not be given by the organization. The ability to influence others is founded on the strength of the leader's or manager's power base. A manager who functions with all five power factors is in the best position to influence workers. Such a situation may be more ideal than real, however. Most leaders find themselves in managerial situations in which they must influence with a limited power base.

> EXAMPLE: Primary nurse Peters has become quite expert in oncology care. For 3 years she has worked part-time while attending the local university to earn a degree in her field of interest. She applies what she has learned to care giving. Returning patients often ask for her to be assigned to them again.
>
> Because she is recognized as an expert, her requests for modification of patient care and special supplies and equipment are rewarded and her suggestions and proposals are put into effect.

MANAGEMENT
Similarities and Differences between Leaders and Managers

Although leadership and management are closely related, they are not identical. A leader may or may not have official appointment or power to lead, whereas a manager is the person who has been appointed to a particular position in the organizational structure and therefore has the power to implement that process of guiding and directing the work of others according to predetermined policies.

Leaders and managers may differ in the concept of their roles. Managers develop through the work of others, whereas leaders depend on inner qualities for personal growth. Managers are interested in maintaining routine and order in a controlled and rational structure, whereas leaders are often interested in risk taking and in exploring new avenues or ways of doing things. Managers tend to treat workers according to their role in the work place (e.g., aide, LVN, head nurse), whereas leaders interact with others as people, considering feelings empathetically. The box below presents a summary of the similarities and differences between leaders and managers.

The Nurse as Leader and Manager

Most nurses have grown accustomed to leading and managing their activities as students and then in professional practice by assuming leadership for the management of their individual work loads and providing nursing care for their patients / clients. Some have consciously applied the management process to their practice; others have acquired managerial skills through trial and error. Effective nurses are those who blend

---

Similarities and Differences between Leaders and Managers
the effective nurse blends the roles

Leaders	Managers
May or may not have official appointment to the position	Are appointed officially to the position
Have power and authority to enforce decisions only so long as followers are willing to be led	Have power and authority to enforce decisions
Influence others toward goal setting, either formally or informally	Carry out predetermined policies, rules, and regulations
Interested in risk taking and exploring new ideas	Maintain an orderly, controlled, rational, and equitable structure
Relate to people personally in an intuitive and empathetic manner	Relate to people according to their roles
Feel rewarded by personal achievements	Feel rewarded when fulfilling organizational mission or goals
May or may not be successful as managers	Are managers as long as the appointment holds

the qualities of both leader and manager, who have followers willing to be influenced by them, and who understand and apply the principles of management to practice.

Definitions of Management

No single definition of management has been universally accepted. Some popular definitions are: "Management is the process of working with and through others to achieve organizational objectives in a changing environment"[4,p.9]; "management is the process of obtaining and organizing resources and of achieving objectives through other people, management is dynamic rather than static"[5,p.27]; "management is planning, directing, coordinating and controlling, including leadership, giving direction, developing staff, monitoring operations, giving rewards fairly and representing both staff members and administration as needed"[7,pp.99-100]; and "management is the process of getting work done through others. Nursing management is the process of working through nursing staff members to provide care, cure and comfort to patients."[8,p.1]

Management Process

The following definition will be used as a basis for discussion of the management process: *The management process consists of achieving organizational objectives through planning, organizing, directing, and controlling human and physical resources and technology.* Management is the art of getting things done through other people. Managers achieve organizational objectives by arranging for others to do things, not by performing all the tasks themselves. A team leader, for example, would assign the work group to care for patients, run errands, be on call for an emergency, and go to lunch at specific times.

The management process can be applied to nursing management as shown in Figure 1-3. Nursing management can be viewed as a relationship of inputs and outputs in which the workers (all members of the health care organization), physical resources, and technology (including buildings, grounds, supplies, and equipment) are merged to bring about the organizational goals for delivery of quality nursing care.

Organizational Structure and Management Functions

When nurses become leaders of formal work groups, they are primarily concerned with carrying forth objectives for the nursing care of a prescribed number of patients/clients. However, all activities are accomplished in an organized structure that provides necessary control. *Organizational structure* is a mechanism through which work is arranged and distributed among the members of the organization so that the goals of the organization can logically be achieved. Most hospitals, for example, function in a highly organized, bureaucratic structure in which control comes from the top down, and

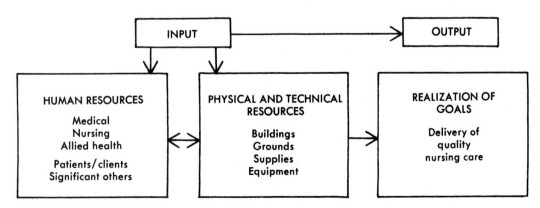

Figure I-3. Planning, organizing, directing, and controlling through human and physical resources for goal realization.

lines of authority are spelled out in detail (e.g., board of directors to director of nursing services to supervisors to head nurses to team leaders to staff nurses and so on.) The most common means of informing nursing personnel of structure is through policies and procedures manuals. An example of structure in nursing is the system used to provide nursing care, such as team nursing, functional nursing, and primary care nursing.

Levels and Types of Managers

Different levels and types of managers are typically found in health organizations. Nurse managers are usually classified by their level in an agency and by their responsibilities. Table 1 shows the basic level of nurse managers.

This book is primarily for first-line managers. Therefore middle and top managers will be discussed only as their roles affect the first-line manager.

The Nurse Management Process

Successful management involves active participation by managers in the four basic managerial functions: planning, organizing, directing, and controlling. These functions are interrelated, and most nurse managers use the components simultaneously to solve problems.

As Figure 1-4 indicates, the nursing management process carried out within the organization structure on a cyclic or continuous basis. First, managers *plan* or focus on deciding what to do. The planning process provides the framework for performance. At this stage, for example, the team leader of a group of nursing personnel would be concerned with the numbers and kinds of patients to be cared for, the

◇ **Table I.** Nurse managers and their responsibilities

LEVEL	RESPONSIBILITY
Top managers	Responsible for the overall operations of nursing services; establish objectives, policies, and strategies; represent the organization in community affairs, business arrangements, and negotiations; typical titles: director of nursing services, chairman, executive vice president
Middle managers	Usually coordinate the nursing activities of several units; receive broad, overall strategies and policies from top managers and translate them into specific objectives and programs; typical titles: supervisor, coordinator
First-line managers	Directly responsible for the actual production of nursing services; act as links between higher level managers and nonmanagers; typical titles: head nurse, team leader, primary care nurse

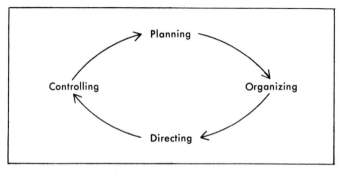

Figure I-4. The nursing management process.

qualifications of the nursing staff to provide that care, the geographical location of the patients, and the physical resources available to get the job done.

Second, the nurse manager must decide how to do it; in other words she must *organize* to establish order and to systematically achieve the goals for provision of care. At this stage the team leader would establish authority to act and responsibility and accountability relationships, informing each person of her assignment.

Third, the nurse manager *directs* performance. In essence she focuses on leading nursing staff in the most effective manner possible. At this point in the management process, the team leader concentrates on how the assignments are being accomplished—on skills, members' knowledge of what they are doing, member motivation, and interpersonal relationships. The team leader examines her own leadership style as it relates to goal achievement.

Fourth, managers *control* or evaluate performance against established standards of performance. This function involves evaluating individual and group performance; examining indicators of effectiveness and efficiency through patients / clients and services rendered; and investigating problems that may have developed in communication, resource allocation, and interpersonal relationships.

Finally, attention is given to *what needs to be changed*. All activities of the management process—planning, organizing, directing, and controlling—are examined to determine what factors or activities may or may not need correction or change so that goals are achieved. The change component generally occurs in each of the four management functions and therefore is not considered as a separate entity. Nurse manager activities are presented in more detail throughout the remainder of the book.

INTERPERSONAL RELATIONSHIPS

In the theory of management much is said about establishing surroundings that promote effective leadership and management. The importance of organizational structure, tasks to be accomplished, and persons and resources to do the job are discussed. But the secret of successful leadership and management lies in attention given to the interpersonal relationships that af-

fect goal attainment. An environment in which individuals working together can perform well must be established and maintained.

Behavioral Science Approach to Management

Maneck Wadia, management consultant and educator, has developed a conceptual framework for management in which he incorporates the behavioral sciences into the management processes of planning, organizing, directing, and controlling.[9] He believes it is important for the manager to understand psychology (study of human behavior), sociology (study of group behavior in modern society), and cultural anthropology (study of effects of culture on human behavior). Managers who know how individuals generally behave, why they behave as they do, and the relationships between human behavior and the environment are better equipped to function in their roles.

Behavioral Science Approach Applied to Nursing Management

Nurses have a great need to understand and apply behavioral sciences to nursing practice both in the care of patients / clients and in leadership and management. Part of Wadia's concepts are adapted for application to nursing management, as shown in Figure 1-5. A series of circles are given. The lower half of the diagram constitutes the objectives the nurse manager needs to obtain; the upper half of the diagram represents the framework within which nursing objectives are achieved. Giving attention to the center circle, one can say that an individual staff member needs to be satisfied so that he or she will work well in a group. It is important to understand human needs and the way they operate to have individual satisfaction. Nurse managers are greatly involved in leading small groups of patients / clients and nursing personnel in the delivery of care; they need to understand behavior to be aware of the constantly changing needs. Chapter 3 provides further discussion of human needs, pointing out Maslow's theory that until the individual (or lower order) needs are met, other higher order needs cannot be addressed.[10]

As depicted in the second circle in Figure 1-5, the nursing group must be motivated to work together successfully, since motivation is

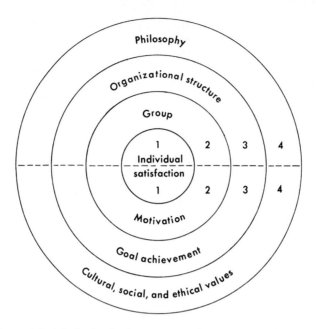

Figure 1-5. A behavioral science approach to nursing management.

closely related to satisfaction and productivity. Most workers seek and find some satisfaction in their jobs. This is particularly true of nurses, as they often enter and remain in the nursing profession because of a desire to serve others in close, personal ways. Evidence shows that individuals are motivated most successfully when a group approach is used by management. Likert, a noted sociologist, makes the following statement: "Every human being earnestly seeks a friendly and supportive relationship and one that gives him a sense of personal worth in the face-to-face groups most important to him."[11] The whole area of group dynamics takes on a significant role for the nurse manager, for if ignored too long, nursing staff will begin to look to sources outside assigned work groups to find fulfillment of individual and group needs.

The third circle in the conceptual scheme for nursing management considers goal achievement and organizational structure. A nurse manager is constantly aware that goal achievement is the primary reason for existence of any organization. A health care organization attempts to establish efficient and effective rela-

tionship among work, individuals, and the setting in which quality nursing care can be delivered. Overall goals are developed for short- and long-term operation, with specific goals developed at different levels in the organization. All goals must be compatible with the organization and the individuals comprising it; hence the inclusion of circles 1 and 2 (individuals and groups) in consideration of structure and goals. The degree of goal achievement in any level affects the degree of goal achievement in any other level.

The fourth or outer circle takes into account cultural, social, and ethical values as they relate to the philosophy of the organization. *Philosophy* in this scheme means the sense of purpose and reasoning behind organizational structure and goals. Health care institutions, whether they be hospitals, clinics, or any other type of facility, have as their primary reason for existence the function of providing the gamut of patient/client services.[12,p.2] These services may include diagnostic, therapeutic (both surgical and nonsurgical), preventive, health promotion, personnel education, and research services. The emphasis given to these various functions varies from agency to agency, depending largely on the people served, the geographical location, and the basic mission of the particular agency.

A *philosophy or mission of nursing service* should closely parallel the philosophy or mission of the agency served. Nursing philosophy or mission may be described as an intentionally chosen set of values or purposes that serves as the basis for determining the means to accomplish nursing objectives. Nursing philosophy is broad and general in terminology (wording), yet directs nursing behavior, giving it a sense of purpose. It goes beyond the everyday routine to look at the ultimate purpose for doing the work.[7,p.52] Areas generally emphasized in a statement of nursing philosophy are quality, quantity, and scope of service; decision making based on factual information; appropriate delegation (giving authority and responsibility at the lowest possible organizational level); achievement of organizational goals; effective communication both vertically and laterally; and flexibility to meet and adapt to the changing needs of the organization, individuals, community, and society in general.

Values refers to beliefs that are important to an individual. Defined broadly, values are abstract ideals that shape an individual's thinking and behavior.[12,p.238]

All values are influenced by (1) *culture,* or the customs and behavioral patterns in existence; (2) *social factors,* or the composition and practices of work groups, and (3) *ethics,* or beliefs about moral principles and standards governing the conduct of workers in a profession. In American culture the ultimate values are generalized as freedom, opportunity, self-realization, and human dignity.[13] These values assume a respect for the rights of others, a concern for justice and order under law, and a responsibility for maintaining and perpetuating systems that make this freedom possible.

Some of the values and assumptions underlying the health care and nursing scene include the beliefs (1) that nurses have the power to shape the kind of future they want if they accept the responsibility for making things happen, (2) that nurses need a vision of the way they would like society to be, (3) that nurses have the ca-

pacity to adapt to change, and (4) that nurses need to believe in a future they can affirm and be realistic about positive and negative forces.[12]

At the departmental level, one of the manager's roles is to manage the culture, social factors, and ethics of the nursing staff. High quality patient care is the traditional and expected outcome to be achieved through individual staff members. Collectively, their shared values, beliefs, and aspirations form the culture that gives the nursing unit its character. The nursing department's culture can be likened to a security blanket for the staff. The members' collective values concerning care determine the lengths to which they will go to achieve them. Knowing staff members' aspirations, the department manager can align them with the mission and goals of the agency and use staff members' values to enrich departmental operations.[14]

In the conceptual scheme presented for nursing management (see Figure 1-5) each smaller circle is part of the larger one, and all areas affect one another. Thus the individual is part of the group, and both the individual and group are part of the organization. The organization affects goal achievement, which in turn is influenced by the philosophy and values held by the organization and its personnel. Depending on the emphasis, a nurse manager could look at these circles from the inside out, from outside in, or from any other point of view. Nurse managers at the direct care giving level are most apt to be concerned primarily with the lower half of the circles, constituting goal achievement; however, they need to be aware of the interrelationships.

Interdependent Relationships in the Management Role

As discussed, management is considered a process, with consideration given to the many factors that may influence the process. Figure 1-6 illustrates the interdependent relationships that exist. The organizational structure, authority and power, management process, resources available, and behavioral components each have a bearing on the other. The effectiveness of the leader / manager depends on her knowledge and ability to function within this framework.

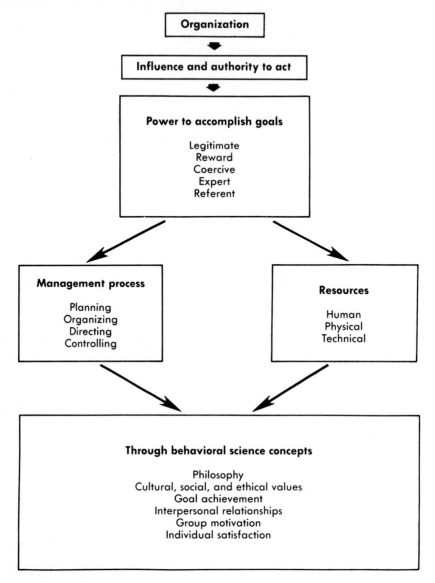

Figure 1-6. The framework for nursing management.

SUMMARY

1. All nurses lead and manage to some degree.
2. Leadership/management is a learned process.
3. A leader can lead only as long as there are followers; a manager has official power to act and may or may not possess leadership qualities.
4. The dynamics of leadership include the leader, the follower(s), and the specific situations.
5. A formal leader is one appointed by administration and given authority to act; an informal leader influences others to act without official sanction.
6. Influence is any attempt by an individual to change behavior of others. This can be accomplished through assertiveness, ingratia-

tion, rationality, sanctions, exchange, upward appeal, blocking, and coalitions.

7. Managerial influence includes motivation, power, leadership, and behavior modification.

8. Authority and power are necessary to achieve organizational goals. Authority is the legitimate right to give commands; power is the ability to influence another through the control over needed resources.

9. There are five different forms of power: legitimate, reward, coercive, expert, and referent. Ideally, the effective nurse uses all five; however, in bureaucratic organizations the nurse functioning in middle- or lower-level positions may not be able to use all forms and may need to consider alternative ways to achieve power.

10. The management process consists of achieving organizational goals through planning, organizing, directing, and controlling human and physical resources. Successful management is evidenced by efficient work output and satisfying human interactions.

11. Nursing management depends on the interrelationships among organizational structure, tasks to be accomplished, and workers and resources to do the job.

12. Three levels and types of managers are typically found in a health agency: *top managers* (who are responsible for overall operations), *middle managers* (who coordinate nursing activities of several units), and *first-line managers* (who are directly responsible for the actual production of nursing services).

13. Behavioral sciences incorporate knowledge of psychology (study of human behavior), sociology (study of group behavior in modern society), and cultural anthropology (study of effects of culture or socially transmitted behaviors on individuals and organizations).

14. Application of behavioral sciences to nursing management increases the nurse manager's effectiveness as a leader.

15. Use of the framework for nursing management, which includes organizational structure, authority and power, the management process, resources, and application of behavioral science concepts, promotes desired outcomes.

 Questions for Study and Discussion

1. Which concepts of leadership and management should be most heavily weighted for managerial success and effectiveness?

2. Explain the difference between formal and informal leadership.

3. Consider the following situation: You are a newly hired primary care RN. As part of your orientation, your department manager remarks that she wants to help you learn as much as possible about the nursing unit. Your assignment for this day is to provide care to four patients who require considerable attention. However, the department manager frequently interrupts your services: "Come see the way we do this procedure," "Take this specimen to the lab—you need to know where it is," "Help Doris with her patient; it will be a good opportunity for you to observe a more experienced nurse," and so on. Because of the frequent interruptions you fall far behind in your work, causing you to work overtime, for which you are reprimanded by the department manager. Referring to this situation, describe a behavior that reflects one of the different influence actions (assertiveness, ingratiation, rationality, sanction, exchange, upward appeal, blocking, and coalition). Not all influence actions are included in the situation.

4. What do the terms *authority* and *power* mean to you? How would you differentiate between the two?

5. Considering the five bases of power (legitimate, reward, coercive, expert, and referent) which tactics do you usually use to influence your parents, instructors, or supervisor? Would it be better to rely on other tactics? Explain.

6. Which base(s) of power do you suppose the first-line department manager of a nursing unit relies on most? Explain.

7. Prepare three columns. Write your own definition of management for you as (1) a student, (2) a staff nurse, and (3) a department manager. How are they the same? How do they differ?

8. Define the behavioral science approach. How does this method apply to nursing management? Give examples.

REFERENCES

1. Sullivan E and Decker P: Effective management in nursing, ed 2, New York, 1988, Addison-Wesley Publishing Company.

2. Davis K: Human behavior at work: organizational behavior, ed 5, New York, 1977, McGraw-Hill Book Co.

3. Kipnis D, Schmidt S, and Wilkinson I: Intraorganizational influence tactics: explorations in getting one's way, J Appl Psychol 4:440-452, 1980.

4. Kreitner R: Management, ed 4, Boston, 1989, Houghton Mifflin Co.

5. Hellriegel D and Slocum J: Management, ed 5, New York, 1989, Addison-Wesley Publishing Co.

6. French J and Raven B: The basis of social power. In Cartwright D and Zander A, editors: Group dynamics, research and theory, ed 3, New York, 1968, Harper & Row, Publishers, Inc., pp 607-623.

7. Tappen R: Nursing leadership and management: concepts and practice, ed 2, Philadelphia, 1989, FA Davis Co.

8. Gillies D: Nursing management: a systems approach, ed 2, Philadelphia, 1989, WB Saunders Co.

9. Wadia M: Management and the behavioral sciences: a conceptual scheme, Calif Man Rev 8(1):65-72, 1965.

10. Maslow A: Motivation and personality, ed 3, New York, 1987, Harper & Row, Publishers (with new material by Ruth Cox and Robert Frazer).

11. Likert R: New patterns of management, New York, 1961, McGraw-Hill Book Co.

12. De Bella S, Martin L, and Siddall S: Nurses' role in health care planning, Norwalk, Conn, 1986, Appleton-Century-Crofts.

13. Robbins S: Organization theory: structure, design, and applications, ed 3, Englewood Cliffs, NJ, 1990, Prentice-Hall.

14. Johnson L: Strategic management: a new dimension of the nurse executive's role, JONA 20(9):7-10, 1990.

SUGGESTED READINGS

Art and science of management: empowerment: change-change: empowerment, Nurs Man 20(6):17, 1989.

Atchison T: Vision-health care leadership's challenge for the 90s, J Healthcare Educ Train 5(1):22-25, 1990.

Barrett G: Are you a winner? a winner has special qualities, Nursing 90 20(9):120, 1990.

Caserta J: Women of the 1990s, Home Healthcare Nurse 8(4):4, 1990.

Cash K: Nursing models and the idea of nursing, Int J Nurs Stud 27(3):249-256, 1990.

Curtin L: The excellence within, Nurs Man 21(10):7, 1990.

Eilers M: How assertive are you? Nursing 90 20(1):124-125, 1990.

Flower J: A conversation with Warren Bennis: the chasm between management and leadership, Healthcare Forum J 33(4):59-62, 1990.

Flower J: Managing quality, Healthcare Forum J 33(5):64-68, 1990.

Grainger R: Self-confidence: a feeling you can create, Am J Nurs 90(10):12, 1990.

Hardy L: Education for nurse administrators, The Canadian Nurse 86(8):33-34, Sept 1990.

Hughes L: Assessing organizational culture: strategies for the external consultant, Nurs Forum 25(1):15-19, 1990.

Jacox A, Pillar B, and Redman B: A classification of nursing technology, Nurs Outlook, 38(2):81-82, 1990.

Johnson L: Strategic management: a new dimension of the nurse executive's role, JONA 20(9):7-10, 1990.

Krackhardt D: Assessing the political landscape: structure, cognition, and power in organizations, Admin Sci Q 35(2):342-369, 1990.

Lee C: Followership: the essence of leadership, Training 28(1):27-35, 1991.

Manthey M: Leadership: accenting the positive, Nurs Man 21(7):40-42, 1990.

Manthey M: Trends: shifting patterns of authority, Nurs Man 21(19):14-15, 1990.

Murphy P and Ellson S: Socialization of women and health care: implications for training, J Healthcare Educ and Train 4(1):7-13, 1990.

News: NICHOL calls for boost to nurse management, Nurs Times 86(38):8, 1990.

Professional growth: how to become a successful leader, Nursing 90 20(12):97, 1990.

Steven D: Profile of a good manager, Nurs Man 22(1):60-61, 1991.

1990 AJN Guide: Finding the job that's right for you, The AJN Guide, Am J Nurs Co 0-937126-268, pp 16-21, 1990 (evaluation of talents, abilities and personality).

2

Styles of Leadership and Management

_____ **BEHAVIORAL OBJECTIVES** _____

On completion of this chapter the student will be prepared to:

☐ Determine what impact personal characteristics and traits have on leadership and management and assess leadership characteristics of self.

☐ Define leadership style and its relationship to the management process.

☐ Differentiate among authoritarian, democratic, and permissive styles of leadership.

☐ Determine the style of leadership that best supports a successful managerial role.

☐ Interpret the process of management by situation.

☐ Explain how a nurse manager can overcome feelings of powerlessness.

In Chapter 1 it was determined that (1) leadership is the ability to inspire and influence others to the attainment of goals through formal and informal procedures and (2) management requires authority and power to implement the organizational goals of planning, organizing, directing, and controlling human and physical resources and technology. In addition, it was noted that effective managers use behavioral science concepts to achieve their purposes.

Another important issue is the wise and systematic *use of self* to get the right things done at the right times. This chapter will discuss leadership style or the *way* in which a leader/manager uses personal influence to achieve the objectives of the organization.

Leaders have many ways of interacting with individuals and work groups. The interactions of individuals and groups represent the most critical relationship in an organization. No matter how large or small the enterprise, each person involved is a leader and/or follower and is part of the work situation. Leadership involves other people, and by their willingness to follow the group leader, group members help to make the leadership/management process possible. How leaders work with followers and how both work with the job situation determine the success of the individual manager, and by extension, the success of the organization. Every nurse leader/manager develops a characteristic style of seeking, wielding, and reacting to power. Studying individual characteristics and the ways in which styles of behavior and nurse leaders/managers affect the health care delivery system allows nurses to interact more productively and more harmoniously to achieve personal and organizational goals.

CHARACTERISTICS OF A LEADER
Trait Theory

During most of recorded history the prevailing theory and assumption was that leaders are born, not made. Leaders such as Abraham Lincoln, F.D.R., and Florence Nightingale were said to have been blessed with an inborn ability to lead. The "great man" approach to leadership eventually gave way to trait theory.

In the 1930s and 1940s, when psychological testing became popular, research on leadership focused on personality traits or distinguishing features of a leader, such as intelligence, shyness or aggressiveness, and ambition or laziness. The leadership theorists intended to isolate a set of characteristics that would describe all effective leaders. Then all an employer need do was compare the applicant with the list of characteristics to determine the worker's acceptability for the job. By 1950 the list had grown to over 100 characteristics identified as essential to successful leadership.[1] It would be highly unrealistic to expect one person to possess all the characteristics that have been named as important to leadership. Presented with such a list, the prospective leader/manager could easily become discouraged and give up before trying, never knowing the challenge that leadership can afford.

Taken seriously, trait theorists are limited because they focus on the leader's personal characteristics and overlook other factors of the leadership-management situation, such as the work setting, its structure and goals, and the myriad people involved.

Characteristic Theory

A more constructive approach is to look closely at personal characteristics that influence a leader's ability to perform the role of manager ef-

fectively. To do this, the factors of group and work situation need to be considered. Taken together, there is good evidence that certain personal qualities favor success in the leadership role.[2,p.472]

Stogdill, a noted authority on leadership studied characteristics of leaders for 22 years (1948 to 1970) and concluded that a selected group of characteristics indicates differences between leaders and followers and effective leaders from ineffective ones. Following are the characteristics he identified as being distinctive of effective leaders[3]:

1. Self-confidence, with a sense of personal identity
2. Strong drive for responsibility
3. Ability to complete tasks (persistence)
4. Energy
5. Willingness to accept consequences of decisions and actions
6. Acceptance of interpersonal stress
7. Tolerance of frustration and delay
8. Ability to influence behavior
9. Ability to structure social interactions to accomplish purposes
10. Venturesomeness and originality
11. Excessive initiative in social situations

Louis Lundborg, one of the nation's most influential banking executives, identifies qualities of leaders by saying that people will follow leaders who they feel (1) know where they are going and how to get there; (2) exercise courage and persistence even in the face of danger, opposition, or discouragement; (3) are believable; (4) do not exploit others for personal advantage; (5) make goals seem important, attainable, and exciting; (6) instill confidence in workers; (7) articulate well; and (8) maintain morale.[4]

Warren Bennis, noted management consultant, is convinced that successful leaders do, in fact, share some common traits.[5] He interviewed 90 highly successful leaders, including corporate and public-sector executives, both male and female. Four common traits or competencies were identified: management of attention, management of meaning, management of trust, and management of self (see box on p. 18).

These characteristics are typical of a successful leader. However, variations exist in the degree to which the characteristics are exhibited in individual leaders. There are wide differences in personalities. Also, not all characteristics are present in each person. Many strong leaders are associated with admirable qualities, but these same leaders may also have significant weaknesses.[3] Experience indicates that only a minority of leaders have great talents. Social science research since the 1930s reveals that only a few outstanding leaders have been identified as unusually gifted people.[3] Most people have strength in one or two areas and need a lot of help in others. Knowledge of the characteristics identified with effective leaders can help the nurse in preparing for the role of leader/manager; however, in the final analysis, leaders and managers are judged to be successful not on their characteristics but rather on what they accomplish.

LEADERSHIP STYLE THEORY

Style is an important factor in the leadership/management process. A style is the way in which something is said or done; it is a particular form of behavior directly associated with an individual. Leadership style is how a leader uses interpersonal influences to accomplish goals. Individual behavior is influenced by formative years and by all the input in a person's life thereafter. Thus the style or approach taken by a nurse manager toward patients/clients, nursing staff members, and other associates strongly reflects prior experiences.

Behavioral Styles

During World War II, the study of leadership took a significant turn. Researchers began to direct their attention from personal traits to patterns of leader behavior, called *leadership styles.* Rather than focusing on *who the leader was,* they observed *how the leader actually behaved.*

The Ohio State leadership studies. In the 1940s a team of Ohio State University researchers identified two dimensions of leadership behavior:

Common Traits of Successful Leaders as Identified by Bennis

1. Management of attention

The leader demonstrates a mix of vision or intelligent foresight and strong personal commitment.

    EXAMPLE: Rene Wilcox, community health nurse, has a mental image of spearheading the establishment of a center for pregnant women in a downtown neighborhood. Her strong personal dedication attracts others and inspires them to join in the fulfillment of her dream.

2. Management of meaning

The leader possesses unusual communication skills.

    EXAMPLE: Rene surveys the environment and proposes a site for the center, determining what is needed to start the program; she then describes enthusiastically and succinctly exactly what is needed and why. Her persuasive ability to communicate the need serves to align others with the cause.

3. Management of trust

The leader remains constant and secure and builds trust by making others aware of his or her steadiness of purpose.

    EXAMPLE: Rene is persistent, even dogmatic, about her intent to initiate a program for pregnant women. She befriends several single mothers while making her survey. In so doing, she lets others know where she stands.

4. Management of self

Successful leaders develop their strengths and learn from their mistakes. They generally reject the idea of failure.

    EXAMPLE: Rene determines that she is best at discussing needs and organizing forces. She believes herself to be weak in generating funds. She compensates for this weakness by using her strong communication skills to enlist support of others talented in fundraising.

initiating structure and consideration.[6,pp.1-40] Literally hundreds of studies have been done in an attempt to determine how these two dimensions relate to leadership effectiveness, group productivity, and group morale. Applied to nursing, the *initiating structure* refers to behavior in which the nurse manager organizes and defines the work to be accomplished and establishes well-defined, routine work patterns, channels of communication, and methods of getting a job done. For example, the nurse manager provides a manual of job descriptions, personnel policies, and procedures. *Consideration* refers to behaviors that convey mutual trust, respect, friendship, warmth, and rapport between the nurse manager and the staff. When there is such a relationship the staff learns to expect that the nurse manager will be open to hearing any message from them. The theory proposed by the Ohio study was that a combination of high structure and high consideration (high-high)

leads to greater leadership effectiveness. Figure 2-1 lists sample behaviors of high initiating structure and high consideration.

The Managerial Grid®. Robert Blake and Jane Mouton developed the Managerial Grid®, a trademarked and widely recognized typology of leadership styles.[7] They too remain convinced that there is one best style of leadership, that of *high concern for people* as well as *high concern for production*. As Figure 2-2 indicates, concern for people involves promoting friendship, maintaining morale, helping co-workers get the job done, and attending to things that matter to people, such as promotions, pay, working conditions, and benefits. Concern for production involves a desire to achieve greater output (e.g., handle greater patient-care loads) and cost effectiveness (e.g., use a minimum of staff and supplies while maintaining optimum care). Blake and Mouton stress that managers and

HIGH INITIATING STRUCTURE	HIGH CONSIDERATION
1. Organizes and defines group activities and makes clear the manager's relation to the group.	1. Promotes mutual trust, respect and rapport.
2. Defines the role expected of each member.	2. Shows concern for group members' needs.
3. Assigns tasks, plans ahead, explains how tasks are to be done.	3. Allows participation in decision making.
4. Pushes for achievement of organizational goals.	4. Encourages two-way communication.

Figure 2-1. Sample behaviors of high initiating structure and high consideration exhibited by a manager. *Adapted from the Ohio State Leadership Studies. From Fleishman E and Hunt J: Current developments in the study of leadership, Carbondale, Ill, 1973, Ohio State University Press, pp 1-40.*

HIGH CONCERN FOR PEOPLE	HIGH CONCERN FOR PRODUCTION
1. Comfortable work tempo and conditions.	1. Task oriented / work accomplishment.
2. Satisfying interpersonal relationships.	2. Interdependence on achieving a common goal.
3. Works for equitable pay, promotions and benefits for workers.	3. Quality and quantity oriented.

Figure 2-2. Sample behaviors of a manager who has high concern for people and high concern for productivity. *Based on the Managerial Grid III® by Blake R and Mouton J: The key to leadership excellence, Houston, 1985, Gulf Publishing Co.*

leaders need to be versatile enough to select the course of action appropriate to a given situation, but that exercising high concern for people as well as high concern for production produces the greatest success.

Although studies seemed to demonstrate a positive relationship between high initiating structure and high consideration (approximately 80%), this premise could not be proved conclusively because other combinations, such as low initiating structure and high consideration, sometimes resulted in higher performance and productivity. It became clear that the work situation also had a profound influence in determining the relationship between leadership behavior and performance.

Learned Behavior

Researchers have come to recognize that unlike characteristics, behaviors can be learned. Therefore it is assumed that individuals who are trained in the appropriate style can lead and manage more effectively.[8,pp.415-421] The fact that a manager's personality or past experience helps form a leadership style does not mean the style is unchangeable. Managers learn that some styles work better for them than others; if a style proves unsatisfactory for a particular situation, the manager can alter it. However, managers who attempt to adopt a style that is greatly inconsistent with their basic personality are unlikely to use that style effectively.

AUTHORITARIAN, PERMISSIVE, AND DEMOCRATIC STYLES OF LEADERSHIP AND MANAGEMENT

Research indicates that styles of leadership employed by leaders and managers vary with organizations and are tailored to fit their needs. There are simply too many kinds of leaders, personnel, tasks, organizations, and environments for one leadership/management style to apply to all cases. Further, numerous ways of classifying styles of leadership/management are employed. Although some theorists label styles differently from others, offering a variety of ranges of behavior representative of a specific style, all describe the authoritarian, democratic, and permissive styles as basic approaches to management.

Authoritarian Style of Leadership/Management

Classic research by Levin, Lippit, and White in 1939 shows that a authoritarian style of leadership range from very rigid to benevolent practices.[9] In the strictest sense authoritarianism functions with high concern for task accomplishment but low concern for the people who perform those tasks. Likert characterizes the authoritarian style of leadership as exploitive, or using the efforts of workers to the best possible advantage of the employer without regard to the workers' interests.[10,11] In the extreme use of authoritarian leadership, communications and activities occur in a closed system, as illustrated in Figure 2-3. Managers make all work-related decisions and order workers to carry them out. Standards and methods of performance are also rigidly set by managers. The autocratic leader frequently exercises power, sometimes with coercion. Failure to meet the manager's goals may result in threats or punishment. The autocratic personality is firm, insistent, self-assured, and dominating with or without intent and keeps at the center of attention. This kind of manager feels little trust or confidence in workers, and workers in turn fear the manager and feel they have little in common with him or her. Douglas McGregor has produced perhaps the most famous description of attitudes

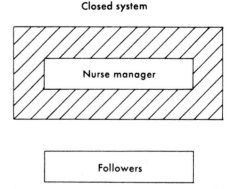

Figure 2-3. Authoritarian style of leadership. Shaded area represents predominant control. *Modified from Eckles R, Carmichael R, Sarchet B: Supervisory management: a short course in supervision, New York, 1975, John Wiley & Sons, Inc, p 81.*

assumed by autocratic leaders.[12] He maintains that autocratic leaders view individuals as naturally lazy, lacking in ambition, disliking responsibility, preferring to be led, self-centered, indifferent to organizational needs, resistant to change, not very bright, and lacking creative potential (see also Chapter 3).

Many managerial leaders take issue with those who believe authoritarian leadership to be a "put-down" of persons. Proponents of a more conservative or benevolent approach to authoritative leadership value workers and their capabilities but believe there is need for strong structure and order. In the benevolent authoritative approach[2] managers still issue orders, but workers have some freedom to comment on those orders. Workers are given some flexibility to carry out their tasks, but within carefully prescribed limits and procedures. A benevolent autocrat may simply give orders, use praise and demand loyalty, or make followers feel they are actually participating in decisions, even though they are doing what the leader wants. In general, these managers have a condescending attitude toward those they lead, and the followers are cautious when dealing with their managers.[11,pp.135-161]

Some form of authoritarian leadership has been used in nursing for many years. It reflects a very directive type of leadership that stresses giving orders by the nurse manager and taking orders by other members of the nursing staff. Authoritarian leadership is particularly suitable in situations of crisis when clear directions are of the highest priority. It is often referred to today as a *directive* or *controlling* style of leadership.[13,p.34]

Certain followers are most productive with authoritarian leadership. They derive a sense of security and satisfaction under this style of management. In turn, this type of management provides strong motivation and psychologic rewards to the leader. Authoritarianism allows for the possibility that the manager is likely to think and act faster and more effectively than others. Leaders with authoritarian styles are known for their ability to excel in times of crisis, to get tough jobs done, and to bring order out of chaos when those around them falter.[14,p.514]

EXAMPLE: Head nurse Fay Getty wants her nursing unit to win the annual hospital award for optimum attendance. She issues a bulletin itemizing her expectations: everyone will report to work on time; there will be no unexcused lateness or absence; and penalties will be assigned for failure to comply.

Fay is making policy without input from her staff. As a result they feel defensive, fearful, and exploited.

EXAMPLE: Ron Dooley enters a room and notes that a patient is having severe respiratory difficulty. He punches the call-light and demands immediate help; when help arrives, he gives appropriate orders.

In this instance, Ron correctly assigns people to clearly defined tasks; there is no thought of exercising participatory decision making. The staff experiences security in the procedure.

Permissive, Ultraliberal, or Laissez-faire Style of Leadership

The permissive style of leadership/management is at the opposite end of the continuum from the authoritarian style. Some would say that calling the permissive style "leadership" is a contradiction in terms, that leadership is absent under this system.[13,p.37] Under the laissez-faire style of leadership, the general climate is one of permissiveness or ultraliberalism in which there is lack of central direction or control. The laissez-faire manager wants everyone to feel good, including the manager. The free-rein leader avoids responsibility by relinquishing power to followers. Liberal leaders permit followers to engage in managerial activities, such as decision making, planning, structuring the organization, setting goals, and controlling the organization.

It has been estimated that fewer than 25% of all employees can operate responsibly with the permissive style and that only 10% of all managers accept and use the laissez-faire, permissive, or ultraliberal leadership style.[10] According to Lewin, permissive leaders believe it is the responsibility of the organization to supply money, materials, equipment, and workers, and that managers have the responsibility to direct their own efforts toward achievement of organizational goals. Permissive leaders assume workers are ambitious and responsible, accept organizational goals, and are dynamic, flexible, intelligent, and creative.[9] Figure 2-4 illustrates how the leader assumes a small role, relinquishing the bulk of the management process to followers. This style can be effective in highly motivated professional groups, such as in research projects in which independent thinking is rewarded. The very liberal style of leadership is oriented to higher social, ego fulfillment, and self-actualization needs. But this style is not generally useful in the highly structured health care delivery system in which organization and control form the baseline of most operations.

> EXAMPLE: Supervisor Carol Ezavedo informed the five department managers under her supervision that they were to assume full responsibility for staffing their stations. Four managers were delighted with the responsibility and followed through well, keeping within agency staff guidelines. The fifth manager staffed her station from day to day according to her desires, but with no regard to guidelines. She allowed her staff to arrive late and leave early for personal reasons. She called in extra help when staff members complained, without investigating the causes of their difficulties. Because there was little control, the staff took more and more liberties, creating inefficiency and chaos. The matter came to a climax when an emergency occurred and there was inadequate staff to handle the crisis.

The supervisor had abdicated her responsibility, allowing the group to drift into an untenable situation.

Democratic, Participative, or Consultive Style of Leadership

In the democratic or participative approach, the manager is "people oriented," focusing attention on human aspects and building effective work groups. Interaction between manager and personnel is open, friendly, and trusting. A collaborative spirit or joint effort exists, allowing for governance through group participation in decision making. Figure 2-5 demonstrates the open system of communication that prevails, the democratic manager consulting with group members and solving problems with them, assuming that others want to be considered in the process. There is a mutual responsiveness to meeting group goals, with work-related decisions made by the group. The democratic manager attempts to develop the group's sense of responsibility for the good of the whole and for individual accomplishments. Thus the goals set by the work group may not always be the ones personally favored. Democratic managers try to give workers feelings of self-worth and importance. Performance standards exist to provide guidelines and permit appraisal of workers,

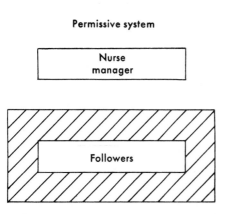

Figure 2-4. Permissive, ultraliberal, or laissez-faire style of leadership. Shaded area represents predominant control. *Modified from Eckles R, Carmichael R, and Sarchet B: Supervisory management: a short course in supervision, New York, 1975, John Wiley & Sons, Inc, p 81.*

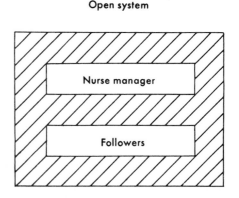

Figure 2-5. Democratic, participative, or consultive style of leadership. Shaded area represents shared control. *Modified from Eckles R, Carmichael R, and Sarchet B: Supervisory management: a short course in supervision, New York, 1975, John Wiley & Sons, Inc, p 81.*

rather than to provide managers with a tool to control workers.

There are some decisions that do not permit the nurse manager to exercise total democracy, but use of the participatory process when possible permits each member to identify with the work setting by establishing challenging goals, providing opportunities to change or improve work methods, pursuing professional and personal growth, recognizing achievement, and helping personnel learn from their mistakes. Likert's research studies revealed that a democratic or participative style of leadership leads to high productivity and is the most desirable form of management in a wide variety of work situations.[10,11]

EXAMPLE: Department manager Martha Zanger delegates authority for care of 26 patients to the primary care nurses. She depends on them to plan and implement appropriate care, utilizing an interdisciplinary approach. Martha retains ultimate responsibility for all outcomes. Thus she maintains an active two-way flow of upward and downward communication, assuring accountability and at the same time providing for flexibility and creativity among the nursing staff.

Comparison of Styles of Leadership

There are many similarities and differences in behavior, attitudes, and conditions present in leadership styles. The box below provides a comparison of authoritarian, democratic, and permissive styles.

As mentioned previously, not all of the behaviors are evident at any one time; however, each of the three styles of leadership is usually consistent within its category. A nurse manager will use all the styles separately or together, depending on the manager's flexibility and the circumstances inherent in each situation.

David Frew[15] has developed a leadership and followership style test to help participants think about the various dimensions of their management styles. In a 5-year period the instrument has been used by more than 3000 persons whose job functions include first-line management in every conceivable kind of organization, including health care. The instrument measures two different dimensions of organizational importance: (1) leadership style, or the idealized approach that a person would prefer to use in supervising, and (2) followership style, or the kind of leadership patterns preferred by an in-

---

Comparative Summary of Democratic, Authoritarian, and Permissive Styles of Leadership

Democratic	Authoritarian	Permissive
Participative	Conservative	Ultraliberal
Group goals	Organizational goals	Individual goals
Open	Defensive	Open
Facilitating	Restrictive	Permissive
Freeing	Coercive, pressure	Abdicating
Encouraging	Discouraging	Frustration, conflict
Accepting	Rejecting	Accepting and rejecting
Variety	Sameness	Differences
Equality	Inequality	Equality
Trusting	Fearing	Indifferent
Available supervision	Constant surveillance	Supervision as requested
Encouragement, assistance	Force	Self-direction
Freedom of choice	Obedience	Freedom of choice
Cooperation, group loyalty	Competition	Limited group alliance
Opportunity	Exploitation	Uncontrolled
Challenge	Threat	Permissive
Recognition	Praise	Acceptance
Self-discipline	Punishment	Self-gratification
Satisfaction	Reward	Acceptance

dividual in his or her boss. Each dimension is conceptualized as existing on a 5-point scale; for example, a person who scores "5" would function in a highly democratic or participative style, whereas a score of "1" would mean the leader prefers to be highly autocratic. This test is easily self-administered, self-scored, and self-interpreted in 15 to 20 minutes. Take the test, score it, and study the interpretations (box on pp. 25-28).

LEADERSHIP AND MANAGEMENT BY SITUATION

A comparative study of leadership styles seems to suggest that a democratic or participative style of leadership is the style of choice in most situations. However, there are too many factors to consider to make so broad an application. Researchers have turned their attention from classifying behaviors that label managers as autocratic, democratic, or permissive to considering management by situation.

Management by Situation

All situational-leadership theorists share one fundamental assumption: successful leadership occurs when the leader's style matches the situation. The premise is that styles of leadership should not be stereotyped as either forceful, participative, or permissive. Rather, management should be viewed as a process composed of a range of possible options in which the manager chooses a leadership style complementary to the need.

Robert Tannenbaum and Warren Schmidt were among the first theorists in 1958 to identify forces they believed should influence a manager's choice of leadership style. Those identified were (1) forces in the manager, (2) forces in the subordinates, and (3) forces in the situation.[16] Although Tannenbaum and Schmidt personally favored the democratic style, they have found that managers need to take certain practical considerations into account before deciding which style of leadership to use. Fred Fiedler and Martin Chemers contingency theory is more explicit in its description of factors to consider when determining a style of leadership. The manager is asked to review (1) the work situation, (2) the manager's leadership style and expectations, and (3) the follower's characteristics and expectations.[17,18,19] Fiedler and Chemers believe that when these three forces are considered and adaptations made, the situation is likely to be harmonious, with a willingness on the part of all those involved to cooperate in accomplishing goals.

The challenge, according to Fiedler and Chemers, is to analyze a leader's basic motivation and then match him or her with a suitable situation to form a productive combination. They believe it is more efficient to move leaders to suitable situations than to tamper with their personalities (for instance, trying to get a task-motivated person to become relationship motivated or vice versa).[17]

EXAMPLE: Nancy Canseda was assigned to be a department manager in an oncology unit where the pace was slow and there was heavy emphasis on emotional and spiritual matters. Nancy believed her primary competencies to be in triage and technical skills. She felt inadequate to the task required of her new assignment. She requested a transfer to either Intensive Care or the Emergency Room. Fiedler and Chemers would have supported this request, rather than encourage her to change her ways, believing that Nancy would be far more efficient if moved to a situation suitable to her personality.

The Health Care Advisory Board maintains that poor management is a greater problem in retaining nurses than most administrators realize.[18] De Crosta[19] says that use of situational leadership, first developed in 1988 by Hersey and Blanchard,[20] can help nurse managers to retain nurses on their staffs. *Situational leadership is a management system based on*

The situation at hand
   + The professional readiness of the staff member

The nurse manager assesses each nurse's needs and determines which leadership behaviors will help that nurse get the job done with the fewest problems. The nurse manager first considers the nurse's ability (knowledge, experience, skill), then determines the nurse's willingness (confidence, commitment, motivation, and energy) to complete a given task.

The next step in Hersey and Blanchard's situational leadership method is to match one of four managerial styles of leadership to the fol-

Leadership and Followership Style Test

Structural leadership profile

The following 20 statements relate to your ideal image of leadership. We ask that as you respond to them, you imagine yourself to be a leader and then answer the questions in a way that would reflect your particular style of leadership. It makes no difference what kind of leadership experience, if any, you have had or are currently involved in. The purpose here is to establish your ideal preference for relating with subordinates.

The format includes a 5-point scale ranging from *strongly agree* to *strongly disagree* for each statement. Please select one point on each scale and mark it as you read the 20 statements relating to leadership. You may omit answers to questions which are confusing or to questions that you feel you cannot answer.

	STRONGLY AGREE	AGREE	MIXED FEELINGS	DISAGREE	STRONGLY DISAGREE
1. When I tell a subordinate to do something I expect him/her to do it with no questions asked. After all, I am responsible for what he/she will do, not the subordinate.	1	2	3	4	5
2. Tight control by a leader usually does more harm than good. People will generally do the best job when they are allowed to exercise self-control.	5	4	3	2	1
3. Although discipline is important in an organization, the effective leader should mediate the use of disciplinary procedures with his/her knowledge of the people and the situation.	1	2	3	4	5
4. A leader must make every effort to subdivide the tasks of the people to the greatest possible extent.	1	2	3	4	5
5. Shared leadership or truly democratic process in a group can only work when there is a recognized leader who assists the process.	1	2	3	4	5
6. As a leader I am ultimately responsible for all of the actions of my group. If our activities result in benefits for the organization I should be rewarded accordingly.	1	2	3	4	5
7. Most persons require only minimum direction on the part of their leader in order to do a good job.	5	4	3	2	1
8. One's subordinates usually require the control of a strict leader.	1	2	3	4	5
9. Leadership might be shared among participants of a group so that at any one time there could be two or more leaders.	5	4	3	2	1
10. Leadership should generally come from the top, but there are some logical exceptions to this rule.	5	4	3	2	1

Continued.

Leadership and Followership Style Test—continued

	STRONGLY AGREE	AGREE	MIXED FEELINGS	DISAGREE	STRONGLY DISAGREE
11. The disciplinary function of the leader is simply to seek democratic opinions regarding problems as they arise.	5	4	3	2	1
12. The engineering problems, the management time, and the worker frustration caused by the division of labor are hardly ever worth the savings. In most cases, workers could do the best job of determining their own job content.	5	4	3	2	1
13. The leader ought to be the group member whom the other members elect to coordinate their activities and to represent the group to the rest of the organization.	5	4	3	2	1
14. A leader needs to exercise some control over his/her people.	1	2	3	4	5
15. There must be one and only one recognized leader in a group.	1	2	3	4	5
16. A good leader must establish and strictly enforce an impersonal system of discipline.	1	2	3	4	5
17. Discipline codes should be flexible and they should allow for individual decisions by the leader, given each particular situation.	5	4	3	2	1
18. Basically, people are responsible for themselves and no one else. Thus a leader cannot be blamed for or take credit for the work of subordinates.	5	4	3	2	1
19. The job of the leader is to relate to subordinates the task to be done, to ask them for the ways in which it can best be accomplished, and then to help arrive at a consensus plan of attack.	5	4	3	2	1
20. A position of leadership implies the general superiority of its incumbent over his/her workers.	1	2	3	4	5

Structural followership profile

This section of the questionnaire includes statements about the type of boss you prefer. Imagine yourself to be in a subordinate position of some kind and use your responses to indicate your preference for the way in which a leader might relate with you. The format will be identical to that within the previous section.

1. I expect my job to be very explicitly outlined for me.	1	2	3	4	5
2. When the boss says to do something, I do it. After all, he/she is the boss.	1	2	3	4	5

Leadership and Followership Style Test—continued

	STRONGLY AGREE	AGREE	MIXED FEELINGS	DISAGREE	STRONGLY DISAGREE
3. Rigid rules and regulations usually cause me to become frustrated and inefficient.	5	4	3	2	1
4. I am ultimately responsible for and capable of self-discipline based upon my contacts with the people around me.	5	4	3	2	1
5. My jobs should be made as short in duration as possible, so that I can achieve efficiency through repetition.	1	2	3	4	5
6. Within reasonable limits I will try to accommodate requests from persons who are not my boss since these requests are typically in the best interest of the company anyhow.	5	4	3	2	1
7. When the boss tells me to do something which is the wrong thing to do, it is his/her fault, not mine when I do it.	1	2	3	4	5
8. It is up to my leader to provide a set of rules by which I can measure my performance.	1	2	3	4	5
9. The boss is the boss. And the fact of that promotion suggests that he/she has something on the ball.	1	2	3	4	5
10. I only accept orders from my boss.	1	2	3	4	5
11. I would prefer for my boss to give me general objectives and guidelines and then allow me to do the job my way.	5	4	3	2	1
12. If I do something which is not right it is my own fault, even if my supervisor told me to do it.	5	4	3	2	1
13. I prefer jobs which are not repetitious, the kind of task which is new and different each time.	5	4	3	2	1
14. My supervisor is in no way superior to me by virtue of position. He/she does a different kind a job, one which includes a lot of managing and coordinating.	5	4	3	2	1
15. I expect my leader to give me disciplinary guidelines.	1	2	3	4	5
16. I prefer to tell my supervisor what I will or at least should be doing. It is I who is ultimately responsible for my own work.	5	4	3	2	1

Continued

Leadership and Followership Style Test—continued

Scoring interpretation

You may score your own leadership and followership styles by simply averaging the numbers below your answers to the individual items. For example, if you scored item number one *strongly agree* you will find the point value of "1" below that answer (Leadership Profile). To obtain your overall leadership style add all the numerical values which are associated with the 20 leadership items and divide by 20. The resulting average is your leadership style.

Interpretations

SCORE	DESCRIPTION	LEADERSHIP STYLE	FOLLOWERSHIP STYLE
Less than 1.9	Very autocratic	Boss decides and announces decisions, rules, orientation	Can't function well without programs and procedures. Needs feedback
2.0–2.4	Moderately autocratic	Announces decisions but asks for questions, makes exceptions to rules	Needs solid structure and feedback but can also carry on independently
2.5–3.4	Mixed	Boss suggests ideas and consults groups, many exceptions to regulations	Mixture of above and below
3.5–4.0	Moderately participative	Group decides on basis of boss's suggestions, rules are few, group proceeds as they see fit	Independent worker, doesn't need close supervision, just a bit of feedback
4.1 and up	Very democratic	Group is in charge of decisions; boss is coordinator, group makes any rules	Self-starter, likes to challenge new things by him/herself

It should be noted that scores on this instrument will vary depending on mood and circumstances. Your leadership or followership style is best described by the range of scores from several different test times.

lower's readiness. Specifically, the nurse manager matches task behaviors to the nurse's ability. These task behaviors are telling, selling, participating, and delegating (see the box on p. 29).

Situational leadership allows the nurse manager to move from one style to another as each situation presents itself. The manager must make transitions carefully, such as moving from a telling to a delegation style through supporting and coaching steps. Easy to learn and effective when applied, situational leadership helps the nurse manager improve staff competency and relationships by applying the appropriate style of leadership to each particular situation.

Manager's Style of Leadership and Expectations

How a manager leads is influenced by that person's background, knowledge, values, and experiences (forces in the manager) and the relationships or interdependency between the manager and the other personnel. The manager is likely to choose a style that complements his or her personality. The greater the manager's need to control the situation, the more likely it is that an authoritarian or conservative leadership style will be selected. The greater the belief in followers' competency and in the ability of members to work responsibly, the more likely a democratic or participative approach to leadership will be taken. The greater the belief that

Hersey and Blanchard's Situational Leadership

The nurse manager uses high amounts of task behavior when the subordinate nurse has little or no ability for the task, and low amounts of task behavior when the subordinate nurse is able to perform the task, as illustrated by the following examples:

1. Telling

EXAMPLE: Cora was new to use of the crash cart. During orientation, she was shown its contents and procedure. When a code was called, Cora assisted the leader and was told what to do each step of the way. After the code, a thorough review of procedure was held.

The leader knew Cora did not have the skill to manage a code, but did have the ability to learn. Through gradual initiation Cora gained competence, moving into a participating style.

2. Selling

EXAMPLE: Lena is resistant to floating to other nursing units when asked to do so and makes life miserable for the nurse manager because of her complaining. The nurse manager explains that there are many benefits to be gained from different environments, such as learning new skills, making new friends, and the possibility of becoming more visible to the agency, an asset in the event that an opportunity for advancement arises.

The nurse manager could have insisted that Lena take her turn, but chose instead to sell the benefits of floating to Lena, knowing that willingness in a worker contributes to high productivity and satisfaction.

3. Participating

EXAMPLE: Sydney, a new employee, was hesitant to administer IV medications to oncology patients because he was afraid of skin erosion due to his lack of experience. He continued to ask for supervision even though the nurse manager believed him to be competent.

A participating nurse manager would compliment Sydney on his competence in giving oncology medication, then suggest that he proceed on his own, asking for help if he felt it was needed. Sydney followed the plan and gradually weaned himself away from a dependent position.

4. Delegating

EXAMPLE: Nurse Aide Theresa was assigned to a surgical nurse unit unfamiliar to her. She was frightened of all the suction equipment, of the IVs, and of touching patients. The nurse manager assigned Theresa to work with an experienced nurse aide for one week, asking that she teach Theresa the art of caring for surgical patients.

Both performance and attitude changed once the new aide understood the situation and her role, and she was able to move quickly to a participatory role.

---

workers have the ability to achieve with minimal structure and direction, the more likely a permissive or ultraliberal style of leadership will be taken.

Followers' Characteristics and Expectations

The characteristics and expectations of followers also must be considered before managers can choose an appropriate leadership style. As demonstrated in the test on leadership and followership styles, followers differ in their response to leadership. Ultimately the response of followers to the manager's leadership determines how effective the manager will be.

Knowledge, competency, and *level of the workers* are important characteristics to consider. For example, capable persons usually require much less supervision than new or inexperienced workers. And less prepared personnel require carefully planned, detailed guidance. The nurse manager's task is to know the qualifications of each member assigned to the nursing team to provide them with the right amount of supervision and guidance.

Attitudes and *needs of followers* are also influencial factors in selecting a leadership style. Some workers are extremely dependent, preferring a highly structured environment in which the follower makes very few decisions about work activities. This kind of worker is most comfortable with an authoritarian manager. Persons fitting into this category may be a great asset to the organization. They may be very reliable and willing workers who gladly perform the most difficult and distasteful assignments. The worker's preference for this structured situation may be temporary. New workers are likely to need a period of close supervision during orientation.

At the opposite end of the continuum is the follower who has a strong need for minimal structure, preferring to chart his or her own activities, and to decide what will be done. This person is less likely to relate closely with a group or team endeavor. This independent personality is usually driven to achieve and to master every situation, desiring a manager who respects individual drives and ambitions and who allows free rein. If the job situation is wrong for such a follower, this person can be harmful to the organization.

Followers who perform best in a moderately structured environment are those who want to have a part in the decision-making process within limits but who allow others to make major decisions. They are usually competent workers who do not want constant overseeing but who prefer democratic or participative leadership that provides reassurance that they are performing correctly and well. In contrast to the follower who wants everything clearly spelled out, the follower who enjoys a participative relationship wants to know the goals but wants also to have a voice in how they will be achieved.

The Work Situation

Fred Fiedler spent 15 years researching leadership in hundreds of work groups. He identifies three elements in the work situation that help determine which style of leadership will be most effective: (1) interpersonal relationships between leader and followers, (2) the task to be accomplished, and (3) the extent of the leader's power.[21,22]

Leader-follower relationships. According to Fiedler, interpersonal relationships between leader and followers are the most important influence on the manager's power and effectiveness. If relationships are good, the manager may not have to rely on formal rank or authority. On the other hand, if the manager is disliked or not trusted, the manager may have to rely heavily on authoritarian methods to accomplish group tasks.

Task accomplishment. Task accomplishment is the second most important variable in the work situation. The nurse manager's responsibility, for example, includes not only providing care for patients/clients, but also managing people where such services are performed. A manager's task also includes planning, organizing, directing, evaluating the work of others, and enforcing the agency's policies and procedures that apply to the manager, followers, and patients/clients. Again, there is a gradation in structure in a work setting, ranging from highly structured to highly unstructured tasks. Highly structured settings are usually desirable in work environments such as specialty care areas, where the job must be done in a certain way, or with workers who have limited preparation for their roles.

Power position. The third factor to consider in a work situation is the power position. Some positions carry a great deal of power and authority. The administrator of a hospital and director of nursing services are examples. Like most upper-level management positions, they have great power over the workers employed by the organization. Generally, the greater the size of the work group, the greater the geographic spread; the greater the time pressures to make a decision, the more likely the use of an autocratic or conservative style of leadership.

Because of their large and complex nature, it is not uncommon for most health care delivery systems to be structured under a high degree of governance, with limited opportunity for nurse managers to proceed under their own direction. As work allotment becomes more decentralized, there is opportunity for nurse managers to adopt a democratic or participative style of leadership.

The nurse manager who overcomes feelings of powerlessness by assuming responsibility for these feelings is on the way to achieving personal power. We cannot change other people, but we can influence situations in a way that prompts other people to change themselves. In his effectiveness course for the American Management Association, George Kushel asked managers for the secret of their success. He learned that most managers do not derive power from their companies or their organizations, but from their own personalities. They succeed because they have a strong sense of personal power. Successful people who view themselves and their careers positively are usually productive people.

Instead of believing there is no hope, the successful manager classifies situations and strategies as either helpful or harmful to their personal or organizational goals, sifts out the harmful and concentrates on helpful plans of action. Successful people have reasonable expectations, take their jobs very seriously, and are totally committed to the organization while on the job. They know that their success and power come from within.[23]

Flexibility of Managers to Use Various Leadership Styles

The ideal situation is for a manager to be able to (1) adequately assess the followers' characteristics and expectations; (2) identify the interpersonal relationships among the leader and followers, the tasks to be accomplished, and the degree of power to do the job; and (3) choose a leadership style that best fits the situation. If managers are relatively inflexible in their leadership style, then they will function well only in certain situations. Such a limitation hampers an individual's career, for to use a manager who has only one leadership style, an organization must adapt the job to the manager, rather than the manager to the job.

Fiedler believes that leadership styles are inflexible and is discouraging when discussing the possibility of reeducating managers to use different styles.[22] Others, however, believe strongly that most managers actually have great potential and flexibility in responding to influences in the work setting and that behavior can be changed. Hersey, Blanchard, and Landy, behavioral scientists, for example, believe that managers can develop the ability to select and use different leadership styles, from making decisions solely on their own through various degrees of group participation, in accordance with their analysis of the needs of the leader, followers, and work situation.[20,24]

This book is based on the assumption that nurses who believe they have the potential to be flexible in their leadership style can learn to be effective as leaders in the different situations a nurse manager encounters.

SUMMARY

1. Characteristics are personality traits or distinguishing features of a person.
2. According to Bennis, four common traits are common in successful leaders: management of attention, management of meaning, management of trust, and management of self.
3. Only a minority of leaders have great talents; becoming an effective leader/manager is the result of hard, systematic work.
4. Style is a particular form of behavior directly associated with an individual; leadership style is the way in which a leader uses interpersonal influences to accomplish goals. The Ohio State study utilizing the Managerial Grid® concluded that a high degree of initiating structure and a high degree of consideration would lead to greater leader effectiveness; they found that although there was an indication that this was true, *situation* proved to be the dominant factor. Blake and Mouton's Managerial Grid® is based on the theory that there is one best style of leadership: concern for both production and people.
5. Since behavior can be learned, appropriate styles of leadership can be learned.
6. An authoritarian style of leadership/management varies from very rigid (highly structured, power ridden, leader oriented, and task centered) to benevolent (strong structure, with some consideration for workers and their preferences). The authoritarian style is most effective in crises when highly specialized skills are required and options for activities are limited.
7. A permissive, ultraliberal, or laissez-faire

style of leadership/management functions with minimal structure in a free-rein environment, with leadership relinquished by the leader to the followers. This style is most effective when independent activity is desired.

8. A participative or democratic style of leadership/management is moderately structured, allowing for group governance through collaboration or joint effort. This style is most useful in situations in which openness and trust prevail, all group members are capable of decision making, and there is time to function by majority rule.

9. Styles of leadership/management may appear separate and distinct, but in practice they are not. A manager functions in one style most of the time, but depending on individual flexibility and circumstance, the leader may use combinations of all styles at one time.

10. One goal of an organization is for its managers to use a style of leadership that promotes a high level of work performance in a wide variety of circumstances, as efficiently as possible, and with the least amount of disruption. Effective nurse managers assess their individual styles, then work toward the adoption of leadership styles that best complement their structural environment, tasks to be accomplished, and personnel involved. Management by situation is a process in which a leader chooses a behavioral approach that best fits the manager's leadership style and expectations, the followers' characteristics and expectations, and the work situation.

11. The task of an effective manager is to work toward bringing all forces that influence the situation as close together as possible.

12. To accomplish the management process, the leader must know self, followers, and the character of the work situation and be flexible enough to make necessary adaptations or changes.

13. Personal power can be achieved by overcoming feelings of powerlessness, by classifying events and situations as either helpful or harmful to one's personal or organizational goals, by making appropriate changes, and by being totally committed to the organization while on the job.

Questions for Study and Discussion

1. Think of the best leader you have ever known personally. In terms of traits, characteristics, style, and situational factors, why was that person a good leader?
2. Do you agree with the situational leadership theorists' claim that there is no one best style of leadership? Why or why not?
3. Summarize what the Ohio State model and the Managerial Grid® have taught managers about leadership.
4. Assume that you are the department manager of a pediatric unit. You have observed that Cynthia, one of your staff RNs, becomes impatient and sometimes angry with noncompliant children. You walk into the room just as the RN shouts at a 4-year-old to "sit down and be quiet or you will be sorry!" State what your approach would be if you were (1) an authoritarian manager, (2) a permissive manager, or (3) a participative manager.
5. Do you ever feel that you have power? Over what situations? Where does the source of your power originate?

REFERENCES

1. Adorno T and others: The authoritarian personality, New York, 1950, Harper & Row, Publishers.
2. Hellriegel D and Slocum, J: Management, ed 5, Reading, Mass, 1989, Addison-Wesley Publishing Co.
3. Stogdill R: Handbook of leadership: a survey of theory and research, New York, 1981, Free Press.
4. Lundborg L: What is leadership? J Nurs Admin 12(5):32-33, 1982.
5. Bennis W: Why leaders can't lead: the uncon-

scious conspiracy continues, ed 1, San Francisco, 1989, Jossey-Bass Publishers.

6. Fleishman E and Hunt J: Current developments in the study of leadership, Carbondale, Ill, 1973, Southern Illinois University Press, pp 1-40.

7. Blake R and Mouton J: The management grid III: the key to leadership excellence, Houston, 1985, Gulf Publishing Co.

8. Landy F: Psychology of work behavior, ed 4, Pacific Grove, Calif, 1989, Brooks/Cole Publishing Co.

9. Lewin K, Lippitt R, and White R: Patterns of aggressive behavior in experimentally created social climates, J Sociol Psychol 10(2):271-299, 1939.

10. Likert R: New patterns of management, New York, 1961, McGraw-Hill Book Co.

11. Sayles L: Leadership: managing in real organizations, ed 2, New York, 1989, McGraw-Hill Book Co.

12. McGregor D: Leadership motivation: essays of Douglas McGregor, Cambridge, 1968, MIT Press. (Edited by Warren Bennis and Edgar Schein with the collaboration of Carolyn McGregor.)

13. Tappen R: Nursing leadership and management: concepts and practice, ed 2, Philadelphia, 1989, FA Davis Co.

14. Kreitner R: Management, ed 4, Boston, 1989, Houghton Mifflin Co.

15. Frew D: Leadership and followership, Personnel J, 56(2):90-96, 1977.

16. Tannenbaum R and Schmidt W: How to choose a leadership pattern, Harv Bus Rev 55(5):162-164, May-June 1973.

17. Fiedler F and Chemers M: Leadership and effective management, Glenview, Ill, 1974, Scott, Foresman and Co.

18. Health Care Advisory Board: Nurse recruitment and retention, Washington, DC, 1987, The Advisory Board Co, p 136.

19. DeCrosta A: Meeting the nurse retention challenge: an interview with Connie Curran, Nursing 89 19(5):170-171, 1989.

20. Hersey P and Blanchard K: Management of organizational behavior: utilizing human resources, ed 5, Englewood Cliffs, NJ, Prentice-Hall, 1988.

21. Fiedler F: Engineer the job to fit the manager, Harv Bus Rev 44:116, Sept-Oct 1965.

22. Fiedler F: Validation and extension of the contingency model of leadership effectiveness, Psychol Bull 76(2):128-148, 1971.

23. Korobow L, Smith R, and Kushel G: Think yourself powerless? Think again, Nursing 89 19(11):103-109, 1989.

24. Landy F: Psychology of work behavior, ed 4, Pacific Grove, Calif, 1989, Brooks/Cole Publishing Co.

SUGGESTED READINGS

Dubnick C and Williams J: Getting peak performance in the knowledge-based organization, Healthcare Forum J 34(1):32-36, 1991.

Flower J: The art and craft of followership, Healthcare Forum J 34(1):56-60, 1991.

Freda M: A role model of leadership and advocacy for nursing, Nursing Forum 24(3,4):9-13, 1989.

Husted G, Miller M, and Wilczynski E: 5 ways to build your self-esteem, Nursing 90 20(5):152-153, 1990.

Jacoby J and Terpstra M: Collaborative governance: model for professional autonomy, Nurs Man 21(2):42-44, 1990.

Weber D: The healthcare forum/3M visionary leadership conference, Healthcare Forum J 34(1):39-45, 1991.

Weiss R: The quiet superstars, Healthcare Forum J 34(1):51-55, 1991.

Zurlinden J, Bongard B, and Magafas M: Situational leadership: a management system to increase staff satisfaction, Orthop Nurs 9(2):47-52, 1990.

3

Organizational Structure and Management Systems

☐ State the purpose of most health institutions.

☐ Differentiate between government-owned, voluntary, and proprietary hospitals.

☐ Describe a hospital merger and its implications for the nurse manager.

☐ Explain the effects of national health policy on health care delivery agencies.

☐ Describe a typical magnet hospital.

☐ Define public health services and explain the role of the community health nurse.

☐ Compare public health departments and community health nursing with home health agencies and the visiting nurse.

☐ Describe a hospital that meets American Hospital Association standards.

☐ Name the primary accrediting bodies that control health care institutions.

☐ Give reasons for organizational structure and its composition. Identify significant factors that influence organizational relationships.

☐ Compare the advantages and disadvantages of the bureaucratic and human relations approaches to organization and management.

☐ Explain the rationale for selecting an organizational structure and management system.

Professional people will spend a good part of their professional lives working in organizations, either as a staff person, manager, or both. This chapter is about organizations—why they are formed and managed, and how nurse managers can best help organizations set and achieve their goals.

Nurses practice in many different types of organizations, most of which focus primarily on the provision of health care services, such as hospitals, clinics, health maintenance organizations (HMOs), public health agencies, nursing homes, skilled nursing facilities, community mental health centers, and neighborhood health centers. Other organizations that have different primary purposes may utilize nurses as one part of their system. For example, nurses are employed in prisons, schools, day-care centers, and businesses and industries. Nursing services vary widely from highly specialized care to preventive treatment. Regardless of the service rendered, the nurse must function within the existing organizational structure, both formal and informal. Because most nurses are employed in hospitals, this chapter focuses primarily on nursing management in hospitals. Where appropriate, other health care settings are also discussed.

FORMAL AND INFORMAL STRUCTURE

Each organization has both a formal and an informal structure that determine work and interpersonal relationships.[1,p.343] The formal structure is usually highly planned and publicized, whereas the informal structure is unplanned and concealed. This chapter focuses on the formal structure. Informal or covert structure is discussed in Chapter 8.

HEALTH CARE INSTITUTIONS AND THE HOSPITAL

A large number of health care organizations in the United States today are acute care hospitals. Health care institutions usually possess a common basis for existence: to serve the health needs of the public. Until recent years the hospital has been a place for care of the sick and the dependent. Today the hospital has become a center of technical services for the sick and the well, with great emphasis on preventive services and health promotion among the general population. Goals are reached in accordance with the type of health setting. Inherent in meeting health needs are (1) administering patient care, (2) educating health agency personnel and the public, (3) engaging in research, and (4) protecting the health of the public. The emphasis given to functions varies from hospital to hospital, depending on the basic philosophy and goals of the particular hospital.

The history of hospitals can be traced to the healing temples of ancient Egypt. The evolution of the modern hospital is usually associated with development of the Christian ethics of faith, humanitarianism, and charity. The hospital in the United States is based essentially on the British prototype, yet has a uniqueness of its own.[2]

The American Hospital Association (AHA) defines a hospital as an institution with the primary function of providing diagnostic and therapeutic patient services for a variety of medical conditions, both surgical and nonsurgical. A number of guidelines are provided by the AHA at the national and state levels to protect the interests of the consumer. These guidelines are concerned with items such as (1) number of beds (no fewer than six); (2) a safe and sanitary environment; (3) an identifiable governing body legally and morally responsible for the conduct of the hospital; (4) a chief executive with continuous responsibility for the operation of the hospital in accordance with established policy; (5) a medical staff accountable for maintaining proper standards; (6) continuous registered nurse supervision of nursing services; and (7) pharmacy, food, x-ray, laboratory, and operating room services.[3] Nursing is the largest department in any hospital.

Health care agencies are of three types: (1) *government owned* at the federal, state, or local levels; (2) *voluntary,* or non–profit-making; and (3) *proprietary,* or profit-making.

Government-Owned Health Agencies

Government-owned health agencies are official bodies providing health services to selected groups of people under the support and direction of the local, state, or federal government. Their services are often provided without cost to the client or are offered at a reduced rate to the medically indigent. These organizations

Examples of Government-Owned Hospitals Operating under Support and Direction of the Voting Public

Federal	State	Local
Army	Psychiatric	County
Navy	Chronic diseases	City/county
Veterans Administration	State university	City
Public Health Service	Medical school	
Indian service	Hospitals	
Marine hospitals	Prisons	
Department of Justice		
Prisons		

Examples of Voluntary Health Care Organizations Operating under the Support of Nonprofit Organizations

Church affiliated	Community	Industrial	Special interest groups
Salvation Army	Any community	Railroad, lumber	Shriners
Roman Catholic		Union	Cancer, muscular dystrophy
Presbyterian		Kaiser-Permanente	Mental retardation
Baptist			Others
Lutheran			
Methodist			
Seventh Day Adventist			
Others			

are directly answerable to the sponsoring governing agency or boards and indirectly responsible to elected officials and taxpayers who support them. The top box above illustrates the kinds of government-owned hospitals operating at different levels. People cared for at the federal level include veterans, military personnel, and their families. These services are usually housed in very large facilities, where the bed capacity ranges from hundreds to thousands. There are also those who need protective services that are available through the U.S. Department of Public Health, such as Indian services and Marine hospitals. The health needs of federal prisoners are also provided for by the federal government.

Voluntary Health Agencies

Voluntary health agencies are nonprofit, tax exempt organizations designed to meet health needs of the general public. Operation without profit does not mean that voluntary agencies do not need to be concerned with their financial well-being. Although they have no stockholders interested in profit, they still must plan for having sufficient money to expand, to be prepared for inflation or depression, and to be able to meet all financial obligations. Consequently, most nonprofit agencies have receipts in excess of expenditures, held for the time when they are needed. These monies differ from profits in that the funds are redirected into the agency for its maintenance and growth, rather than routed into the hands of stockholders. The second box above lists the major classifications of owners of this type of agency, including church affiliated, community, industrial, and special interest groups. Basic support for an important part of a voluntary agency's capital budget depends on income from clients, determined on an individual basis, and gifts. Orientation is toward service for religious, ethnic, economic, or special interests.

Generally speaking, services established by large corporations are fairly secure in their finances, but health care agencies established by

Examples of Proprietary Health Agencies Operating as Profit-Making Organizations

Individual owner
Partnership
Corporation
Multisystem
Single
Chain

local governmental agencies for those who cannot pay for their own care have always been severely underfinanced and understaffed. This causes frustration for health care providers as they see the need for their services but are hampered by lack of funds.[4]

Proprietary Health Agencies

Proprietary health agencies operate for profit. They serve people who can pay for their services, directly or indirectly. These privately owned corporations function under the direction of stockholders, such as physicians, a corporation, or a board of trustees. The box above gives examples of owners of private health agencies. Personnel practices, client services, growth, and emphasis on quality or quantity of care vary among agencies. Many proprietary agencies receive supplementary funds through private and public funding for provision of health care, research, and special services and are in a position to provide some financial assistance to eligible clients who can afford ordinary care but cannot handle catastrophic illness. Hemodialysis and transplantation of human organs are examples of services that are financially out of reach for the average citizen but can be made available by special arrangement.

COMMUNITY HOSPITAL MERGERS

Multihospital systems are becoming increasingly common. Nursing homes, psychiatric facilities, HMOs, and home care agencies are often part of multiunit systems.[5]

In the 1980s, 23,000 hospital mergers and acquisitions incorporated groups of hospitals into new organizational relationships. The major goal of such mergers was to increase hospital system's power in highly competitive marketplaces. Even with the mergers, one third to one half of all transactions failed to meet the financial expectations.[5] The box on p. 38 describes four types of mergers.

Merger and the Nurse Manager

Mergers affect all nurses—staff members begin to worry about their place in the new structure. Unless plans for the merger are clarified quickly and nurses understand how it will affect them, they will gradually resist and withdraw from their original commitment to the workplace. The role of nurse managers is to help their staffs to overcome negative influences. Before this goal can be accomplished, nurse managers must first resolve any negative feelings they might be experiencing themselves. Gathering information and establishing a power base within the enlarged system becomes vital.

Managers can best accomplish staff adjustment to a merger through persuasion, helping staff to see that the change is inevitable and that it can have positive outcomes for the worker. The key to an effective merger is expert horizontal and vertical communication in areas of productivity, momentum, teamwork, power distribution, self-preservation activities, commitment levels, and staff attrition.

Neither a fast-paced nor a slow-paced rate of change is desirable in a merger. Fast-paced changes add stress, and slow-paced changes drag out the trauma. Overall, a moderate rate of change seems advisable—fast enough to reduce anxiety, and slow enough to provide thorough communication during the process.[7] The appropriate rate of change is in effect when all parties concerned understand the process and are moving forward with the plans for merger.

Compatibility of merging organizations will have to be determined. Each organization involved in the merger is at a different level of development; therefore, attention must be directed toward finding a common ground. See Chapter 11 for an example of the process used to cope with a major change.

HEALTH CARE REIMBURSEMENT SYSTEMS

It would be difficult to overstate the extent of change affecting health care delivery systems in

The Merger Process[6]

Pritchett proposes four ways to merge organizations:

1. The rescue posture	The agency in trouble welcomes help from a purchaser
2. The collaborative posture	The most common merger procedure; occurs in an environment where each party desires to merge and there is a feeling of mutual respect and interest in working together
3. The contested merger	Only one agency or party has a strong desire to merge, but both parties see some gain to be had from the merger
4. The raid posture	One organization takes over another by surprise, thus producing shock and antagonism.

the last decade. In the early 1980s, hospitals and community health agencies experienced a revenue squeeze imposed by third-party payers. Hospitals, both nonprofit and others, struggled with rapidly increasing labor and technology costs accompanied by declining inpatient revenues. Added to this has been competition from groups such as health maintenance organizations (HMOs), private sector delivery systems (e.g., surgicenters, urgent care units, diagnostic facilities, and outpatient clinics).

Retrospective Payment Systems

Retrospective payment for health services is reimbursement made to health care providers *after* the services have been given. Some governmental services as well as private insurance companies have used this system. An example of retrospective payment is the Johnson administration's "Great Society" program, resulting in Public Law No. 89-97, the Social Security Amendments of 1965, which established Titles XVIII (Medicare) and XIX (Medicaid) of the Social Security Act.[8] Private-sector organizations—health insurance agencies such as Blue Cross and Blue Shield, health maintenance organizations (HMOs), and preferred provider organizations (PPOs)—also received retroactive payments. Under the retrospective payment plan, hospitals were encouraged to promote extended hospital stays, for the longer patients were hospitalized, the higher the revenue received and the greater the profits. Physicians also reaped benefits from extended stays through greater reimbursement for services.[9]

The author has attended meetings sponsored by government officials and addressed to physicians and hospital administrators, admonishing them to curtail the length of hospital stay (LOS) of their patients and to seek ways to reduce costs during hospitalization. Physicians and hospital administrators were warned that unless they found ways to resolve the problem, the government would find a solution. Hospitals, however, were slow to respond.

Prospective Payment System (PPS) Diagnosis-Related Groups (DRGs)

In 1983, Public Law 98-21, a Social Security Amendment, was passed, providing hospital reimbursement under Part A of the Medicare program. This bill revolutionized the health care system, as it provided for *prospective* payment for hospital services given to Medicare patients, rather than the previous method of *retrospective* reimbursement, by which most health care bills were covered. The new payment system was gradually phased into hospitals beginning in 1983, setting payment levels on services *before* they were provided. Four hundred sixty-seven different diagnosis-related groups (DRGs) were identified. The Health Care Financing Administration (HCFA) used Medicare data from previous years to determine a fixed payment for each DRG. Under this system, a hospital is paid a flat fee for the treatment of a patient with a given diagnosis. As a result, hospitals now have an incentive to control costs, for if their costs are below the prospective payment reimbursement, they may keep the difference; if the costs are higher, hospitals must absorb the difference, thus facing a break-even or lose situation.[2,p.19] At the end of fiscal year 1988, the prospective payment system covered 5626, or 84%, of all hospitals.[10] The prospective payment system firmly moved the delivery of health care into the business world, where the ability to compete is essential to survival. The implications for nursing service are grave.[11] Nurse managers are challenged to seek ways to provide quality care within a stringent budget. See Chapter 10 for a discussion of this problem.

Preferred Provider Organizations (PPOs)[12]

A PPO is a health financing and delivery arrangement by which a group of health care providers (e.g., hospitals and physicians) offers its services on a predetermined financial basis to health care purchasers (employers of large numbers of people) under terms that encourage the selection of the providers to supply services to sponsored individuals. Hospitals seek to develop PPOs in order to protect or expand the volume of services they provide. Hospitals may perceive that their market shares are threatened by an oversupply of services and providers and by aggressive marketing by HMOs and by other PPOs. By sponsoring their own PPOs, they hope to offer employers and potential consumers some of the advantages of an HMO without giving up traditional payment systems or their own autonomy. Both nonprofit and for-profit corporations can offer PPOs. Hospital-sponsored plans usually form a separate for-profit or not-for-profit corporation. A PPO steering committee typically includes hospital administration, nursing administration, financial officer, planner, legal counsel, board of director representatives, and medical staff representatives.

The Omnibus Budget Reconciliation Act (OBRA)

Since 1966 health care policy has been left to the whim of the congressional budget process, culminating in the 1980s with annual budget reconciliation acts. The Omnibus Budget Reconciliation Act (OBRA) of 1989 affects most areas of health policy.[13] The purpose of the budget reconciliation process is to bring spending that is not controlled through the regular congressional appropriations process into conformity with the annual budget resolution. Since passage of the Social Security Amendments of 1983, the act that established the Prospective Payment System, the Secretary of Health and Human Services, in consultation with the Prospective Payment Assessment Commission, is required to make annual adjustments to the rates paid to hospitals covered by the Social Security Act. Although an annual increase was promised, no such increase has ever been approved by Congress or set by the Secretary.[14] This situation adds further to the financial stress on hospitals.

Adaptations to Reimbursement Systems

Nonprofit, tax-exempt hospitals are adapting to the new environment, as are their investor-owner counterparts. There is currently a trend toward reducing the number of nonpaying patients. Another is to recruit, retain, and reward physicians in order to gain access to those physicians' patients. To this end, hospitals offer improved facilities, increased power, and financial incentives. Both proprietary and nonprofit hospitals have banded together into chains and alliances, with varying degrees of centralized control. Financial managers have assumed more important roles with the advent of computerized data systems designed to maximize revenues through the prospective payment system and preferred provider organizations. The case manager role has emerged as a direct outgrowth of the need to relate the PPS and PPOs to provision of care. (See Chapters 5 and 7.) The businesslike attitudes and strategies now embraced by nonprofit hospitals have created the perception in some circles that the distinctions between nonprofit and for-profit hospitals are disappearing.[15]

MAGNET HOSPITALS[16,17]

Magnet hospitals are urban, medium-to-large community hospitals or medical centers that have a reputation for higher rates of retention of nurses and for excellence in nursing practice. A late 1989 follow-up of an American Nurses' Association-sponsored study of 741 hospitals across the United States reveals that their nursing staffs are composed of a high median percentage of RNs (81%) and that they typically have few middle managers concerned with clinical decision making. Because the nursing staffs are educated, experienced, and clinically competent, they assume responsibility for patient care with the help of clinical nurse specialists. As a result, a nurse manager's span of control can increase. (See Chapter 4 for a discussion of the clinical nurse specialist [CNS].) For example, where formerly there might have been assistant directors of medical-surgical nursing, parent-child nursing, and so on, who actively supervised the nursing care given on these units, now there are fewer nursing directors. The nurse managers appointed are specialists in budget and financial planning, in strategic and operational planning, and in education and research. Evening and night supervisors are no longer needed to supervise responsible, autonomous staff nurses. In one of the 16 magnet hospitals surveyed, head nurses are on beeper call for consultation on any nursing problem the staff cannot handle. In all but three of the magnet hospitals studied, scheduling and staff replacements are decentralized to the nursing unit for the RN staff to manage. The nursing care delivery system is flexible and ever changing, dictated primarily by patient needs. Eight-hour total patient care and case management are the dominant delivery systems.

In magnet hospitals nursing units generally operate autonomously, are self-governing, and participate in nurse-physician collaboration in department-wide issues that relate to them.

PUBLIC HEALTH SERVICES

Health services can be defined as helpful actions specifically intended to improve health. *Public health services* are those conducted on a community basis for the public good, such as communicable disease control, collection and analysis of health statistics, and environmental health services, including such activities as radiation and air pollution control. *Personal health services* are those provided to individuals and include promotion of health, prevention of illness, diagnosis, treatment, and rehabilitation.[18,p.19] Public health's mission is to fulfill society's interest in ensuring conditions under which people can be healthy.[19]

COMMUNITY HEALTH NURSING

Nursing theory recommends that nursing practice focus on the whole patient. Likewise, community health nursing focuses on the health of the whole community. An ad hoc committee of the American Public Health Association defined the role of public health nursing in the delivery of health care as

a systematic process by which: (1) the health and care needs of a population are assessed in collaboration with other disciplines in order to identify subpopulations, families, and individuals at increased risk of illness, disability, or premature death; (2) a plan for intervention is developed to meet these needs which includes resources available and those activities that contribute to health and its recovery, and the prevention of illness, disability and premature death; (3) a health care plan is implemented effectively, efficiently, and equitably; and (4) an evaluation is made to determine the extent to which these activities have an impact on the health status of the population.[20]

PUBLIC HEALTH ORGANIZATIONAL STRUCTURE

The structure of a public health care system includes the resources (e.g., money, people, physical plant, and technology) and the organizational configurations necessary to transform these resources into health services.[2,p.2] Ideally, there would be a single, coherent organization with all public health groups in organizational alignment. In reality, public health is practiced in a complex set of organizational and jurisdictional relationships. In the United States, each state has ultimate responsibility for the health of its residents; however, public health activities are usually delegated to local health departments. About half the states have combined health and social service agencies. In some states there is a super- or umbrella-agency structure, causing public health services to become predominantly a welfare program, and the broad vision of public health is overshadowed.[20] Figure 3-1 provides an example of a typical organizational structure of a public health department. The city or county is divided into districts. The Director of Public Health Nursing is responsible for all functions, which are delegated through assistant directors. For each district there is a Public Health Nurse Specialist

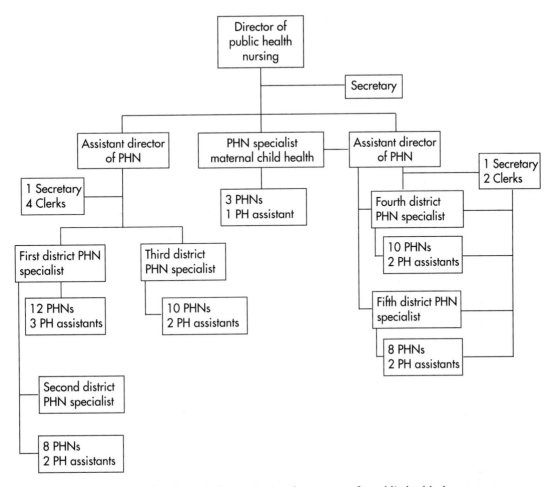

Figure 3-1. Example of a typical organizational structure of a public health department.

who directs and supervises the Public Health Nurses and who is available for sharing her expertise with all the staff. Secretaries and clerks are available to PHNs for administrative services. One specialty area is singled out in this sample chart (maternal-child health); however, there could be more specialties or none if the director elects to incorporate all services into the daily activities of the districts.

HOME HEALTH CARE/VISITING NURSE SERVICES[21,pp.276-293]
Origin

Home health care in the United States began with the visiting nurse service approximately 100 years ago. Visiting nurse societies were originally managed by nonnurses, but by 1900 the organizations had hired nurses to supervise the nursing staff. They were financed by charities, public boards, churches, and voluntary boards. Fees for services were charged if the client could pay. By 1920 a large number of health insurance carriers covered client charges. In 1966, when Title XVIII of the Social Security Act was implemented, Medicare began funding home health care for the aged and disabled. Provision for home health care shifted from private and charitable sectors to the third-party payment modes, with Medicare as the primary source of reimbursement.

Services Provided

Traditional services provided by home health care agencies included skilled nursing, home health aide service, physical therapy, occupational therapy, speech pathology, and medical social services. In recent years more comprehensive services have been instituted, including respiratory therapy and parenteral nutrition, intravenous therapy, chemotherapy, home ventilator management, apnea therapy, cardiac monitoring, and high-risk pediatric home care.

Home health care agencies are either voluntary, proprietary, or hospital based. The services provided follow a physician-approved plan of treatment. Another component of home health care is hospice services, which specialize in care of the terminally ill. Hospices are commonly asociated with visiting nurse services and agencies under the auspices of religious organizations. Accreditation and monitoring of home health care agencies varies greatly according to state regulation. There are more than 10,000 home health agencies in the United States, over half having Medicare certification. The JCAHO, NIN and the American Public Health Association also accredit home health care agencies.

Organization

According to Medicare regulations, the director of nursing of a home health care agency (who is also the administrator, executive director, or president in some agencies) must be a registered nurse. The ANA standard for a home health nursing care director requires a professional nurse with a master's degree. The administrator is responsible for administration and direction of all client care activities and is charged with fostering the professional growth of the clinical staff. As the home health care industry has begun to mature, it has not been uncommon to see home health agencies being managed by administrators with business, public administration, health care, or hospital administration degrees, experience, or both. Figure 3-2 provides an example of the organizational structure of a typical home health care agency.

ACCREDITATION

Control of health care institutions first occurs at municipal (city and county) and state levels. Each facility providing health care services is required to meet minimal standards established by authoritative bodies, usually through city, county, and state public health commissions or departments. Beyond this basic precautionary assurance of safety to the public, a hospital that desires to be accredited at the national level usually seeks sanction from the

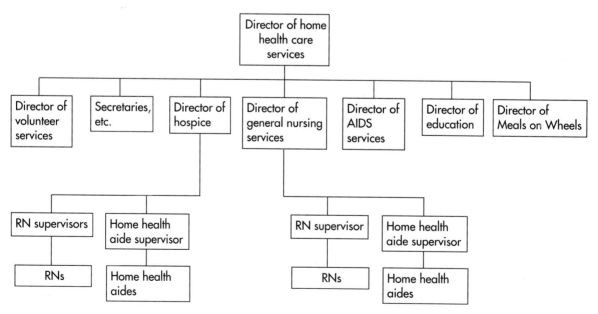

Figure 3-2. Example of the organizational structure of a typical home health care agency.

JCAHO, the primary body at the national level for evaluation of health care institutions. This group provides guidelines that are essential standards for facilities, services, and organizations.[22] This organization is subscribed to by the AHA, the American Medical Association (AMA), the American College of Physicians (ACP), American Association of Homes for the Aging (AAHA), and the American Nursing Home Association (ANHA). Additional criteria, through means of other voluntary accreditation bodies, are required by some groups or agencies before they will fund or use routine or special health care services. Federal funds are major sources of income provided through such avenues as Medicare, construction grants, and education appropriations for medical residencies and internships and nursing education and practice.

The quality of nursing service care is influenced by and closely associated with the quality of hospital and medical care. Although nursing services are reviewed in accordance with specific criteria established by the JCAHO, the American Nurses' Association (ANA) has not been successful in gaining professional representation on the commission.

ORGANIZATION AND ORGANIZATIONAL STRUCTURE
Organization

An organization signifies an institution or functional group, such as a business, government agency, or hospital, with a formal intentional structure of roles or positions. *Organization* also refers to the process of organizing, or the way in which work is arranged and allocated among the members of an institution or business so that the goals of the enterprise can be efficiently achieved. Organizations are a vital element of society, since they enable goals to be accomplished that could not be achieved as well by individual effort.

The strength of an organization lies in its ability to marshal resources to attain a goal, while remaining flexible enough to allow for creativity and growth. The purpose and goals of an organization determine the way it is organized. For example, businesses are created to sell goods and services, and hospitals are created to provide health care. Both accomplish these goals by dividing the work among groups and individuals and linking the subparts together. Providing health care services requires the combined knowledge, coordination, and control of enormous numbers of people and resources, enabling goals to be met that would otherwise be difficult or even impossible to reach. The box lists groups of people and services common to hospital organization.

Organizational Structure

Organizational structure refers to the process or way a group is formed, its channels of authority, span of control, and lines of communication. The establishment of formal organizational patterns through departmentalization and division of work is an attempt for orderliness in administration. A well-organized enterprise results in effective functioning through departments in which each individual is responsible for and performs a specified set of activities. The successful accomplishment of organizational structure, then, makes it possible for an organization to achieve its purposes: (1) to coordinate effort, (2) to have common goals or purposes, (3) to divide

---

◇   **Services, Resources, and People Common to Hospital Organization**   ◇

Services	Resources	People
Medical services	Medical records	Administrators
Nursing services	Pharmacy	Controller
Inservice education and training	Radiology	Admitting officer
Educational offerings	Pathology	Purchasing agent
Social service	Food services	Engineer
Occupational therapy	Volunteers	
Physical therapy	Housekeeping	
	Laundry	

labor, and (4) to establish a functional hierarchy of authority.[1,p.345]

Organizational chart. In small organizations, where there are only a few employees, the manager can verbally explain organizational relationships and changes in relationships to employees as needed. In larger, more formally structured organizations the chain of command is too complex for verbal communication alone; therefore an organizational chart is drawn, in which each position, department, or function is diagrammed and the relationships among them shown. The separate units of the organization usually appear in boxes, which are connected to each other by solid lines that indicate the official chain of command or by broken lines to indicate an unofficial relationship. Most large organizations develop organizational charts and find them very helpful in defining managerial authority, responsibility, and accountability.

Organizational charts have five major characteristics:[23,p.345] (1) division of work, in which each box represents an individual or subunit responsible for a given part of the organization's work load; (2) chain of command, with lines indicating who reports to whom and by what authority; (3) the type of work performed, indicated by the labels or descriptions for the boxes; (4) the grouping of work segments, shown by the clusters of work groups (e.g., departments, single units); and (5) the levels of management, which indicate individual and entire management hierarchy, regardless of where an individual appears on the chart.

Horizontal and circular charts may be used, but the most common format for a large health facility to describe relationships is the vertical chart, constructed to reflect the hierarchical chain of command from the top down.

Hierarchy. *Hierarchy* refers to a body of persons or things organized or classified in pyramidal fashion according to rank, capacity, or authority, with authority assigned to vertical levels with offices ranked in grades, orders, or classes, one above the other. Those with the greatest decision-making authorization are at the top, and those with the least authority are at the bottom.

Span of management. The *span of management* can be defined as the number of persons who report directly to the manager. Considerations that enter into the question of how many managers are needed for a specific number of workers include: (1) the level in the organization in which the work takes place, (2) geographic location, (3) the nature of the work being performed, (4) the abilities and availability of the managers, and (5) the capacities and self-direction of the followers. For nurses the span of control is usually well delineated through decentralization. In the typical structure nursing directors have assistants reporting to them, area coordinators or supervisors reporting to the assistants, and on down the line in the chain of command, with charge nurses or head nurses, nurse case managers, team leaders or primary care nurses, and other staff nurses. The ratio of nurse managers to followers varies with rank or level. The higher the rank or level, the greater the number of employees for which the manager is responsible (as with the director of nursing services). The lower the rank or level (e.g., team leader), the fewer persons there are assigned to the manager's span of control.

The span of management is controlled to allow improved communication, efficiency, and coordination. Too wide a span may mean the managers are overextending themselves and the workers or followers are receiving too little guidance or control. The managers may feel harassed and frustrated, trying to deal as best they can with all their responsibilities. Too narrow a span of management may mean that managers are underused and their workers or followers are overcontrolled, resulting in a waste of human resources.

Typical hospital organizational chart. Figure 3-3 presents a sample organizational chart typically used by hospitals. The chart helps in visualizing the formal organizational structure and is either available on request or placed in policy manuals for employees. Organizational levels are identified as top (e.g., governing board, administrator), intermediate (e.g., directors, supervisors), and bottom (e.g., staff nurses); units of each level are named (e.g., divisions, departments); and titles of positions are assigned. Such a chart shows what activities are performed and

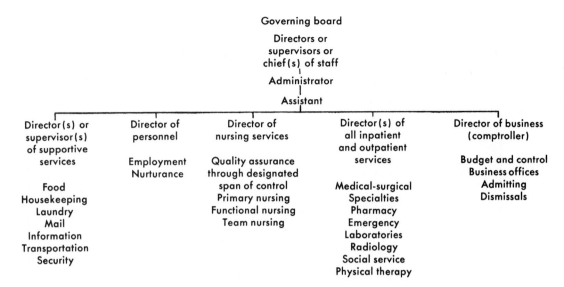

Figure 3-3. Typical hospital organizational chart.

by whom, the groupings of activities, and their relationships.

Organizational relationships are represented by uninterrupted lines between units, showing who reports to whom. The formal authority is represented by the administrative hierarchy and by some health professionals. The medical staff is excluded, as it does not have official status. Only those persons whose salaries are paid by the institution typically fit into the formal pyramid represented by the unbroken lines. When a power relationship is partial or informal, it is represented by a broken or dotted line. Advisory boards, physicians and dentists, and auxiliary and volunteer workers are among those who fit into this category. For example, if a nurse manager reports to a physician but is responsible to the nurse supervisor, a dotted line runs from the nurse to the physician, and an unbroken line from the nurse to the supervisor.

CENTRALIZATION, DECENTRALIZATION, AND MATRIX SYSTEMS

The two major forms of organizational structure are (1) *centralized control* and (2) a *decentralized* or *participatory* approach with occasional use of the matrix system. The centralized model is the most common in hospitals; however, de-

centralized organizational structures are gaining popularity. Emphasis is concentrated on traditional nursing departments, rules, and procedures, with control emanating from the top down (see Figure 3-3). The functional arrangement is by such activities as transportation; food; budget control; personnel; and various specialties in nursing services, including surgical, medical, and pediatric.

The advantages of the centralized form are twofold. First, it can be highly cost-effective, because the special services are grouped together, which eliminates duplication of effort. Second, it makes management easier, because managers have to be experts in only a concentrated range of skills.

The disadvantage of the centralized structure is that as the organization becomes larger and more complex, the hierarchical arrangement can prove cumbersome. For example, a hospital may have a single department of nursing, yet within the department there may be specialties such as open heart surgery, oncology, burn center, trauma nurses, and neonatal intensive care. These many responsibilities in the hands of a single department head dilute the attention one leader can give to each department. Another drawback is that this arrangement does not readily adapt to change. Obtaining quick decisions or actions on specific problems may re-

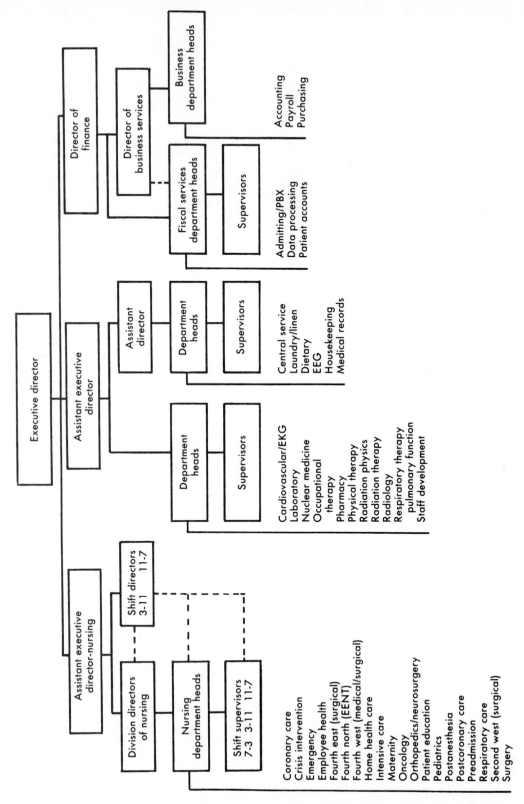

Figure 3-4. Sample of organizational structure under a decentralized or participatory approach. *From Cox CL: Supervisor Nurs 11(3):32, 1980.*

quire more time, because such decisions have to be made by higher-level managers.

The *decentralized* or *participatory* approach is a behavioral system whereby the large structures are broken down into smaller units, and authority is delegated to those closer to the majority of workers.[20] Traditional nursing specialties (e.g., medical, surgical, pediatrics, labor and delivery, each under the control of its supervisor and director of nursing services) are made into departments in themselves on a par with other hospital departments, such as laboratory, dietary, and social services (Figure 3-4). Top management still retains ultimate responsibility for the operations of the various hospital departments, but planning and implementation for each department is carried out by the department head who functions autonomously with authority to administer that department 24 hours a day. The types of decisions to be decentralized are important. They include who controls the budget, who has power over hiring and firing, who handles disciplinary measures, promotions, and transfers, and who handles disputes between staff and management.

The advantages of decentralization can be very positive. As middle managers, the department heads can (1) reflect their interests and have a voice in decision making, (2) improve quality of care through 24-hour continuity, (3) increase communication departmentally and interdepartmentally, (4) have better interpersonal relationships, and (5) problem solve with greater imagination and creativity, because the members know what improves patient care in their areas.

One disadvantage of decentralization could be the initial cost in developing managers and staff training; however, turnover rate under decentralization has been found to be low, and the time, effort, and skill needed to make the system work has proved advantageous. The most serious problem that can occur is a communication breakdown.[24] Nurses who worked at El Camino Hospital during the implementation of decentralization concluded, "There can be no responsiveness in a decentralized system unless there is communication. Effective communication cannot occur without the free exchange of information among all concerned parties."[25] Problems with role clarification can also occur.

Until the system is established, there may be some questions as to who has authority.

In actuality, most systems have some components of both centralization and decentralization. For example, a hospital may maintain its hierarchy but assign control of nursing care delivery to the head nurses, including ancillary and support services. Any degree of flattening of organizational structure will produce benefits, providing adequate planning and preparation have occurred.

Another less commonly used form of organizational structure is the *matrix system,* in which the benefits of both centralized and decentralized control are used. The matrix plan provides for both hierarchical (vertical) coordination in the separate departments, as well as lateral (horizontal) coordination across departments. Every matrix contains three unique sets of relationships: (1) the unit or department manager, who heads and balances the dual lines of authority (e.g., the head nurse); (2) the matrix manager, who shares workers (e.g., a project manager in charge of cost control); and (3) the staff, who report to these two different managers (Figure 3-5). Advantages of the matrix system are that management can apply specialized skills to solve a problem and interdisciplinary cooperation is encouraged. One disadvantage is that all members must possess good interpersonal skills to receive orders from two different bosses.[1]

Significance of Organizational Charts

An organizational chart is meaningful only to the extent that the system represented on paper is a reality. Its precision sometimes masks what is actually taking place in an institution. Hierarchies are far more complex than the average description would indicate. Most observers agree the dynamic levels throughout the hos-

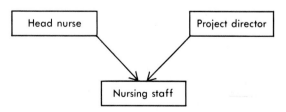

Figure 3-5. Organizational structure using the matrix system.

pital organization are those that occur through informal day-to-day interactions, not by periodic maneuvering of structural arrangements. Questions of importance are to what degree is the formal organization consistent with what actually takes place, and to what degree does hierarchy obstruct or serve organizational purpose?[26,pp.90-94]

Understanding of the organizational structure in which work occurs can be tested by using the form provided in Figure 3-6. Assume that you are a team leader. List those persons with whom you have professional contact in a given day or time, and identify the nature of your relationship with them within the organizational structure of the agency. If a formal organizational chart in which you function is unavailable to you, then use the typical organizational structure provided in Figure 3-3. This relationship or experience may consist of exchanges as follows:

Team leader and dietitian	Discussion of need for change in diet for a patient who is not tolerating present food
Team leader and nurse aide	Discussion about aide's failure to ambulate a patient
Team leader and physician	Telephone conversation about patient's progress
Team leader and director of nursing service	Discussion about general work conditions
Team leader and head or charge nurse	Discussion about need for more nursing personnel on health care team

On completion of the exercise, if you discover that there is some haziness about some lines of authority and uncertainty as to which of the responses is appropriate, then the organizational structure provided is inoperative, and further clarification is needed.

The use of an exercise such as this can dramatize the large number and wide variety of relationships existing in an organization that are neither shown nor suggested by the conventional organizational chart. Such an exercise may also clearly indicate that a large part of an individual's time is oriented at the same level or downward, rather than upward, where authority is thought to be. Analysis also suggests that

authority does not always reside at the top of the organization, as the typical organizational structure would indicate; rather, it may be found at all levels. There is immense power throughout any organizational structure. The nurse manager needs to be aware of the system and its significance in relation to activities inherent in the role.

ORGANIZATIONAL DESIGNS
Bureaucratic Approach to Management

Sociologist Max Weber[29] and management writers Frederick Taylor[30] and Henri Fayol[27,28] were major contributors to the so-called classical approach of bureaucracy, a hierarchical structure based on legalized, formal authority. Most hospitals are structured according to this design, as modern managers believe the bureaucratic format offers a model for placing large numbers of people with diversified skills and abilities into a structure that can be easily identified and programmed. Members of a bureaucratic organization are guided in their actions by (1) rules and regulations, (2) specialization of tasks and division of labor, (3) appointment by merit, and (4) an impersonal climate. Weber praised bureaucracy as an organizational design for its rationality, its clear chain of command, and impartiality. He also admired the clear specification of authority and responsibility, which he believed made it easier for the organization to evaluate performance and distribute rewards fairly.

Rules and regulations. Weber saw the need for a consistent system of rules and regulations pertaining to the rights and duties of personnel in different positions. All bureaucracies have rules and regulations for each office, which ensures accountability and promotes impersonality. The system usually takes the form of policies, bylaws, procedures, and committees. Ideally, each office has representation in the formulation of the rules and regulations, which provides uniformity and coordination. The basic rationale for rules and regulations is that the manager can use them to promote efficiency, which is the overpowering and central goal of bureaucracy, and to eliminate uncertainty in task performance because of differences in individuals. When employees know who is to do what, and

1	2	3	4	5
Name of person with whom you had contact	His or her role in the organization	Who made the initial contact?	Reason for the communication	Relationship within the organizational structure*
Joan Atkins	Pharmacist	Pharmacist	Drug requested not available	b, c

*Place the letter(s) of your response in column 5.

a. Above me in chain of command, but I do not report directly to him/her.

b. Above me in chain of command, and I report directly to him/her.

c. An associate, on the same level with me.

d. He/she is under my direct control.

e. I guide this person's activities, but he/she reports to another person.

f. This person is a part of the organization, but I have no formal control over him/her or he/she over me.

g. A patient, client, or representative.

Figure 3-6. Analysis of contracts with hospital personnel in relation to organizational structure. *Modified from Brown D: Looking into nursing leadership. In The professional nurse looks at authority and hierarchy, Washington, DC, 1966, Leadership Resources, Inc, p 15.*

when and how they are to do it, they feel more secure.

Policy and procedural manuals are common in hospitals. Various formats are used, but each supplies information on policy and on each ma-

jor job, outlining its requirements, limitations, and relationships to other jobs in the enterprise. This is particularly important in nursing because of the vast differences in preparation, titles, and licensing. Among the personnel are aides, assistants, licensed practical or vocational nurses, and registered nurses. Although there is much overlap in nursing functions, there is a need to establish guidelines to ensure that nurses function at their capacity based on educational preparation and within legal limits. The bureaucratic manager needs to know the precise limits of the sphere of responsibility and competency to avoid infringing on that of others. The nurse manager, for example, can exercise leadership with assurance when it is known where responsibility begins and ends.

Specialization and division of labor. One goal of specialization and division of labor in the hierarchical structure is to produce more and better work with the same effort, in the belief that it is a natural means for personnel to become expert in their jobs and to be held responsible for the performance of their specific duties.[28] Technical ability qualifies a person for a given office and secures his or her position in the hierarchy with protection against arbitrary dismissal. The need for division of labor is probably the primary reason for establishing organizational structure. When there is more to be accomplished than any one person can do, the usual procedure is to assess the necessary activities for accomplishment of overall objectives, divide them, and apportion them to departments that perform the specialized functions. This is called *departmentalization* or *decentralization,* demonstrated in the typical organizational structure shown in Figure 3-4. As with span of management, departmentalization should be considered according to (1) purpose, (2) functions, (3) persons and things, and (4) territory or geographical location.[2] Almost without exception, however, in health care facilities departmentalization or decentralization is made on a functional or task-oriented basis, as it incorporates the benefits of specialization, such as operating room, radiologic, medical, surgical, nursing services, and so on. A disadvantage of departmentalization or decentralization is that sometimes little kingdoms are established, and vested interests take precedence over attainment of institutional goals, thus creating conflicts. Also, problems of coordination become more complex as changes occur and departments multiply.

Appointment by merit. Employment and promotions in a bureaucracy are made on the basis of seniority and achievement. Employees who accept the objectives of the organization and produce the quality and quantity of services desired receive higher financial reward, benefits, and status.

Impersonality. Weber believed that a manager should be formal in attitudes, without affection or enthusiasm.[27] He thought that emotional attachments interfere with rational decisions. Weber's ideas of relationships with people neglect the human aspects of organization members, who are assumed to be motivated only by basic economic incentives. As the educational levels, affluence, and work expectations of organization members have risen over time, this criticism of Weber's ideas has become more severe.

HUMAN RELATIONS OR PARTICIPATORY APPROACH TO MANAGEMENT
Human Relations

The human relations movement was a pointed effort to make managers more sensitive to their employees' needs. It came into being as a result of two very different historic influences; unionization and studies of human relations.

Unionization. From the late 1800s to the 1920s, U.S. industry increased rapidly in an attempt to meet the many demands of a burgeoning population. Cheap labor was readily available, and there was a seller's market for finished goods. Then came the Great Depression of the 1930s which left millions unemployed. Many considered business the culprit, causing sympathy to turn from management to labor. Congress passed the Wagner Act in 1935, legalizing union-management collective bargaining. Management began to seek ways to quell the pressure for all-out unionization. Unionization began to filter into the ranks of nursing, although at a much slower rate than in industry.[29]

Human relations. Early human relations researchers and behavioral scientists attempted to deal with what they saw as the major inadequacy of the classic bureaucratic model—the neglect of the human element in the organization. They argued that an industrial organization has two objectives: economic effectiveness *and* employee satisfaction.[30,pp.35-44] The basic principle of the human relations approach is that when things go well for the worker, the organization profits. Two factors are distinguishable in the human resource approach. First, certain leadership characteristics are associated with productivity and good management. Second, emphasis is placed on the worker, particularly as a member of a work group.[30] Study of the human relations approach began in the late nineteenth century, focusing on democratic structure, multidirectional communications, and promotion of general satisfaction of the worker. Self-development, individualization, initiative, and creativity were identified as attributes to be promoted and encouraged. Several researchers have made significant contributions to the humanistic approach.

Mayo-Hawthorne studies. Elton Mayo and his Harvard associates conducted the famous Hawthorne studies of human behavior in work situations in a Western Electric plant from 1927 to 1932. This researcher discovered that when special attention is given to workers by management, productivity is likely to increase, regardless of changes in the working conditions. He also found that informal work groups and an informal social environment among employees, which allow for group decision making, have a great influence on productivity. For Mayo the concept of the social man wanting on-the-job relationships had to replace Weber's concept of the rational man motivated by personal economic needs. Mayo did not argue against the bureaucratic structure but proposed that improvements be made by making the structure less formal and by permitting more employee participation in decision making.[31]

Follett studies. Mary Parker Follett, whose background was in law, political science, and philosophy served as a management consultant until her death in 1933.[32] She had strong conviction that managers should be aware that each employee is a complex collection of emotions, beliefs, attitudes, and habits. To get employees to work harder, she felt, managers had to recognize the motivating desires of the individual. Follett urged managers to motivate performance rather than simply demand it. (See Figure 3-7.) Historians credit Mary Parker Follett with being decades ahead of her time.[33]

McGregor studies. As mentioned in Chapter 2, Douglas McGregor believes that the vertical division of labor that characterizes bureaucratic organizations is based in part on a set of negative assumptions many managers have about workers. He refers to these assumptions as Theory X, in which managers believe that workers have little ambition, desire security above all, and avoid work unless coerced. A rigid, formal hierarchy is designed to control employees. McGregor suggests that organizations can meet their goals much more effectively if they attend to the human needs of organization members and use their potential. He developed a set of assumptions about the worker, called Theory Y, which is compatible with the human relations approach. According to Theory Y, workers can enjoy work, and if conditions are favorable, they will exercise self-control over their performance. Individuals are motivated to do a good job by opportunities to interact with their superiors rather than by financial rewards alone. According to McGregor, personal goals can be achieved through formal organizational structure, policies, and goals.[34]

Chris Argyris's structure. Chris Argyris points out that managers in most formal organizations

Figure 3-7. Follett's concept of motivation and management.

have near-total responsibility for planning, organizing, directing, and evaluating the work of their employees. For example, bureaucratic managers often have complete authority to set work schedules and reward and discipline or dismiss employees. Argyris contends that such domination causes workers to lose heart and become passive and dependent. He maintains that when human needs for self-reliance, self-expression, and self-fulfillment are not met, workers will become dissatisfied, frustrated, cause trouble, or leave, thus increasing costs. Argyris suggests an organizational design that allows workers a much greater degree of independence and decision-making power and creates a more informal and flexible organizational climate. He also favors the formation of teams of work on special projects. This is the matrix organizational structure.[35]

Maslow's theory. Dr. Abraham Maslow, noted psychologist and the father of motivation theory, determined that people can best be understood through the study of human needs and their influence on behavior.[36] His theory has probably received more attention and application to organizational environments than any other, for his classifications have direct implications for managing human behavior in organization. Maslow says that humans are ever-wanting creatures. As one need is satisfied, another appears to take its place. The individual is then motivated to satisfy the new need. Maslow developed a hierarchy of needs based on clinical experience. Figure 3-8 provides an example of these needs with suggestions as to how they relate to a member of an organization.

Note that the hierarchy is arranged in the form of a triangle that illustrates the needs of each person: (1) physiological need, (2) security or safety need, (3) social need, (4) ego or self-esteem need, and (5) self-actualization or self-fulfillment need. The hierarchy of needs theory indicates that the individual must first satisfy the lower level needs before realizing higher level needs. It is possible to move in and out of the levels, according to needs present at any given time. The strength and priority of these needs will vary with each person. What motivates a person at one time may have no motivation for

that person at another period in life. Another way to look at the pyramid is to vary the thickness of the layers according to different attitudes, values, and perceptions of life.

Likert's studies. Rensis Likert shares the views of McGregor, Argyris, and Maslow. In his research on effective group performance he found that traditional authoritarian managers are less able to motivate their staff to high standards of achievement than are managers who promote their staff's feelings of worth and importance. Likert created a model for organizational design that provides for bureaucratic methods in which organizations and managers are held accountable for their group's performance but also provides for a system in which (1) supportive relationships are encouraged, (2) group decision making occurs when appropriate, and (3) high performance goals are set. The principle of supportive relationships suggests that attending to one another's needs should add to the sense of personal worth and importance of individual members. Through the use of group decision making and high performance goals, managers can help group members feel that they are responsible for decisions affecting them and that they are an integral part of the organization. The setting and attainment of high goals enable organization members to develop a sense of pride and accomplishment.[37,38]

Advantages of the human relations approach to management. Above all else, the behavioral approach makes it clear that people are the key to productivity. According to the advocates of the behavioral approach, technology, work rules, and standards do not guarantee good job performance. Success depends on motivated and skilled individuals who are committed to organizational objectives. Only a manager's sensitivity to individual concerns can foster the cooperation necessary for high productivity.[39,pp.80-81]

Limitations of the human relations approach to management. A common criticism of the human relations approach to management is that most managers function in a bureaucratic environment in which one organizational design is

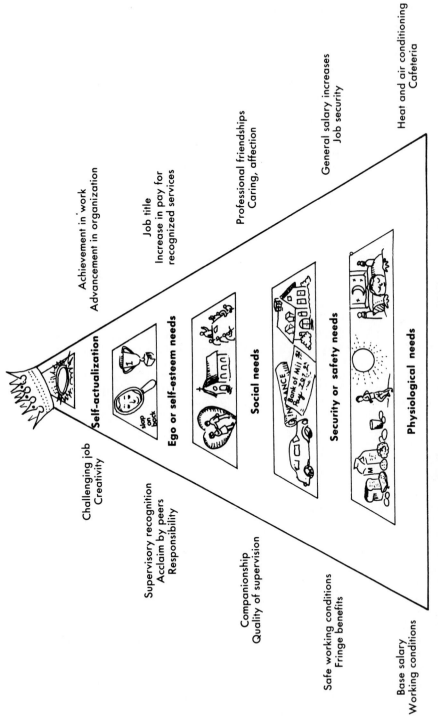

Figure 3-8. Maslow's hierarchy of needs applied to members of an organization. *Modified from Szilagyi A: Management and performance, Santa Monica, Calif, 1981, Goodyear Publishing Co.*

adopted and little enthusiasm is given by administration for individuality. Also, opponents of the human relations approach believe that a truly democratic approach is time-consuming and that work goals may not be met, particularly when the objectives of lower-level employees are not consistent with the goals at the top level or power base of the organization. Further, individual differences are overlooked, as not everyone can or wants to work in a moderately structured environment. Some persons prefer the security of strong control with clearly defined activities and limits.

ADOPTION OF AN APPROPRIATE ORGANIZATIONAL STRUCTURE AND MANAGEMENT SYSTEM

Selection of an organizational structure and management system that is right for an agency

is crucial to efficiency and effectiveness of the organization. The structure and system selected must match the purposes and goals of the organization and be compatible with the needs of those charged with fulfillment of those purposes and goals. The consequences of an inappropriate structure and management system can be inefficiency, high cost, unrest, dissatisfaction, or even outright failure of the organization. Rarely is one structure or system used exclusively, and after selection there can be many changes, for organization is a dynamic process with continuous need for appraisal and adaptation. The box compares the major characteristics of the bureaucratic and human relations approach. Each system is represented in the extreme. One can readily see that parts of each system are present in any organized structure and management system.

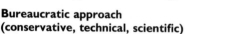

Comparison of Characteristics of Bureaucratic and Human Relations Approaches to Organizational Structure and Management Systems

Bureaucratic approach (conservative, technical, scientific)

Control is organizational.
Leaders are appointed by head(s) or hierarchy.
Directions are one-way; nonquestioning obedience is demanded.
Organization manipulates needs of employer and serves its goals; loyalty to organizational goals.

Workers at each level are viewed mechanically as objects to be used interchangeably to get the work done.
Manager is controller.
Personnel are manipulated; management defines objectives.
Class and class status structure lead to job satisfaction.
Physiological factors (strength, speed, skill, and so on) produce fluctuations in production.
Workers relate to organization individually.

Job fragmentation and specialization occur.
Economic factors are primary motivation; emphasis on quantity output in least amount of time.

Human relations approach (democratic, participative, liberal)

Control is democratic or participatory.
Leaders are approved by followers.
Communication system is open, multidirectional.

Goals are consistent with individual goals; otherwise workers' first loyalty is to profession; second to organization.
Workers are matched carefully with work assignment; value is given to individualism, self-control, initiative, and creativity.
Manager is a facilitator.
Natural work groups define own objectives.

Acceptance as part of a stable group leads to satisfaction.
Social conditions (acceptance, common interests, and so on) determine level of production.
Members of small groups relate to one another and then to the organization.
Individual behavior is subject to the group.
Social forces and quality of service are more important than economic factors.

SUMMARY

1. Each health organization has both a formal structure (highly planned and publicized) and an informal structure (unplanned and concealed).
2. The purpose of most health institutions is to serve four primary needs of the public: (1) patient care, (2) education, (3) research, and (4) protection of public health.
3. The American Hospital Association (AHA) defines a hospital as an institution whose major purpose is to provide patient services. Guidelines are provided at national and state levels to protect the interest of the consumer.
4. There are three types of health care organizations: (1) government owned, (2) voluntary or non-profit-making, and (3) proprietary or profit-making.
5. Voluntary health agencies are nonprofit, tax-exempt organizations designed to meet the health needs of the general public.
6. Proprietary health agencies operate for profit.
7. Community hospital mergers consist of incorporating groups of hospitals under one umbrella. The major goal is to increase hospital systems' power in highly competitive marketplaces. There are four types of mergers: (1) rescue, (2) collaborative, (3) contested, and (4) raid.
8. Increased labor and technology costs accompanied by declining inpatient revenues and competition from health maintenance organizations (HMOs), private sector systems, and other hospitals have caused great changes in health care institutions.
9. Retrospective payment for health services is reimbursement after the services have been provided.
10. Prospective payment involves setting payment levels for services before they are provided.
11. Diagnoses-related groups (DRGs) are the basis of a prospective payment system (PPS) for hospital services given Medicare patients.
12. The Prospective Payment System (PPS) established in 1983 sets fixed fees for services to Medicare-covered inpatients, based strictly on diagnosis without regard to treatment choices or the actual cost of an individual patient's care. Under this system, hospitals fare better financially by providing fewer services to more patients.
13. A Preferred Provider Organization (PPO) is a health financing and delivery arrangement in which a group of health care providers (e.g., physicians, hospitals) offer their services on a predetermined financial basis to health care providers.
14. The Omnibus Budget Reconciliation Act (OBRA) of 1989 was designed to bring spending for Medicare and Medicaide, which is not controlled through the regular congressional appropriations process, into conformity with the annual budget.
15. Health care agencies are adapting to new reimbursement systems by reducing the number of nonpaying patients, rewarding physicians with incentives, making alliances with other health care agencies, and employing stricter financial controls.
16. Magnet hospitals are urban, medium-to-large-size community hospitals or medical centers that have a reputation for high retention of nurses and excellence of nursing practice. They often have a system of autonomous, self-governed operation at the unit level. The nurse manager's role is typically broad in scope.
17. JCAHO is the primary body at the national level for evaluation of health care institutions. It has support from most health professional organizations. The American Nurses' Association (ANA) does not yet have representation.
18. Organization is done to attain organizational purpose and overall goals that could not be performed by one person alone.
19. Organization involves setting up a mechanism to coordinate the work of organization members into a unified, orderly, and harmonious whole.
20. The composition of an organization includes channels of authority, span of control, and lines of communication.
21. There are two major forms of organizational structure: centralized control and the decentralized or participatory approach. A

third system, called matrix, combines the best of the centralized and decentralized forms.

22. Formal organization common among existing hospitals is a hierarchical, pyramid-like structure, with authority assigned along vertical lines. The greatest decision-making power is at the top and those with the least authority are at the bottom.

23. Authority is found at all levels. A large part of a nurse manager's time is spent with people at the same level or at a lower level in the organization.

24. Public health services are those conducted on a community basis for the public good. Public health's mission is to fulfill society's interest in assuring conditions in which people can live healthy lives.

25. Community health nursing focuses on the health of the whole community. The community health nurse engages in the nursing process of assessment with other disciplines to identify problems, develops plans for intervention, implements plans, and evaluates their impact on the health status of those served.

26. Public health organizational structure includes resources (money, people, physical plant, and technology) and the organizational configuration necessary to transform these resources into health services.

27. The Director of Public Health Nursing is responsible for all functions, which are delegated through assistant directors.

28. Home health care services/visiting nurse associations include traditional services such as skilled nursing, home health aide services, varied therapists, and medical social services. In recent years, more comprehensive services have been included, such as respiratory therapy, parenteral nutrition, intravenous therapy, and chemotherapy.

29. Home health care agencies are either voluntary, proprietary, or hospital based. The services follow a physician-approved plan of treatment.

30. The human relations movement was a pointed effort to make managers more sensitive to employee needs. Unionization and human relation studies served as impetus to the movement.

31. There are basically two approaches to organization and management: bureaucratic and human relations.

32. Bureaucracy is the classic approach, based on a hierarchical structure with legalized, formal authority. Common characteristics are (1) rules and regulations, (2) specialization of tasks and division of labor, (3) appointment by merit, and (4) an impersonal climate. Most hospitals have a bureaucratic structure.

33. Criticisms of the classic bureaucratic form of organization and management are: (1) it neglects the human aspects of organization members, who are assumed to be motivated only by economic incentives; (2) it does not take into account rapidly changing and uncertain environments; (3) as the organization grows in size, top managers become progressively out of touch with realities at the lower levels of the organization; and (4) there may be a breakdown in communications between managers and followers, permitting counterproductive personal insecurities to flourish.

34. Advantages of the human relations approach to management include key emphasis on people, which results in a staff of motivated individuals committed to organizational objectives.

35. Criticisms of the human relations approach to organization and management are: (1) most persons function in a bureaucratic environment, making it difficult to apply a participatory approach to management; (2) it is time-consuming; (3) organizational goals may not be met; and (4) not everyone likes to work in a moderately structured environment.

36. In selecting an organizational structure and management system, one must consider what is best for agency efficiency and effectiveness in relation to its purposes and overall goals and congruency of the workers.

Questions for Study and Discussion

1. How is the college/university you attend owned and organized? Can your educational institution be compared with one kind of health care agency structure? Which one? In what way?

2. Compare the similarities and differences among health care delivery systems that are government owned, nonprofit, and proprietary.

3. Give the rationale for the merging of health care agencies. What are the advantages and disadvantages of merging?

4. Explain the differences between retrospective and prospective payment systems. Which system is currently most popular? Why?

5. What is a Preferred Provider Organization (PPO)? Who belongs to PPOs? Why do health agencies vie for health care providing purchasers' business?

6. List several ways health care agencies can adapt to reimbursement systems. Are you disturbed by any of the means suggested? Explain.

7. Upon graduation from your nursing program, would you consider applying for a staff position at a magnet hospital? What are your reasons for applying? For not applying?

8. Define the terms "public health services" and "community health nursing." What are the differences in scope of practice?

9. Explain the differences between the roles of a public health nurse and a home health care nurse.

10. What is meant by "span of control?" What is your span of control as a student? If you were a staff nurse, what would be your span of control?

11. Select a place of employment (past or present) in which you worked. Diagram to whom you would go with a problem and to whom that person would go with a problem, and so on to the top. Are there any gaps you cannot complete? If applicable, why do you think you did not know the lines of authority from the lowest level to the top?

12. Would you rather work in a centralized or in a decentralized organization? For what reasons?

13. What are the characteristics of a bureaucracy? In your opinion, how applicable are these characteristics to most health care delivery systems today? What is your rationale?

14. What do unionization and the human relations approach to management have in common?

15. Select one human relations expert and explain his or her philosophy of management. Do you agree with this person? Explain why.

REFERENCES

1. Hellriegal D and Slocum J: Management, ed 5, Reading, Mass, 1989, Addison-Wesley Publishing Co.
2. Longest B: Management practices for the health professional, ed 4, Norwalk, Conn, 1990, Appleton & Lange.
3. American Hospital Association: Hospital terminology, Chicago, 1988, The Association.
4. Sullivan E and Decker J: Effective management in nursing, ed 2, Menlo Park, Calif, 1988, Addison-Wesley Publishing Co.
5. Robino D and DeMeuse K: Corporate mergers and acquisitions: their impact on HRM, Personnel Administrator, 30(11):33-34, 1989.
6. Pritchett P: After the merger: managing the shock-waves, New York, 1985, Dow-Jones-Irwin.
7. Kaye G: Multies, mergers, acquisitions and the health care provider, Nurs Man 20(4):56, 1989.
8. The Health Insurance for the Aged Act, The Social Security Amendments of 1965, p. 1, 89-97, 42 USC.
9. Sullivan T and Moore V: A critical look at recent developments in tax exempt hospitals, J Health Hosp Law 23(3):65-80, 1990.
10. Pointer D and Pointer T: Case-based prospective price reimbursement, Nurs Man 20(4):30-33, 1989.

11. Van Hoesen N and Ericksen L: The impact of diagnoses-related groups on patient acuity, quality of care, and length of stay, JONA 20(9):20-23, 1990.
12. Jones K: Feasibility analysis of preferred provider organizations, J Nurs Adm 20(1):28-33, 1990.
13. The Omnibus Budget Reconciliation Act of 1989, Conference report no. 101-386, 1st session. P. L. 101-239, 1989.
14. Epstein J: An examination of the Omnibus Budget Reconciliation Act of 1989: the evolution of national health policy, J Health Hosp Law 23(2):53-59, 1990.
15. Horwitz D: Corporate reorganization: the last gasp or last clear chance for the tax-exempt, non profit hospital? Am J Law Med 13(5):527, 1988.
16. Kramer M: Trends to watch at the magnet hospital, Nursing 90 20(6):67-74, 1990.
17. Kramer M: The magnet hospitals: excellence revisited, JONA 20(9):35-44, 1990.
18. Institute of Medicine: The future of public health, Washington DC, 1988, National Academy Press.
19. Josten L: Wanted: leaders for public health, Nurs Outlook 37(5):230-232, Sept-Oct, 1989.
20. Ad Hoc Committee on Public Health Nursing Definition and Practice, Public Health Nursing Section: The definition and role of public health nursing in the delivery of health care, Washington, 1980, American Public Health Association.
21. Brault G: Home health care nursing: the changing picture. In Bullough B and Bullough V: Nursing in the community, St. Louis, 1990, Mosby–Year Book, Inc.
22. Joint Commission on Accreditation of Healthcare Organizations: Accreditation manual for hospitals, Chicago, 1988, The Commission.
23. Kreitner R: Management, ed 4, Boston, 1989, Houghton-Mifflin Co.
24. Gillies D: Nursing management: a systems approach, ed 2, Philadelphia, 1989, W. B. Saunders Co.
25. Althaus J: Nursing decentralization: the El Camino experience, Wakefield, Mass, 1981, Nursing Resources, pp. 5-133.
26. Wheelen T and Hunger J: Strategic management, ed 3, Reading, Mass, 1990, Addison-Wesley Publishing Co.
27. Weber M: Economy and society, New York, 1968, Bedminster Press.
28. Taylor F: Scientific organization, New York, 1947, Harper & Brothers.
29. Wilson N, Hamilton C, and Murphy E: Union dynamics in nursing, JONA 20(2):35-39, 1990.
30. Weber M: Theory of social and economic organization, New York, 1947, The Free Press (Translated by A M Henderson and T Parsons).
31. Mayo E: The human problems of an industrialized civilization, New York, 1953, Macmillan.
32. Parker L: Control in organizational life: the constitution of Mary Parker Follett, Acad Man Rev 9(19):736-745, 1984.
33. Bluedorn A: The classics of management, Acad Man Rev 11(4):451-454, 1986.
34. McGregor D: The human side of enterprise, New York, 1960, McGraw-Hill Book Co.
35. Argyris C: Integrating the individual and the organization, New York, 1964, John Wiley & Sons.
36. Maslow A: Motivation and personality, ed 2, New York, 1970, Harper & Row, Publishers.
37. Likert R: New patterns of management, New York, 1961, McGraw-Hill Book Co.
38. Likert R: The human organization, New York, 1967, McGraw-Hill Book Co.
39. Sayles L: Leadership: managing in real organizations, ed 2, New York, 1989, McGraw-Hill Book Co.

SUGGESTED READINGS

Adamson G and Emswiller T: Communicating the vision, Healthcare Forum J 34(1):12-15, 1991.

Alidina M and Funke-Furber J: First line nurse managers: optimizing the span of control, JONA 18(5):34-39, 1988.

Cohen W and Levinthae D: Absorptive capacity: a new perspective on learning and innovation, Adm Sci Q 35(1):128-152, March 1990.

Gilmore T: Effective leadership during organizational transitions, Nurs Econ 8(3):135-141, 1990.

Jaques J, Gillies D, and Biordi D: Outpatient surgery: a case study, Nurs Man 21(10):88i-88k, 1990.

McCreight L: The future of public health, Nurs Outlook 37(5):219-225, 1989.

Mitchell P, Krueger J, and Moody L: The crisis of the health care nonsystem, Nurs Outlook 38(5):214-217, 1990.

News: Push to "reform": long-term care seen "starting off on crutches," Am J Nurs 91(1):85-88, 1991 (Omnibus Budget Act).

Olliver C: Visions communicated, Healthcare Forum J 34(1):17-21, 1991.

Pappas C and Van-Scoy-Mosher C: Establishing a profitable outpatient community nursing center, JONA 18(5):31-33, 1988.

Ramirez D: Culture in nursing service organization, Nurs Man 21(1):14-17, 1990.

Reynolds L: Will government force a healthcare marriage? Man Rev 79(4):28-29, 1990.

Rooks J: Let's admit we ration health care—then set priorities, Am J Nurs 90(6):39-43, 1990.

Sands R: Hospital governance: nurse trustee vis-a-vis nurse executive, Nurs Man 21(12):14-16, 1990.

Sawin K: The AHCPR effectiveness initiatives: opportunities for rehabilitation nursing, Rehab Nurs 15(5):264-266, 1990.

Steel P: Surviving organizational change, Nurs Man 21(12):50-51, 1990.

Simpson R: The Joint Commission did what you wouldn't, Nurs Man 22(1):26-27, 1991.

Townsend M: A participative approach to administrative reorganization, JONA 20(2):11-14, 1990.

Turner S: Dealing with medical staff: it's time to do it differently, Nurs Man 21(2):52-53, 1990.

Viau J: Theory 2: "magic potion" for decentralized management? Nurs Man 21(12):34-36, 1990.

Ward D: National health insurance: where do nurses fit in? Nurs Outlook 38(5):206-207, 1990.

4

Nursing Personnel and Their Roles

☐ Define the meaning of role analysis and identify factors that affect role in nursing practice.

☐ List and explain the functional roles of nurse managers.

☐ Explain the different levels of nursing education.

☐ Describe the problems encountered by foreign registered nurses seeking licensure in the United States.

☐ Identify the major categories of nursing personnel and the preparation and education required for each position.

☐ Describe the role expectations for the common categories of licensed nursing personnel.

☐ Define the expanded role of the nurse case manager.

In preceding chapters the leadership and management process, styles of leadership and management that best support a successful managerial role, organizational structure, and management sytems have been discussed. The manager also needs to know about types of nursing personnel and their roles. This chapter discusses role theory and role expectation in the typical organizational structure, nurse population, nurse education, nurse registration, and the expanded role of the nurse. Armed with knowledge about these topics, the nurse leader / manager can better fulfill the responsibilities of the position.

ROLES OF NURSING PRACTICE

A role is a group of related activities carried out by an individual. The concept of *role* is drawn from the behavioral sciences and has been defined as a prescribed way of behaving, or a social prescription for a person who has a specific position within a group.[1,p.571] In a healthy organization, everyone knows his or her role, and those roles mesh in a way that encourages cooperation and reduces dysfunctional conflict. For this reason, *role analysis,* which is *the systematic clarification of interdependent tasks and job behavior* is of vital importance.

Role Characteristics

Certain features characterize a role: (1) it requires that a person who accepts a role behave in a certain way; (2) it implies transaction with others as social interaction occurs; (3) it involves expectations and perception by both the role enactor and those with whom he or she relates; (4) it depends on social norms regarding values, judgments, and feelings; (5) it leads to conformity, as boundaries for pactice are usually established; and (6) it may place demands on an individual that he or she may not be able to fulfill or that are incompatible with his or her personal preferences,[2,pp.585,587; 3,pp.68-69] thus creating conflict.

The Nurse's Role

The nurse's perceived role is determined in part by *sources of roles* and the existence of multiple roles. Sources that form a nurse's role are institutional requirements (rules and regulations, job descriptions), patient/client expectations (patients, rights), peer expectations (group norms), and the nurse's conception of what behaviors the role implies based on professional values and attitudes (see the box below).

A second key characteristic of a nurse's role is that there are *multiple roles* to perform during a typical day. In nurse case management, for example, the nurse is a manager (planner, organizer, director, controller); coordinator; collaborator; expert clinician; and communicator with patients, families, and all others who influence care. Each member of a role set (e.g., nursing group or team) is influenced by his or her own performance and the actions of others. Members may be rewarded or punished because of one person's behavior and may require certain actions (role expectations) from that person to perform his or her own tasks.

The sources for role expectation and the varied roles in which a nurse engages can give rise to role problems in organizations if there are unclear or ambiguous messages. Problems also arise if the nurse receives different directions from several sources (e.g., physician, supervisor, patient, interdisciplinary personnel), who all expect compliance. This leads to role conflict. Another problem occurs if a nurse is unwilling or unable to accept the norms associated with the role. Unless the problem is identified and resolved, stress and job dissatisfaction will result. In a healthy organization, everyone knows his or her role, and those roles mesh in a way that encourage cooperation and reduce dysfunctional conflict.

The Nurse Manager's Role

As nursing service departments become decentralized, the role of head nurses is changing from a clinical to a management focus. Increasingly, head nurses are expected to assume responsibility for the management of a number of nursing units. Adjusting to the role changes from centralized to decentralized management requires a certain level of expertise. This may be accomplished through mentoring, inservice education, and formal education. Managerial tasks of the role need to be clearly identified. See the box on p. 62.

NURSE LICENSURE

A license is a legal document that permits a person to offer his or her skills and knowledge

---

Role Definition and Expectations of a Nurse

Role definition

Organized set of expected behaviors of a nurse in any given position

Expectations of a nurse from various sources

Meets institutional requirements (rules, regulations, job descriptions)
Meets patient/client needs (patient's rights)
Maintains professional values and attitudes
Works within group norms
Establishes effective communication strategies and social interaction

◇ **Seven Roles in Nursing Management as Identified by Sherman** ◇

Sherman identified seven functional roles in nursing management which were further identified in a research study of 48 head nurses and 20 nursing supervisors employed at six hospitals in Wisconsin.[4,5]

1. **Planning** for self, for the nursing unit(s) and for emergencies.
2. **Organizing,** ranging from arranging one's own and others' work loads to participating in analysis of wages, working conditions, and procedures for handling supplies, drugs, and equipment.
3. **Staffing,** including interviewing and orienting new staff, as well as being involved in inservice programs.
4. **Leading,** being familiar with the agency's mission, philosophy and goals, coordinating activities of nursing personnel, and providing advice on nursing practice, as needed.
5. **Communicating,** listening to all personnel, maintaining effective horizontal and vertical relationships and publicizing staff's achievements to higher management.
6. **Decision making,** including problem solving and selling major change ideas to supervisors.
7. **Controlling,** including safety and quality assurance activities.

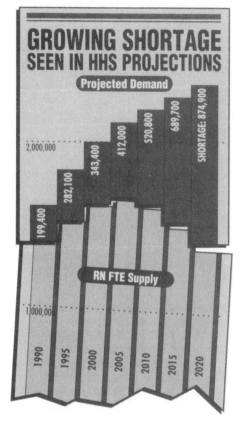

Figure 4-1. Health and Human Services projections regarding RN supply between 1990 and 2020. *From News: RN population seen declining after the year 2000: HHS predicts shortage could top 800,000 by 2020, AJN 90(9):97, 1990.*

to the public in a particular jurisdiction, where such practice would be unlawful without a license. The purpose of nursing licensure is to protect society from unskilled and incompetent persons who would practice or offer to practice nursing. All professional nurses who practice for hire are required to have a license. To accomplish this, it is necessary to define the scope of practice in the field coming under control. Each state has the responsibility to develop its own nurse practice act and to establish regulatory measures for implementation. Students or nurses should obtain a copy of the nurse practice act of their state and study it for professional guidelines and implications.

NURSE POPULATION[6]

According to a 1989 sample survey prepared by Evelyn Moses, chief of the federal Division of

Nursing's Data & Analysis Staff for the Department of Health and Human Services (HHS), the RN population is 2,118,900. The number of working nurses is 1,687,000, with a full time equivalent supply of 1,414,800. In the HHS projection, increasing nurse shortages will occur in nursing, public health, and allied health over the next 30 years. The report paints an alarming picture of growing deficits of nursing personnel. As Figure 4-1 indicates, the shortfall of RNs will swell from 199,400 in 1990 to 874,900 in the year 2020. There is presently a downtrend in the number of graduates from nursing schools and an escalation in demand for RNs. Moses cautions readers not to view the forecast as fact, but rather as a framework for reading trends. The HHS study indicates RNs' median age to be 39, but the age distribution is changing. In 1988, 14.4% of nurses were between ages 70 and 74 and 97.8% between ages 20 and 24. Employment of those over age 50 was 26.8%. Only 8.5% of employed RNs were from ethnic/minority backgrounds, a matter of concern to HHS. The report had little to say about future prospects for the LPN/LVN population since no recent data have been collected on that group. The number of LPN/LVN programs peaked at 1319 in 1977. Since that time the number has decreased over 21%. In 1977-1978 there were 45,350 graduates from LPN/LVN programs, and in 1986-1987 there were only 27,285. The expert panel guesses that demand for LPNs/LVNs will decline in the long run, whereas jobs for nurses' aides will continue to grow. A contrasting view from the Bureau of Labor Statistics calculates that needs for LPNs will expand by 38% between 1986 and 2000.

FOREIGN NURSE LICENSURE

With backing from the American Nurses' Association and the National League for Nursing, the Commission on Graduates of Foreign Nursing Schools (CGFNS) was created in 1978 to administer a twice-a-year test of nursing and English language competencies.[6] By now, 43 of the 53 state registered nurse boards (includes Guam, Puerto Rico, and Virgin Islands) insist on CGFNS certification. The Immigration and Naturalization Service (INS) and the Department of Labor also require certification for an H-1 visa. It is estimated that now approximately 10,000 foreign nurses enter the United States each year with temporary H-1 visas. These are issued after a sponsoring employer submits proof to the INS that the "alien" is a duly licensed professional registered nurse. A large number of foreign nurses come from the Philippines.

Because of the nursing shortage, some states (such as New York and California, which currently have the largest numbers of foreign applicants for the licensure test) do not comply with ANA and NLN recommendations. The national passing rate for foreign nurse graduates first taking the RN licensure examination ranged from 35% in February 1983 to 50% in July 1986. Twenty thousand foreign nursing students took the RN licensure examination in 1989.[7] An RN advisory committee in California is recommending to the legislature that the state adopt the CGFNS requirement. They propose that schools sponsor remedial courses and urge employers to help foreign-trained nurses to improve their communications skills so they can more easily move into the U.S. nursing arena and can ensure greater patient safety and quality care.[7]

NURSING EDUCATION

Nursing education for registered nurses in the United States had its beginning in the latter half of the nineteenth century in New York. The English ideals of nursing were followed, with the school run by nurses, affiliated with the hospital, and service training an integral part of the education. The course generally involved 1 year of training, followed by 1 to 3 years of employment at the hospital. Lectures were given by physicians' bedside training was provided by nurses.[8]

The number of such nursing schools grew rapidly in the late nineteenth century as the number of hospitals increased, demanding the free labor that student nurses provided. Exploitation of students led nurses to join forces to upgrade their status, forming organizations that were the precursors to the National League for Nursing (NLN) and the American Nurses' Association (ANA). This mobilization led to improving nursing education through registration and accreditation of schools. Nursing licensure was accomplished in every state by 1923.[9]

Today registered nursing education programs operate with specific goals and guidelines to enable graduates to meet the licensure requirements of their respective states, which are usually comparable with other states with the aid of endorsement or reciprocity.

Nursing Schools: Number and Types

As of 1987, there are about 1465 nursing schools in the United States with 70,561 graduates annually. These schools offer a total of 789 associate degree, 209 diploma, and 467 generic baccalaureate programs. In addition, there are 194 master's programs and 45 doctoral programs.[10] Table 2 describes the various categories of nursing education programs in the United States,

◇ **Table 2.** Nursing education program in the United States

CATEGORY	PROGRAM BASE	LENGTH OF PROGRAM	STATE LICENSURE REQUIREMENTS	RECOGNITION
Aides, assistants, orderlies, attendants	Hospital, adult education, community colleges, private schools	3-6 months	No	Certification optional— required in most states
Practical nurse or vocational nurse	Hospital or hospital/ community college	1-1½ years	Yes (LPN/ LVN)	Certification
Diploma programs	Hospital or hospital/ community college	3 years	Yes (RN)	Certification
Associate degree programs	Community college/ hospital	2 years	Yes (RN)	Associate in arts degree (AA)
Baccalaureate degree programs	College or university	4-5 years	Yes (RN)	Bachelor of science degree in nursing (BSN, BS)
Master's degree in clinical nursing or nursing education programs	University	1½-2 years	Varies with individual state	Master's degree in nursing in specialty area (MSN, MS)
Doctoral programs in nursing	University	3-4 years	Varies with individual state	Doctoral degree in nursing in specialty area (PhD, EdD)

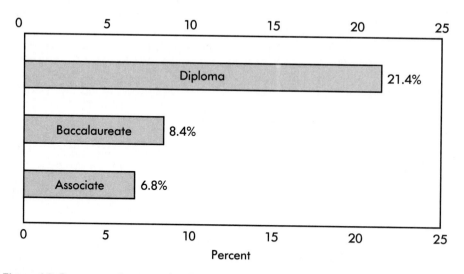

Figure 4-2. Percentage decrease of *graduates* from basic nursing programs from 1977 to 1988. *Adapted from National League for Nursing data review 19-2290, New York, 1988, The League.*

indicating program base, length of study, state licensure requirements, and the recognition granted.

From the years 1977 to 1988, the number of graduates from most nursing programs has de- creased: 8.4% for baccalaureate, 6.8% for associate, and 21.4% for diploma programs. (See Figure 4-2.) Speculation regarding the decrease in enrollment in basic nursing education programs focuses on the "new age" with its multiple and varied opportunities for women to pursue other professional careers. Diploma programs have been hardest hit, as students switched to college-based programs and hospitals closed schools.[10]

Enrollment Upswing in Basic Nursing Education

A 1989-1990 report by the American Association of Colleges indicates that the trend for admissions to nursing programs has changed from negative to positive. As Figure 4-3 indicates, diploma schools led the growth with a 10.3% advance. AD programs followed with a 6.4% rise, and BSN programs contributed a 3.7% increase. There are fewer diploma programs, but the number of enrolling students has increased.[11]

Enrollment Upswing in RNs Returning to BSN Programs and Graduate Education

Enrollment in master's degree programs was up 8.2% in 1989, and in doctoral programs up 9.2%. The number of RNs returning for BSN degrees increased by 44.7% in the last 5 years.[11] (See Figure 4-4.)

TECHNICAL VERSUS PROFESSIONAL NURSING PRACTICE (AD VERSUS BSN)

Major nursing organizations espouse the belief that different technical and professional levels of nursing exist, and nursing curricula for the two levels—bachelor of science in nursing (BSN) and associate degree (AD)—vary in length and content. In practice, this belief is often not carried out in staff assignment.[12] Much research has been conducted to find evidence of the differences between BSN and AD graduates in skills and practice, but there are flaws in the research. Very little has been done to differentiate the complexity of clinical judgment required to make clinically competent, knowledge-based practice decisions in the management of patients' care, probably because there is a lack of concensus on the identifiable body of knowledge required to practice any level of professional nursing.[13] Yet there is bias on the part of the persons ranking nurses of various levels. Those who have not earned bachelor's degrees themselves are less likely to rank BSN graduates higher than AD graduates.[13] Although most hospital job descriptions do not

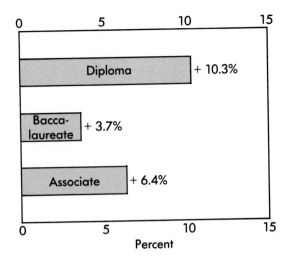

Figure 4-3. Upward trend of enrollment in basic nursing programs in fall of 1988. *Adapted from News: diploma schools are reviving as enrollments surge, AJN 90(9):104, 1990.*

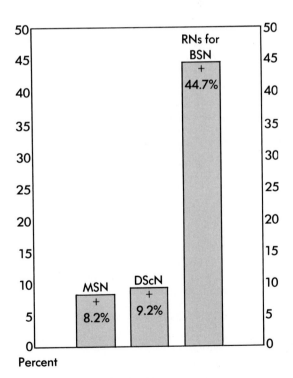

Figure 4-4. Report of enrollment in gradute programs in nursing and for RNs returning for a baccalaureate degree. *Adapted from a report on 1989-1990 enrollment and graduations in baccalaureate and graduate programs in nursing, Washington, DC, 1990, AACN.*

specify a requirement for a baccalaureate degree, the majority list the BSN degree as preferred. Job descriptions for almost all nurse managerial positions specify baccalaureate or master's level preparation as required or preferred.

Arenas, Not Levels, of Practice

Leah Curtin, editor of *Nursing Management* magazine, states that nursing practice is being differentiated by necessity and by demand. (This trend is reflected in the thoughts of other nursing leaders.) She proposes that, for the 1990s and beyond, levels of practice such as "professional" versus "technical" no longer be considered, but "arenas" of practice be considered instead, using the following categories.[14]

Arena 1. Clinical nurses, who work in health care agencies, whose role will be to plan and deliver direct care to the majority of people who become ill, need surgery, or reside in elder-care facilities. For patients who require complex care or who are at high risk, clinical nurses will collaborate with nurse case managers in the design and delivery of direct care. Clinical nurses will be prepared at the associate and baccalaureate levels.

Arena 2. Nurse specialists, who limit their practices to specific areas of care, such as midwives, anesthetists, and nurse practitioners. Nurse specialists will work in a variety of settings and will be prepared at master's and doctoral levels.

Arena 3. Nurse case managers, who will coordinate with primary nurses, physicians, social workers, home health nurses, and so on, in the design, delivery and evaluation of care for high-risk patients in the hospital and in the community. Employed by hospitals and community agencies, these nurses will be prepared at baccalaureate and master's levels.

CERTIFICATION PROGRAMS

Certification is a credential issued by a professional body that helps protect the consumer by affirming a person's excellence in a particular area. The American Nurses' Association tests and certifies seven types of nurse clinicians at the RN generalist level: (1) medical/surgical, (2) gerontologic, (3) psychiatric/mental health, (4) maternal/child, (5) child and adolescent, (6) high-risk perinatal, and (7) community health. The ANA certifies four clinical specialties at the master's level: (1) medical/surgical, (2) child and adolescent, (3) adult psychiatric/mental health, and (4) child and adolescent mental health.[15] In the last few years, some nursing specialists have moved into the community, serving as expert clinicians and consultants to private insurance companies, HMOs, physician groups, clinics, home health agencies, and public health departments. Several independent specialty organizations certify nurses who work in the community, such as the Association of Rehabilitation Nurses and the International Association of Enterostomal Therapy.[16,17]

Professional certification fosters responsibility in demonstrating professional accountability. Nurse professional organizations use their expertise to determine universal standards, and examinations are given on a regular basis. Certification is valid for a specified time period, and a renewal process is designated, usually requiring work experience in the field of certification and evidence of continuing education.[18]

SCOPE OF RN PRACTICE

As long ago as the early 1950s, nurses recognized a need to accept greater responsibility and provide health care services to an increased number of persons at a reasonable cost. The explosion of medical knowledge had a profound effect on medical procedures, patterns and organization of patient care, and increased effectiveness for the patient. Similarly, registered nurse preparation and skills have expanded, allowing the nurse to move into primary health care roles with different and distinctive kinds of activities.

Major changes in the environment in which nurses practice have brought about drastic changes in nurses' roles. Sources of change are many and complex. The roles of the physician and nurse are becoming parallel, supportive, and complementary. Patients/clients are taking a greater part in the management of their own care. Costs have escalated in an unstable socioeconomic environment, creating a highly competitive spirit among health care providers. The health care industry has become labor intensive because of the introduction of advanced medical technology. Women are staying in the profession, rather than leaving to rear children. These women want to plan their careers, update their knowledge, and advance toward the realization of their career goals. Emphasis is on flexible working hours, job-sharing, and part-time employment.

Martha Rogers, nurse scientist and leader from New York University, says that expanding the scope of nursing practice is not defined as adding technical skills and machine manipulation, it rather means adding new knowledge and skills and having deep commitment to human service, which will revolutionize the health delivery system. She advocates a collaborative relationship between nurses and physicians and other health professionals. It means a commitment to serve in the field of human health and welfare for the "young and old, rich and poor, in home, hospital, school, business, clinic, ghetto and country club—all these fall within the scope of nursing."[19]

Following are examples of the variety of roles in which nurses are presently engaged. This list is meant to be representative, not all-inclusive.

Staff Nurse

RNs engaged at the staff level provide the bulk of primary nursing practice. Licensed graduates from diploma, AD, and BSN programs are eligible to function as beginning practitioners in acute, intermediate, long-term, and ambulatory health care facilities, and, depending on preparation for certification, in home health care and community health agencies. All should be able to apply the nursing process of assessment, planning, implementation, and evaluation. Placement of new RN graduates depends upon interest, aptitude, and availability of position. Given experience, education, and training, RNs may advance to the many diverse avenues of practice.

Critical Care Nurse (CCN)[20, 21]

Critical care has progressed from a "do the best you can" approach into an enormous specialty backed with a solid body of scientific knowledge and intricate skills. The critical care nurse uses the primary nursing delivery system, which allows a certain independence of practice, while serving as a full-fledged team member in

patient management. CCNs monitor complicated systems such as balloon angioplasty, pacemakers, hemodynamics, intraaortic balloon pumping, bedside hemodialysis, and advanced neurological and surgical procedures, often teaching physicians, primarily interns and residents in teaching hospitals, about caring for critically ill patients. Critical care nurses have input into the design and purchase of equipment, including bedside computers. They also help design products and techniques for practice. Some CCNs have become politically involved with right-to-die and living-will legislation and the right of nurses to pronounce death in the absence of a physician. Critical care nurses are fast moving toward the case-management approach to critically ill patients. When a CCN is constantly in attendance, many agree that this nurse is best able to manage total care of the patient in concert with all disciplines involved. The American Association of Critical Nurses (AACN) is the CCNs official organization.

Critical care nurses preferably have a BSN and advanced preparation in critical care nursing. Many nursing schools and colleges offer 4- to 12-month programs in critical care nursing in conjunction with hands-on experience in critical care units. Before enrolling in such a program, a nurse should have 2 to 3 years of clinical practice. Master's-level programs in critical care are also available, providing a thorough grounding in the basic sciences, indepth preparation in gerontology, interpersonal focus, and preparation to work collaboratively with professional nurse case managers, physicians, and other interdisciplinary personnel. Graduates from these advanced degree programs are prime candidates for managerial roles.

Clinical Nurse Specialist/Nurse Clinician (CNS/NC)

The role of clinical nurse specialist evolved in response to a need. As hospitals developed numbers of specialty care units, such as critical care, trauma care, diabetic treatment centers, oncology, and so forth, nurses became experts in providing nursing care for patients with particular sets of needs.[22] The Nurse Training Act of 1964 assisted many schools to establish expanded programs and master's degree programs, and clinical specialization became the primary focus of new curricula.[23] Bullough and Bullough define the CNS as a specialist in nursing who has a master's degree, whereas NC is a general term that describes a specialist who may or may not have a master's degree.[16] The American Association of Critical Care Nurses (AACCN) is one of the many accrediting agencies that certifies nurses in specialty areas. A CCRN certification is available through this organization upon proof of experience and successful completion of a written examination.[24]

> EXAMPLE: Sara, a clinical nurse specialist, is assigned to an oncology unit. She is called to see Mary, a 32-year-old with a diagnosis of leg sarcoma, who is experiencing intense stress and is threatening to give up all treatment. Sara spends time talking with Mary and her husband, then performs an initial assessment and determines what approach to follow. She arranges for a visit with the hospital psychiatrist, and together they learn that Mary believes there is no hope for her; she prefers to spend the rest of her life with her husband and two children. Sara confers with the physician, then explains to Mary that she has an excellent chance of recovery if she follows the prescribed therapy. The CNS helps Mary to understand the treatment and resolve her anxieties. The CNS administers Mary's next few chemotherapy treatments. Sara follows Mary's course of stay until dismissal, offering support to Mary and guidance to the nursing staff.

The role of the CNS is evolving rapidly in two directions: one toward an almost total blending with that of the nurse practitioner, and the other toward the role of the professional nurse case manager. Leah Curtin, editor of *Nursing Management,* believes the clinical nurse specialist's role will most likely be combined with those of the nurse practitioner and nurse case manager by the end of the 1990s.

Operating Room Nurse (ORN)[24]

In hospitals, where patients are admitted prior to and/or following surgery, the ORN monitors client progress from the time of entry into the operating room until the patient is dismissed to the staff nurse in attendance. In outpatient settings, the ORN is engaged in preoperative patient assessment, patient preparation for surgery, setting up for surgery and assisting the surgeon during the procedure, managing the recovery of patients, and follow-up of patients in their homes and workplaces by telephone or home visit.

As surgical procedures become more complex, and surgery is increasingly performed in outpatient settings, the ORN needs more advanced skills for the role. Most ORN staffs are made up of nurses prepared with diplomas and ADs, and some with BSN degrees. The American Association of Operating Room Nurses (AAORN) support the ANA's position that baccalaureate nursing education should be the entry-level preparation for operating room nurses. The AAORN helped support the JCAHO standards for nursing in operating rooms, specifically stating that supervisors, head nurses, and circulating nurses in surgical and obstetrical services must be qualified, registered nurses.

Community Health Nurse

A community may be defined as a group of people living in the same locality and under the same government, and/or who have shared interests and needs. The function of a community is to provide safety, security, mutual protection and support, a means for socialization, and avenues for finding assistance for specific needs. A community health nurse/public health nurse functions within this communal framework. It is the PHN's role to serve the health needs of the portion of the public to which she or he is assigned.[16]

Need for expansion of community health services. By tradition, the focus of community health nursing is on preventive health care. Although prevention remains first priority, additional roles are being added to the community health nurse. When the federal Health Care Financing Administration implemented its Prospective Payment System (PPS) in 1983, based on Diagnosis Related Groups (DRGs) for Medicare, and Health Maintenance Organizations (HMOs) and other managed-care options came into being, early discharge of hospitalized patients was encouraged. The work of the community health care nurse was impacted across the country, causing nurses to expand and increase their efforts to meet the challenges. The community health caregiving process has been complicated further by the increased age of patients, increased patient acuity levels, decreased length of hospital stays, geographic distances between family members, and inadequacy of funds.[25]

In addition to the traditional community health nursing role, other community-focused nursing roles have evolved. Examples of such roles are the nurse practitioner, nurse midwife, occupational health nurse, and school nurse, all of which require special skills and abilities.[16]

Nursing leadership in community health nursing. Nursing leadership in the community is important, necessitating an understanding of the basic power structure of a community, the process of community action, and strategies for influencing the flow of power and decision making in the community.[22] A study of the future of public health carried out by the Institute of Medicine (IOM), an arm of the National Academy of Sciences and supported by the Kellogg Foundation, was released in August 1988.[26] The report contains recommendations for the practice of public health nursing. The IOM affirmed that public health's mission is to fulfill society's interest in assuring conditions in which people can be healthy, but they expressed concern about the dearth of effective nursing leadership within the discipline. This problem was identified as most crucial because of the chronic lack of funding to carry out the mission of public health and the lack of leadership skills required to overcome the myriad problems. The IOM challenged nursing leaders to become better prepared in order to ensure that public health activities are consistent with those a community perceives it needs.[27] Public health nurse education for leaders must emphasize an examination of the health of a community from the epidemiological perspective, but must also consider other sciences such as sociology, psychology, anthropology, economics, and political science. Continuing education must be carried out vigorously by the present community health nurse population as well as those who join the ranks.[28] Following are some of the roles that community health nurses practice.

Community Health/Public Health Nurse (PHN)[16]

Bullough and Bullough describe the community health nurse as focusing primarily on disease prevention and health promotion. The PHN delivers care to the community as a whole, to populations within the community, to families, and to individuals. The overall goal of the community health nurse is to improve the health of the entire community by identifying people who are at high risk for illness, disability, or death. Selection of clients is based on epidemiologic studies and referrals by physicians and other health-related personnel. The community health nurse works closely with the interdisciplinary health team, which includes physicians, sanitarians, nutritionists, and health educators. Community health nurses provide little hands-on care to clients; instead, they focus their attention on other areas, for example, prenatal care, substance abuse, and communicable diseases such as acquired immunodeficiency syndrome (AIDS).

The PHN usually works out of a state, city, or county public health department, carrying a "case load" of families or individuals, depending on assignment. Public health nursing includes independent roles and responsibilities described as *primary* (the prevention of illness before it has a chance to occur), *secondary* (early detection of actual or potential health hazards), and *tertiary* (avoiding further deterioration of an existing problem). The PHN maintains records of patient progress and health needs of clients, makes assessments, provides health care education, and makes referrals for other necessary health-related services. Preparation for this role is a BSN degree in nursing that has a basic component of community health nursing. A PHN certificate is issued by the state upon completion of the program and several years of hospital nursing experience. Master's and doctoral programs in community health nursing are available in many major universities.

Home Health Care Nurse/Visiting Nurse

While community/public health nursing is based on a wellness model, home health care has evolved as a medical model. Home health is the largest employer of nurses within community-based nursing roles.[16,p.276] A report by the Department of Health and Human Services makes the assumption that home health visits will increase by 66% by the year 2020, because of the belief that almost one half of United States citizens will belong to HMOs by that time.[29,30]

Most home health care nurses are employed by visiting nurse associations (VNAs) located in large cities and small towns across the country, primarily funded by federal monies. Proprietary agencies employ home health care nurses for services such as private duty nursing. Industries may offer home health services to their employees, and some hospitals offer home health care as extended care services.

A core of services is generally provided by any home health care agency following a physician-approved plan of treatment. The nurse's role in home health care is to visit a designated number of clients a day, assess the needs, provide hands-on care such as bed bath, change of dressing/tubes, provide emotional and psychological support, determine patient progress, and maintain records. The desired preparation for this role is a BSN; however, requirements for the home health nurse vary greatly from state-to-state. As the acuity level of home care clients increases, there is greater need for the clinical nurse specialist and nurse practitioner to participate in home health care as teachers and consultants.[21]

Nurse Practitioner (NP)[16,31]

The nurse practitioner is a health care provider who is responsible for providing comprehensive care to both well and ill patients. The nurse practitioner educates patients and/or their families in order to promote wellness, prevent health problems, maintain current health, and intervene in acute or chronic illness. All functions are completed within standardized guidelines, and orders developed and sanctioned by the employing agency's governing body. Typical roles include (1) conducting comprehensive or episodic health assessments, (2) making medical diagnoses, (3) writing orders for diagnostic studies and therapeutic procedures, (4) prescribing and regulating medications in conjunction with physician agreement, (5) maintaining records and documents, and (6) utilizing effective communication skills through teaching and counseling.

An NP may establish an independent practice or work in collaboration with other nurses and/or physicians, or may choose to work in a health maintenance organization (HMO), physician's office, outpatient department, clinic, geriatric facility, public health agency, business or industry, university, or a voluntary agency.

Since 1965 preparation for an NP has evolved from a few-month certification program to a master of science degree in nursing (MSN), which includes 1 to 2 years of specialized classroom and experiential learning as a nurse practitioner. Upon graduation, the nurse practitioner must take the appropriate certification examination. The American Nurses' Association certifies family nurse practitioners, adult nurse practitioners geriatric nurse practitioners, and pediatric nurse practitioners. Most pediatric nurse practitioners are certified by a separate organization, the National Association of Pediatric Nurse Associates and Practitioners. Obstetric-gynecologic nurse practitioners are certified only by the Nurses' Association of the American College of Obstetricians and Gynecologists. Each of these certifying bodies requires registered nurse licensure, graduation from a recognized nurse practitioner program, and successful completion of a certifying examination. Most employers recommend that NPs have several years of clinical practice in hospitals before enrolling in nurse practitioner programs.

Nurse Midwife

A nurse midwife follows the birthing process from inception through delivery. The nurse midwife gives prenatal care, attends labor and delivery, and cares for mothers and infants in the postpartum period. Midwives have a deep interest in preventive health measures and enlist client participation in care. Midwives generally function within the community in birthing centers HMOs, and in hard-to-reach areas, and/or practice among high-risk groups. Nurse midwives have experienced great difficulty in achieving acceptance, particularly by physicians who may have felt their practices threatened. Resistance remains high in some states, such as California. Studies by such groups as the ANA and the Institute of Medicine report that the neonatal morality rate has dropped significantly as a result of attendance by nurse midwives.[16] There are 32 educational programs accredited by the College of Nurse-Midwifery. Of this group, 16 are at the master's level, 15 are certificate programs, and one awards a doctor of nursing science degree.[32]

> EXAMPLE: Fern, nurse midwife, worked out of a neighborhood family practice center. There she encountered Sandra, a 14-year-old girl who was 6 months pregnant. Fern established rapport with Sandra and her family, then conducted a physical assessment. She determined that Sandra was anemic and undernourished and also had many dental caries. Fern asked a social worker in the agency about Sandra's home conditions, and together they worked out a plan for dietary supplements and dental care. Fern followed Sandra's progress carefully and made plans for the desired home delivery. Sandra and her family chose to put the baby up for adoption, and arrangements were made with a local agency. Fern delivered a healthy 6 lb 2 oz boy without difficulty, knowing that she had access to a nearby hospital and physician if necessary. The nurse midwife followed through with filling the birth certificate and placement of the infant with an adoption agency. She attended Sandra throughout her postpartal period. Fern referred the young mother to Planned Parenthood classes.

Occupational Health Nurse (OHN)[16]

Business and industry are seeing the value of employing competent nurses to provide health services for their companies. Occupational health nurses help monitor the safety in the workplace, examine and advise ill workers and their families, provide first aid, attend those who are injured, and facilitate good health among workers and their families. They maintain records of clients, and plan and implement educational programs, using resources such as clinical nurse specialists, industrial hygienists, safety engineers, and consultants. The OHN evaluates safety and health programs and conducts studies to identify potential health problems. Occupational health nurses are now supporting drug and alcohol programs, obesity clinics, smoking cessation programs, and exercise programs.

There are now an estimated 25,000 occupational health nurses. Their professional society is the American Association of Occupational Health Nurses (AAOHN). Most members of this organization are diploma graduates or nurses who received their training in hospital programs. The educational level of the group is escalating, moving toward the baccalaureate degree. Nearly 2000 AAOHN members have AAOHN certification, representing additional education earned in degree or continuing education programs. Formal, organized specialty training is available in only a few universities.

School Nurse[16,33]

The goal of school nursing is to support the educational process by helping students keep healthy and by teaching students and teachers preventive practices. The school nurse may be responsible for one or more schools. Responsibilities may include first aid, screening, follow-up, control of communicable diseases, immunizations, teaching health classes, identifying ways of transmitting knowledge that supports healthful behavior, conducting health-related studies, and responding to calls from other schools. School nurses may also act as student advocates and consultants. Preparation for the school nurse includes a bachelor of science degree in nursing (BSN) plus a school health credential, awarded by the state upon successful completion of a designated number of prescribed courses taken beyond the baccalaureate level. A small number of school nurses have become school nurse practitioners, making physical examinations and following ill children in the home, especially in schools where there is no contact with physicians.

Professional Nurse Case Manager (PNCM)

Case management is designed to provide quality care while curtailing the cost of that care. In some respects, a nurse case manager is a combination of manager, primary care nurse, clinical specialist, nurse practitioner, and community health nurse, for all the skills required to fill this one role are embodied in these five categories.[34] The PNCM moves beyond the traditional discipline boundaries of time or shift and geographic or nursing-unit orientation. The case management model attempts to integrate nursing and all other interdisciplinary services for the patient's total illness episode in the hospital, as well as in the community.[35]

A nurse case manager's effectiveness relies on the nurse's use of knowledge, judgment, attention, and skill to bring about the greatest improvements in care outcomes. See Chapter 5 for a description of the nurse case management delivery systems. The ANA publication, *Nursing Case Management,* recommends a baccalaureate degree in nursing as the minimal level of educational preparation for a nurse case manager and strongly recommends preparation at the graduate level.[35]

Licensed Practical Nurses/Licensed Vocational Nurses and Other Categories of Nurse Caregivers

The development of licensed practical nurses or licensed vocational nurses has occurred in this century. As late as the 1920s, most registered nurses were private duty nurses working in homes. In hospitals with nursing schools, student nurses provided the labor. Hospitals without schools employed untrained or "practical" nurses. By 1940 health care delivery had shifted from home to the hospital, and as a result RNs as well as practical nurses became the major source of labor. The resulting competition between these two groups increased the pressure by the ANA and other interested groups for licensure of practical nurses. After considerable struggle, stratification of nursing was first formalized in 1938 with the passage of a nursing licensure act in New York State. This act required licensing of all who nursed for hire and established two levels of nursing—registered (RN) and practical (PN)—restricting nursing functions to members of these two groups. All states subsequently passed similar acts. By 1955 all states had licensing boards of licensed practical nurses (LPNs).[36]

Marie Manthey, one of the founders of the LPN/LVN technical program, lists criteria that are helpful in determining which patients are to be cared for by the LPN/LVN:

1. Patient requires routine and standardized care
2. Patient outcomes are predictable
3. Patient's reaction to illness and hospitalization is not threatening to the sense of self and does not upset his or her emotional equilibrium.

Within the framework of these parameters, an LPN/LVN follows the care plan designed by the RN and can be assigned to perform total care during a tour of duty.[37]

Ever since World War II when the number of LPNs increased astronomically (from eight schools before the war to over a thousand after) LPNs have gradually widened their scope of practice. In the beginning, LPNs were not allowed to administer medications in acute-care hositals; later, they could give oral medication but not intramuscular injections. Gradually they advanced to regulating the flow of IVs, but not adding medications to the IV. This is the situation today. LPNs/LVNs seek to expand their role; this effort creates conflict between LPNs/LVNs and RNs. LPNs/LVNs feel demeaned when they believe there is a narrow, illogical differentiation strategy used to restrict their functions, whereas RNs fear that their roles may be taken over by nurses ill-equiped to perform them.[37,38]

Assistive Nursing Personnel

A variety of health care workers perform designated nursing and support services for patients/clients that do not require RN/LPN licensure. These persons are designated as nurses' aides, nurse assistants, orderlies, and attendants, depending on the kind of facility that employs them and the type of services they perform. Short training programs offered in orientation programs and/or preemployment training programs, adult education, community colleges, and private schools provide the necessary preparation for these occupations.

Standardization and regulation of course content or employment requirements rests with each state and the individual hiring practices of the particular facility. Many states require that unlicensed nursing personnel be certified to practice, having fulfilled certain requirements, such as completion of an approved program and employment as a nurses' aide for at least 2 years.

Need for the Nurse Assistant (NA)

Nurse assistants are being used increasingly in health agencies. One major reason for this trend is the current nurse shortage. Another reason is cost. Nursing homes, for example, average 6.5 nursing assistants for every 100 beds, with 1 full-time equivalent RN and 1.5 LPNs/LVNs.[39] Nurse assistants' pay averages $4.50 per hour in major metropolitan areas, considerably less than LPN/LVN or RN pay. Most large hospitals and health care agencies try to staff as few nurse assistants as possible, believing that quality of care suffers without professional staff in the primary roles. In hospitals and other agencies, the scope of practice and job responsibilities for ancillary staff must be clearly defined. To help ensure adequate supervision and quality care by nurse assistants, the Tri Council, composed of the Association of Colleges of Nursing, the American Organization of Nurse Executives, the American Nurses' Association, and the National League for Nursing, believes the nursing profession should determine the educational preparation necessary for nurse assistants, as well as define their specific responsibilities. The Tri Council also believes that assistive nursing personnel should be regulated by licensure.[40]

SUMMARY

1. A role is the organized set of expected behaviors of a nurse in any given position. A nurse performs multiple roles in a typical day.
2. Role characteristics include behaving in a prescribed way; social interaction; mutual expectations; and perceptions by role enactor and those with whom he or she relates; social norms regarding values, judgments, and feelings; and conformity.
3. Sources that define a nurse's role are institutional requirements, patient/client expectations, peer pressure, and the nurse's conception of what the role implies.
4. Functional roles in nursing management include planning, organizing, staffing, leading, communicating, decision making, and controlling.
5. A license is a legal document that permits a person to offer his or her skills and knowledge to the public in a particular jurisdiction. The purpose of licensure is to protect society from unskilled and incompetent persons who would practice or who would offer to practice nursing.
6. As of 1989, there were 2,118,900 RNs in the United States with a full-time equivalent of 1,414,000.

7. The Department of Health and Human Services (HHS) predicts that by the year 2020 there will be a shortage of 874,900 RNs.
8. Only 8.5% of employed RNs in 1988 were from ethnic/minority groups.
9. Certification is a credential issued by a professional body that helps protect the consumer from harm by affirming excellence in a particular area. The ANA certifies seven types of nurse specialists at the RN generalist level, and four clinical specialty areas at the master's level. Several independent specialty organizations certify qualified nurses who work in the community.
10. The Commission on Graduates of Foreign Nursing Schools (CGFNS) administers a twice-a-year test of nursing and English language competencies. Most of the state Registered Nurse Boards require CGFNS certification. There are approximately 10,000 foreign nurses who enter the United States each year with temporary visas (H-1). About 20,000 foreign nurses take the RN licensure examination each year.
11. The United States has almost 1500 nursing schools, 789 AD programs, 467 generic BSN programs, and 45 doctoral programs. There was a significant decrease for all basic nursing programs from 1983 to 1988, and an increase in master's and doctoral programs. Since 1989, nursing school enrollments in BSN programs have increased with a large number of RNs returning for BSN degrees.
12. There are various technical and professional levels of nursing; however, it is difficult to measure differences between diploma, AD, and BSN graduates because of role blurring. Job descriptions for most nurse managerial positions specify BSN or MSN preparation preferred.
13. Because it is difficult to differentiate theory and practice skills between associate, diploma, and baccalaureate graduates, a recommendation has been made by Leah Curtin, editor of *Nursing Management,* that nursing no longer consider levels of practice such as "technical" and "professional" but consider arenas of practice such as (1) clinical nurse, prepared at the associate, diploma, and baccalaureate levels, (2) nurse specialist, prepared at masters' and doctoral

levels, and (3) nurse case manager, prepared at baccalaureate and master's levels.

14. The expanding scope of nursing practice is characterized by the addition of new knowledge and skills, deep commitment to human service, and a collaborative relationship with physicians and other health care professionals who wish to serve in human health and welfare programs for all people.

15. Staff nurses provide the major share of primary nursing practice. They function in acute, intermediate, long-term, and ambulatory health care facilities. All staff nurses should be able to apply nursing process to practice.

16. The critical care nurse (CCN) is a hospital-based RN with advanced preparation and experience in critical care. The CCN may or may not be certified.

17. The clinical nurse specialist (CNS) is a certified RN who provides expert care for patients with particular sets of needs. The CNS expands the scope of nursing practice in inpatient care by providing direct patient care with greater comprehensiveness, continuity, and coordination of all patient services.

18. The operating room nurse (ORN) functions in both inpatient and outpatient settings. Skills include expertise in assessment, preparation, and assisting, and in recovery of patients. ORNs sometimes follow-up on patients in their homes and workplaces and oversee services in recovery care centers.

19. The community health nurse/public health nurse (PHN) works within a framework of community whose purpose is to provide safety, security, mutual protection and support, a means for socialization, and avenues for finding assistance for specific health needs. The PHN performs independent roles while providing primary, secondary, and tertiary care.

20. The advent of the Prospective Payment System (PPS) in 1983 affected the work of the CHN by increasing the number and acuity of individuals needing community health services.

21. The home health care nurse/visiting nurse provides a core of home health services to patients following a physician-approved plan of treatment.

22. Nurse practitioners (NPs) are registered nurses who provide primary patient care and who have special training beyond that required for nursing licensure in medical history taking, physical assessment skills, and patient management. All functions are completed within standardized guidelines and orders developed by and sanctioned by an appropriate governing body. Common classifications are family nurse practitioner, pediatric nurse practitioner, obstetric-gynecological nurse practitioner, and psychiatric-mental health nurse practitioner.

23. A nurse midwife follows the birthing process from inception through delivery. Nurse midwives generally function in the community in birthing centers, in HMOs, in hard-to-reach areas and/or practice among high-risk groups.

24. Occupational health nurses (OHNs) (sometimes called industrial nurses) provide consultation services, assess environmental hazards, complete preemployment histories and physical examinations, provide health education and are on staff as full- or part-time nurses available to employees.

25. A school nurse supports the educational process by helping students maintain health and by teaching students and teachers preventive practices.

26. The concept of nurse case manager (NCM) emerged in the mid-1980s and is rapidly gathering momentum. The ANA describes nursing case management as "a healthcare delivery process whose goals are to provide quality healthcare, decrease fragmentation, enhance the client's quality of life and contain costs." Nurse case management is multidisciplinary in scope and includes case management prior to hospital admission through at least 2 weeks of monitoring following a patient's dismissal. NCMs are beginning to function in the community, employed by businesses and public-health-oriented agencies.

27. Licensed practical or licensed vocational nurses (LPNs/LVNs) are prepared in vocational schools, which stress clinical experiences in various health care settings

with focus on nursing process, caregiving, and health teaching. As the practice of nursing becomes more complex, the number of LPN/LVN schools is gradually declining.

28. Assistive nursing personnel (nurses' aides, nurse assistants, orderlies, and attendants) perform designated nursing and support services for patients that do not require RN/LPN licensure. Nurses, aides increasingly are being used in health agencies, both in and out of hospitals, as a result of the current nurse shortage and economic factors.

Questions for Study and Discussion

1. If you accept the role of staff nurse, what personal characteristics would be expected of you? Do you think you would have a problem meeting any of these expectations? Please explain.

2. Describe the roles of nurse manager. In which of these roles do you believe yourself to have the most potential? Do any of the roles have negative connotations for you? Please explain.

3. What is the purpose of RN licensure? Do you think each state should have the right to develop its own criteria for nursing practice, rather than the national government developing criteria for all states?

4. What, if anything, do you think should be done to increase the very low percentage of ethnic and minority RNs? If you are caucasian, would you be willing to give up your space in a nursing program for an equally qualified student from an ethnic/minority background? Why?

5. Do you believe that there should be two levels of practice for the staff nurse? If so, should there be a salary differentiation between the technical and the professional nurse? Please give the rationale for your opinion.

6. Explain the purpose of nurse certification. Who is the primary certifying association?

7. Select the nursing role you would like to practice in the future. Explain the preparation required for the role and its scope of practice. What sparks your interest in this field?

8. Does the role of professional nurse case manager appeal to you? In what ways? If not, why is the role not inviting?

9. Explain the difference in scope of practice between the RN and the LPN/LVN. Do you believe this latter category of nurse is necessary to the profession? Why?

REFERENCES

1. Landy F: Psychology of work behavior, ed 4, Pacific Grove, Calif, 1989, Brooks/Cole Publishing Co.
2. Kreitner R: Management, ed 4, Boston, 1989, Houghton Mifflin Co.
3. Wheelen T and Hunger J: Strategic Management, ed 3, Reading, Mass, 1990, Addison-Wesley Publishing Co.
4. Sherman V: Nursing's management crisis, Supervisor Nurs 11(10):31-33, 1989.
5. O'Neil K and Gajdostik K: The head nurse's managerial role, Nurs Man 20(6):39-41, 1989.
6. Washington, DC News: Rn population seen declining after the year 2000: HHS predicts shortage could top 800,000 by 2020, Am J Nurs 90(9):97-110, 1990.
7. Management briefs: Foreign nurses: pending legislation may slow immigration procedures, Nurs Man 20(11):19-20, 1989.
8. Watson J: The evolution of nursing education in the US: 100 years of a profession for women, J Nurs Educ 16(7):31-37.
9. McCloskey J and Grace H: Current issues in nursing, ed 3, St Louis, 1990, Times Mirror/Mosby College Publishing.
10. National League for Nursing: Nursing data review, New York, 1988, The League.
11. Report on 1989-1990 enrollment and graduations in baccalaureate and graduate programs in nursing, Washington, DC, Am Assoc College Nurs, 1990.
12. Sortet J: Incongruencies in the nursing profession, Nurs Man 20(5):64, 1989.

13. Schumann L: Attitudes regarding basic nursing programs: ratings of baccalaureate, associate degree and diploma prepared RNs in the Northwest, J Nurs Educ 20(2):71-78, 1990.
14. Curtin L: Designing new roles: nursing in the 90s and beyond, Nurs Man 21(2):9, 1990.
15. American Nurses' Association: The career credential: professional certification, the 1987 catalog of certification requirements, Kansas City, MO, 1987b, The Association.
16. Bullough B and Bullough V: Nursing in the community, St. Louis, 1990, Times Mirror/Mosby College Publishing.
17. NLN perspective: Interview with Jeanette C. Hartshorn, project director, committee for the national board of nursing specialities, Nurs & Health Care 10(5):276-279, 1990.
18. McCloskey J and Grace H: Current issues in nursing, ed 3, St Louis, 1990, Times Mirror/Mosby College Publishing.
19. Freda M: A role model of leadership in and advocacy for nursing, Nurs Forum, 24(3,4):9-13, 1989.
20. Wilson V: From sentinels to specialists, AM J Nurs 90(10):32-43, 1990.
21. Cyr L: The clinical nurse specialists in a home healthcare setting, Home Healthcare Nurse 8(1):34-39, 1990.
22. Tappen R: Nursing leadership and management: concepts and practice, ed 2, Philadelphia, 1989, FA Davis Co.
23. Kalisch P and Kalisch B: The advance of American nursing, Boston, 1987, Little, Brown and Co. Inc.
24. McCloskey J and Grace H: Current issues in nursing, ed 2, Boston, 1985, Blackwell Scientific Publications.
25. Harris M: Restructuring: specifics for home health, Nurs Econ 8(4):257-271, 1990.
26. Institute of Medicine: The future of public health, Washington DC, 1988, National Academy Press.
27. Josten L: Wanted: leaders for public health, Nurs Outlook 37(5):231-232, 1989.
28. Anderson E: Public health content in nursing curricula, Nurs Outlook 37(5):233-235, 1989.
29. Department of Health and Human Services: Secretary's Commission on Nursing: interim report, Washington DC, 1988, The Department.
30. News: RN population seen declining after the year 2000: HHS predicts shortages could top 800,000 by 2020, Am J Nurs 90(9):97;110, 1990.
31. Taylor S, Pickens J, and Geden E: Interactional styles of nurse practitioners and physicians regarding decision making, Nurs Res 38(1):50-55, 1989.
32. American Colleges of Nurse-Midwives: Education programs accredited by the division of accreditation, ACNM, J Nurse-Midwifery 29(2):173, 1984b.
33. Lewis K and Thomson H: Manual of school health, Menlo Park, Calif, 1986, Addison-Wesley Publishing Co.
34. Del Togno-Armanasco V, Olivas G, and Harter S: Developing an integrated nursing case management model, Nurs Man 20(10):27, 1989.
35. American Nurses' Association: Nursing case management, NS-32 2.5M, Kansas City Mo, 1988, The Association.
36. State-approved schools of nursing LPN/LVN 1990, ed 32, NLN Pub Div Res 19-2334; 2-70, 1990.
37. Manthey M: The role of the LPN or . . . the problem of two levels, Nurs Man 20(2):26;28, 1990.
38. LPNs widen their role: disagreement grows, Am J Nurs 90(2):16-19, 1990.
39. Nursing Home Assistants: facts and figures, Nursing 90 20(3):11, 1990.
40. Nursing News: defining their role clearly, Nursing 90 20(7):14, 1990.

SUGGESTED READINGS

AACN: Finally . . . enrollments are up, Nursing 90 90(2):10, 1990.
Ball G: Perspectives on developing, marketing, and implementing a new clinical specialist position, Clin Nurs Spec 4(1):33-36, 1990.
Barnum B: Interview with Jeanette C Hartshorn, Project Director, Committee for the National Board of Nursing Specialities, Nursing & Health Care 10(5):276-279, 1990.
Becker K and others: A nurse practitioner job description, Nurs Man 20(6):42-44, 1989.
Brider P: The struggle for just compensation, Am J Nurs 90(10):77-88, 1990.
Carr P: Needs to know, wants to know, ought to know, Home Healthcare 8(4):34-36, 1990.
Chamings P and others: Anesthesia nursing: a collaborative model for graduate education 10(5):271-274, 1990.
Chisholm M: Consultations in the CNS often affects development of the organization itself, Clin Nurs Spec 4(1):37, 1990.

Controversies in care: foreign nurse screening: cause for alarm? Am J Nurs 90(10):18; 22, 1990.

Coombs J: Creating a healing environment: nurse case managers address pregnant teenagers' needs—physical, emotional and spiritual, Health Progress, 7(14):38-41, May 1990.

Flaherty M and DeMoya D: An entrepreneurial role for the nurse consultant, Nurs Health Care 10(5):259-261, 1990.

Florida Nurses' Association: Choosing your employment setting, Nursing 90 20(5):156-159, 1990.

Ford M: The nurse specialist: a cornerstone of quality patient care, J Med Assoc Ga, 79(2):101-103, 1990.

Harrington C and Culbertson R: Nurses left out of health care reimbursement reform, Nurs Outlook 36(4):156-158, 1990.

Headline News: Foreign nurses face new threat of deportation, Am J Nurs 90(7):11, 1990.

Holt F: Managed care and the clinical nurse specialist, Clin Nurs Spec 4(1):27, 1990.

Huston C: What makes the difference? attributes of the exceptional nurse, Nursing 90 20(5):170-173, 1990.

Jonker V: The midwives' role in general practice maternity care, Midwives Chronicle 103(1226):84, March, 1990.

Kinsey D: Mentorship and influence in nursing, Nurs Man 21(5):45-46, 1990.

Kroll C: Registered nurse students: academic admission and progression, J Cont Educ Nurs 21(4):160-162, 1990.

McCreight L: The future of public health, Nurs Outlook 37(5):219-225, 1989.

Mechanic H: Redefining the expanded role, Nurs Outlook 36(6):280-284, 1990.

Morse G: Resurgence of nurse assistants in acute care, Nurs Man 21(3):21; 35-56, 1990.

Myles S: Nurse liaison: bridging the gap, Nurs Man 21(3):28-29, 1990.

News: Staff shortages hurting nursing homes the most, Am J Nurs 91(1):85;90, 1991.

Pearson L: 25 years later: 25 exceptional NPs look at the movement's evolution and consider future challenges for the role, Nurs Practitioner 15(9):14-28, 1990.

Phillips E and others: DRG ripple and the shifting burden of care to home health, Nurs Health Care 10(6):325-327, 1990.

Powills S: Educational system responds to similar dilemma, Hospitals 63(9):36-37, 1989.

Rawson D and Harman K: Nursing exchange: a new experience (hospice nursing), Nurs Man 21(3):30-31, 1990.

Rich J: In pursuit of a BSN, Nursing 90 20(2):118-120, 1990.

Rooks J: Nurse midwifery: the window is wide open, Am J Nurs 90(12):30-36, 1990.

Salmon M: Public health nursing: the neglected specialty, Nurs Outlook 37(5):226-229, 1989.

Storfjell J: How valuable are nurses' skills? a case for fair pricing in home health care, Nurs Health Care 10(6):311-313, 1990.

Styles M: On specialization in nursing; toward a new empowerment, Nurs Health Care 10(5):281-282, 1990.

Sullivan N and Quaintance M: A unique LPN to ADN bridge program, Nurs Man 21(3):14-15, 1990.

Wolf G: Clinical nurse specialists: the second generation, JONA 20(5):7-8, 1990.

5

Staffing Process and Nursing Care Delivery Systems

————————————— **BEHAVIORAL OBJECTIVES** —————————————
On completion of this chapter the student will be prepared to:

☐ Explain the staffing process of recruitment, selection, and placement of personnel.
☐ List the criteria important to the staffing process and identify major components of each.
☐ Define the systems used to deliver nursing care—total care, functional, team, primary, modular, and nurse case management—and determine advantages and disadvantages of each.

An important part of management is placing the right people in the right jobs. An organizational structure may be designed on paper, but to come to life it must be staffed with people. These efforts are referred to as *staffing,* a separate and fundamental function of management. Staffing is the process of assigning competent people to fill the roles designed for the organizational structure through recruitment, selection, and development of personnel.

Human resource planning requires a systematic approach to staffing. Today's rapidly changing conditions necessitate (1) a foresighted, systematic approach that provides the right number of people to fill the roles designed for the organization, (2) proper utilization of personnel, and (3) planning for personnel needed to satisfy future needs.[1,p.348] This chapter discusses employment procedures, criteria important to the staffing process, and nursing care delivery systems, all of vital significance to effective management.

NURSE SUPPLY

The last 2 decades have seen the number of working nurses grow from 750,000 in 1970 to 1.69 million in 1989, but this number is insufficient to meet the present need. According to the Health and Human Services Secretary's Commission on Nursing, approximately 200,000 nurses are needed to fill current vacancies. The critical care and medical-surgical hospital units are hardest hit by the shortfall.[2]

The Commonwealth Fund commissioned an interdisciplinary study that focused on the nursing shortage. The study team surveyed hospital administration, nurses, and educators in six urban areas from east to west that together serve more than one third of the U.S. population. They found a definite trend toward increasing the RN population and reducing the number of LPNs/LVNs.[3] This is not surprising since the use of complex technology has grown, patient acuity has risen and RNs are generally more capable of providing complex care.

NURSE TURNOVER

Rapid turnover of nursing personnel is a significant problem. The average 40% national turnover rate for RNs compromises the quality of patient care and places a significant financial strain on hospitals. A study by Prescott and Bowen stated that the dollar cost for one RN turnover can be over $10,000. This includes the cost of advertising, recruiting, unfilled positions, hiring, termination, orientation and training, and decreased new RN productivity.[4] Forty-seven% of working nurses expect to be working at different hospitals or other health agencies in 3 years. Therefore, it behooves employers to investigate causal factors for nurse turnover and to seek ways to rectify the situation. Marketing theory predicts that hospitals could recruit nurses more effectively if they had a clearer understanding of what nurses in their labor markets are looking for in jobs.[5]

A NLN study asked 38,227 newly licensed RNs if they were satisfied with their current jobs. Only 64% of hospital nurses responded affirmatively. Reasons given for dissatisfaction include inadequate salary (32%), poor working conditions (18.1%), understaffing or too much work (14.1%), poor staff relations (9.7%), dissatisfaction with hours (4.8%), and underutilization of skills (3.0%).[6] In a recent conversation with the author, Paula, a staff nurse in a metropolitan hospital, explained her concerns.

> Here the stress is high all the time. I only work 40 hours a week but I don't know how much longer I can take it. I'm thinking of working in a clinic. The pay is the same and I don't have to work as hard, nor feel the pain.

All nurses are not alike, nor are their employment needs. Attention to periodic market surveys can help employers keep in touch with preferences of nurses in their local labor markets and make offers that will meet these needs.

RN WORK PRIORITIES

Researchers Kramer and Hafner studied categories that are most often cited as first priorities in selecting a new job.[7] They found that work schedule, salary, benefits, and low degree of stress were most often rated as very important by nurses in their selection of a new job. Part-time nurses indicated they would increase their work hours for better wages, child care, weekend pay differentials, opportunity for salary increases, and schedule flexibility. Part-time nurses were more likely to be married and to have many more family-related responsibilities. There was a significant difference in priorities between master's-prepared staff nurses and nurses at all other levels. Of the master's-prepared RNs, 35% ranked professional rewards, such as autonomy and time to engage in research, first.

GRADUATING SENIORS' PRIORITIES

Another study surveyed BSN seniors at an NLN-accredited state university nursing program one week prior to graduation. Students were asked to rank 39 characteristics in order of importance in choosing a hospital for employment. They selected the following as very important (1) quality of patient care, (2) treatment of nurses as professionals, (3) adequate staffing, and (4) low patient-to-nurse ratios. The students did not particularly care about characteristics that appeal more commonly to the older married nurse, such as child care, bonuses, profit-sharing plans, relocation assistance, and tuition reimbursement.[8] Employers seeking new graduates would do well to focus on these items.

SALARIES FOR EXPERIENCED NURSES

The average maximum salary for staff nurses nationally rose to $34,000 in 1990, according to a personnel officer who recruits nurses throughout the United States. The average minimum salary reached $25,900. Salaries for emergency department and surgical nurses reached an average maximum of $37,600, and those for head nurses climbed to $46,000.[9]

SALARIES FOR NEW GRADUATES

Salaries for new graduates are usually predetermined by financial controllers; however, there are various compensation benefit packages offered, including such things as bonuses, shift differentials, tuition reimbursement, flextime in shifts, opportunity to work in another hospital for several months each year in the locale of the employee's choice (with the initial employer responsible for all arrangements and no loss of benefits for the nurse), a 9-month work year with full-time status, mentoring programs, and career ladders. Employers are becoming more creative in meeting the needs and desires of new graduates, hoping they will be satisfied with the agency and will plan to stay.[10]

EMPLOYMENT PROCEDURES
Recruitment

There are various ways to recruit nurses: one can fill vacancies from within the agency; hire graduates from schools and colleges; place advertisements and announcements; and use nurse employment agencies, both professional and private, national and international. Less formal means are recommendations by employees and friends. Some applicants initiate their own contacts. Geographic location plays an important part in nurses' decisions as to where they will work. For example, magnet hospitals such as large municpal hospitals associated with educational institutions are very appealing to nurses, particularly new graduates, as large health facilities have a wide range of offerings in their agencies and ready access to the attractions of urban life.

Driven by the increasing nursing shortage, many health agencies are trying to recruit as many new graduates and experienced nurses as possible (see box). Many hospitals have converted general beds to intensive care beds to reflect changes in patient care needs. Intensive care units employ four to six times as many nurses per bed as do general units. This development creates a cycle of demand. As physicians aggressively treat very ill patients, there is a need to use more technology, which places greater demands on nurses. Shortened hospi-

Major Factors Contributing to RN Demand

The four major factors contributing to the demand for RNs are
1. Increased intensity of medical practice
2. Changes in patient characteristics
3. Nurse professional goals
4. Economic incentives

talizations for many patients have not only increased patient acuity in hospitals, but have also raised the demand for skilled and extended-care facility beds. Each of these agencies is scrambling for its share of nursing personnel. Thus prospective employers are forced to determine which recruitment and retention activities are most likely to be effective in enticing nurses to their institutions.[10]

Employers' Recruitment Strategies

In 1988 hospitals spent an estimated $3.2 billion in recruiting nurses, which equals about $1 million per hospital. Connie Curran, prominent nursing consultant, suggests that if health agencies were to put their money into making jobs more desirable, such as improving salaries, working conditions, and opportunities for professional development, they would not have the large nursing turnover that exists today.[10]

Experienced Nurses

Nurses who have practiced for a number of years and become expert in their fields have more clout with recruiters. Salaries and work schedules, as well as other benefits important to them, can be negotiated. Some employers will trade health insurance for child care if the staff member's spouse has health insurance. If the prospective employee is relocating, the employer may offer a mortgage subsidy program or arrange for a lower rate of interest in the purchase of a home, and pay moving expenses. Recruiters assess the nurse's potential value to the agency, then devise a plan they hope will attract that nurse.[11]

In today's world, nurses must learn to become entrepreneurs, to catalog their achievements, to shop around for the best wage and benefit package in the kind of environment desired, to sell themselves to recruiters, and to bargain for the best offer possible.

Registry Nurses

Nurse registries are private agencies that hire nurses to provide a pool of nursing staff for employers who wish to supplement their nursing personnel, such as hospitals, home health care agencies, private homes, and communities. Nurse registries have become a popular alternative for nurses today, who often are motivated by a desire for higher wages, flexible scheduling, and benefit packages at a reasonable fee.[12] Because hospitals can call on registry nurses, they can maintain minimal nursing staffs commensurate with their average daily patient census. Then, when the census increases, they can augment their staffs with registry nurses. This plan allows hospitals to avoid the problem of having more staff than needed during times of low census. Yet, unless exercised carefully, the option to use registry nurses can be very disruptive to the provision of quality care.[13] Consistency and continuity of services may be broken and there may be need for continual orientation. Nurse managers are well aware of these issues but often face the urgency of finding nurses to fill positions.

Registry personnel should be screened as carefully as other hospital-employed nurses. A critical need for nurses does not justify failure to exercise reasonable care in screening registry nurses or hiring temporary nurses. If the nurse manager knows that the registry nurse is incompetent and fails to act upon that knowledge, liability to the user of RN services may follow. The nurse manager also has a legal duty to communicate any pertinent information about a registry nurse's performance to the registry employing the nurse[14] (see box at right).

Nurse registries are a part of the health care system because the marketplace demands them. Establishment of guidelines such as those mentioned in the box can help to offset serious problems that jeopardize patients care.

Responsibility for Selection of Nursing Personnel

The responsibility for staffing an organization with nursing personnel rests with every man-

Recommendations Regarding the Use of Registry Nurses

The Harvard Risk Management Foundation recently provided a number of excellent recommendations for hospitals and other health agencies to consider when using the services of registry nurses.[14]
1. Contract with a select group of agencies that have been carefully screened. Ascertain that each agency has a thorough evaluation program for its nurse employees.
2. Have a written contract between the health agency and the registry, addressing the issue of liability.
3. Require the registry and/or the nurses to carry sufficient malpractice insurance (minimum individual limits of $1,000,000).
4. Have an orientation program, which includes an evaluation of the level of competence, for all registry nurses who work in the health facility.
5. Let patients know they are being cared for by registry nurses.
6. Minimize use of registry personnel as much as possible and try to assign them to low-risk settings.
7. Make it clear to registry nurses that they are to identify any portion of their assignments beyond their abilities.
8. Independently verify the registry nurse's licensure status, previous references, and disciplinary and malpractice history.

ager at every level. Figure 5-1 illustrates the procedure typically used. Staffing requires coordination between the personnel department and nursing services. The personnel department ordinarily provides staff to departments in accordance with requests received. The usual custom is for the personnel department to screen the applicant for information such as valid licensure, education, experience, preferences, and health status. The nursing service personnel are then responsible for making the selection and placement to a specific job. Top-, middle-, and lower- or first-level managers collaborate to select the best person for each position.

The prospective employee should know about the salary and wage plan, fringe benefits, working conditions, agency expectations of the

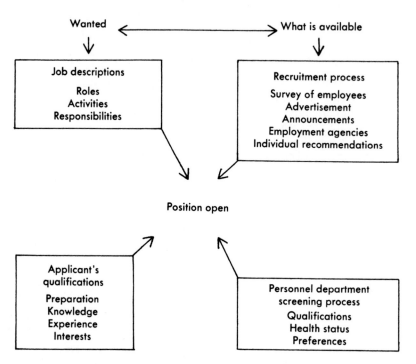

Figure 5-1. Typical employment procedure used by health care agencies in matching applicants with job openings.

applicant, working hours and time off, the possibility of having individual requests considered, orientation to the job, evaluation procedures, promotional policies, and opportunity for inservice and continuing education. Standards of nursing care adopted by the health facility should be reviewed and clarified, along with an explanation of the methods used for delivery of patient/client care. The climate of the interview should be such that the prospective employee feels comfortable in discussing any matter pertaining to employment. Acquisition of as much knowledge as possible about the agency and the job before employment reduces the probability of dissatisfaction and short-term employment, thereby contributing to increased quality of care provided and cost-effectiveness.

Induction and Orientation

Induction consists of those formal procedures an employee goes through immediately after employment. This includes (1) getting on the payroll, (2) arranging for deductions (income tax, health insurance, and so on), and (3) completing routine records.

Orientation is the formal process of apprising the new employee of the organization and her place in it. The new worker must become aware of her part in meeting goals of the organization. The amount of time and emphasis devoted to orientation varies with the size of the agency, scope of services offered, and provision for training. This takes the form of (1) teaching personnel, (2) equipment and other teaching resources, (3) availability of space for classes and practice, (4) needs of the new employee, and (5) urgency for the new worker to be on the job. A successful orientation helps speed the transition process by building the nurse's identification with the agency, helping the nurse become acquainted with fellow personnel, and providing the nurse with important information about the organization.

CRITERIA IMPORTANT TO THE STAFFING PROCESS

Staffing criteria are unique to each organization; however, all health care facilities have certain basic criteria.

Staffing carries forward the structure and goals of the organization. The organizational chart, in conjunction with job specifications, will indicate the numbers and types of workers needed to fill the various nursing positions. For example, however desirable it may be, it is not possible to employ an additional nurse to provide specialized care to ileostomy patients unless that position is incorporated into the total organizational plan through proper channels. Nurse staffing depends on existing structure and standards. If agency standards adopt professional nursing standards as prescribed by the American Nurses' Association (ANA), for example, they must require individualized nursing care; effective communication among nurses, physicians, staff, and patients/clients, their families, and community at all levels; participation in decisions influencing their role in the nursing care; and provision for continuing education. Therefore staffing must include an adequate number of qualified professional and nonprofessional personnel to meet these standards.

Job specifications are clear and in writing. For practical purposes, staffing an organization begins with identification of roles and a written record of minimal requirements necessary to perform the job. *Job descriptions* or *performance responsibilities* spell out precise job content, including duties, activities to be performed, responsibilities, and results expected from the various roles by the agency. Job descriptions cannot possibly include all duties and responsibilities; to do so would make the list cumbersome and impractical. Job descriptions simply spell out minimal requirements for fulfillment of the job. Further, the job description is always subject to interpretation, and with time, the typical nurse modifies the role to some degree; this modification is a natural result of individuality and change. Following is an example of a typical job description or performance responsibilities for a primary care nurse and a clinical nurse specialist.

Typical Performance Responsibilities for a Primary Care Nurse*

1. Assess patient's needs by giving direct nursing care, collecting data about the patient from patient and family, observing and inspecting patient, reviewing the clinical records, knowing the medical diagnosis, and positively seeking information from the physician and other personnel caring for patient
2. Records patient needs and problems and writes appropriate nursing directives for activities, techniques, equipment, or supportive measures
3. Coordinates the medical care plan with the nursing care plan, interpreting physician's orders to achieve the most effective results; relates physician's orders to appropriate measures; assumes responsibility for the execution of the physician's orders; solicits patient's cooperation in planning and implementing plan of care
4. Makes rounds, alone and with physicians of primary patients; plans patient care with physician and the patient; communicates patient's needs and problems to physician as necessary
5. Encourages and uses reported observations and suggestions of all levels of nursing personnel in planning nursing care
6. Gives recognition to the real and potential contribution of family and significant others in planning patient care
7. Coordinates preparation and planning of patient discharge, which begins on admission and includes patient and family in necessary teaching and learning activities
8. Assists other RNs, LPNs/LVNs, aides, and technicians in following through with all information and directives on the nursing care plan
9. Communicates with nursing staff regarding their adherence to the plan of care or changes in plans

*Modified from Ganong J and Ganong W: Help with primary nursing: accountability through the nursing process, Chapel Hill, NC, 1977, WL Ganong Co, pp 45-48. Used by permission. This pattern of nursing care requires a decentralized structure in which the nurse is given greater freedom to act than is the case in a centralized bureaucratic hierarchy.

10. Listens to, evaluates, and acts on needs, problems, and suggestions of patients, visitors, physicians, and others
11. Checks own documentation process, evaluates effectiveness of care plan, comfort and safety of nursing care, and degree to which patient's needs and problems are being met
12. Assists with teaching and planning activities at bedside, conferences, inservice education, and staff development programs
13. Develops, implements, and revises teaching program for primary patients as necessary while hospitalized as well as for continued care at home
14. Assumes responsibility for hospital, department, and unit policies and practices directly related to patients/clients for whom she is caring
15. Promotes and maintains good interpersonal relationships with patients; families; medical, nursing, and other personnel; and the public
16. Gives brief report to head nurse or charge nurse (and/or associate nurse) at end of shift for continuity

Typical Performance Responsibilities for a Clinical Nurse Specialist in a Middle Management Role[15]

1. Sets standards for clinical nursing practice
2. Evaluates the quality of nursing services
3. Acts as a clinical role model and maintains clinical proficiency
4. Collaborates with other health care professionals
5. Evaluates staff performance
6. Develops staffing patterns collaboratively with top administrative personnel
7. Makes budget recommendations
8. Monitors physical environment

Note that each of the job descriptions or performance responsibilities are written in the form of behavioral objectives, each of which can be measured for evaluation.

Staff members are matched to their assignments as well as possible. Correlation between the abilities and potential abilities of nursing personnel and their job assignments is often overlooked. This oversight results in unused resources, boredom, and dissatisfaction. The agency, worker, and patient/client are the los-

ers. Assessment of general ability, intelligence, aptitude, skills, interests, personality, and experience at time of employment and beyond is an excellent use of time. Sometimes proper attention to placement is not given partly because the work demands are so crucial and partly because personnel on staff have not reached the degree of sophistication necessary for testing.

The worker who feels misassigned may fail to make a problem known. One resource open to the nurse who is experiencing stress from an inappropriate matching of abilities and interests is self-assertion.

Malcolm Shaw, leader of human resources development programs, maintains that one's desire to act and to defend oneself are the energizing forces that can move a person from where he is to where he wants to be. But these feelings must be channeled into specific actions that are effective and fulfilling. Assertive behavior that is open, honest, clear, goal-oriented, and respectful of all people's rights can accomplish desired goals and leave the individual feeling human and free from guilt.[16,p.63]

STAFFING PROCESS

Today's nurse manager is faced with many challenges in negotiating the health care environment. What is appropriate for one health care agency may not work well for another. There are guidelines and models available to nurse managers that can be used or modified to meet individual agency requirements and conditions. In brief, the process is as follows.

Data Collection

The initial step in implementation of a staffing system is to develop a means for data collection. Ideally, the nurse who is responsible for seeing that care is delivered to a unit (usually the head nurse is the best source of information). The objectives for an inpatient facility and an ambulatory care center are essentially the same: (1) to match patient care needs with available resources, (2) to ensure cost-effectiveness, (3) to provide a basis for budgetary justification of needed positions, (4) to measure efficiency of care delivery, (5) to assess quality and quantity of care delivered, and (6) to ensure equitable patient care assignments.[17,18]

First studied in hospitals are patient census

figures; average length of stay in the hospital; patient discharges and admissions as they relate to seasons, months of the year, and days of the week. An analysis of these data will reveal definite patterns. In some units, such as surgical, there may be more patients admitted at the beginning of the week, whereas a geriatric unit may have more admissions at the end of the week or before holidays. The census in most agencies generally drops significantly around Christmas and picks up after the first of the year until summer vacation time begins. Other factors influencing hospital census are physicians' vacations or conventions; demographic information, such as age of population; and the economic status of the community.

Patient Classification Systems

"A patient classification system is a method of grouping patients according to the amount and complexity of their nursing care requirements. In most classifications, patients are grouped according to caretaker time and ability required to provide care."[19,p.290] Lewis and Carini cite three types of patient classification systems: (1) descriptive, which is a narrative description of various degrees of care required by a particular patient, (2) checklist, which simply lists patient problems according to patient acuity, and (3) time-based systems, which list patient needs according to level of acuity (e.g., minimal, partial, acute, or complex) and ascribe the amount of

nurse-time needed to fulfill the needs.[20] The delivery system in effect (e.g., modular, team, total care, or primary nursing) and the mix of nursing personnel (e.g., RNs, LPNs/LVNs, nurses' aides) influence staff allocation. Some projectors of staff needed use a point system (e.g., 1 to 9 points for minimal care, 10 to 20 points for partical care, and 21 to 30 points for total care) or ascribe hours of care needed (e.g., 1 to 2 hours for minimal care, 3 to 4 hours for partial care, and 5 to 7 hours for total care). The 24-hour figures are then computed and prorated according to shifts, depending on when the bulk of nursing care is given. Table 3 offers a sample of one form that may be used for staff projection after necessary data have been gathered. Other data unique to a specific unit may be added as desired. If, for example, there are 22 patients on the day shift, either read on the chart or compute as follows:

Three required minimal care:	$3 \times 0.17 = 0.51$
Fourteen required partial care:	$14 \times 0.27 = 3.78$
Five required total care:	$5 \times 0.36 = \underline{1.80}$
Total number of nursing personnel needed to staff the day shift:	6.09

Compute the number of nursing personnel needed to staff the evening and night shifts using Table 3 and the following information:

Table 3. Numbers of nursing personnel needed to staff a unit*

NUMBER OF PATIENTS	CLASSIFICATION OF PATIENTS								
	MINIMAL			PARTIAL			TOTAL		
	DAY	PM	NIGHT	DAY	PM	NIGHT	DAY	PM	NIGHT
1	0.17	0.14	0.10	0.27	0.15	0.07	0.36	0.30	0.20
2	0.34	0.28	0.20	0.54	0.30	0.14	0.72	0.60	0.40
3	0.51	0.42	0.30	0.81	0.45	0.21	1.08	0.90	0.60
21	3.57	2.94	2.10	5.67	3.15	1.47	7.56	6.30	4.20
22	3.74	3.08	2.20	5.94	3.30	1.54	7.92	6.60	4.40
23	3.91	3.22	2.30	6.21	3.45	1.61	8.28	6.90	4.60
24	4.08	3.36	2.40	6.48	4.00	1.68	8.64	7.20	4.80

*Formula: for the number of staff needed, the number of nursing personnel required to care for one patient (according to classification) is multiplied by the number of patients in that classification.

1. There are 24 patients on the evening shift classified as follows:

Five require minimal care: × =

Sixteen require partial care: × =

Three require total care: × =

Total number of nursing personnel needed to staff the evening shift:

2. There are 26 patients on the night shift classified as follows:

Seven require minimal care   × =

Fourteen require partial care   × =

Five require total care: × =

Total number of nursing personnel needed to staff the night shift:

Unless the classification of care of patient population remains fairly stable, the projector will need to classify patients each day before determining the numbers of staff needed. Of course, estimates will be projected for at least 2 weeks to make out the staff schedule. Necessary adjustments will be made from day to day, depending on the differences between projection and actuality.

Classification by computer. Patient classification can be simplified greatly by use of computers. The classficiation system can be programmed and brought up onto the screen for instant viewing and alteration.

Disadvantages of classification systems. Staff shortages can complicate the use of a patient classification system. Staffing in nursing homes is often determined on the basis of the patients' needs, and not the care they get, because of lack of staff. The problem is perpetuated if future staffing is based on previous allotments.[19]

There is little information on what actually happens when there is a shortage of staff. Reports indicate that some tasks are dropped and others curtailed. Blurring of nursing roles can also occur in classification systems. For example, nursing homes often lump together RNs, LPNs, and NAs. Disregarding type or level of personnel may have serious implications for funding.[19]

Staff Mix

A further assessment is that of determining the ratio or mix of nursing personnel who will provide the care. Again, this decision depends on the philosophy of the institution and the kind of delivery of care (functional, modular, team, total, primary). It is generally agreed that for acute care facilities, the highest percentage of staff should consist of registered nurses, then LPNs/LVNs, and last, assistants.

Staff Scheduling

Schedules for work and time off should meet organizational goals with fairness and equity among personnel. Basically, a schedule for a nursing staff pattern adheres to the following criteria:

1. The policies, standards, and practices of the employing agency on use of professional and paraprofessional nursing personnel
2. Appropriate ratio or balance between professional and paraprofessional or supportive staff
3. Continuity of services (For the promotion of quality care, nurses must care for the same patients/clients over time and work with the same nursing personnel.)
4. Approved master staffing budget with effective and economical assignment of personnel through avoidance of maldistribution and overstaffing
5. Satisfaction of staff members in their work
6. Consideration of vacations and other scheduled time off, which needs to be planned well in advance to provide for year round distribution
7. Allowance for adjustments in case of illness, emergencies, or changes in care needs
8. Staff members informed of their work schedules at least 2 weeks in advance of implementation
9. Protection of the rights of individuals against discriminatory action because of sex, ethnic differences, or religious beliefs

Centralized versus decentralized staffing systems. Work schedules can be developed on centralized systems, or decentralized systems, or a combination. A *centralized* staffing system is impersonal, done by the director of nursing services or designate, who develops a master plan for nursing personnel in the health facility. *Decentralized* staffing is a more personal approach. The middle and lower or first levels of management determine staffing. There are advantages and disadvantages to each system, as illustrated in Table 4. Most systems have some components of both centralization and decentralization; for example, a centralized organization may have decentralized staffing.[21]

Traditionally, head nurses or their counterparts at the lower or first level of management develop a schedule for their units, with the supervisor (middle level) filling any vacant spots from her greater number of units. The staffing person in the director of nursing services office (top level) allocates any additional personnel necessary, drawing on nurses from other units, the float list (if one exists), part-time nurses who will work on call, or outside agencies. Regardless of the staffing system in effect, a master plan for the entire facility is maintained for overall control.

Scheduling in advance. Schedules provide workers with advance notice. Like other members of the work force, nurses appreciate knowing their work schedules well in advance. The nurse population is predominantly female, with a median age of 37.7 years; 70% are married, and there is a high proportion of young nurses. Thus problems related to spouses' schedules, child

care, and social activities may weigh heavily on nurses' minds. They must know their schedules to maintain harmony in their homes and to meet individual needs.

An erratic or poorly planned schedule creates confusion and anger among the staff. Interpersonal relationships suffer because of such chronic happenings as posting the work schedule immediately before it goes into effect, last-minute changes in days off, overtime, long stretches without relief, split days off, few weekends free, and preferential treatment of some workers. Dissatisfaction is evidenced by dissension and reduced work performance. Lateness, increased absences, lethargy, and dropouts are natural consequences. These undesirable circumstances can be avoided by developing carefully planned work schedules well in advance of implementation and considering all criteria necessary for good scheduling.

The traditional way to schedule nursing personnel is to arrange coverage for each nursing department for 7 days a week, with a 5-day work week for round-the-clock service—a mammoth task. One expert has approached the problems of RN assignment by computation. With full-time employment and the usual hol-

◇ **Table 4.** Comparison of the advantages and disadvantages of the centralized and decentralized staffing systems

STAFFING SYSTEM	ADVANTAGES	DISADVANTAGES
Centralized	Conserves time Scheduler familiar with overall situation Easier to handle need for help in times of illness, absence, or emergency with qualified personnel Less frequent requests for special privileges Compatible with computerization	Denies head nurse the right to make staffing decisions Minimal opportunity for personal contact with staff Limited knowledge of workers' abilities, interests, and needs Limited knowledge of nursing care needs in the separate departments and units of nursing
Decentralized	Head nurse accountable for staffing decisions Scheduling based on knowledge of personnel and patient/client needs Greater control of activities; can rearrange schedule quickly as needed Fresh ideas generated for improvement of system	May be time consuming Sometimes results in lack of sufficient numbers of qualified personnel necessary to meet unforeseen needs Increased number of requests for special privileges

idays and vacations, no matter the mix, there are either too few or too many nurses to cover the staffing positions. The traditional staffing pattern tends to underuse nursing resources on some days and overuse them on weekends and holidays. The typical 2-week work schedule shown below for nursing personnel is an illustration of the traditional system. This schedule was made with a given directive that there must be at least two RNs assigned to any one day. Note that RNs A and B have a weekend off, while RN C has none. (A schedule for a longer time would allow rotation.) Monday was selected as the overstaffed day, as this day is generally most demanding of nursing services in hospitals. Analyze the schedule for process and problems; then plan an alternative schedule to see if problems can be minimized. This hypothetical schedule does not take into account other important scheduling criteria, such as meeting needs of individual patients/clients, workers, and the environment. An example illustrates the point. In past years, common practice has been for nurses to work two weekends out of every three. Current problems in acquiring and retraining staff have caused many hospitals to give every other weekend off. A quick perusal of the sample work schedule reveals that more RN personnel are needed to supply this one concession.

	RN TEAM LEADER		
DAY	**A**	**B**	**C**
S	x	Off	x
M	x	x	x
T	Off	x	x
W	x	Off	x
Th	x	x	Off
F	x	x	Off
Sa	Off	x	x
S	Off	x	x
M	x	x	x
T	x	x	Off
W	x	x	Off
Th	Off	x	x
F	x	Off	x
Sa	x	Off	x

Cyclical staffing system. A better way to designate work time is to develop a cyclical plan, in which workdays and time off are regularly repeated for 4-, 6-, 7-, or 12-week periods. To be suc-

cessful, the system requires centralization, sufficient numbers of full-time, qualified staff, and other groups of nursing personnel who are willing to work part-time, float, and be on call for emergencies. In this system the staff is treated fairly and equally. Everyone can have the same number of weekend days off, and the problems of overstaffing or understaffing are solved. This preprogrammed system also works well on the computer. The disadvantages of centralized staffing, outlined in Table 5 also apply to cyclical staffing. Figure 5-2 presents a master time schedule for a 4-week cycle.

Other staffing patterns being tried by nurse managers are the 40-hour, 4-day work week and a 7 days on, 7 days off plan. These and other options will continue to be studied in the hope that assignment of nursing personnel will be simplified and improved. Table 5 presents a description of four methods of staffing patterns and the advantages and disadvantages of each.

A computer program can be developed to create staffing schedules taking into account such factors as shift variations, staff/patient ratios, and staff requests. Whereas nurse managers previously spent as much as 8 hours devising the work schedule for a single unit, with the computer a completed schedule can be developed in less than an hour.

NURSING CARE DELIVERY SYSTEMS

A nursing care delivery system is an approach devised to deliver nursing care effectively and efficiently to patient populations. Each method has certain advantages and disadvantages. Nursing care delivery systems often have not kept pace with the rapid and complex changes in health care. Historically, four basic delivery services were utilized: (1) total care (previously referred to as *case nursing*), (2) functional, (3) team, and (4) primary nursing. These more common nursing care delivery systems will be discussed, as well as two more recent innovations: modular nursing and nurse case management.

Need for an Effective Contemporary Nursing Care Delivery System

According to Marlene Kramer, noted nurse educator and researcher, "Probably the biggest change that will occur in hospital nursing in the 1990s is the system for delivery of nursing

◇ **Table 5.** Four methods of staffing patterns

METHOD	DESCRIPTION	ADVANTAGES	DISADVANTAGES
Conventional	Centralized-decentralized combination is the oldest and most common. Head nurse makes up staffing pattern for particular unit; it is then incorporated and centralized in master plan in nursing office.	Pattern can be altered at central office to best meet needs; head nurse can use the "float concept" to her advantage; the precise measurement of nursing hours needed per patient population is measurable with this pattern.	If there is too much decentralization, cohesiveness and order will be lost.
Cyclical	Staffing pattern repeats itself every 4-6, 7-12 weeks.	Pattern provides for float personnel to fortify staff when need arises; there is a fair distribution of good and bad hours among all staff, therefore no favoritism is shown; each person knows her pattern and can plan ahead; once a cyclical pattern is established, layperson can work with it.	A constant, sufficient number of the appropriate mix of personnel is required for it to work.
Forty hours; 4 days	Forty hours a week is worked in 4 days, followed by a block of off-duty time.	The large time block off may offset the possibility of fatigue; staff may have more weekends off; overlapping may provide for better coverage at meal time.	Fatigue is possible, resulting in poorer quality of care; studies in other disciplines have shown an increase in accidents and a lack of overall productivity.
Seven days off; 7 on	A 10-hour day is worked for 7 days, followed by 7 days off.	Nurses are paid for 8 hours with no vacation or holidays allowed; they are given 70 hours of sick leave; better continuity of care is achieved because the same staff may cover almost an entire hospitalization of a patient; there is better communication with physicians and other staff; inservice program is strengthened.	Pattern may be too hard on personnel physically; staff may desire holidays and vacation time.

Modified from Holle ML: Staffing: what the books don't tell you, Nurs Man 13(3):15, 1982.

Elements: Every other weekend off   Number of split days off each period: 2
Maximum days worked: 4   Operates in multiples of 4, 8, 12, ...
Minimum days worked: 2   Schedule repeats itself every 4 weeks

☐ Scheduled day off

Position	Name	Week I							Week II							Week III							Week IV							
		S	M	T	W	T	F	S	S	M	T	W	T	F	S	S	M	T	W	T	F	S	S	M	T	W	T	F	S
Full time	R.N. 1																												
Full time	R.N. 2																												
Full time	R.N. 3																												
Full time	R.N. 4																												
Full time	R.N. 5																												
Full time	R.N. 6																												
Full time	R.N. 7																												
Full time	R.N. 8																												
Part time	8 hrs/week R.N. 9	ON													ON								ON						
Part time	8 hrs/week R.N. 10	ON													ON								ON						
Part time	8 hrs/week R.N. 11							ON	ON													ON							ON
Part time	8 hrs/week R.N. 12							ON	ON													ON							ON
	Total R.N.s on duty each day	6	7	7	6	6	6	6	6	7	7	6	6	6	6	6	7	7	6	6	6	6	6	7	7	6	6	6	6

Figure 5-2. Example of cyclical scheduling. Master time schedule for 4-week cycle. *From Eusanio PL: J Nurs Admin 8:12-17, Jan 1978.*

care—who will delivery it (staff mix) and in what way." [22] A serious issue today is the need to develop nursing care services that will match quality of care with cost and reimbursement for services.

Total Care Nursing

Total care nursing is the oldest of the care systems. One nurse is assigned to one patient/client for the delivery of total care. The nurse functions within the system of nursing care used by all staff (Figure 5-3). The one-to-one pattern is common assignment for student nurses, private duty nurses, and for special circumstances in which single care is needed (e.g., isolation, intensive care units). In total care nursing it is possible for one nurse to be assigned to more than one patient/client, providing that nurse can meet the objectives of the assignment. Note the broken and unbroken lines in Figure 5-3. For the student nurse there is a dual allegiance between instructor and charge nurse. While the student meets individual learning needs through the instructor's guidance, the ultimate responsibility for patient/client care rests with the charge nurse officially employed. Because nurse assistants cannot give medications or administer many treatments, and because in many instances their assessment skills are inadequate for the delivery of total care, individual nursing is no longer possible in most hospitals as a major pattern of care.

Functional Nursing

Functional nursing is a system of care borrowed from industry that concentrates on duties or activities. This pattern of care involves an assembly-line approach, with major tasks delegated by the charge nurse to individual members of the work group. One member may be assigned to desk work, another to pass medications, another to administer all treatments and/or monitor IVs, another to give hygienic care, and so on. Each member of the working group is highly dependent on the others for completion of the group's total assignments. Established protocol and procedure manuals are followed closely. Figure 5-4 diagrams the channels of authority existing under this controlled system. Nursing care plans provide an important link

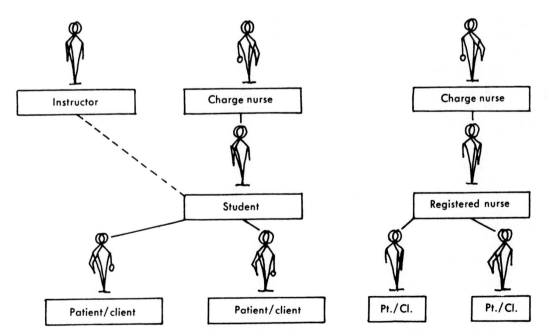

Figure 5-3. Lines of authority in a typical health care facility with total care nursing.

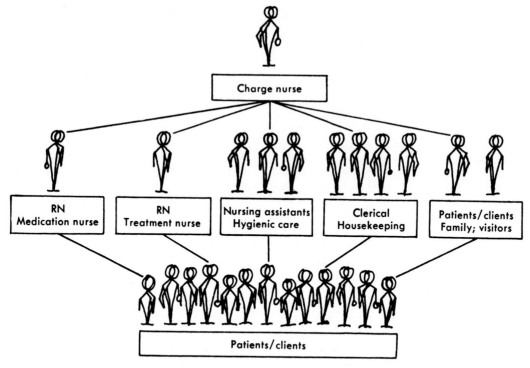

Figure 5-4. Lines of authority in a typical health care facility with functional nursing.

between the workers and quality of care given, as there is limited opportunity for members of the nursing group to meet for coordination of efforts.

Advantages and disadvantages of the functional system are controversial among nurses and hospital administrators. Many hospital administrators consider the functional system the most economical way to deliver nursing services. This may be true if consideration is given to meeting minimal health care standards with as few nursing personnel as possible. Another advantage named is that the nurse manager (or head nurse) maintains greater control over work activities. In this autocratic system the manager bears responsibility for all activities of those persons assigned to provide care, as well as for the quality of care given. As chief of all activities, the charge nurse is barraged with input from all sides: physicians, nursing staff, students, patients/clients, visitors, and the public. In addition, the nurse manager must complete administrative functions as well. The dichotomy

of roles often becomes overwhelming, causing the nurse to be inadequate in the fulfillment of job expectations.

Some workers feel more secure in the dependent role necessary to functional care. The manager may enjoy telling people what to do, and some workers are comfortable in following orders and in performing repetitive tasks. However, the more significant issue is that of patient/client care. The functional design is aimed at work production with conservation of workers and cost. Psychological and sociological needs are often overlooked, thus defeating the very purpose of care systems.

Team Nursing

Team nursing is a system of care in which a professional nurse leads a group of health care personnel in providing for the health needs of an individual or group of people through collaborative and cooperative effort. Team nursing was developed in the 1950s because of social and technological changes. World War II drew many nurses away from hospitals, leaving gaps. Services, procedures, and equipment became more extensive and complicated, requiring specialization at every turn. One attempt to meet increased demands for nursing services, better use of knowledge and skills of professional nurses, and increased patient/client and worker satisfaction was team nursing.[23]

In the 1950s Eleanor Lambertson, with the aid of a Kellogg grant, studied the system of team nursing in a large hospital in New York City.[24] She concluded that team nursing, if properly used, could serve as one good answer to effective use of nursing personnel who had diversified backgrounds and skills. Dorothy Newcomb focused her attention on helping head nurses to see the value of team nursing and later expanded her writing to include the entire team.[25] Others, such as Kron[26] and Douglass,[27] have contributed to the body of knowledge of team nursing.

Team nursing is based on a philosophy of certain beliefs and values: (1) the worth of every individual, (2) the need for a qualified person to be the overall coordinator and interpreter of plans for care, (3) emphasis on co-equal status with minimal hierarchical lines of demarcation between the leader and followers, and (4) sensitivity and responsiveness to the need for adaptability and change.

Team nursing can be identified by specific characteristics. A nursing team (1) is always led by a nurse licensed to practice; (2) functions wherever there are health needs focusing on the patient's total needs; (3) includes the patient in the development and implementation of care plans whenever possible; (4) is changeable and adaptable; and (5) recognizes and appropriately uses each individual's talents, abilities, and interests to the fullest.

A clear line of organization structure is needed for the nursing team to provide a mechanism for horizontal and vertical communication. As Figure 5-5 illustrates, when team nursing is used, an organizational pattern is employed whereby the charge nurse or designated person delegates leadership responsibility to a nurse leader for a specific group of patients/clients. Team members relate to the team leader, who in turn relates directly to the charge nurse. The charge nurse's role changes from that of an organizer and manager of tasks to a coordinator, consultant, and evaluator.

Team nursing is one form of decentralization. The intent is to bring decision-making authority, responsibility, and accountability to an operational level. This is accomplished by reducing the degree of vertical control held at the top level and developing increased horizontal communications at lower levels. In this system the team leader can employ any or all patterns of nursing care according to the needs of the patients/clients and the capabilities and desires of the caregivers.

Determination of size of a nursing team lies within each setting. How many members and the mix of staff needed to assure provision of quality care to a specific group of patients/clients relates to the patient group and its nursing needs. In general units, nursing team cares for 10 to 20 patients, with three to five nursing staff members assigned to their care.

A nurse's task is more complex with team nursing than with the functional approach, as more managerial skills are required. The team leader is challenged to include all members of the team in the problem-solving approach according to their abilities. Inherent in the philosophy of team nursing is a belief that all members have the right to be entrusted with responsibility, to be given authority to act, and to be accountable for their actions. At the heart of team nursing is the communication system, which is important for providing direction, giving reports of assignments in progress and those completed, focusing on patient/client care, acquiring information, and assessing team relationships.

Team nursing has the advantages of involvement of all team members in planning, executing, and evaluating. When all parts are working satisfactorily, this involvement provides job enrichment and job expansion to all workers, especially at lower levels on the team.

Disadvantages of team nursing are viewed from different perspectives. Some believe this method of assignment to be more costly, because the overall efficiency of the nursing unit is reduced by fragmented distribution of personnel. Others point to the increased amount of time necessary for several team leaders to perform similar managerial tasks of assessment,

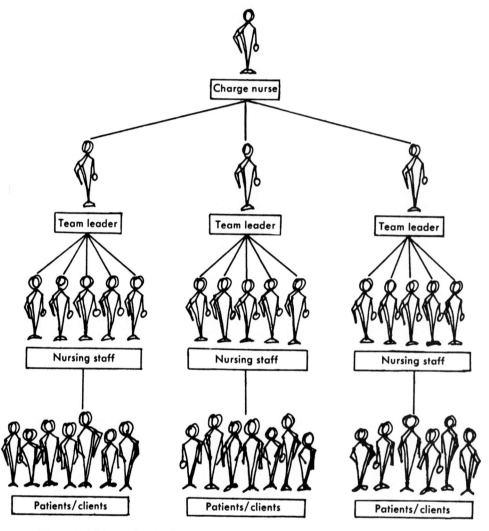

Figure 5-5. Lines of authority in a typical health care facility with team nursing.

delegation, and controlling of work groups. The element of error is another factor to consider. There are risks with decentralization of responsibility; confusion may occur when several people are receiving orders (e.g., from head nurse to team leader to nursing staff members). Also, some nurses may not wish to take on the responsibility of leading a group, preferring a more independent or dependent system.

Primary Nursing

Primary nursing is both a philosophy of nursing care and a model of organizing that care in a hospital to achieve high-quality care outcomes. Its goals are to achieve patient-centered, individualized care that is comprehensive in scope, coordinated, and continuous from patient/client admission to discharge. Staffing for primary nursing usually requires that one RN primary nurse be assigned four to six patients (depending on patient acuity), two or more of these patients being the nurse's primary patients. Primary nurses have accountability, authority, and autonomy for the care of their primary patients and attention to patient's families from admission to discharge.[18] Primary nurses are account-

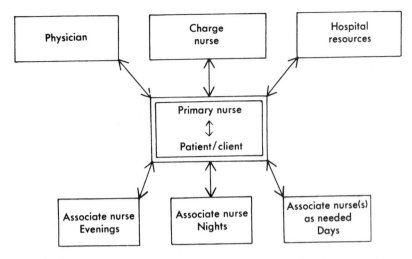

Figure 5-6. Lines of authority in a typical hospital with primary nursing.

able for the outcomes of the nursing care given, not just for the fact that care is given.[28]

The primary nurse may provide nursing care services to the patient/client individually or through coordination of care with associates. This is accomplished through direct communication (on the job or by telephone), nursing care plans, notes, and other records. Figure 5-6 illustrates the direct lines of authority necessary for primary care nursing. The primary nurse, physician, and head nurse control the quality of care the patient/client receives by maintaining an effective communication system. This system is accomplished through regular meetings to discuss and agree on the rationale for care, to plan comprehensive care, to solve problems, and to evaluate and coordinate patient/client care. Figure 5-6 illustrates the peer or colleague relationship among the nurse, physician, head nurse, and all others. It also demonstrates that the patient/client is the center of focus for all functions.

The quality of care given depends on the ongoing nursing care plans, clarity of directions, and the ability of the primary care nurse. Selection of nurses who are qualified to function in the primary pattern of care is important factor to successful achievement of purposes. For best results the primary nurse should be a registered professional nurse prepared for the role. Primary nurses are expected to be clinically competent, take nursing histories do all initial as-

sessments, develop care plans, problem solve effectively, and accept a new role of independence for planning and providing comprehensive care.[29]

Primary nursing has the advantage of focusing on knowing the needs of patients/clients and increasing care and effectiveness. The patients/clients are more satisfied, because they can identify with one nurse who they believe has a vested interest in their welfare. The communication system between patients/clients and the nurse and the nurse and physician and other health team members is improved, as there are fewer channels to go through to get things done. Nurses have opportunity to function autonomously as professionals and use their capacities, which may lead to greater satisfaction with hospital nursing, thus resulting in less employee turnover.[29]

Disadvantages of primary nursing are related to cost, implementation, role confusion, and poor communication. Cost becomes an issue wherever primary care nursing is considered as primary nursing requires a much higher proportion of professional nurses to ancillary personnel. Some top-level administrators, physicians, and nurses feel that changing to primary nursing increases costs. Others counter, however, that primary care nursing can be accomplished without any increases in the budget.[30]

Overall administrative efficiency may be reduced with primary nursing, as each nurse's leadership is restricted to a small group of patients/clients. There is also the factor of nurses' preparation for and interest in primary nursing. Role confusion can occur when LPNs/LVNs are assigned patient care. They are not assigned primary patients but are used as associate nurses under the supervision of the RNs. In practice their roles overlap frequently. Communication problems may arise between the primary nurse and other nursing staff.

Modular Nursing[31]

Modular nursing is a modification of team and primary nursing. Modular nursing is a geographic assignment of patients that encourages continuity of care by organizing a group of staff to work with a group of patients in the same locale. For example, a module might consist of five or six rooms side by side along one hall, or a group of rooms or cubicles that surround a nursing station. The fixed geographic area typically represents 10 to 12 patients per module. This nursing care delivery system is sometimes used when there are not enough registered nurses to practice primary nursing. With financial constraints and census fluctuations plaguing hospitals, ways are being sought to provide a more effecient delivery system that ensures quality patient care and promotes professional nursing. Unlike team nursing, whereby the RN directs care given by members of the team, in modular nursing each RN, assisted by paraprofessionals, delivers direct care to a group of patients. In addition to care giving, the RN plans

care for all patients in the module and directs paraprofessionals in the more technical aspects of care.

The Medical Center of Delaware had delivered nursing care according to a primary nursing model for 12 years. With the average length of stay shortened and patient acuity increased, RNs had little time to supervise LPNs and nurse assistants. They convened a task force of key nurse management and staff members to assess the situation and to develop a modular system. Even though the number of RNs and LPNs decreased and the number of nurses' aides increased, it was felt that RNs and paraprofessionals were better satisfied, because there was improved unit efficiency. The box indicates the advantages and disadvantages of the modular system as compared with primary and team nursing.

Nursing Case Management

The term *case manager* began to appear in the nursing literature in the mid-1980s, and the concept has been gathering momentum ever since. Case management is based on the concept of providing managed care on a continuum for persons with episodic or chronic illnesses.[31] The American Nurses' Association describes nursing case management as "a healthcare delivery process whose goals are to provide quality healthcare, decrease fragmentation, enhance the clients' quality of life and contain costs."[32] The professional nurse case manager "is responsible for assessment of patient and family, establish-

Advantages and Disadvantages

	MODULAR	PRIMARY	TEAM
Continuity of care	Yes	Yes	No
Close nurse/patient relationship	Yes	Yes	No
Patient knows nurse	Yes	Yes	No
Increased coordination time	Yes	No	Yes
Combines nurse's skills	Yes	No	No
Reduces time for RN in indirect activities	Yes	No	No
Lunch/break coverage	Yes	No	Yes
RN performs RN/Rx	Yes	Yes	No
Decreased time looking for assistance	Yes	No	No

From Bennett M and Hylton J: Modular nursing: partners in professional practice, Nurs Man 20(2):24, 1990.

ment of the nursing diagnosis, development of the nursing care plan, delegation of nursing care to associates, activation of interventions, coordination and collaboration with the interdisciplinary team and evaluation of outcomes."[33] In institutions, these activities occur prior to admission through at least 2 weeks after discharge. In communities, activities occur in any setting—the home, clinic, extended care facilities, or hospital—for as long as necessary.[34] The best-known examples of those who utilize nurse case managers are prepaid health care plans, health maintenance organizations (HMOs), and Preferred Provider Organizations (PPOs). This consumer trend of choosing managed care systems reflects support for services that are cost-effective yet maintain quality outcomes.[35] Figure 5-7 provides an example of the organizational structure of a health care delivery system in an acute care health agency utilizing the nurse case manager. In this setting, the professional nurse case manager (PNCM) carries an active caseload of approximately 40 patients: 10 in the acute care setting and 30 followup patients in the community. The case manager may have another 40 to 50 patients who have stabilized and require only a monthly telephone call for ongoing outcome evaluation.[32]

Initially, the PNCM spends time with the patient and family to establish an open, working relationship and to gather information about previous health, causal factors for hospitalization, previous and current levels of physical, psychological, and spiritual functioning and coping abilities, and availability of resources and social supports. With this data, the PNCM, together with the patient and family, primary nurse, and physician, identify potential and current problems, prescribe a course of nursing treatment during the in-hospital stay, and formulate a discharge plan.[36]

The PNCM is also responsible for collaborating with the multidisciplinary health care team and with community agencies to facilitate the achievement of agreed-upon health outcomes. Within the home and community settings, the PNCM continues to assess patient and family health care needs and suggests or arranges for interventions as appropriate. The PNCM teaches, counsels, and collaborates with other health care professionals.[32] See the box on p. 98 for a summary of case management models.

The growing complexity of the community health care delivery system has created some negative consequences, such as clients becoming lost in the system or receiving duplication of services, primarily as a result of lack of coordination of services. Case managers are now being employed in a variety of health care settings. They help clients navigate the maze of

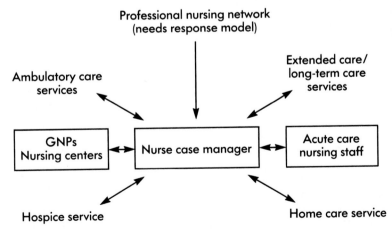

Figure 5-7. Organizational structure of a delivery system in an acute care agency utilizing the nurse case manager. *Reprinted with permission from Ethridge P and Lamb G: Professional nurse case management improves quality, access and costs, Nurs Man 20(3):30, 1989.*

Case Management Models

Curtain describes four models of case management usually practiced in a hospital setting:[37]

1. **The North Eastern model** (unit-based primary care giver) is an extension of primary nursing. The primary nurse initiates the relationship before admission when possible, actively engages in discharge planning, coordinates all inpatient activities, and follows the patient for 2 weeks or more after discharge.

2. **The Arizona model** (nurse case manager) establishes criteria for the selection of high-risk patients in each clinical area. These patients are referred to a case manager, at least baccalaureate prepared, who is already in a management position (head nurse or supervisor). The case manager monitors and coordinates the patient's care with the primary nurse, physician, and other appropriate health care providers. The case manager participates in discharge planning and follows patients through discharge, nursing home, home health agency, physician's office, and/or clinic for an indefinite but extended period of time.

3. **The HMO model** (monitoring system) coordinates care with hospital personnel in an attempt to control expenditures while delivering quality care. High-risk patients are followed over time in an effort to control resource utilization.

4. **The insurance-based and state-based (medical) model** (monitoring system) is designed to cut costs. Here the case manager reviews records and progress, identifies problem areas, and follows them over time.

---

health care providers as they move from one level of care to another. Private insurance companies such as Blue Cross/Blue Shield and HMOs have found that case managers can save companies money, as well as provide better service. Case managers are becoming important in the field of mental health as they work with the mentally ill population to secure needed care and funds for survival.[38]

SUMMARY

1. There are over one half million working nurses in the United States, but this number is insufficient to meet the need. Critical care and medical-surgical hospital units are hardest hit by the shortage.

2. Rapid turnover of nursing personnel is a significant problem. Attention to periodic market surveys can help employers keep in touch with employment preferences of nurses.

3. Categories most often cited by experienced RNs as first priorities in selecting new jobs are work schedule, salary and benefits, and low degree of stress.

4. Graduating seniors selected quality of patient care, treatment of nurses as professionals, adequate staffing, and low patient-to-nurse ratios as their priorities in job selection.

5. The average maximum salary in 1990 for staff nurses nationally was $34,000; the average minimum salary was $25,900.

6. New graduates and experienced nurses often are enticed to new jobs through such things as negotiation of work schedules, benefits, and incentives.

7. Major factors contributing to the demand for RNs are increased intensity of medical practice, changes in patient characteristics, nurses' professional goals, and economic incentives.

8. A nurse registry provides a pool of nursing staff for employers who wish to use supplementary nursing personnel. Registry staff should be screened carefully and oriented to the employing agency carefully to avoid disruptions in service and to maintain provision of quality care.

9. Staffing follows the structure, goals, and standards of the organization served.

10. Job specifications must be clear and in writing.

11. Description of performance responsibilities should spell out job content for each of the roles in the agency.

12. Staff members are to be matched to their jobs as well as possible, with attention to abilities, apitude, interest, and need.

13. The nurse employee is responsible for mak-

ing personal requests for placement known to the proper authorities.

14. The numbers of RNs and paraprofessionals should be correlated depending on the philosophy of the agency, patient / client needs, methods used in provision of nursing care, availability of qualified nursing personnel, and any problems unique to the agency.

15. Work schedules are developed through a centralized system, decentralized system, or combination.

16. Centralized work schedules are developed at the top level of management for the entire work force. Advantages are conservation of time, knowledge of overall situation, ability to handle unforeseen circumstances more easily, easy computerization, and less frequent requests for special privileges. Disadvantages are minimal opportunity for personal attention and limited knowledge of workers and the specific nursing care needed by individual patients / clients.

17. Decentralized scheduling is accomplished at the middle and lower levels of management. Advantages are knowledge of personnel and patients / clients served and greater control of on-the-job activities, allowing the schedule to be altered more quickly. Disadvantages include length of time needed for scheduling, lack of sufficient qualified personnel necessary to meet all nursing situations, and increased number of requests for special privileges.

18. The staffing system most commonly employed is a combination of centralized and decentralized planning, with cooperative efforts among schedulers.

19. Schedules provide workers with advance notice. They are planned for either 2-, 4-, 7-, or 12-week periods.

20. Traditional scheduling is based on the 5-day work week with round-the-clock coverage. Whatever the mix, with fulltime employment there will either be overstaffing or understaffing. Problems can be minimized through use of part-time help and sharing personnel among departments and units.

21. The cyclical staffing system is recommended. In this system, days and time off are regularly repeated on a 4-, 6-, 7-, or 12-week basis. Sufficient numbers of qualified staff are needed to assure success of the system.

22. Total care nursing is the assignment of one nurse to one patient / client for the provision of total care. Student nurses and private duty nurses are examples.

23. Functional nursing is a task-oriented system of care with an assembly-line approach, functioning under an autocratic system, with concentration on conservation of workers and cost. Great responsibility rests with the charge nurse for coordinating and supervising all activities. The patient / client suffers for lack of individual attention.

24. Team nursing is a plan of care in which a group of nursing personnel are led by a qualified nurse to plan, direct, and evaluate the delivery of care to a group of patients / clients. The system focuses on total patient / client care, includes the patient / client in the planning process, is adaptable, and recognizes and uses individual members' talents, abilities, and interests to the fullest extent possible.

25. Primary nursing is a continuous and coordinated nursing process in which a registered nurse provides the initial patient / care assessment and assumes accountability for planning comprehensive 24-hour care for an individual patient / client for the length of hospitalizaion, or for the duration of care needed.

26. Modular nursing is a modification of team and primary nursing. It is a geographic assignment of patients that encourages continuity of care by organizing a group of staff (RNS and paraprofessionals) to work with a group of patients.

27. The professional case manager is responsible for assessment of patient and family, establishment of the nursing diagnosis, development of the nursing care plan, delegation of nursing care to associates, activation of interventions, coordination and collaboration with the interdisciplinary team, and evaluation of outcomes prior to admission through at least 2 weeks after dismissal.

28. Leah Curtin describes four models of case management usually practiced in a hospital setting: (1) the North Eastern model (unit-based primary care givers), (2) the Arizona model (at least baccalaureate-prepared nursing case managers working with patients, nursing associates and interdisciplinary personnel from before admission to after discharge), (3) the HMO model (a monitoring system by the case manager), and (4) the insurance-based and state-based medical model wherein the case manager reviews records and progress in an effort to reduce costs.

29. To be positive, relationships must be nurtured between the case manager and physicians, primary nurses, public health nurses, and other interdisciplinary staff.

30. There are varying standards for preparation of the nurse case manager. The ANA recommends a BSN as minimal level of education.

31. Experimentation is under way regarding the use of health professionals other than nurses to act as case managers.

 Questions for Study and Discussion

1. Explain why nurse turnover is so expensive.
2. What are your priorities in selecting a job as an RN? How do they compare with those of other graduating seniors in the class? With graduating seniors' priorities listed in the text?
3. What plans would you make to find employment as an RN?
4. Assume that as department manager of a postsurgical nursing department, you are to staff the unit with nursing personnel. What are the basic guidelines you will use to decide on the numbers and kinds of staff?
5. Define a patient classification system. Explain one system commonly used.
6. What is a nursing care delivery system? Choose one system to define, and describe the RN's role in that system.

REFERENCES

1. Kreitner R: Management, ed 4, Boston, 1989, Houghton Mifflin Co.
2. US Health and Human Services Department, Nursng Analysis staff: Selected findings from the 1988 national sample survey of registered nurses, Washington DC, The Department.
3. American Hospital Association: Hospital statistics, Chicago, 1988, The Association.
4. Jones C: Staff nurse turnover costs. II. Measurements and results, JONA 20(5):27-31, 1990.
5. Cohn J and Lowell L: Market research gives nursing administrators an edge, Nurs Man 20(5):44-46, 1989.
6. Minnick A and others: What do nurses want? priorities for action, Nurs Outlook 37(5):214-217, 1989.
7. Kramer M and Hafner L: Shared values: impact on staff nurse job satisfaction and perceived productivity, Nurs Res 38(3):172-177, 1989.
8. Orr R: Factors important to BSN graduating seniors in employment decisions, Nurs Man 20(6):68-70, 1989.
9. The good news: Where are nursing salaries going in 1990? The AJN Guide, p 15, 1990.
10. Theisen B and Pelfrey S: Using employee benefit plans to fight the nursing shortage, JONA 20(9):24-28, 1990.
11. Barigar D and Sheafor M: Recruiting staff nurses: a marketing approach, Nurs Man 21(1):27-29, 1990.
12. Smith S and Dvoren-Baker T: The registry dilemma, Nurs Man 20(11):56-57, 1989.
13. Coss T: Nursing registries and economic efficiency, Nurs Man 20(1):50-51, 1989.
14. Fiesta J: Law for the nurse manager: agency nurses—whose liability? Nurs Man 20(3):16, 1989.
15. Mills M: Clinical nurse specialist organizational value and role support, Clin Nurs Spec 3(4):186-187, 1989.
16. Shaw M: Assertive-responsive management: a personal handbook, Reading, Mass, 1988, Addison-Wesley Publishing Co.
17. Smith S and Elesha-Adams M: Allocating nurs-

ing resources in ambulatory care, Nurs Man 20(1):61-64, 1989.

18. Gillies D: Nursing management: a systems approach, ed 2, Philadelphia, 1989, WB Saunders Co.

19. Helberg J: Reliability of the nursing classification index for homehealth care, Nurs Man 20(3):48-56, 1989.

20. Lewis E and Carini P: Nurse staffing and patient classification, Rockville, Md, 1984, Aspen Systems.

21. Willington M: Decentralization: how it affects nurses, Nurs Outlook 34(1):37, 1986.

22. Kramer M: Trends to watch at the magnet hospitals, Nursing 90 20(6):70, 1990.

23. Marriner-Tomey A: Guide to nursing management, ed 3, St Louis, 1988, Times Mirror/Mosby College Publishing.

24. Lambertsen E: Nursing team: organizational and functional, New York, 1953, Columbia University Press.

25. Newcomb D: The team plan, New York, 1953, G P Putnam's Sons.

26. Kron T: The management of patient care: putting leadership skills to work, ed 6, Philadelphia, 1987, WB Saunders Co.

27. Douglass L: The effective nurse: leader and manager, ed 3, St Louis, 1988, Times Mirror/Mosby College Publishing.

28. Zander K: Second generation primary nursing: a new agenda, J Nurs Adm 15(3):18-24, 1985.

29. Tappen R: Nursing leadership and management: concepts and practice, ed 2, Philadelphia, 1989, FA Davis Co.

30. Johnson M and McCloskey J: Series on nursing administration, vol 2, Changing organizational structures, Redwood City, Calif, 1989, Addison-Wesley Publishing Co.

31. Bennett M and Hylton J: Modular nursing: partners in professional practice, Nurs Man 20(3):20-24, 1990.

32. Ethridge P and Lamb G: Professional nursing care management improves quality, access and costs, Nurs Man 20(3):30, 1989.

33. Zander K: Managed care within acute care settings: design and implementations via nursing case management, Health Care Super (2):27-43, 1988.

34. Zander K: Nursing case management: strategic management of cost and quality outcomes, J Nurs Adm 18(5):23-30, 1988.

35. McKenzie C, Torkelson N, and Holt M: Care and cost: nursing case management improves both, Nurs Man 20(10):30-34, 1989.

36. Olivas G and others: Case management: a bottom line case delivery model. I. The concept, J Nurs Adm 19(11):16-20, 1989.

37. Curtin L: Editorial opinion: the news from the front, Nurs Man 20(3):7-8, 1989.

38. Smith G: Using the public agenda to shape PHN practice, Nurs Outlook 37(2):72, 1989.

SUGGESTED READINGS

Adams-Ender C and Hudock J: The army nursing care team, Nurs Man 20(3):63-64, 1989.

Bailey B: How to float safely and effectively, Nursing 90 20(2):113-116, 1990.

Barigar D and Sheafor M: Recruiting staff nurses: a marketing approach, Nurs Man 21(1):27-29, 1990.

Becker and others: A nurse practitioner's job description, Nurs Man 20(6):42-44, 1989.

Betancourt E and Lombardi J: Job sharing in nursing management: it can work, Nurs Man 21(1):47-49, 1990.

Corcoran L and Diers D: Nursing intensity in cardiac surgical care, Nurs Man 20(2):80I-80P, 1989.

Day L: Automated staff scheduling in long-term care facilities, Nurs Man 20(30):76-78, 1989.

Dunsmore C and Houston R: Traveling nurses—a valuable resource, Nurs Man 21(10):79-81, 1990.

Elliott T: Cost analysis of alternative scheduling, Nurs Man 20(4):42-46, 1989.

Faught D and Staunton V: Marketing nursing to men, Nurs Man 20(6):74, 1989.

iesta J: The nursing shortage: whose liability problem? Part II, Nurs Man 21(2):22-23, 1990.

Fondiller S: How case management is changing the picture, Amer J Nurs 91(1):64-74, 1991.

Fuszard B, Slocum L, and Wiggers D: Surviving the nurse shortage, Part II, JONA 20(5):41-45, 1990.

Gulotta K and Matlack K: Recruitment: combining work and school, Nurs Man 21(10):71-78, 1990.

Houston R: Twelve-hour shifts: answer to job satisfaction? Nurs Man 21(10):88F-88H, 1990.

Jacobson E: Three new ways to deliver care, Am J Nurs 90(7):24-26, 1990.

Jones K and others: An agency-staffed nursing unit project, Nurs Man 21(10):36-40, 1990.

Kaplow R, Ackerman N, and Outlaw E: Co-primary nursing in the intensive care unit, Nurs Man 20(12):41-43, 1989.

Kostreva M and Genevier P: Nurse preferences vs circadian rhythms in scheduling, Nurs Man 20(7):50-62, 1990.

Malloch K, Milton D, and Jobes M: A model for differentiated nursing practice, JONA 20(2):20-26, 1990.

Manthey M: Delivery systems and practice models: a dynamic balance Nurs Man 22(1):28-30, 1991.

Mueller J and Lavandero R: Interim nursing management as temporary employment, Nurs Man 21(1):43-46, 1990.

Myles S: Nurse liaison:bridging the gap (oncology), Nurs Man 21(3):28-29, 1990.

Newton G: Designing and implementing a supplemental staffing system, Nurs Man 21(10):30-32, 1990.

O'Malley J, Loveridge C, and Cummings S: The new nursing organization: the changing environment challenges us to redesign nursing care delivery systems, Nurs Man 20(2):29-32, 1989.

Ouellette J and others: Clustering:decentralization and resource sharing, Nurs Man 21(6):31-35, 1990.

Quillen T: How to reduce absenteeism: strategies that work, Nursing 90 90(6):32CC-32LL, 1990.

Ringerman E and Luz S: A psychiatric patient classification system, Nurs Man 21(10):66-71, 1990.

Roscoe J and Haig N: Planning shift patterns, Nursing Times 86(38):31-33, Sept 19, 1990.

Sadler C: Shift work: beat the clock, Nursing Times 86(38):28-30, Sept 19, 1990.

Salmond S: In-hospital case management: responses to common questions and concerns, Orthop Nurs 9(1):38-40, 1990.

Schwamb J: A maternity patient classification system, Nurs Man 20(11):66-71, 1989.

Wake M: Nursing care delivery systems: status and vision, JONA 20(5):47-51, 1990.

Weis D: 10 questions recruiters will ask, Nursing 90 20(3):116-118, 1990.

White S: Symposium on successful recruitment and retention strategies in critical care, heart and lung: J Crit Care 19(3):219-242, May 1990.

Wolcott M: Ambulatory surgery (staffing pattern), Nurs Educ 15(4):36-39, 1990.

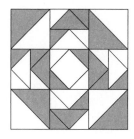

6

Planning and Decision Making: Fundamental Processes

On completion of this chapter the student will be prepared to:

☐ Define the overall planning process and apply it to organizational planning.
☐ Name five factors that contribute to manager resistance to the planning process.
☐ List six valid reasons for using the planning process.
☐ Compare and contrast the scope of planning for top-, middle-, and lower or first-level managers.
☐ Define decision making and explain the variables present in the process.
☐ Discuss the scientific, intuitive, emotional, and pragmatic approaches to decision making.
☐ State the functions of group decision making, compare the advantages with disadvantages, and discuss group decision makers' power.
☐ Explain the purpose and procedure of management by objectives.
☐ Indicate how plans are developed to achieve objectives.
☐ Identify the components of a written nursing care plan and explain its value to nursing practice.
☐ Explain the evaluation or controlling process as part of the planning process.

Planning is basically nothing more than deciding in advance what will be done and what will not be done in the next minutes, hours, days, months, or years. Not to plan is a plan in itself. It has been well said, "If you don't care where you are going, any road will take you there." Planning bridges the gap between where you are and where you want to go. It answers in advance the questions of who, what, when where, why, and how of future actions. Plans affect how people will work and for how long. Plans determine rate, effectiveness, and quality of program. Planning takes into account the seen and unseen, recognizing that all factors have influence on one another.

Planning is having a specific aim or purpose and mapping out a program or method *beforehand* for accomplishment of the goal. There is a difference between planning and purpose. Purpose is making a resolution or intending to accomplish something. As with New Year's resolutions, unless specific steps are taken to achieve the resolution or purpose, nothing will happen. Planning is making a commitment and establishing tools that can measure the outcome.

As the population of the world grows and our means of communicating with one another become more sophisticated, the opportunity for working together grows at an ever-increasing rate. The number of interactions and possibilities for overlap and duplication in plans and confusion among different people, structures, and organizations multiply at a fantastic rate. If we are not clear in deciding where we are going and how we plan to get there, we will find ourselves continually colliding with other people's plans. By announcing our goals and clearly indicating the steps we plan to take to achieve them, we establish points of communication with others who are also making new plans and working with old ones.

Every manager has a planning function to perform. Planning is not concentrated only among top-level managers. Although it is true that top managers may devote more of their time to planning and work with more vital issues than do managers at the middle and lower levels, the fact remains that every manager has planning to perform within his or her particular area of activities, and the planner is the one with the greatest opportunity to bring together all

the resources of an enterprise into a more effective unit.

This chapter should prove helpful to nurses who hope to influence their environment and make things happen. It is designed for the nurse who is seeking more effective means of improving current and future performance. It offers principles of planning and decision making and guides to using them in nursing practice. It deals with those aspects of planning and decision making that directly affect the nurse manager on a personal as well as an organizational level. The chapter focuses on key elements of the processes, presenting them in a way that will illustrate the interdependence of the processes of planning and decision making in the total activity of managing.

In general, planning is an intellectual process based on facts and information, not on emotions or wishes. Planning is a continuous process of assessing, establishing goals and objectives, and implementing and evaluating or controlling them, which is subject to change as new facts are known. If plans are considered as fixed and unchangeable, then most likely they will fail. In the planning process the necessary steps are mapped out, pointing toward the goal, but as each major step is taken, a reevaluation or feedback occurs that calls for examination of progress against set standards that measure performance. As conditions change, plans are revised and updated.[1]

In organizations the primary management function is planning for results. Organizational planning is using the continuous process of assessing, establishing goals, and implementing and evaluating them to ensure that decisions about the use of people, resources, and environment help achieve agency goals for the present and the future (Figure 6-1).[1] See the box on p. 106, which explains reasons for planning.

SCOPE OF PLANNING

Scope is defined as the breadth or opportunity to function. In management *scope of planning* means how far the manager can go in developing plans for self and others. Understanding scope of planning becomes more critical at higher levels of an organization, for it is top management that sets overall policies and goals of the organization. The further down the or-

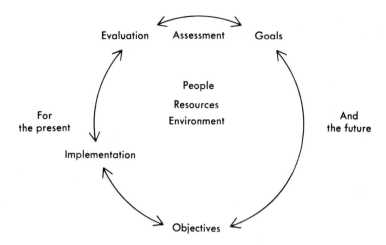

Figure 6-1. The continuous planning process applied to management.

ganizational hierarchy managers are, the smaller their scope of responsibility and the greater the likelihood that the scope of planning will gradually decrease to involve only particular subunit activities.

Nurses can be classified by their level in the health organization as top-, middle-, and lower- or first-level managers. The box on p. 107 illustrates the levels of management in nursing.

Top-Level Managers

Top-level managers comprise a comparatively small group of executives who make up the highest classification of managers. Top management's scope of responsibility is the overall management of the organization. Top managers establish operating policies and guide the organization's interactions with its environment. Top managers are typically titled president or director. Nurse executives managing at the top level are commonly named director of nursing services or associate administrator. The nursing director is responsible for all activities of the facility that require nursing services; therefore the scope of planning is broad and general in nature.

Middle-Level Managers

Middle-level managers can encompass many levels in an organization, depending on size and philosophy of the institution. Middle managers direct the activities of other managers. Super-

visor and coordinator are common titles for middle managers in nursing. Supervisors report to the director of nursing, and head nurses or department managers to supervisors. A nursing supervisor should be responsible for only the number of head nurses with whom she or he can maintain adequate contact. One of the principle responsibilities of middle managers is to direct the activities that will actually implement the broad operating policies of the organization. A nursing supervisor, for example, coordinates the overall staffing and delivery of services of those units controlled by the head nurses. The head nurses or department managers in turn manage staffing and delivery of services for their individual units. The case manager coordinates and oversees the work of nurses and other interdisciplinary personnel in and out of the health agency in the interest of a selected group of patients.

Lower- or First-Level Managers

Lower- or first-level managers constitute the lowest level in an organization at which individuals are responsible for the work of others. Examples of lower- or first-level managers in business and industry are the clerical supervisor in an office and the foreman in a manufacturing plant. Examples in nursing are the department manager, team leader, or primary nurse. The scope of activity for lower- or first-level nurses is responsibility for management of all care

Reasons for Planning

The necessity of planning has been emphasized by many people in many ways. Both conceptual and practical reasons have been given. Following is a compilation of reasons given by Douglas Gehrman, manager of the Exxon Company U.S.A.,[2] that aptly applies to nursing administration.

1. *Planning increases chances of success by focusing on results, not activities.* Most studies on planning have been done in the business sector and have shown that although planning does not guarantee success, planners consistently outperform nonplanners. Planning helps focus on objectives, and employees can see the result of their labor. Knowing the objectives of the enterprise helps employees relate what they are doing to meaningful outcomes. This principle can be applied to hospitals and other health care agencies. Although most are nonprofit systems, nonprofit does not mean they aren't concerned with making a profit. The delivery of care is a big industry with the problem of providing many intangible or difficult-to-measure services. These facilities could experience greatly improved results if they were to rely on effective planning procedures.

2. *Planning forces analytical thinking and evaluation of alternatives, thus improving decisions.* Through the reasoning process the manager seeks to minimize risk and maximize opportunity.

3. *Planning establishes a framework for decision making consistent with top management's objectives.* The overall planning process in any organization is a top-to-bottom proposition. Top managers set broader objectives with longer time horizons than do lower-level managers. In effect, this downward flow of objectives creates a mean-end chain.

4. *Planning orients people to action instead of reaction.* For any given period, the best use is made of available resources. Guesswork is eliminated, and the manager can successfully direct his or her activities with foresight, influence, and action.

5. *Planning includes day-to-day managing as well as future-focused managing.* The daily pressures of determining how specific tasks can best be accomplished on time with available resources are important and must be addressed, but the manager must look beyond the immediate focus to the future and plan how to pursue the organization's long-term goals.

6. *Planning helps avoid crisis management and provides decision-making flexibility.* When plans anticipate emergencies, they allow the worker to function more calmly and efficiently when an actual crisis occurs. For example, when staff can respond to a fire by proper reporting procedure, protection of environment, and use of emergency equipment, tragedy may be averted. When personnel know signs and symptoms of conditions for hypoxia or alkalosis versus acidosis, they may be able to prevent irreparable damage or even save a life.

7. *Planning provides a basis for measuring organizational and individual performance.* Managers can evaluate the environment, resources, and employees' effectiveness when the expected is known. The entire planning process leads to a continuous inspection of assessment, goal and objective setting, and implementation of plans.

8. *Planning increases employee involvement and improves communications.* Although time-consuming, employee involvement in how things are to be done and by whom creates a feeling of ownership and therefore a strong commitment to goal achievement.

9. *Planning helps one discover the need for change.* Planning can point out opportunities for new or different services. It guides management thinking to future desirable activities, indicates how best to make change, and directs attainment of goals. Change is occurring in all sectors, and certainly in the health field, which has become one of the biggest industries in the United States. As the industry grows, the amount of lead time for planning becomes longer.

10. *Planning is cost-effective.* Costs of health services are accelerating at a rapid rate. Although many fiscal matters are beyond the manager's control, particularly at the lower levels of management, some costs can be contained through planning for efficient operation. For example, projecting the number of nurses needed to care for a group of patients or ordering enough surgical supplies for one nursing unit to provide an even flow of work without excess are important in the total scheme of agency operation.

◻   Top-level managers
(director of nursing services)
↓
Middle-level managers (supervisors)
↓
Lower- or first-level managers
(head nurse, team leader, primary nurse)   ◻

___

given in the nursing unit or for administering direct nursing care to one or more patients/clients. The nurses combine personnel and resources to accomplish immediate goals. Many nurses prefer this level of performance to more prestigious ones, because they experience great satisfaction in seeing the immediate results of their efforts. Others enjoy the one-to-one relationship possible at this level, with greater opportunity to administer direct patient care. Figure 6-2 presents the scope of planning for nurses who function at the top, middle, and lower or first levels of nursing. The chart shows that each management person has responsibilities specific to each role, but that the responsibilities are interrelated and ongoing.

DECISION-MAKING PROCESS

Decision making is the process of developing a commitment to a particular course of action. Decision making pervades all of the basic man-agement functions: planning, organizing, directing, and controlling. Lee Iacocca has made the statement, "If I had to sum up in one word the qualities that make a good manager, I'd say that it all comes down to decisions."[3]

Variables Present in Decision Making

Although decision making has never been easy, it is especially challenging for today's nurse managers because of such major issues as nurse shortages and economic pressures. Today's decision makers face three difficult changes: (1) complexity, (2) uncertainty, and (3) the need to use different information-processing styles.[4]

The following situation will be used in discussing the variables present in decision making: The nurse manager is faced with the dilemma of whether or not to introduce overlapping shift patterns. She has decided that an overlap in staff at crucial times on all shifts would benefit the patients served, as well as improve the managerial process. Now she must sell the idea to nursing staff and administrators.

Complexity. For managers, complexity is a self-perpetuating cycle consisting of multiple criteria, intangibles, risk and uncertainty, long-term implications, interdisciplinary input, and value judgments. (See Figure 6-3.)

Multiple criteria. Typically, a decision must satisfy a number of criteria representing different interests. In the case of a change to overlap in

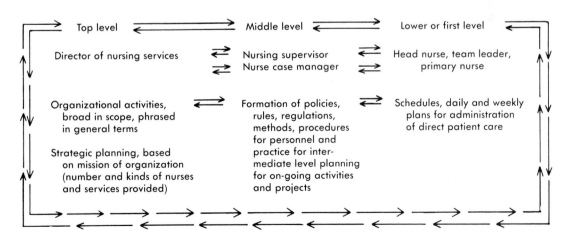

Figure 6-2. Scope of planning for nurse managers in a health care organization.

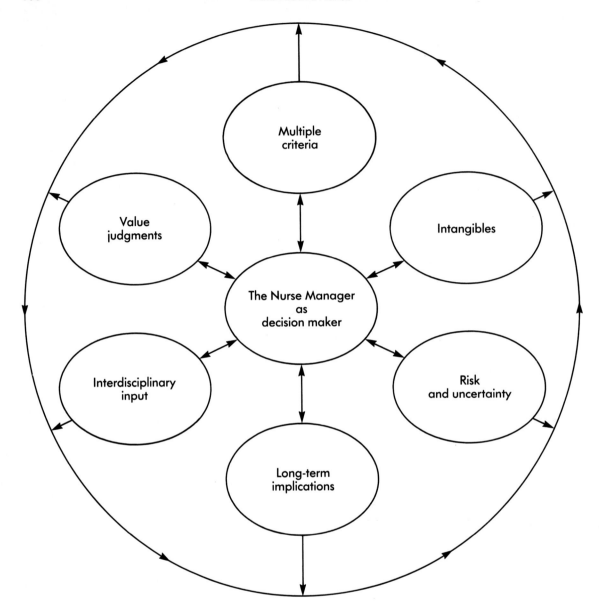

Figure 6-3. Sources of complexity for today's managerial decision makers. *Adapted from Kreitner R: Management, ed 4, Boston, 1989, Houghton Mifflin Company, pp 226-228.*

shifts, agreement must first come from nursing staff who would be involved in the change, nursing administrators who have the power to sanction change, and the financial officer who controls the purse strings. Hospital standards of patient care must be assured continuously. Balancing conflicting interests is a major challenge for the nurse manager.

Intangibles. Factors such as employee morale and bureaucracy, although difficult to measure, often determine decision alternatives. Some staff nurses, for example, may perceive that they have less opportunity for promotion if their skills and competencies are not evaluated by a single manager. Others may feel they are losing close touch with their peers by

A Strategy for Decision Making under Risk and Uncertainty

Situation: Addition of nursing shifts that overlap to cover high-intensity time periods.

Risk of situation

1. Nurses may resent having to come to work at odd hours and may refuse to cooperate.
2. Nurses may feel fragmented when they cannot finish all the tasks they began.
3. Nurses will have to rearrange their home and child-care schedules, which may not always work out to their satisfaction.
4. Nurses may feel they are losing close relationships by having their time split between two shifts at peak hours.
5. It may become difficult to share ownership of assignments.
6. Nurses may be in conflict with their peers because of differing opinions on how to manage patient care.
7. Quality of care may decrease.
8. The budget may not continue to provide for a sufficient number of nurses.

Value of situation

1. Nursing loads will lighten, resulting in fewer errors and improved patient care.
2. Nurses will be more satisfied with the overall outcomes of their jobs.
3. Some nurses may come to like the flexibility and learn to be creative in their time management.
4. Nurses will have the opportunity to expand the boundaries of their relationships and choose which ones to nurture.
5. Nurses will learn to collaborate and will get off duty on time.
6. Nurses will develop stronger interpersonal and interdependent skills and relationships.
7. The level of skills and knowledge will increase as nurses learn from one another.
8. Adjustments can be built into the system.

---

working with two sets of staff at only peak times.

Risk and uncertainty. Unfortunately, the outcome of a situation cannot always be known in advance. A nurse manager is functioning in a situation of risk if there is some possibility of loss, harm, or danger to either property or person, physically or psychologically. Reasonably accurate probabilities based on historical data and past experiences can often be calculated. The decision maker is advised to consider each situation, list the risks against the value or possible good outcome of the situation for self and others, then choose the alternative that has the least negative variables among its outcomes. The box offers a decision-making strategy for a situation in which risk and uncertainty are involved. The nurse manager studies the situation and considers the variables. In this case, the manager chooses to go along with the addition of overlap staffing, for she reasons that the risks are manageable. Pre-planning sessions with nursing staff and concerned administrative personnel can resolve most of the possible risks of shift change. Ongoing evaluation of the new staffing pattern, another risk-averting ap-

proach, will help identify problem areas so that they may be solved before becoming major issues. If the nurse manager had concluded that the risks outweighed the advantages, she would have either given up the idea or gone back to the drawing board.

Long-term implications. Managers are increasingly becoming aware that their decisions have not only an intended short-term impact but also an unintended long-term impact. Both immediate and future outcomes must be considered. Overlap coverage for all shifts alleviates the pressure on the nursing staff as a result of the high intensity of patient care during specific time periods. If patient census changes and less coverage is needed, nurses may resent having to rearrange their schedules, as they have already planned child care and family life around the former schedule and may experience difficulties with change.

Interdisciplinary input. Rarely is one manager totally responsible for an entire package of decisions. A single decision is usually a link in a chain that has passed from one person to another. For example, in her proposal for shift overlap, the nurse manager would meet with nursing staff and administrators, because what affects one nursing unit affects all. Nurse administrators would also meet with financial and personnel officers to work out details. These are all vital but time-consuming steps.

Value judgments. A value is a conception, clearly defined or implied, indicating what an individual or group considers desirable. Values play an important role in the decision-making process. People are not born with values but acquire them early in life. Parents, teachers, relatives, friends, and acquaintances influence an individual's values. As a result, every nurse manager and staff member brings a certain set of values to the workplace.

Uncertainty.[5] We are all aware of varying degrees of uncertainty in our daily personal lives. We attach high degrees of certainty and confidence to the prospect that the sun will rise tomorrow, that our family will love us, that our friends will be there for us when needed. But our confidence wanes when circumstances become more uncertain. Events such as the death of a loved one or a friend's moving away fill us with uncertainty. Unfortunately, life is filled with uncertainties, including those of the workplace, and nurse managers are expected to make the best decisions they can in spite of uncertain circumstances.

Managers who are able to assess the degree of certainty in a situation are able to make more effective decisions. A condition of certainty exists when there is no doubt about the facts of a situation and its outcome. For example, given facts, there is certainty that the hospital will be open round-the-clock for years to come, requiring nursing staff. There is some uncertainty regarding the actions of the nursing staff. Although there is always attrition to be expected, more nurses than usual may resign from the hospital if they are displeased with the staffing pattern.

Decision-Making Styles

Newell and Simon studied information-processing theory, reaching the conclusion that effective problem solving depends on the ability of the problem solvers to adapt to the human limitations of short-term memory when they are processing information.[5] Nurses are re-

The Manager's Decision-Making Process

Intelligence

Searching the environment for conditions requiring a decision

Design

Inventing, developing, analyzing possible courses of action

Choice

Actual selection of a particular course of action

Adapted from Simon H: The new science of management decisions, New York, 1960, Harper & Row, p 12.

quired to process a vast quantity of information. Experienced nurses learn to cluster or group pieces of information to simplify complex situations. This skill requires time and practice. Benner identified five levels of nursing proficiency: (1) novice, (2) advanced beginner, (3) competent, (4) proficient, and (5) expert.[7] She describes an expert as one who has an immediate, intuitive grasp of a whole situation, focuses directly on the problem, and takes immediate action. Only after a decision has been made is it likely that an expert will separate all the components of the whole and analyze them separately. Since the nursing staff ranges from novices to experts it is necessary for the nurse manager to be able to make effective decisions consistently so that she may serve as a role model and teacher.

The scientific approach to decision making. Herbert Simon, Nobel prize winner[7] has described the manager's decision process in three stages: (1) intelligence, (2) design, and (3) choice, which is called the scientific approach to management. As the box demonstrates, *the intelligence stage* involves searching the environment for conditions requiring a decision (for example, one nurse has failed to report for work, a patient requires crash-cart services—leaving the attending nurses' patients uncovered—and a nurse-doctor conflict is in progress). *The design stage* entails inventing, devel-

The Scientific Approach to Decision Making, Applied

Problem (Intelligence Stage)	Design Stage
1. One nurse has failed to report for work.	a. Increase the work load of the existing staff. b. Ask supervisor for staff coverage. c. Ask a nurse to return from another unit. d. Seek help from the registry.
2. A patient requires crash-cart services; this causes the nurse's other patients to be left unattended.	a. Take the nurse's place while she is otherwise occupied. b. Ask other nursing staff on the unit to cover the patients during the emergency. c. Ask for coverage from another unit.
3. A nurse-doctor conflict is in progress in the nursing unit.	a. Order the two to stop the conflict immediately. b. Report them to your immediate superior. c. Ask them to step into your office and stay with them until they do.

The final step in Simon's decision-making process is *choice,* referring to the actual selection of a particular course of action.

Problem	Choice
1. One nurse has failed to report for work.	Call a nurse from the registry to avoid overtaxing the remaining staff on duty, and to avoid interfering with a nurse's regularly scheduled day off, as this may perpetuate the problem.
2. A patient requires crash-cart services; this causes the nurse's other patients to be left unattended.	Request other nurses on duty to cover for the nurse immediately. If the situation becomes prolonged, seek help from another unit. The manager needs to be free to circulate.
3. There is a nurse-doctor conflict in progress in the nursing unit.	Ask the two to step into your office, guiding the way, thus avoiding a public scene and allowing for resolution in private.

oping, and analyzing possible courses of action, and *the choice stage* entails selecting a specific course of action. The box provides an example of how the scientific approach to decision making is applied to the examples given.

Analyzing the decision process by stages emphasizes the difference between management and nonmanagement decisions. Nonmanagement decisions are concentrated on the choice stage only. For example, the nurse's aide has to make a choice only as to which patient, from the assigned six, she will care for first and what supplies, from already ordered stock, are needed. Management decisions place greater

emphasis on the intelligence and design stages (making the overall assignments and ordering all supplies). Managers who rely predominantly on the scientific approach tend to be logical, precise, and objective.

The intuitive approach to decision making. Intuition involves scanning a situation, anticipating changes, and taking risks without benefit of rational processes. Intuition is a capacity for guessing accurately, with sharp insight. Managers who depend solely on intuition for decision making, however, are treading on dangerous ground. Unless their decisions are guided by scientific knowledge, factual information, observation, and practical experience, they are apt to be rife with error. When managers make decisions solely on hunches and intuition, they are practicing management as if it were an art based on feelings.

The emotional approach to decision making. Unfortunately, some nurse managers become so emotionally attached to certain positions that almost nothing will change their minds. Consider the nurse manager who has selected June, a personal friend, to take charge in her absence. Despite June's numerous mistakes and many complaints by nursing staff regarding June's poor performance as an administrator of services, the nurse manager continues to believe that adverse conditions and lack of staff support are the causes of June's problems.

Under such circumstances, managers develop an attitude that says, "Don't bother me with the facts, my mind is made up." Such emotional attachments can have serious consequences for an organization. One solution is for the nurse manager to become aware of her bias. This can be accomplished through a group meeting with presentation of facts. This method can be successful, however, only if the manager is willing to listen with an open mind and to make necessary changes. A second suggestion is that the nurse manager seek out independent opinions. The manager might ask her nursing supervisor to assess June's performance on several consecutive days. Seeking the opinion of a qualified person who has no vested interest in the situation is good practice.

A most important factor to recognize is that managers approach decision making and problem solving in very different ways, depending on their information and processing styles. Nurse managers must learn how to acquire systematically as much valid information about a given situation as possible, as well as skill in coupling this knowledge with intuitive talents to make the best decisions. When both logical, "thinking" skills and intuitive, creative skills are appreciated as valid alternative styles, they can be cultivated to complement each other.

The pragmatic approach to decision making. According to Toffler, "the very speed of change introduces a new element into management,

forcing executives, already nervous in an unfamiliar environment, to make more and more decisions at a faster and faster pace. Response times are honed to a minimum."[8] The health care industry is no exception. With accelerating change and the impetus to get patients in and out of the system as quickly as possible, nurses are forced to make decisions for highly acute, complex patients when time is of the essence. Figure 6-4 outlines a system for decision making that can be used in all circumstances: (1) identify the problem, (2) generate alternative solutions, (3) select a solution, (4) implement the solution, and (5) evaluate the results of the solution. The following situation will be used to illustrate the pragmatic approach to problem solving.

> Helen, nurse manager of a medical unit has two patients with a diagnosis of AIDS (acquired immunodeficiency syndrome). One is confined to bed with a catheter and IV therapy; the other is ambulatory, drinking from the common water fountain and receiving meals in the usual manner from the kitchen. Three members of the nursing staff refuse to care for these patients, as they do not want to "catch" the disease. The remaining 24 nurses on the three shifts accept the assignment, but with expressions of fear. For the most part, the AIDS patients are shunned.

1. Identify the problem. As strange as it may seem, the most common problem solving difficulty lies in the identification of the problem. Busy managers have a tendency to rush into generating and selecting alternative solutions before they have actually isolated and understood the problem. According to Drucker, a respected management scholar, "the most common source of mistakes in management decisions, is emphasis on finding the right answers rather than the right questions."[9]

Referring to Figure 6-4, the first question to ask is, What is the actual situation? (Patients are shunned, nurses are unhappy, and three nurses refuse to take assignment.) As for a desired situation, Helen wants the AIDS patients to receive quality care, which includes acceptance and nurturance. In addition, she desires all nurses to participate in the care of these patients and to feel safe in the process. The next question to address is, What caused the situation, or what or who is responsible for the situation? In this case, the nurse manager convenes the nurses,

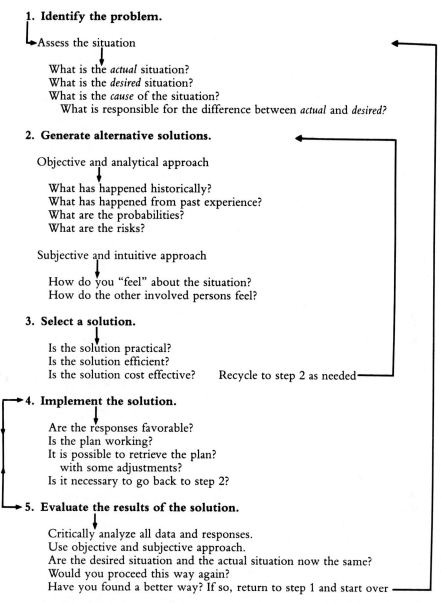

1. Identify the problem.

Assess the situation

What is the *actual* situation?
What is the *desired* situation?
What is the *cause* of the situation?
What is responsible for the difference between *actual* and *desired*?

2. Generate alternative solutions.

Objective and analytical approach

What has happened historically?
What has happened from past experience?
What are the probabilities?
What are the risks?

Subjective and intuitive approach

How do you "feel" about the situation?
How do the other involved persons feel?

3. Select a solution.

Is the solution practical?
Is the solution efficient?
Is the solution cost effective?   Recycle to step 2 as needed

4. Implement the solution.

Are the responses favorable?
Is the plan working?
It is possible to retrieve the plan?
    with some adjustments?
Is it necessary to go back to step 2?

5. Evaluate the results of the solution.

Critically analyze all data and responses.
Use objective and subjective approach.
Are the desired situation and the actual situation now the same?
Would you proceed this way again?
Have you found a better way? If so, return to step 1 and start over

Figure 6-4. An assessment and decision making process. *Adapted from Kreitner R: Management, ed 4, Boston, 1989, Houghton Mifflin Company, p 249.*

seeking some answers. She learns that most nurses know something about AIDS but not enough to overcome their reluctance and fear. One nurse says, "I don't care what scientists say about how AIDS is spread, I'm not taking any chances." Most of the group express concern for the AIDS patients and regret that they be-lieve it necessary to separate themselves from them. As an outcome of this meeting, the nurse manager might identify the problem as fear, poor patient care, noncooperative nurses, or closed minds; but these are symptoms of the problem, not the cause. Instead, she determines the cause to be *lack of sufficient knowledge and understanding about AIDS by staff members,* believing that once educated, the staff nurses will cooperate in providing quality care to all patients.

2. Generate alternative solutions. The nurse manager knows from a historical perspective that this situation typifies a common problem: AIDS patients have suffered widespread repulsion and rejection. Helen knows the problem is growing. It is estimated that by 1991, 145,000 Americans will be ill with AIDS and 54,000 AIDS victims will die.[10] She knows the virus is primarily spread through sexual contact, by infected blood products and by mothers infecting their unborn children. The risk involved for the nurse is in coming in contact with infected blood products, which is preventable through the use of gloves. The fear of acquiring AIDS by sharing drinking fountains, kitchen facilities, tools, and rest rooms is unfounded. Helen feels she knows the nursing staff well enough to believe that once they are informed and understand the facts of the disease, their fear will abate and they will give the desired care.

Helen engages in a brainstorming session with the hospital nurse education department to generate educational options available to the staff. The possibilities include: (1) providing inservice education, (2) offering symposia or workshops, (3) arranging for staff to meet with nurses who routinely care for AIDS patients, (4) assigning reading to staff members and making related articles and references available to staff, (5) bringing in a therapist for group sessions to discuss the staffs' fears, (6) conducting group sessions, and (7) firing the nurses who refuse to accept the assignment of working with AIDS patients.

3. Select a solution. Helen has identified the problem as lack of education and understanding about AIDS. She considers the options available to her and, through the process of elimination, decides to (1) ask the nursing education department to provide inservices on AIDS to the staff and provide articles on AIDS for the unit, (2) send the three hesitant nurses from the unit to an AIDS symposium, (3) arrange for a hospital therapist to meet with the nursing staff to allow the staff to express their feelings about the disease and caring for AIDS patients, and (4) ask nurses from other units in the hospital

who routinely care for AIDS patients to share their feelings and experiences with the staff. The solution is practical in that a hospital educational department is in place, a therapist is employed by the agency, there is provision for paid attendance at educational conferences, and there are nurses in the agency who routinely care for AIDS patients. As for efficiency and cost-effectiveness, there will be a need for nursing coverage while the staff is attending educational group therapy sessions, pay for staff members while they are away, and provision for seminar expenses. These costs are a necessary part of orienting staff members to new experiences and must be absorbed into the budget. If the nurse manager did not have access to a nurse educator, she could seek help from the local health department, the American Red Cross, or AIDS service providers.

4. Implement the solution. Helen brings the staff together and shares the plan for increased education and understanding. She asks for their cooperation throughout the training program, stating that upon completion of the sessions, no staff members will be forced to care for AIDS patients if they still hold to their views, but that failure to comply will mean a transfer to another unit or resignation. She arranges for classes, reading material, symposia, and therapy sessions to occur over a period of 2 months, covering all shifts. During the 2-month period, the nurse manager is attuned to staff response. In the first month of the educational process, the three nurses who refused to care for AIDS patients still refuse. There is, however, greater acceptance of the patients by most of the staff; they are spending more time with them and attending to their emotional needs. Near the end of the second month, two of the three resistive nurses accept assignments to AIDS patients. Helen believes that, on the whole, the plan is working. As to the nurse who refuses to take the assignment, Helen arranges for her to transfer to another department, knowing that allowing a staff member special privilege creates hostility and resentment among peers.

5. Evaluate the results of the solution. It is necessary to analyze the results of the decided-upon solution. In this case the following questions should be asked: Are AIDS patients receiving quality care? Are all staff nurses participating in giving care to AIDS patients? Do these nurses feel "safe" providing this care? In analyzing critically all the data and staff responses, the nurse manager concludes that progress has been good, but that the desired goal has not yet been reached. Helen concludes that the educational plan has been successful, but sees a need to continue group therapy sessions twice a month for support and increased understanding among the nurses. In retrospect, a far better approach would have been to develop a strategy for educating nurses before AIDS patients were admitted to the unit. As the arrows in Figure 6-4 indicate, the problem solver is advised to return to any step in the decision-making process when the plan is not working well.

Group Decision Making

Decision making, like any other organizational activity, does not take place in a vacuum. Groups can aid in the decision-making process through committees, study groups, review panels, or task teams. The following aspects of the decision process can be assigned to groups:
1. Analyzing the problem
2. Identifying facts and subjective data that contribute to the problem
3. Determining probabilities, feasibilities, time and cost estimates
4. Selecting possible solutions
5. Weighing risk factors of each possible solution against values
6. Choosing a solution to the problem
7. Establishing an evaluative system to test the solution

Group development. We have all experienced the uneasiness associated with the first meeting of a new group, be it a club, a sorority or fraternity pledge class, or a committee. Initially, there is little mutual understanding, trust, or commitment between the new group members, because of uncertainty over objectives, roles, and leadership. A working knowledge of the characteristics of a mature group can help the manager systematically manage group development. If and when a group takes on the following characteristics, it can be called a mature group:[4]
1. Members become aware of their own and one another's strengths and weaknesses.

2. Individual differences are accepted without being labeled good or bad.
3. The group develops authority and interpersonal relationships that are recognized and accepted by the members.
4. Group decisions are made through rational discussion.
5. Conflict is generated by only important issues, such as group goals and the effectiveness and efficiency of various means for achieving those goals. Conflict produced by emotional issues is at a minimum.
6. Members are aware of the group's process and their own roles within the process.

Advantages of group decision making. Group decision making has further benefits. Group participation increases members' acceptance of decisions and decreases the problems inherent in persuading the group to accept decisions. This is especially true when a change is being implemented within an organization. A case in point is the situation that occurs when a group of nurses want to join a union. Such a serious step requires input from the agency's entire nurse population. The best way to manage this matter is to disseminate information, hold a general meeting, then meet in small groups whose compositions represent their constituency's wishes.

Disadvantages of group decision making. The negative aspects of group decision making may be that (1) one individual may dominate or control the group, (2) social pressures to conform can inhibit members, (3) competition can develop to such an extent that winning becomes more important than the issue itself, and (4) groups may accept the first potentially positive solution, while giving little attention to other possible solutions.

Power of group decision makers. True group decision making can occur only when the agency agrees to relinquish authority to the group. When decisions are made by groups for organizations, they are usually presented in the form of recommendations. Managers must maintain ultimate accountability for a decision when:
1. The decision has a significant impact on the success or failure of the unit or organization

(such as whether or not to purchase a desk computer for each nurse, as budget allocation is out of the group's control)
2. The decision has legal ramifications (such as a nurse's refusing to care for AIDS patients)
3. A competitive reward is tied to a successful decision (for example, if only one nurse is eligible to receive a promotion)

In less critical areas, the group itself may be responsible for actually making decisions (such as designing and developing standardized nursing care plans, or deciding the best procedure to follow in a unit emergency).

MANAGEMENT BY OBJECTIVES
Goals and Objectives

By definition the initial step in planning is to determine goals and objectives. Goals are statements of intent derived from purposes of the organization. They are usually stated broadly and in general terms. Objectives are specific aims, purposes, or targets set for accomplishment. There should be a harmonious blending of objectives in every enterprise. For example, top-level managers (president, director of nursing services), with the aid of the planning staff, establish major or overall goals for the entire organization. They decide what resources the organization will need to make its goals feasible (people, facilities, and equipment) and how these resources will be allocated among the various divisions or departments. Within the framework of the overall plan, middle-level managers (supervisors, case managers) formulate goals and objectives for their divisions or departments. They decide how the resources of the areas under their control will be used to help the organization achieve its overall goals.

The lower or first-level managers (head nurse, team leader, or primary care nurse) develop individual and group objectives to carry out the purposes of individual and group goals.

Process of Management by Objectives

The management process begins with goals and objectives and ends with an assessment of how well they were accomplished. Peter Drucker, a noted authority on management, introduced the phrase "management by objectives" (MBO) in 1954 to emphasize the importance of accomplishment in keeping with objectives.[9] Since that time MBO has received a great deal of discussion, application, and evaluation. Management by objectives is not a panacea for all management problems, but the system works well in managing nursing activities. Most nurses are familiar with objectives, having used them during their educational process and professional practice. This book is an example of the MBO design. Objectives are given, corresponding content is presented, and evaluation is offered. In this cyclical process the learner can move backward or forward at any point during achievement of the goals.

The MBO concept is simply that every person or group in a work setting has specific, attainable, and measureable objectives that are in harmony with those of the organization.[9] Further, MBO involves managers and workers meeting to establish specific objectives, developing alternative means of reaching them, and periodically reviewing progress toward those objectives. It is based on McGregor's set of assumptions of the Theory Y personality, that under the proper conditions people will find satisfaction in work and will accept responsibility for their results (see Chapters 2 and 7).

From director of nursing services to case manager, team leader, or primary nurse, nurse managers need to take the lead in using and guiding MBO, as it is the managers themselves who, more than anyone else, influence the organizational climate, employee morale, and motivation.

Guidelines for Management by Objectives

MBO programs can vary enormously. Some are designed for the organization as a whole and are broad in nature (e.g., to provide quality care, to maintain currency in the health field, and to engage in research). Others are designed for use in a small subunit of an organization and are more specific (e.g., to implement primary nursing in the intensive care unit on the fourth floor in 6 weeks and to develop a plan whereby each patient on the medical department of the sixth floor can participate in the management of his or her care in 3 months). Whether broad or narrow in scope, there are common elements in MBO systems that contribute to their success. Objectives should:
1. Be in harmony with those goals of the total

organization and committed to the MBO approach at all levels of the organization

2. Take into account the technical and human side of planning
3. Be formulated by those who will have a part in their implementation. (Vested interest and understanding of their importance lead to increased effort and goal achievement.)
4. Answer the questions, What is to be done? Who is responsible? How much is to be accomplished? When and where is the task to be accomplished? What is the cost in time, money, energy, resources, emotions?
5. Be measurable, stated in observable or behavioral terms, and allow for a realistic evaluation of outcomes
6. Establish a means of accountability, provided through clearly defined responsibilities fixed before goals are established. (Stating objectives in behavioral terms requires performance criteria, sometimes called *job descriptions*. These lists of expected activities

must relate directly to the stated objectives, otherwise it will be difficult to see the relationship between them and evaluate performance.)

7. Have regular, periodic meetings (oral and written) between manager and other participants to review progress toward the previously set objectives
8. Be flexible enough to allow for changes or elimination of objectives when no longer useful. (Once the objectives have been set and agreed on within normal constraints of organizational policies, managers should have the freedom to develop and implement programs to achieve their goals.)

Management by Objectives in Nursing Management

Examples of goals and behavioral objectives formulated by top-, middle-, and lower- or first-level managers are given in Table 6. Their effectiveness in the planning process are dis-

 Table 6. Goals and objectives of top-, middle-, and lower- or first-level managers

OBJECTIVES	IMPLICATIONS
Top level	
1. To provide quality nursing care to all patients or clients in each setting by professional nurses and ancillary personnel 2. To manage patient/client services efficiently and effectively	1. These overall goals are stated in broad terms and tell the nurse manager the agency is intent on meeting standards beyond minimal or legal requirements. The nurse manager needs to define "quality nursing" (ANA standards, agency determined standards, or combination of both). 2. The manager knows there is to be no discriminatory or preferential treatment of patients/clients and that everywhere nursing is practiced, planning is to occur. 3. The nurse manager needs to understand management skills. If such understanding is lacking, the nurse will seek help (on-the-job, inservice, advanced education). 4. Performance criteria must be available for all nursing personnel (job descriptions, procedure manual, and so on). 5. Top-level management (director of nursing services or designated representative) will appoint a middle-level manager (supervisor) to chair a standards committee and another to monitor management process (in small organizations, may be the same person).

Continued.

Table 6. Goals and objectives of top-, middle-, and lower- or first-level managers

OBJECTIVES	IMPLICATIONS
Middle level	

1. To establish a standards committee composed of one member from the professional nurses group and one from ancillary personnel from each subunit (floors, stations, ICU, and so on) whose purpose is to:
  a. Reach a common understanding of what is meant by "quality nursing"
  b. Compare present standards with agreed-upon definition of quality care
  c. Make necessary additions, changes, or deletions
2. To devise a plan whereby all nursing personnel have opportunity to exchange ideas and provide input into the work of the committee and to receive feedback concerning progress
3. To determine if nursing personnel have opportunity to exchange ideas and provide input into the work of the committee and to receive feedback concerning progress
4. To determine if nursing personnel have the necessary competencies to administer quality nursing care as defined by the committee
5. To complete the initial project in 6 months; then establish an ongoing review committee
	1. Actions become more specific. The chairman of the standards committee will contact other middle-level managers (supervisors) for selection of members to serve on the committee. Before the meeting, available data will be gathered and duplicated so that each person can have a copy (present standards, job descriptions, and so on). Other resources or persons will be used as needed.
	2. Times for meeting will be set well in advance to allow lower or first-level managers to plan schedules. Meetings will start and stop on time.
	3. Objectives will be formulated and acted on. For example, a part of the usual definition for quality care is that written nursing care plans are prepared for each patient/client. This specific activity would be one of the first for consideration.
	4. The nurse manager will develop a plan for involvement of all members whom she represents (input and feedback).
	5. A plan for assessing nursing competencies against accepted criteria for evaluation will be developed.
	6. The chairman of the committee(s) will maintain a two-way flow of information between the standards committee and top-level management (director of nursing services or representative).

Lower or first level	
1. To appoint representatives from the small work group to the standards committee 2. To meet the standards committee at regularly scheduled times 3. To set up weekly meetings for one-half hour with members of the small work group to keep them informed and to hear their views 4. To make sure that members' opinions are fairly represented at committee meetings 5. To assess each member's understanding of "quality care" as defined by the committee 6. To determine each member's ability to provide "quality care" 7. To devise a plan for helping each member to acquire necessary knowledge and skills needed to give care expected	1. At this level the nurse manager works with details that put overall goals and plans into effect. 2. Team leaders and other members appointed to the standards committee will arrange with their immediate supervisor (head nurse or substitute) for times to meet with all nursing staff to discuss content and to receive their input (head nurse will attend). 3. Notes will be taken and referred to at each meeting of the committee. 4. Agreed-on evaluation tools will be used to gain the needed information. The lower or first-level manager will cooperate in implementing the methods decided on (participate in evaluation procedure, arrange time and place for assessment between nurse and patient/client, or use of other facilities).

cussed. Other examples of behavioral objectives for team leader activities are given in more detail in Chapter 4.

Achieving these goals requires commitment of time and energy on the part of all concerned. Each member of the nursing staff must become involved in the overall planning for the outcome to be a success. Note that the objectives presented begin with broad, overall goals that can lead to MBO. Each set of the objectives given in the example will be broken down further to allow for guidelines every step of the way. Thus objectives become the basis for management of all nursing activity. Methods for implementation of objectives flow easily out of the plan, resulting in improved performance and higher morale. The nurse manager works toward a successful blending of goals and objectives of the organization in patient care management, operations of physical environment, and human resources management.

IMPLEMENTATION OF THE PLAN
Developing Alternative Courses of Action

Objectives should include a plan of action for accomplishing needs or desired results. Planning involves developing various choices or alternative courses of action and choosing the most satisfactory alternative. Assume, for example, that a part of the nursing team's plan is to increase its knowledge of quality nursing care. The objective may be for every team member to satisfactorily pass a test in cardiopulmonary resuscitation every 6 months. Alternative plans for consideration might be that (1) each team member assumes responsibility for content and testing at a local Red Cross center, (2) education and testing be provided through inservice education at a centralized level in the employing agency, or (3) each team member be taught and tested on the job by arrangement with the head nurse or similar person. After the alternatives have been drawn up, they are evaluated with a view to costs and benefits to agency and personnel and to the probability of 100% success. Total compliance is necessary in this situation because the objective is of prime importance, as lack of such knowledge in a single team member becomes life threatening to the patients/clients.

Nursing Care Planning

An excellent way to plan for nursing care is through written care plans. The nursing care plan is a record of nursing needs for a particular patient. Also included are expected outcomes and nursing interventions necessary to help the patient reach desired goals. Nursing care plans provide for continuity, communication, coordination, individualization, and documentation of nursing care.[11] Even though optimal nursing care cannot be ensured through the use of patient care plans, it can never be achieved without such a plan.[12]

Individualized nursing care plans are based on the premise that each person is unique in some way; therefore it is necessary to develop a plan for each individual that addresses his or her specific needs. Preparation of an individual care plan for each patient/client is difficult. Time constraints, lack of impetus, and varying abilities of nursing personnel to formulate plans often prevent them from using nursing care plans. The nurse manager can lead the way in teaching how to prepare and use the plans. A list of common diagnoses or nursing problems most common to the agency can be compiled and standard care plans developed for each. Examples might be coronary insufficiency, cardiovascular accident, anemia, anxiety, and pneumonia. The prepared standard care plans could be duplicated and made available to the nurses on their respective units. When a patient is admitted, the nurse can take the nursing history and pull the standard care plan that most closely relates to the patient, activate with the date, circle or check those problems that pertain to the patient, and add any other unique patient needs. An example of one form of standard care plan is given in the box on p. 120. Note that only those problems present at the time of admission are activated. Others may be dated and checked if they occur. Other forms of standard care plans may be used. Standard nursing care plans can be accessed manually or by computer.

Nurses on all shifts use the nursing care plan as a basis for practice. Those who are unfamiliar with the patient will find there is far more continuity and comprehensiveness of care with a written plan. Care planning may include all significant persons: the patient, family, physician,

Patient Care Plan

diagnosis: colitis

Discharge criteria: 1. Verbalizes understanding of and willingness to follow M.D.'s outpatient regimen. 2. Verbalizes understanding of and willingness to follow diet at home and make correct selection from a food list. 3. Demonstrates understanding of medication regimen. 4. Relates realistic plans for coping with stressful situations after discharge (job, family, recreation, etc.).

DATE	PROBLEM	EXPECTED OUTCOMES	NURSING INTERVENTIONS
	① Diarrhea and abd. cramps due to colitis.	① Decrease in no. of stools to 1-2 daily; stools of normal consistency.	① Document color, consistency, and time of all stools. Notify M.D. of gross change in stools.
	② Weight loss due to anorexia, nausea, and/or vomiting.	② Maintain admission weight. Take meals without n. or v.; verbalize understanding of diet.	② Weigh daily at _____ a.m. ✔Contact dietitian for a patient conference. ✔Reinforce teaching. ✔Give antiemetics as needed. ✔Check one hour before each meal, and p.r.n.
	③ Dehydration due to electrolyte imbalance.	③ Intake at least 2000 cc per day. Moist mucous membranes; good skin turgor.	③ Record I&O q 8 hr. Force fluids to 2000 cc. 1800 cc day and p.m. shifts; 200 cc noc.
	④ Possible perianal discomfort, skin breakdown, or rectal bleeding due to diarrhea	④ Healthy skin around anus. No rectal bleeding	4 If needed, get order for Sitz bath; medication for excoriation. ✔Instruct in cleansing procedure after each b.m.
	5 Weakness due to gastrointestinal malabsorption.	5 Ambulate without assistance. Does own activities of daily living.	5 Establish plan for daily care with patient. Encourage self-help as much as possible. Allow for frequent rest periods. Increase ambulation gradually. Record plan and indicate progress on each shift.
	6 Frustration and anxiety due to diarrhea and interruption of life-style.	⑥ Tolerance for situation. Verbalize realistic plans for coping.	⑥ Spend at least 15 min/day with pt. Listen, guide, and support in therapeutic plans.
	7 Potential development of complications: hemorrhage and/or perforation.	7 Stable vital signs. Normal temperature. No severe pain or sudden increase in pain.	7 Check at least every _____ hours for ↑ temperature, pulse and respirations. Listen for hyperactive bowel sounds, check for blood in stool and excessive pain.

Adapted from a Standard Care Plan used at The Good Samaritan Hospital of Santa Clara Valley, San Jose, California.

dietitian, physical therapist, clergyman, and so on. The plan is kept up to date and used as a basis for documentation and for transfer or discharge summary and planning. Nursing care plans provide evidence that standards of care have been maintained and that nurses have assumed responsibility and accountability for professional nursing practice.

EVALUATION OR CONTROLLING THE PLAN

Planning has been described as a process that requires cognitive skills (thinking and decision making). The process does not end with a plan, however, for there is a direct link between plans and evaluating or controlling outcomes. To have practical effects, plans must be implemented and monitored. Evaluation or control is the ongoing process of making sure that performance meets specific goals and objectives. Planning and evaluating are closely interrelated. No evaluation or control can take place unless a plan exists, and the success of the plan is uncertain at best unless some effort is made to monitor its progress.[13]

Results of Evaluation or Control Process

Not only does planning lead to evaluation or controlling, but the reverse is often true. A nurse manager who is evaluating an activity often sees the need to alter the original plan to meet changing or unforeseen conditions.

Again, if there is employee participation in the evaluation process, members will be more likely to control their own activities to make sure the objectives are met. For example, if all team members agree to satisfactorily pass a cardiopulmonary resuscitation class every 6 months, they might voluntarily spend extra time and effort to complete the task well and on time. Evaluation or control of activities is discussed in greater detail in Chapter 10.

SUMMARY

1. Planning is an intellectual, continuous process of assessing, establishing goals and objectives, and implementing and evaluating them to determine if changes are needed.
2. The organizational planning process is applied to people, resources, and environment for the present and future.
3. The manager can enter and exit the planning process at any point in the process, according to need.
4. Managers who understand why resistance to the planning process occurs in themselves or others can more realistically anticipate and/or cope with the problems.
5. Some reasons that managers may not want to engage in the planning process are lack of knowledge of the organization and of the value of planning, time and work factors, desire to deal with immediate instead of future situations, fear of failure, and resistance to change.
6. Reasons for planning include success in achieving goals and objectives; giving meaning to work; effective use of personnel, resources, and environment; cost control; preparation for crises; readiness for change; and continuous evaluation of the management process.
7. Scope of planning is defined as how far one can go in developing plans for self and others.
8. The widest scope of responsibility for planning lies with top managers, who have responsibility for the overall policies and goals of the organization. Responsibility decreases in proportion to the size of the territory and the tasks assigned, as with middle and lower or first levels of management.
9. Top managers are the highest managers, typically called presidents or directors. A nursing manager at this level is commonly called director or administrator of nursing services. Planning is broad and general.
10. An example of a middle manager is the nursing supervisor who is responsible for several other nurse managers, usually head nurses. Nursing supervisors are concerned with formation of policies, procedures, and objectives that will realize organizational purposes. Case managers are categorized as middle managers.
11. Lower or first-level managers are at the lowest level of the managerial structure. They put overall organizational goals and supervisors' plans into effect at the front line. Team leaders and primary nurses are examples of lower or first-level managers.

12. All management participates in the planning process, which is interwoven and circular, allowing any member in the organization to communicate with another, depending on purpose and need.

13. Decision making is the process of developing a commitment to a course of action and pervades all basic management functions.

14. Variables present in decision making are complexity, uncertainty, and the need to use different information-processing styles.

15. Complexity in management is a self-perpetuating cycle consisting of multiple criteria, intangibles, risk and uncertainty, long-term implications, interdisciplinary input, and value judgments.

16. Nurse managers who are able to assess the degree of uncertainty in a situation are better able to make effective decisions than are those who cannot.

17. Experienced nurses learn to cluster pieces of information for processing complex situations.

18. The scientific approach to decision making includes using one's intelligence, considering the design and possible courses of action, and making an educated choice.

19. Intuitive decision making relies on personal perceptions, hunches, biases, and personal values.

20. Nurse managers need to learn how to combine the scientific approach with intuition, because the two methods can complement each other.

21. The pragmatic approach to decision making can be used in all circumstances: (1) identify the problem, (2) generate alternative solutions, (3) select a solution, (4) implement the solution, and (4) evaluate the results of the solution. One may return to any step at any given time.

22. Groups can aid in the decision-making process through committees, study groups, review panels, or task teams.

23. Given a mix of people who are knowledgeable and interested, group performance is frequently better than that of a single member.

24. Group participation increases acceptance of decisions made by the participants.

25. Negative aspects of group decision making may be (1) dominance by one individual over the group, (2) social pressure to conform, and (3) competition.

26. True group decision making can occur when the agency agrees to relinquish authority to the group.

27. Goals are statements of intent derived from purposes of the organization; objectives are specific aims, purposes, or targets set for accomplishment.

28. Objectives stem from goals and are specific aims or purposes.

29. In management by objectives (MBO), every person or group in a work setting has specific, attainable, and measurable objectives that are in harmony with those of the organization.

30. Objectives should include a plan of action to facilitate the accomplishment of needs or desired results.

31. Alternatives or choices are judged by costs and benefits to the agency and personnel and the probability of success.

32. MBO is easily adaptable to each phase of nursing practice.

33. Objectives should answer the questions who, what, where, when, and why and be flexible enough to allow for changes or elimination when they are no longer useful.

34. MBO requires commitment by the agency and all personnel.

35. Plans must be implemented and monitored to have practical results.

36. Nursing care is best carried out through the use of a written care plan, which is a record of nursing assessment (nursing problems), expected outcomes, and nursing interventions.

37. Nursing care plans provide for continuity, communication, coordination, individualization, and documentation for round-the-clock care.

38. Use of standard care plans helps to ensure care planning and provides for a quick review of the usual problems encountered with a particular diagnosis.

39. Evaluation or control is the ongoing process of making sure that performance meets specific goals and objectives.

40. Planning leads to evaluation, and evaluation leads to altering the original plan as needed to meet changing or unforeseen conditions.

Questions for Study and Discussion

1. Why is planning a primary management function, and why is it particularly important for nurse managers today?
2. Write three behavioral objectives for things you intend to accomplish in the next 6 months.
3. Do you think your personal value system would affect the way you would perform as a department manager? Explain.
4. Explain the differences between first-level, middle-level, and top-level managers.
5. Assume you are the supervisor in a home health care agency. You have 6 RNs and 12 home health aides under your jurisdiction. You believe all staff have maximum assignments. The director of the home health care agency announces that, as a result of government cutbacks, each nurse and aide will have to add two clients per day to their caseloads. Identify the problem; then use the complexity chart given on Figure 6-3 to itemize your reactions to each of the sources of complexity.
6. As a new staff nurse, you have a problem. Upon employment, you were promised verbally by a personnel administrator that you could continue advanced studies in nursing at the local university. You are entering your third month of employment and already have had to miss five classes because of a conflict of schedules. Your department man-

ager says that she made no promises—her first priority is to cover the needs of the nursing unit. Use the scientific approach (see the box on p. 111) to identify the problem, design possible courses of action, and select a course of action.
7. Explain why the use of intuition alone in decision making is not sound.
8. Review the pragmatic assessment and decision-making process presented in Figure 6-4; then work through the following situation: You are the department manager of a labor and delivery area where the philosophy is to allow family members to attend the mother from time of admission until dismissal. The only exclusion is during delivery, when only two adults are allowed at the mother's side. There is continual noise and disruption around the nurses' station by family members who want frequent information, special privileges (food, drink, extra chairs, sleeping cots, and so on). Small children create confusion, and you are not sure that they are always safe within the environment. You believe that families should be together, but that there should be some control. Work with items 1 to 3 of Figure 6-4 to solve the situation.
9. Are there any decisions in which a group of nursing staff could not make a decision for their nursing department? Explain.

REFERENCES

1. Bittel L: The McGraw-Hill 36-hour management course, New York, 1989, McGraw-Hill Publishing Co.
2. Gehrman D: Why plan. In Kreitner R: Management, ed 4, Boston, 1989, Houghton Mifflin Co.
3. Iacocca L: An autobiography, New York, 1984, Bantam.
4. Kreitner R: Management, ed 4, Boston, 1989, Houghton Mifflin Co.
5. Newell A and Simon H: Human problem solving, Englewood Cliffs, NJ, 1972, Prentice-Hall, Inc.
6. Benner P: From novice to expert, Menlo Park, Calif, 1984, Addison-Wesley Publishing Co Inc.
7. Simon H: The new science of management decision, New York, 1960, Harper & Row.
8. Toffler A: The third wave, New York, 1980, Bantam Publishing House.
9. Drucker P: The practice of management, New York, 1954, Harper & Row.
10. Singer I: AIDS in the workplace, Nation's Business 75:36, August, 1987.
11. Kron T and Gray A: The management of patient care: putting leadership skills to work, ed 6, Philadelphia, 1986, WB Saunders Co.
12. DeBella S, Martin L, and Siddall S: Nurses' role in health care planning, Norwalk, Conn, 1986, Appleton-Century-Crofts.
13. Brubakken K: The nursing care plan: monitoring for, J Nurs Qual Assur 1(3):79-80, 1987.

SUGGESTED READINGS

Ala M and Jones C: Decision making styles of nurses, Nurs Man 20(10)52-54, 1989.

Anvaripour P: A nursing department can and should plan for the future, Nurs Health Care 11(4):207-209, 1990.

Bailey J and Hendricks D: Decisions made easy, Nursing 90 20(1):120-122, 1990.

Curtin L: Strategic planning: asking the right questions, Nurs Man 22(1):7-8, 1991.

Goldman E: Planning for success in ambulatory care, Healthcare Forum J 34(1):29-31, 1991.

Golightly C, Wright L, and Pogue L: A model to facilitate interactive planning, JONA 20(9):16-19, 1990.

Ives J: Articulating values and assumptions for strategic planning, Nurs Man 22(1):38-39, 1991.

Johnson J, Holdwick C, and Fredericksen S: A nontraditional approach to wage adjustment (conceptual thinking), Nurs Man 20(11):35-39, 1989.

Mehmert P, Dickel C, and McKeighen R: Computerizing nursing diagnosis, Nurs Man 20(7):24-30, 1989.

New N and New R: Quality assurance that works (problem-solving), Nurs Man 21(6):21-24, 1990.

O'Neil K and Gajdostik K: The head nurse's managerial role (planning), Nurs Man 20(6):39-41, 1989.

Ouellette J and others: Clustering: decentralization and resource sharing, Nurs Man 21(6):31-35, 1990.

Parsons M, Scaltrito S, and Vondle D: A program to manage nurse staffing costs (problem-solving process), Nurs Man 21(10):42-44, 1990.

Pillar B, Jacox A, and Redman B: Technology, its assessment, and nursing, Nurs Outlook 38(1):16-19, Jan/Feb, 1990.

Predd C: Great tips for setting priorities, Nursing 89 19(10):120-126, 1989.

Schmieding N: Do head nurses include staff nurses in problem-solving? Nurs Man 21(3):21N-210, 1990.

Steves J: Step-by-step implementation of PCA therapy (planning, development, implementation and control), Nurs Man 20(12):35-38, 1989.

Storlie F and Leon J: Make the most of your time . . . by trusting yourself (priority setting), Nursing 90 20(3):124-133, 1990.

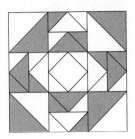

7

Direction

BEHAVIORAL OBJECTIVES

On completion of this chapter the student will be prepared to:

☐ Define direction giving and explain the implications for nursing direction at the lower or first level of management.
☐ Identify factors that determine size of a work group, the span of control, and the physical support system.
☐ Explain guidelines necessary for effective delegation of activities to a group of nursing personnel who are to provide care to a group of patients.
☐ Demonstrate ability to identify priorities in assignment making.
☐ Differentiate between delegation of responsibility in team, functional, primary, modular, and case nursing.
☐ Identify criteria important to giving directions for accomplishment of a nursing assignment.

Earlier chapters have considered organization as a system, referring to the overall structure in a hospital or health facility in which all personnel relate to each other through specific channels. This chapter presents the organizational process of directing at the lower or decentralized level, with the nurse manager working with a small group of nursing personnel, coordinating persons, equipment, and supplies in a designated environment for direction of some specific purpose or work. Directing is the connecting link between organizing for work and getting the job done. In general, *directing* is the issuance of assignments, orders, and instructions that permit the worker to understand what is expected of him or her and the guidance and overseeing of the worker so that he or she can contribute effectively and efficiently to the attainment of organizational objectives.

It is assumed that at this point the nurse manager has knowledge of the organizational structure, policies, standards, and job descriptions of the agency. For the purpose of clarity the concept of direction is divided into two chapters: technical aspects and interpersonal relationships. This chapter discusses the technical activities, methods, and materials employed by the nurse manager at the lower or first level of management. Work flow, equipment, techniques, and procedures used to complete work assignments will be discussed. Chapter 8 focuses on the interpersonal aspect of management. In reality, technical activities cannot and should not be separated from human considerations. For this reason there will be some overlap in discussion.

Other chapters have described many important determinants in the organizational process—people and their values, resources, and the environment in which the organization operates—emphasizing that there is no one best way for all organizations to be designed. The most desirable structure will vary from one organization to the next. The same concepts hold true for the direction-giving process.

This chapter presents information that can be applied to any health care delivery system. Illustrations are given as to how the major concepts of direction giving can be accomplished at the lower or first level of management.

SIZE AND MIX OF THE WORK GROUP: SPAN OF MANAGEMENT

A nurse manager has many tasks with many possible combinations. The nurse is expected to plan, organize, direct, and control quality nursing care given by a group of nursing personnel having diversified abilities and personalities. In addition, that nurse is to possess technical knowledge and expertise that may be applied in any situation. The leader is to be teacher, counselor, and role model.

At lower- or first-level management, the number of people who report directly to a manager represents the managerial span of control. Managers with a narrow span of control oversee the work of a few people, such as a three-bed dialysis unit, whereas those managers with a wide span of control have more people reporting to them, such as supervisors, department manager, case manager, and functional or team leader (Figure 7-1). The larger the span of control, the fewer managers needed; the larger the span of control, the greater the hierarchy. For a narrow span of control, there is greater decentralization.

Factors Influencing Number of Workers and Span of Control

Ideally, the right span of control strikes an efficient balance between too little and too much supervision.

Selecting an appropriate number of people for the nurse to lead as well as the span of management is important to effective operation, since in certain cases a wider or narrower span can make it more difficult for the nurse manager to integrate the activities of group members or the group's activities with other personnel. Following are factors that most affect the numbers of workers and choice of span of control[1]:

1. Standards for care adopted by the health care-providing agency
2. Number and similarity of clients/patients and functions supervised—the degree to which the care and support services for which the nurse manager is responsible are alike or different (e.g., long-term care versus immediate postsurgical care)
3. Number and mix of nursing personnel and the degree of supervision that group members require (e.g., nursing assistants or new graduates versus experienced nurses)
4. Complexity of functions supervised—the nature of the patients/clients and functions for which the nurse manager is responsible (e.g., multiple diagnoses, technical equipment)
5. Planning required of the nurse manager—the degree to which the manager must program and review the activities of the subunit (e.g., daily, weekly, or monthly schedules; audits of care; evaluation of personnel; budget)
6. Coordination required of the nurse manager or the degree to which the nurse must try to integrate functions or tasks within the subunit or between the subunit and other parts of the organization (e.g., dietary, pharmacy, x-ray, OT, PT)
7. Organizational assistance received by the nurse manager or how much help from assistants and other support personnel the manager can rely on (e.g., head nurse, ward manager, clerk, auxiliary services)

Attempting to assign precise numbers and mix of workers that will be appropriate for ad-

Narrow span of control

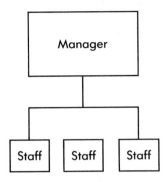

Wide span of control

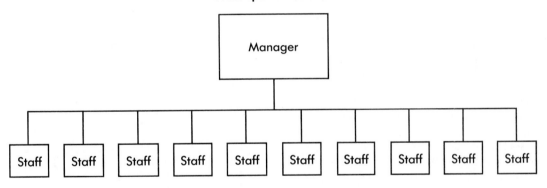

Figure 7-1. Narrow and wide spans of control.

ministering nursing care at a given level in the organization ignores the need for adjustments to accommodate specific situations.

Criteria for Assurance of Quality Care

A more dependable procedure is to determine how many staff members are needed by considering the criteria used to assure provision of quality care to a specific group of patients/clients. Criteria for care are stated in standards and behavioral objectives by accrediting agencies. Whatever the circumstances, enough staff must be employed so that (1) the needs of the patients/clients are met, (2) all time periods are covered adequately, (3) patient care does not

suffer seriously if any member is absent, and (4) enough latitude is allowed for growth and development of the nursing staff.

In many cases the location and purpose of care provide the answer to staffing size and span of control. A 6-bed intensive care unit, a 10-bed recovery room, a 15-bed pediatric area, and a community health agency are cases in point; each of these has its own specific needs. In some general care areas of a hospital, however, the span of management is usually less definitive. For example, a 45-bed medical unit could have a number of possible spans of control. The unit could be treated as one large entity or be divided into two, three, or more subunits. One or any combination of care delivery systems could be applied—total care, functional, team, primary care or case management. Smaller groupings usually bring the best nursing care results, with the directional process occurring as near the point of action as possible.

Physical Support System

Work organization and direction giving are affected by the space, equipment, and physical environment available for support of nursing care. Some facilities are barely adequate, whereas others have every possible convenience and innovation. Resources range from cramped quarters with simple necessities, such as beds and other furniture, linens, and wheelchairs, to large, airy, and attractive surroundings filled with modern equipment and automated devices that lift, turn, breathe, move, and monitor almost every bodily function. Installation of complex computerized informational systems is on the increase, supplying almost limitless amounts of information. With the addition of each piece of equipment comes the responsibility to know how to operate it or to apply the information supplied.

Malfunctioning equipment, excessive cold or heat, noise, darkness, poor sanitation, and odors are examples of factors that make for unpleasant physical working conditions. The more of these present, the less pleasant most workers will find the job, which may reduce the probability of their optimum performance or even remaining on the staff.

The challenges in direction for a nurse manager of a subunit in a small health facility are different from those faced by a nurse manager in a university center in a large city. Regardless of the nature of the health care agency or nursing care setting, the nurse is to perform within prevailing circumstances while working toward adaptations or changes as desired.

SIGNIFICANCE OF THE DELEGATION PROCESS

Managers stand to gain a great deal by adopting the habit of delegating. By passing along well-defined tasks and responsibilities to staff members, managers can free more of their time for other important activities, such as planning and evaluating. Regarding what should be dele-

gated, Andrew Grove, chief executive officer of a leading high-tech electronics company, has made the following recommendation: "Because it is easier to monitor something with which you are familiar, if you have a choice you should delegate those activities you know best."[2] Grove cautions that delegators who follow his advice will experience some psychological discomfort because they will quite naturally want to continue doing what they know best.

In addition to freeing valuable managerial time, delegation is also a helpful management training and developmental tool. Moreover, staff members who desire greater challenge generally become more committed and satisfied when they are given opportunities to tackle significant tasks or challenges. Conversely, a lack of delegation can stifle staff initiative.

> EXAMPLE: Consider the situation of Carolyn, a staff nurse who is enrolled in a managerial program at the local university, and who aspires to become a head nurse. The unit manager offers to allow Carolyn to put some of the theory she is learning into practice in the clinical area. She assigns Carolyn the preparation of the time schedule for a 2-week period and the making of clinical assignments for a 1-week period. Carolyn is delighted. However, the unit manager hovers over her, critical of every move. "You should do it this way"; "That will never work"; "Oh, don't assign Mary to that patient—it's not a good match." Initially, Carolyn tries harder and harder to please the unit manager, to no avail. Before the 2 weeks are up, she asks the unit manager to take back the given authority. Upon evaluation, the unit manager records that Carolyn lacked initiative and gave up before she had ample opportunity to prove herself. Said one observer, "Carolyn won't be here long, you can be sure. She'll get her education and be long gone."

A manager who never allows others to make decisions will have to cope with staff unrest and rapid turnover.

Barriers to Delegation

There are several reasons why managers generally do not delegate as much as they should[3]:
1. Belief in the fallacy "If you want it done right, do it yourself"
2. Lack of confidence and trust in workers
3. Low self-confidence

4. Fear of being thought lazy
5. Vague job definition
6. Fear of competition
7. Reluctance to take the risks involved in depending on others
8. Lack of controls that provide early warning of problems with delegated duties
9. Poor examples set by other managers who do not delegate

Nurse managers can go a long way toward effective delegation by recognizing and correcting these tendencies both in themselves and in their fellow managers. Since successful delegation is habit-forming, the first step is usually the hardest. Properly prepared and motivated staff members, who respond favorably to challenging work, generally reward a manager's trust with a job well done.

RESPONSIBILITIES OF DIRECTION GIVING

The central task of direction giving is to demonstrate that the goals of the health service organization and the goals of staff members are compatible. There are certain managerial responsibilities common to health care agencies: (1) to preserve the regulatory, day-by-day activities that make the system productive—by far the major share of a nurse manager's activity (regulatory), (2) to correct any dysfunction in the system after it has occurred, (corrective), (3) to prevent problems and difficulties by anticipation (preventive), and (4) to promote ways and means for improvement of personnel and the system (promotive).

Guidelines for Implementation of Responsibility

These four types of managerial direction are applied by nurse managers according to the individual situation. The following objectives incorporate the regulatory, corrective, preventive, and promotive components and can serve as guidelines to the nurse in delegation of day-to-day activities.[3] The lower- or first-level nurse manager:

1. Formulates objectives for care that are realistic for the health agency, patient/client, and nursing personnel
2. Gives first priority to the needs of the patients/clients assigned to the nursing staff

3. Provides for coordination and efficiency among departments that provide support services
4. Identifies responsibility for all activities for which the nursing staff is responsible
5. Provides for safe, continuous care
6. Considers need for variety in task assignment and for development of personnel
7. Provides for leader's availability to staff members for assistance, teaching, counsel, and evaluation
8. Trusts members to follow through with their assignments
9. Interprets protocol for responding to incidental requests
10. Explains procedure to be followed in emergencies
11. Gives clear, concise formal and informal directions
12. Uses a management control process that assesses the quality of care given and evaluates individual and group performance given by nursing personnel

Adherence to these guidelines allows goals to be accomplished with order and precision within the bounds of safety, yet in an environment that promotes individual and group initiative and creativity. A brief discussion of each guideline follows.

Formulating objectives for care that are realistic for the health agency, patients/clients, and nursing personnel. Previous discussions in this book have emphasized the importance of agency, subunits, and nursing personnel managing by objectives, based on mutually acceptable standards. Guidelines for formulating objectives for care that may apply to a nursing group at the lower or first level include the following:

1. Provides a holistic approach to care that is comprehensive and continuous. (The patient/client is the central focus for assessing, planning, implementing, and evaluating care.)
2. Initiates and keeps current a written nursing care plan that includes physical, emotional, psychosocial, and religious needs and problems; assignment of priorities of care; and alternatives to meet needs.
3. Assigns staff to patients/clients according to accepted criteria.

4. Ensures safety of patient/client.
5. Assigns staff members according to their legal and professional ability to perform.

Giving first priority to the needs of the patients/clients assigned to the nursing staff. The nurse manager works with a number of patients/clients and therefore needs to determine what should be done in order of importance. To achieve the primary goal of nursing, the providers of nursing must come to terms with what constitutes quality care. After nursing standards are accepted by the agency, each nursing department and/or subunit determines how they will be implemented. Nursing care plans offer the best way for assistance of quality care. Assessing needs and problems, deciding how they are to be met, controlling the process, and evaluating the results provide the mechanism for adherence to priority.

Through nursing care plans the nurse manager benefits from input of all who have participated in the formation of the plans since the patient's/client's admission—the recipient of care, medical and nursing staff, and supportive services. Having a means for centralizing information (the nursing care plan) offers a definite advantage to the nurse manager whose time for direction giving is often limited. Nursing care plans constitute the basis for work assignments. The nurse can check through the nursing care plans quickly for needs and priorities pertinent to direction giving. The nurse delegator then ranks them in order of priority, from life-threatening problems to those of lesser importance, from short-term, immediate needs to long-term needs. Through assessment of problems and formulation of nursing care plans, priority setting helps the nurse manager to organize and direct care with a rational and realistic approach.

Providing for coordination and efficiency among departments that provide support services. An enterprise is said to exist in a complex environment if the number of factors it must deal with is large. This is the case with most health facilities, as there is great dependence and interdependence on forces that meet the many needs of the consumer. Essential support services include departments such as personnel, admitting, records, dietary, pharmacy, x-ray, laboratory, laundry, housekeeping, maintenance, and business or budget control. Unlike the common market, where competition is high, health care agencies have only one source for each major service, which results in great dependence of each department or subunit on the others.

There are two major supply systems used in health agencies: those that meet requests on a one-to-one basis (dietary, pharmacy, treatment, and so on) and those that respond to requests based on an estimation of what will be needed (linens, stock supplies of drugs, equipment for treatments, paper products, and so on).[4] When the work is divided or decentralized into departments and subunits, a greater need is created for coordination of these services. For example, the pharmacy would have no way of knowing when the medications for the day are needed in each area unless the activities of the various departments and subunits are coordinated. Unless alerted, the laboratory would not be aware of a need for drawing blood samples and providing results at specific times throughout the hospital.

Tools and methods are devised by each support service to facilitate its work. Nurses deal with myriad forms and computerized information and messages. For example, a primary nurse contacts the pharmacist about a specific drug needed for a patient, whereas a problem of repeated delay in service is given to the charge nurse for resolution.

The overall communication structure is set forth in organizational charts from top levels of administration on down to the lower or first level. It is the task of managers at all levels to work within the system. Because of the high degree of dependence on others for services in large organizations, the nurse needs to develop the habit of frequent reference to agency policy and to acquire and use skills of coordination and negotiation. The charge nurse bears responsibility for overall management of the individual nursing department and therefore engages in communications with departments that provide service about major matters of control. In turn, lower or first-level managers oversee activities of their assignment and keep the charge nurse informed of significant matters, according to policies.

The demands on the nurse to accommodate

each support service are lessened if clerical assistance is provided. Computers also reduce the work load greatly. With sufficient physical and technical help in coordination of services, the nurse manager can be free to spend time and energy meeting goals in providing quality care.

Identifying responsibility and accountability for all activities for which the nursing staff is responsible. Delegation is the foundation of organization. The leader/manager first must know the patients/clients assigned for care and the workers available to provide that care, grasp the nursing situation as a whole, determine what needs to be done, and subdivide the whole into manageable parts. The leader assigns tasks in such a way that cooperation is reciprocal, high standards of performance and conduct are possible, and sound decisions are made.

Effective direction is best carried out by one person for one group. When nursing service is given through a group of personnel with varied preparations and backgrounds, such as a nursing team or functional group, the leader is the centralizing force. This leader receives directions from the charge nurse as to patient/client load, staff appropriation, group responsibilities, and special assignments, and in turn routes these directions to the team or group members for implementation. It is important that the team leader maintain control of activities of the group assigned. Nurse leaders are the closest professional link between patients/clients and caregivers and should be able to determine the ideal patient-staff relationships. Group members should receive instructions from their leader and be accountable to that leader for their enactment.

Good direction is not dictatorship. Caregivers expect to be given needed information on quantity, quality, and time limits of work. Nurses expect the information to include what is to be done, who is to do it, when and where the activity will take place, and, when necessary, how and why. Assignments are expected to be within the workers' skills and abilities, and materials necessary to completion of the task are to be provided. Assignment making considers two general categories: provision of patient/client care and support services.

To be effective as a delegator, the nurse leader

must have authority to act. Authority is having the power to achieve an end; sanction is given to the nurse leader by a higher authority in the organization. With this power the nurse has the right and obligation to define limits within which others must function to achieve goals. Responsibility follows, with the nurse leader accepting accountability for individual performance as well as for the performance of those who are led.[5]

Determination of who gives care to whom in nursing depends on the system of care in effect. The one-to-one system of nursing care (total care or primary care) may be used effectively as described in Chapter 5. The following discussion focuses on functional, team, primary nursing, modular, and nurse case management, since these are the most commonly used systems; however, principles of effective assignment making and direction giving can be applied to all nursing care delivery situations.

A survey of 987 U.S. hospitals by Madeline Wake of Marquette University reported that team nursing was the most frequently used system (59%) and primary nursing second (29%). Case management is at 3% but rapidly moving up as a viable nursing care delivery system.[6]

Functional nursing. In functional nursing the head nurse or charge nurse assigns the work for all nursing personnel in the department or subunit. Work organization and personnel assignment are simplified with a specialty or task-oriented approach. Personnel are programmed into fixed slots of role designation (e.g., medication or treatment nurse) or assigned to blocks of rooms for production efficiency. The charge nurse first assigns the RNs or LPNs/LVNs to those tasks that require licensure for fulfillment, as do medication and some treatments. The RN or LPN/LVN may be assigned desk work or major care to critical patients.

The next step is to assign hygienic care. The patient/client load is divided among the remaining staff. For example, if there are 45 patients/clients in a nursing department with seven nursing personnel to give hygienic care, three workers would be assigned six patients/clients and three workers would be assigned seven patients/clients. Usually the division of labor is not exact, necessitating a decision as to which worker(s) should be assigned more and which less. The nursing staff is assigned to rooms primarily by territory; that is, each assignment covers as little space as possible to avoid expenditure of excessive energy and waste of time. Additional general areas of responsibility and times for coffee and lunch breaks are posted at the top of the assignment sheet, with specific room assignments given below. Extra assignments and times for breaks from the work area may be posted on a separate sheet. Assignments should be posted in a place easily accessible to the staff. Figure 7-2 provides an illustration of assignments made by a charge nurse for nursing staff appropriated to one department using the functional system.

A fairly rigid plan for assignment making has been presented for study. Note that this task-centered plan considers coverage from the vantage of roles (RNs, LPNs, nursing assistants) and geographic location. It attempts to divide

the categories of workers as equally as possible, with equal coverage during break times. Registered nurse activities are confined to administration of medications for 45 patients/clients. The charge nurse assigned the RN administration of treatments and care of two patients, judging the latter's work load, as administering treatment would not require the nurse's full attention. Dividing the number of patients/clients remaining (43) by the number of nursing personnel left to give hygienic care (7), the nurse-patient ratio is 1:6, with one nurse having seven patients. Because circumstances in health care delivery are not fixed, there will be some deviation from the formula, as with the sample provided below. The nurse–patient ratio* is as follows:

*Formula: divide number of patients by number of nursing staff.

Nurse	Assignment	Break		Lunch
RN X	Medication nurse	RN X	9:40-10	12-12:30
RN Y	Treatments and rooms 1 and 3	RN Y	10-10:20	12:30-1
		LPN A	9:40-10	11:30-12
Nursing assistant 2	Treatment room	LPN B	10:10-10:30	12-12:30
Nursing assistant 3	Kitchen	NA 1	9:30-9:50	11:30-12
Nursing assistant 4	2 PM TPRs/BPs	NA 2	9:50-10:10	12-12:30
		NA 3	9:30-9:50	11:30-12
		NA 4	9:30-9:50	12-12:30
		NA 5	9:50-10:10	11:30-12

Nurse	Rm. no.	No. pts./rm.	Nurse	Rm. no.	No. pts./rm.
RN X	1	1	RN Y	2	1
LPN A	3	1	LPN B	4	1
LPN A	5	1	LPN B	6	1
LPN A	7	2	LPN B	8	2
NA 1	9	4	NA 5	10	4
LPN A	11	2	NA 5	12	4
NA 1	13	2	NA 4	14	2
NA 1	15	2	NA 4	16	2
NA 2	17	2	NA 4	18	2
NA 2	19	2	NA 3	20	2
NA 2	21	2	NA 3	22	2
NA 3	23	2			

Figure 7-2. Sample assignment made by a charge nurse using functional nursing.

RN	1	None	NA 1	1:8
RN	2	1:2	NA 2	1:6
LPN	A	1:6	NA 3	1:6
LPN	B	1:4	NA 4	1:6
			NA 5	1:8

The charge nurse begins assignment making with the formula in mind. Then judgment is needed. The nurse manager rationalizes that patients/clients in private rooms generally have critical needs or special problems that require special competencies or more time than normal. Conversely, those in rooms accommodating numbers of patients/clients are more apt to need intermediate care. This factor, coupled with easier accessibility to patients/clients and supplies, enables the care provider to complete the assignment more quickly. Licensed practical nurse A and nurse assistant 1 have their assignments distributed over a wider territory than do other staff members. The charge nurse wanted the LPN to care for the more critical patients/clients in rooms 3 and 5. If the assignment ended with room 7, the LPN would have had only four patients/clients assigned; if room 9 were added, the load would have increased to eight. Not wishing to place two nurses in a four-bed unit and create unnecessary complications of vying for space and creating confusion among patients as to who was assigned to whom, the choice was made to extend the parameter of the assignment for LPN A and nurses' aide 1. The staff members with lighter patient/client loads are given the support assignments of keeping the kitchen and treatment room in order and taking afternoon vital signs.

It is possible in the functional system to give attention to individual needs of the patients/clients and workers, but the task is more difficult than with use of a more personalized system. The charge nurse has less opportunity and time to become aware of the many ramifications that are significant to a complex nursing situation.

Team nursing. In team nursing, rather than the charge nurse making assignments of patients/clients to personnel, each team leader is given the responsibility for that team. Members receive directions from the team leader and are accountable to that leader for their implementation. The major responsibility of a team leader is to provide quality care to a group of patients/clients, primarily through the work of others. This role of catalyst requires translating the needs of a nursing team into goals and objectives that are realistic, clearly defined, and reflect nursing and agency purposes. As Chapter 6 states, in determination of needs the nurse manager focuses on two major goals: (1) the provision of optimal nursing care for all patients/clients through assessment, problem identification, formulation of plans for nursing action, implementation, and planning for evaluation of care and (2) the provision of nursing care through an effective management process. Following are certain behavioral objectives the leader of a nursing team can follow to provide coordination and efficiency of service.

1. *Determine the number and characteristics of patients/clients assigned to the nursing team.* This is accomplished by reviewing the orders and nursing care plans; consultation with individual patients/clients, significant others, and physicians; reviewing clients' records; and listening to reports from nursing team members as they leave at the end of their shift. At first this procedure can seem overwhelming to a novice leader. The amount of data available can blur into meaningless content until the nurse practices extracting information that has the most relevance to the situation. An experienced nurse soon learns to accomplish this task quickly and well. A worksheet for sorting information is suggested. Color-coding priority activities helps the nurse to see them at a glance when making assignments. Figure 7-3 offers a portion of one such worksheet that may be used by a nursing team leader.

2. *Assess priority of care for all patients/clients,* beginning with those who need the greatest amount of care. Establishing needs in order of priority serves as an indicator for action. Each need is considered as to its importance to the patient/client and to the nursing work group using the criteria of (1) preservation of life, dignity, and integrity; (2) avoidance of destructive changes; and (3) continuance of normal growth and development.[7] The team leader can use distinguishing marks, such as an "X" or "★," beside the patient's/client's name to indicate immediate or special attention. The team leader will scan a worksheet quickly and note the need

Staff member to be assigned	Room no.	Name/physician	Age	Diagnosis	Diet	Activity	TPR BP	I & O	IVs	Treatments and special meds	Needs and problems
	60	Janet Kirgan / Dr. Green	22	Tubal emboism		Amb.				Air studies 2 pm	Worried
	62	Laura Cott / Dr. Foy	48	Sig. abd. Ca c̄ mets	30 bed rest 1-2		✓	✓ Foley		Perineal care p.r.n. Irrig. Foley 10	Force fl. No visitors Psych. support
	64	Mrs. Hasten / Dr. Bell	66	Cataract ® op 1/6	Reg.	Bed rest	✓			Eye shields ® op	Skin fragile 20% vision ® eye
	66	Ray Smith / Dr. Toms	41	Terminal Ca lung	Ca 20.	Bed rest B.R.P.	✓	✓		Maintain airway Cough suction d.t. Turn q 2 h.	No cure Fact Encourage family
	68a	Mr. Fletcher / Dr. Able	71	Burger's disease	Salt free 1000 cal.	Bed rest	✓	✓		Pedal pulses 10-2 Soak feet + knees 10 Burn exercises 10-2	Team managed c̄ physical med. Depressed often Needs help to turn
	68b	Sam Vega / Dr. Kant	55	Aortic bypass graft 1-7	Lo fat	Bed rest			5% D.W. 2 KCl 100 cc q h.	Encour. d.t. On Valium	
	70a	Elaine McEvoy / Dr. Buxton	68	Ca colon	Lo fiber Kosher	Amb. bathrm	✓				Colostomy tomorrow Pre-op teaching visit rabbi
	70b	Lela Smith / Dr. Scott	71	Diabetic ulcer	Soft force fl.	Amb.					Hard of hearing

Figure 7-3. Sample of a partially completed worksheet used by a nursing team leader to record pertinent information about patients/clients in preparation for assignment making and for reference during guidance of team activities. Additional abbreviations may be used to conserve space.

for special tests and procedures and their specific times, reverse isolation or isolation technique, intravenous fluids, planning around routing of patients/clients to other departments for special services, blood transfusions, and so on. The assigner will assess the number of total care patients, those who require intermediate help, and those who are fairly independent. Attention will be given to psychological, sociological, and spiritual needs, which may be of highest priority with some patients/clients.

3. *Review available staff and consider their roles, competencies, and preferences.* Delegation of roles and tasks is simplified if the nursing staff is composed of all licensed personnel. However, many health agencies use the services of technical or semiskilled workers, such as nursing assistants. Ideally, team leaders participate in selection of all staff who serve on the nursing team. With time and attention the team leader becomes well acquainted with the nursing staff. Preparation and experience are weighed against the responsibilities of the assignment. Individual preferences are taken into account as much as possible. The team leader keeps in mind the matter of licensure requirements for certain activities, such as medication and some treatments.

4. *Assign patients/clients who require the most skilled attention to the most qualified staff member(s).* A major goal in assignment making is to divide the total load into a number of activities that can logically and comfortably be performed by one person. People cannot be assigned tasks for which they are not suited, and they should not carry a work load that is either too heavy or too light. A too-heavy work load could mean the job will not be completed well or on time, whereas a work load that is too light could result in idleness and inefficiency. The philosophy of team nursing subscribes to "team" effort, each person helping the others to achieve common goals. Although it is expected that underassigned personnel will help the overassigned member(s), problems may be created that could be averted with careful preplanning.

The team leader may need to assume responsibility for administering medications and monitoring intravenous fluids. Assigning the leader to these activities provides additional opportunity for moving among the patients/clients and nursing staff. Patients/clients who

need treatments that require licensed personnel may be assigned to a licensed member for care, or the team leader can assign the hygienic care to another member and the treatment to a licensed person if it is believed that the licensed member is needed more elsewhere. The leader attempts to match the greatest need with the person best prepared to meet that need; then this team member is assigned to other patients/clients nearby in consideration of the geographical and physical setting. This system calls for some compromises in matching abilities of staff members to the needs of patients/clients. If the criteria for assignment making were followed exactly, staff assignments might consist of one patient/client at the far end of a hall, two in the middle, and three on a side, with two or more staff members providing care in one room. Fragmented assignments are at odds with criteria for provision of quality care and run the risk of patient/client hostility because of inadequate attention. In turn, the team member becomes overtired because of confusion and unnecessary activity.

Some delegators advocate that the team leader administer care to the most acutely ill patient-client on the team or that the leader care for the one who requires the most complex nursing care. Rationale for this suggestion is that the team leader is the most qualified for the task, and the patient will derive the greatest benefit from the leader's services. Also, the leader will be serving as a role model to the team members. When team functioning is viewed realistically, it becomes apparent that if the leader is assigned to an area that requires undivided attention, it then becomes impossible to fulfill other team commitments. A compromise in delegation of activities is suggested. The patient/client with high priority needs is assigned to a qualified member of the team who has less skill than the team leader, and the team leader assists with the patient's/client's care at those times when special expertise is required. The nurse leader is then available to the patient/client needing special care as well as to all of the other patients/clients assigned to the team

5. *Double-assign a patient/client or groups of patients/clients if it is anticipated that assistance with care will be needed.* Sometimes provision of care for a patient/client requires more than one per-

son (lifting, turning, treatments, and so on). If possible, the member who is working in an adjoining room or adjacent area is given a double assignment so she will be easily accessible and can provide the necessary help with minimal loss of time and energy.

6. *Note coverage for breaks from the work scene.* Times are appropriated for coffee breaks, meals, and conferences to ensure continued supervision and care by qualified personnel. For example, there must be continuous coverage by a registered nurse, and each team should have equal staff coverage as much as is possible. Planning with other team leaders, and perhaps with the head nurse, is necessary to see that adequate personnel are available to all teams continuously. Arrangements such as these take the leader's time, especially in a complex setting, but in the end staff time will be conserved, team functioning will be smoother, and patients/clients will receive the necessary constant supervision.

In addition to patient/client care assignment, many health facilities expect nursing personnel to perform supportive services, such as keeping the unit in order (cleaning up kitchen and utility room, straightening linen closets, transporting patients, and preparing vacated rooms for new admissions). The requirements for this kind of ancillary service usually depend on the size of the hospital and the availability and distribution of personnel. It is certainly advocated that the nurses' time *not* be spent in these activities. Large hospitals and other health facilities usually maintain a separate staff for housekeeping duties and another for distribution of supplies. Many hospitals have auxiliary groups who perform varied services, such as caring for flowers, transporting patients, and running errands. Figure 7-4 gives an example of an assignment of nursing personnel using the team system for delivery of nursing care to a group of patients/clients.

Figure 7-4 demonstrates that major purposes of assignment making have been carried out. At the top of the sheet are the name and role of each staff member, along with times for breaks. Continuous coverage for each team is provided for, as well as assuring RN coverage for alternate teams for coffee, lunch, and conference times. Supportive services are assigned, with

sharing of duties between teams. These responsibilities will be rotated between teams from week to week. The patients are not divided equally among the nursing staff, as consideration was given to established criteria. The RN will assume responsibility for medications and care of patient Kirzan in room 60. The patient is near the nurses' station, needs minimal nursing care, yet has need for teaching and emotional support. The LPN is assigned treatments and the care of the most critical patients, with assistance provided for care of patients Snell and Fletcher. Nursing assistant 2 has a greater number of patients, but the total work load is considered equitable. All workers are kept in as close proximity as possible. The team leader will be circulating during the shift to make observations and adjustments as necessary.

Primary nursing. In primary nursing it is the head nurse's responsibility to assign patients to nursing staff. To be effective in this function, there are major principles to consider:

1. Patients/clients must be assigned a primary nurse at admission or within the first 24 hours. The RN or LPN/LVN is delegated responsibility and accountability for planning, giving, and communicating all phases of care for one or more patients/clients from the time of admission through discharge.[8] If it is not possible to make a primary nursing assignment when the patient is admitted, a total care assignment is made in which one nurse is assigned to provide all nursing care needed during one shift. The total care concept is continued until a primary nurse is selected. Responsibilities for the nurse for one shift include assessment of nursing needs, medications, treatments, hygiene and comfort measures, teaching, providing support, and communicating through charting, reporting, and care planning.

2. There should be optimum match of patient/client need with staff preference and competency. Some nursing units maintain a master board near the nursing station with the names and diagnoses of new patients/clients recorded as they are admitted. Staff members are invited to state their preferences by filling in their names beside those of new patients/clients. As much as possible, the head nurse

Team A

	AM break	Lunch	Conferences	Special assignment
RNT Ldr: Marge Singer	9:45-10:05	12-12:30	7:30-7:50 2:00-2:30	
LPN: Ruth Telfer	9:30-9:50	11:30-12		
NA 1: Jean Rass	9:30-9:50	11:30-12		Kitchen NA 1
NA 2: Tam Spivey	9:50-10:10	12-12:30		Rx room

Date: ___
Charge nurse: ___

Team B

	AM break	Lunch	Conferences	Special assignment
RNT Ldr: Cleo Hastings	10:05-10:25	12:30-1:00	7:50-8:10 2:30-3:00	
LPN: Bea Kindall	9:30-9:50	11:30-12		
NA 1: Vici Wilson	9:50-10:10	11:30-12		Kitchen
NA 2: Linda Grace	10-10:20	12-12:30		Rx room NA 2

Team A assignments

Meds — Assignment	Room no.	Rxs — Patient	Other — Diagnosis
	61		
	63		
	65		
	67		
	69a		
	69b		
	71a		
	71b		
	73a		
	73b		
	75a		
	75b		
	77a		
	77b		
	79a		
	79b		
	79c		
	79d		

Team B assignments

Meds — Assignment	Room no.	Rxs — Patient	Other — Diagnosis
RN	60	June Kerzan	Tube Occu.
LPN	62	Laura Cobb	Ca Cx
LPN	64	Mrs. Heather	Cat. (L)eye
LPN/NA 1	66	Roy Snell	Ca Lung
LPN/NA 1	68a	Mr. Fletcher	Buerger's
LPN	68b	Lem Vargas	Aortic ByPass Graft
NA 1	70a	Elaine Metz	Ca Colon
NA 1	70b	Lela Smith	Pneumonia
NA 1	72a	Reva Farrell	Mastectomy (R)
NA 1	72b	Barb Brink	Cholecystomy
NA 2	74a	Terry Erbb	Prostatectomy
NA 2	74b	John Baker	CHD
NA 2	76a	Angela Castro	Bunionectomy/Diabetes
NA 2	76b	Terry Meltzer	Hysterectomy
NA 2	78a	Bob Perry	Fx (L) Leg
NA 2	78b	Sam Frieson	x-rays BL Studies
NA 2	78c	David Cooper	Laminectomy
NA 2	78d	Larry Berg	Duodenal ulcer

Figure 7-4. Sample assignment sheet for a two-team nursing unit indicating patient assignment for team B and cooperative assignments for breaks and other activities.

complies with the request.* Another plan is to have the head nurse assign staff to a group of adjacent rooms. As patients/clients are admitted to these rooms, nurses choose their own patients/clients, which allows for retention of decentralization of decisions, autonomy of the primary nurse, and improved efficiency.

3. Geography of the unit is considered. For conservation of energy and cost-effectiveness, patient/client assignments should be consolidated in one general area. Initially, following the concept of decentralization of nursing services, nurses were given the option to choose patients/clients anywhere in the unit. The result was that a primary nurse could have patients/clients from one end of the unit to the other, requiring much travel time and loss in efficiency.

4. Each nurse should have a case load equitable to those of other nurses, not necessarily in terms of numbers of patients/clients, but in time and energy required to complete the assignment.

5. The assignment remains throughout the patient's/client's stay on the unit unless (a) his or her condition changes beyond the capability of the primary nurse, (b) there are patient-nurse conflicts that cannot be resolved, (c) nurse or patient/client requests a change (if the nurse requests the change, the reasons must be reviewed carefully before a decision is made), (d) the nurse rotates to a block of night shifts or goes on vacation or leave, or (e) the patient/client is transferred to a room that is geographically inconvenient for the primary nurse.

6. Nurses should care for a variety of patient/client problems to ensure professional growth.

7. The nurse should be identified and visible to patient/client, family, physicians, and other health care providers. This can be accomplished by simply introducing the patient/client to the nurse and by posting the primary nurse-patient assignments in a prominent place so that everyone can easily and quickly see which nurse is in charge of the care of a particular patient/client.

8. As much as possible, the same associate nurses should be on alternate shifts and on the primary nurse's days off, since it is their task to carry out the plan of care initiated by the primary nurse and to suggest or make changes as necessary. The greater the continuity of care, the better the quality of care.

Modular nursing. Modular nursing is a modification of team and primary nursing, used most often when there are not enough RNs to cover the scope of care.[9]

1. Patients are identified within the total group of patients in the module who would most benefit by 24-hour primary nursing care. Depending on the number of primary nurses available, these patients are assigned to such care, in order of priority.

2. The remaining patients are assigned in clusters of RNs/nurses' aides, LPNs/LVNs/nurses' aides where the registered nurse delivers direct care to the patients with the help of ancillary personnel.

Case management. Weil describes delegation in case management as a "set of logical steps and a process of interaction with service networks which assures that a patient receives needed services in a supportive, efficient, and cost effective manner."[10]

One of the three components of the case management model is the development of monitoring systems that guide the case manager in evaluating patient progress against preestablished expectations. This monitoring system is commonly referred to as "critical pathway" or a case management plan.[11] One proven system is utilized at Hillcrest Medical Center in Tulsa, Oklahoma.[12] This facility aims, by case-type, to achieve a purposeful and controlled connection between the quality of care and the cost of that care through delegating and monitoring, by the case manager, of all care the client receives. Delegation of responsibilities extend beyond the traditional nursing unit (in which the needs of the client are met only during hospitalization) by developing a focus on the patient's entire episode of illness from before admission, through the hospital stay, to care following dismissal. The hospital is likely to gain the greatest

*This system is practiced successfully at The Good Samaritan Hospital of Santa Clara Valley, San Jose, California.

benefit from case managing patients who fit into Diagnosis Related Groups (DRGs) or who have specific diseases or problems, for by constant surveillance, duplication of services is avoided and the patient's stay is kept at a minimum. Examples of DRGs are Diseases of the Circulatory System and Coronary Artery Bypass Graft with Catheterization. Patients who fit into these categories are covered by Medicare, with specific governmental restrictions. A predetermined number of days is allotted for each DRG along with a fixed rate of reimbursement. If a patient exceeds the allotted number of days or accrues bills beyond the prescribed limit, or if a patient does not have additional insurance to cover the costs, the hospital is responsible for the excess amount. Under the guidelines of Prospective Payment Systems, unless a patient remains out of the hospital for a specified period of time, reimbursement for readmissions may not be provided. Thus health care agencies are pressed to achieve a purposeful and controlled connection between the quality of care given and cost implications. Case managers must keep abreast of current guidelines from all agencies that have a significant impact on the patients they manage.[12]

The case manager is assigned, or selects, patients and is expected to exercise full professional accountability for clinical practice. The first step in the delegation process is to meet with the patient and family, either in person or by telephone, prior to admission or at least on the day of admission. Once assessment has been made and needs identified, the case manager collaborates with individuals (e.g., primary care nurse) or groups (respiratory therapist, physician) to prepare a case management plan. To facilitate the process, case management plans should be preprepared for the targeted DRGs, based on an analysis of historical clinical and financial data, which can then be adapted to the needs of the individual patient. These are similar to the sample standardized care plan shown in Figure 7-5. The plan includes the anticipated length of stay (LOS) and all tests, procedures, and medications prescribed, with target dates for accomplishment and completion and date of dismissal. The case manager can then note the line of progress and follow up on any deviations

from the norm. For example, if the patient's laboratory or pharmacy charges are in excess of the hospital average, the case manager would evaluate the number and types of tests and medications to determine whether there is test duplication or whether generic drugs could be issued rather than brand sources. The case manager would also monitor the hospital length of stay, using historical care data for the patient's DRG.

The case manager monitors patient care and satisfaction through the caregiver and the patient and family. For example, Thelma, nurse case manager, meets Mr. and Mrs. Amber at time of preadmission screening. Mrs. Amber is to have a knee replacement. Thelma explains the nurse case management concept, letting the husband and wife know what Mrs. Amber can expect while she is in the hospital. She explains that for a knee replacement, Mrs. Amber can anticipate about a 7-day stay in the hospital and, although Thelma will not give direct care, she will coordinate and monitor Mrs. Amber's care during and after her hospital stay. At this point Thelma plans for Mrs. Amber's discharge requirements, ensuring that home needs are properly met. A home health aide will be needed, so Thelma contacts the Visiting Nurse Association; a bedside commode and walker will be necessary, so she orders these commodities from a supply house, to be delivered on the day of Mrs. Amber's return home. Upon her admission to the hospital, Thelma plans Mrs. Amber's care with the primary nurse who will give the nursing care. A predeveloped care plan for a knee replacement patient will be utilized. She fills in target dates for completion of tests, procedures, medications, and discharge. She meets with the respiratory and occupational therapists to plan for hospital and follow-up treatment. Thelma makes a daily review of progress, conferring with any person or group when necessary. In addition to monitoring these activities, Thelma makes sure that supplies and services used for Mrs. Amber's care are within normal guidelines. If guidelines are exceeded, she records justification or attempts to correct the situation. Upon Mrs. Amber's dismissal, Thelma maintains contact with her and the home health aide by telephone. If a home visit

Case-Managed Care

Harper-Grace Hospitals
Detroit, Michigan

☐ Harper Hospital Division (48201)   BPH with TURP
☐ Grace Hospital Division (48235)

NURSING CARE PLAN

DISCHARGE PLAN

Discharge to ☐ Home ☐ Nursing Home ☐ Other _____ ☐

Expected Patient Behaviors on Discharge ___ Pt. will void clear urine per urethra after Foley catheter is removed. PT. will state
intention to drink 2 liters fluid/day at home. PT. will state S&S to report to physician e.g. acute pain, hematuria.

Patient Teaching Needs _____

Referrals Made (Date/Name)

Dietary _____   Pastoral Care _____   Social Service _____

Home Care _____   Patient Education _____   Other _____

Nurse Consultant _____   Pharmacy _____

	NURSING DIAGNOSIS/ CLINICAL PROBLEM	Date	Initials	NURSING DIAGNOSIS/ CLINICAL PROBLEM	Date	Initials
NURSING DIAGNOSIS/ CLINICAL PROBLEM	Knowledge deficit: pre & post-op regimen			PC: Hematuria/retained clots		
EXPECTED OUTCOMES	Verbalize pre & post-op regimen for TURP			Has clear straw-color urine 30 cc/hr.		
PLAN/INTERVENTIONS	1. Teach pt/family about TURP surgical experience & document response 2. Give prostate book 3. Show prostate film strip 4. Discuss Foley cath care/fluid intake 5. Ask pt. perceptions of pre/post-op care 6. Answer questions/clarify misperceptions			1. Maintain Foley cath tension for tamponade— release on: _____ 2. Force oral fluids to 2000 cc/day 3. Strict intake & output 4. Run NS bladder irrigation fast enough to keep urine clear 5. Monitor color of urine/clot formation 6. Monitor Hbg & Hct & lytes		

	REVISIONS	Date	Initials	REVISIONS	Date	Initials
EXPECTED OUTCOMES	7. Teach S&S to report to physician			7. Notify physician of bleeding		
PLAN/ INTERVENTIONS						
	RESOLVED	Date	Initials	**RESOLVED**	Date	Initials

INITIAL	SIGNATURE & PROFESSIONAL DESIGNATION	INITIAL	SIGNATURE & PROFESSIONAL DESIGNATION	INITIAL	SIGNATURE & PROFESSIONAL DESIGNATION	INITIAL	SIGNATURE & PROFESSIONAL DESIGNATION

Figure 7-5. Sample of a case-managed standardized care plan. *From Cronin C and Maklebust J: Case managed care: capitalizing on the CNS, Nurs Man 20(3):44-46, 1989.*

NURSING DIAGNOSIS/ CLINICAL PROBLEM	Date	Initials	NURSING DIAGNOSIS/ CLINICAL PROBLEM	Date	Initials

NURSING DIAGNOSIS/ CLINICAL PROBLEM

PC: Acute pain/bladder spasms

EXPECTED OUTCOMES

Displays no signs/symptoms of acute pain/ bladder spasms

PLAN/INTERVENTIONS

1. Monitor for S&S of bladder spasm
   a. acute pain
   b. need to defecate
   c. leakage around catheter
   d. GU irrigant won't run on wide open
   e. can't manually irrigate bladder
      because of increased pressure

REVISIONS	Date	Initials	REVISIONS	Date	Initials

EXPECTED OUTCOMES

2. Administer B + O suppository q 6 h prn
3. Administer pain med prn
4. Manually extract retained clots

PLAN/INTERVENTIONS

   a. instill 100 cc normal saline
   b. withdraw same
   c. repeat until urine clear or until
      patient verbalizes relief of pain/
      spasm
5. Notify physician if unable to extract clots

RESOLVED	Date	Initials	RESOLVED	Date	Initials

INITIAL	SIGNATURE & PROFESSIONAL DESIGNATION	INITIAL	SIGNATURE & PROFESSIONAL DESIGNATION	INITIAL	SIGNATURE & PROFESSIONAL DESIGNATION	INITIAL	SIGNATURE & PROFESSIONAL DESIGNATION

DISCHARGE SUMMARY Date _____ Signature _____

Summary of unresolved problems and follow-up _____

_____

_____

Patient/family understanding of discharge instruction _____

Diet Instruction Given   □ No □ Yes Type _____   Activity Reviewed   □ No □ Yes

Prescriptions Reviewed   □ No □ Yes Type(s) _____   Type _____

_____   Home Care Arranged   □ No □ Yes

_____   Type _____

_____   Supplies Arranged   □ No □ Yes

                                                 Type _____

Follow-Up Appointment □ No □ Yes Type _____   Type _____

Discharge Via □ Walking □ Wheelchair □ Ambulance □ Accompanied By _____

            Belongings Sent _____   Discharged To _____

Continued.

Figure 7-5, continued.

Case-Managed Care—continued

Date					
Day of Adm.	**1**	**2**	**3**	**4**	**5**
Discharge planning/ Teaching	Prostate booklet pre-op Prostate film pre-op Foley catheter care --▷ Fluid requirements --▷ Signs/symptoms to report --▷				Discharge
Functional level/ Activity	Up ad lib	Flat for 6 hours post spinal	Up --▷		
Nutrition/ Diet	Reg as tolerated NPO at midnight	NPO pre-op Reg as tol. post-op Force fluids --▷	Regular --▷		
Consults	Medical clearance if indicated				
Noninvasive tests	CXR ECG				
Invasive tests/OR		OR-TURP Spinal anesthesia			
Labs	CBC, Lytes, PT, PTT SMA$_{18}$, Acid Phos. U/A	CBC & Lytes in PAR	CBC & Lytes		
Treatments	Fleet enema hs	Compression stockings Foley →Tension GU irrigation --▷	DC stockings Release Foley Tension	Foley DD	D.C. Foley
Meds		IV for 24° ---------------- B&O suppository prn --▷ Analgesic IM Stool softener	DC IV Analgesia p.o.		

Expected Patient Outcome: Patient will void clear urine per urethra after Foley is removed. Patient will
verbalize intention to drink 2000 cc/day at home, and identify signs & symptoms to report to physician.

Critical Pathway for: TRANSURETHRAL RESECTION OF PROSTATE

Case Manager: _____

12/03/87, 12/20/87

Figure 7-5, continued.

is required, she arranges for the services of a visiting nurse. Mr. Amber is unable to manage cleaning and meals, so she arranges for home-maker services and Meals on Wheels. When nursing care and other assistance is no longer required, Thelma contacts the Public Health Nursing Department for follow-up visits in the home and continued surveillance.

Development of a critical path plan, which is reviewed for effeciency and necessity, tailored to each patient's needs results in cost-effectiveness and patient and nurse satisfaction.

Providing for safe, continuous care. Each health care facility must meet minimal safety regulations established by law, as well as those adopted by the agency to meet its unique needs. The nurse manager learns of these regulations during orientation to the job, as do all staff members, and assumes responsibility to learn of new changes. The leader is responsible for assessing at regular intervals each member's understanding of safety regulations should a fire, earthquake, tornado, or other disaster occur. Instruction in handling equipment, using proper procedures, and working with dangerous drugs requires reinforcement, as unused knowledge and skills are quickly forgotten.

Considering need for variety in assignment and for development of personnel. Primary consideration is given to assigning staff members to patients / clients so that the most effective use is made of each member's knowledge and abilities. In addition, the nurse leader is concerned with the growth in knowledge and improvement of skills of each member. Variation in assignment provides nurses with the opportunity to "expand their capabilities, enrich their day-to-day work experience, increase their self esteem, and enhance their career potential.[13]" Further, employees who perform multiple assignments demonstrate increased motivation and productivity as well as increased interest in the organization in general. The leader may also arrange for each member to spend some time in advanced preparation through on-the-job instruction, inservice classes, or workshops. An assignment that is limited to a narrow span of care inhibits growth of the staff member and proves costly to the institution, because the employee's potential is not being used.

Providing for leader's availability to staff members for assistance, teaching, counsel, and evaluation. The process of overseeing nursing activities requires the presence of the nurse in the area of action. For a nurse leader, being available means being accessible and of some value to others. The leader is to be ready and willing to provide assistance whenever necessary (or delegate the needed help to another) to teach a procedure, relay knowledge, supervise a nursing function about which a member feels insecure, offer advice with patient / client or staff problems, and evaluate the member's performance. It is for these reasons that the leader's personal assign-

ment should be restricted to activities that will permit being in the mainstream of activity, such as administering medications or giving treatments.

Trusting members to follow through with their assignments. It is possible for a nurse manager who assigns roles and tasks to nursing staff according to sound criteria to feel secure in the knowledge that directions will be carried out to the best of the members' abilities. But success in directing others depends greatly on the attitude of the nurse manager toward the nursing personnel led, as the manager's attitude will dictate the approach taken. As McGregor's Theories X and Y suggest,[14] one manager may be convinced that most human beings have an inherent dislike of work and will seek to avoid it. Another may believe nursing staff enjoy their work and in fact want to work as a part of their basic nature. These differing opinions will result in one manager's using coercion to get work done whereas another manager relies to a larger extent on trusting the member's own initiative.

The attitudes of most nurse managers probably lie somewhere between these opposites. Promotion of an atmosphere of trust allows team members to function on an independent-dependent basis. The staff member is independent in the sense that after the assignment is given, task accomplishment can proceed with some liberty in deciding such things as in what order tasks will be done and in using individual judgment about matters that are not programmed already. The staff member is dependent in the sense that the nurse leader still controls the management of the work group and is available for help and guidance.

Interpreting protocol for responding to incidental requests. All tasks that require much time and have not already been delegated, such as incidental requests from physicians, special technicians, and other staff members, should be channeled through the charge nurse or team leader as appropriate for distribution. The practice of centralized control of these incidental requests by the lower or first-level manager (1) identifies a single channel for command to staff members, (2) keeps the nurse leader informed of all activities, (3) allows for allocation of tasks to the most capable and/or available person, and (4) protects staff members from excessive demands on their time and energy. A physician who asks a favorite nurse to assist with an extensive treatment for a patient not assigned to her disrupts the completion of assignment if the nurse complies without consulting with the charge nurse or team leader.

Explaining procedure to be followed in emergencies. There are always some uncertainties in nursing. This is particularly true in acute treatment areas, but no unit is exempt from crises. Anything can happen—an accident, a hemorrhage, an extreme reaction to a medication or treatment, or a cardiac arrest. It is extremely important for nursing staff members to know that in times of emergency, autocratic rule prevails. The nurse in charge (head nurse, team leader, or other) assumes command of the situation, directing activities until the crisis is past. If this person is not available, the next best qualified person takes over. Other staff members are to remain in their assigned areas, ready to respond for service as needed. Excited personnel do little to alleviate already tense situations in patient/client care areas.

Members of the nursing staff need to know in advance what their responsibilities are in case of emergency. Specific instructions are given at regular intervals in conferences and in special sessions, such as fire and disaster drills. In times of patient/client emergency the staff member present at the time of emergency calls for help on the intercommunication system. If there is no other way to get assistance, another person can be sent for aid, or the staff member can simply call out for help. In the meantime, that staff member will begin emergency measures as appropriate according to protocol and capability, especially when a life may be threatened for lack of action.

Giving clear and concise formal and informal directions. Individual and group effort requires direction if it is to be successful in attaining individual and group ends. Each member of the nursing group must have the information required to execute her assignment. To this end, the information needed for good performance is made known to all staff members through

instructions and orders that are recognized as official. Instructions are given through formal procedures, such as the assignment sheet, one-to-one instructions, records, and the direction-giving conference. Other methods of direction giving are informal, such as orders given to the members by the leader as incidental needs arise. Whether written or verbal, given formally or informally, all orders imparted from a nurse leader to a group member are to elicit response.

Complete and undistorted communication between two or more people is more an ideal than a reality; yet there are many concepts and techniques that can be used to improve communication in the process of giving instruction (see Chapter 8).

A report from nursing staff going off duty usually involves staff members listening to the report from the off-duty staff, jotting down notes about individual assignments, and recording information pertaining to all other patients assigned to the nursing team. Ideally, staff members of the team going off duty provide coverage for the incoming staff so that they may listen to the report without interruption. A conference room where all members can be seated facing each other increases the probability of note taking and encourages free exchange of information. The report of the staff going off duty usually takes approximately 20 minutes for a team taking care of about 15 patients, depending on the complexity of the cases and characteristics of the nurses giving and receiving the report. The procedure is helped by following a routine format for giving information (e.g., room number, patient's/client's name, diagnosis, physician, treatments, medications, nursing care problems, and so on). Clarification of details can occur as each patient is discussed. Care must be taken to allow time for adequate coverage of priority items. A more detailed account of conference technique is presented later in this chapter.

Taping shift reports is an inexpensive and simple mechanism that can be used to provide information and direction about patients/clients and to alert the incoming shift as to needs. These tapes can be prepared at a time convenient to the staff and can be listened to by the incoming staff without the usual distractions that often occur during report time (telephone, last-minute medications, and so on). Taping shift reports saves time, because nurses tend to organize their reports more concisely when they know their voices will be recorded, and irrelevant chatter is absent. In total, primary, and functional nursing systems each incoming staff/nurse listens to the taped report and takes notes on the assigned patients/clients. In team nursing only the team leaders listen, as relevant information about all patients/clients assigned to the team will be relayed by the leader to the team members during the direction-giving conferences. Time for questions, answers, and clarification with the staff going off duty is set aside after the report.

There are further advantages to taping a shift report. If there is need for clarification, the questioner can replay the tape for the answer, and if a staff member's tour of duty begins after the report was listened to, she can hear the report individually. The recorder should follow these guidelines when taping reports:

1. Organize report well before beginning.
2. Introduce self at beginning of tape.
3. Speak slowly and clearly so that accurate notes can be taken.
4. Give patient's/client's room number, name, age (if appropriate), diagnosis, and physician's name.
5. Provide a brief systematic account of each patient's/client's condition, including new or changed orders.
6. Refer to vital signs, temperature elevations, intravenous fluids, and intake and output, as relevant.
7. Indicate names of all pain medications, number of times they should be given, and last time they were given.
8. Cover necessary information about preoperative patients/clients; that is, chart in order, preoperative teaching done, time of preoperative medications, and so on.
9. Give information about postoperative patients/clients; for example, time of arrival from operating or recovery room; general condition; vital signs; IVs (kind, rate of flow, fluids to follow, and so on); dressings; voiding; diet; tolerance; nature of breathing; coughing; and number, position, and patency of tubes.
10. Sign off, noting any issues you may have overlooked or would like to discuss with incoming staff members after they have heard the recording.

After the report is given, a nurse who is learning how to tape-record properly should take a worksheet, listen to the report and record necessary information as if she were the nurse receiving the information for the incoming shift. This exercise will help identify strengths and weaknesses for improvement in report giving. These same guidelines for presenting comprehensive coverage for a group of patients/clients can be used by a nurse leader in giving information face-to-face. The didactic method presents information matter-of-factly and clearly, enabling the incoming leader and staff to apply the information to individual and group plans.

Nurse-to-nurse communication can be upgraded significantly by reporting and discussing patient care at the bedside during *walking rounds* rather than by reporting from nurse to nurse in an isolated patient's room. This method is more easily accomplished in primary nursing, because fewer people are involved, but it is possible to manage with modifications with larger groups (e.g., the team leader could have walking rounds with an LPN or aide).

In the direction-giving conference the nurse leader meets with the entire nursing group for 15 to 20 minutes in a quiet, undisturbed environment to apprise the members more fully of their assignments for the day. These assignments will have been posted as quickly as possible after staff members, coming on duty to allow them to begin the rudiments of their work while waiting for more specific instructions. Members of an alternate nursing team or group will cover for these members during their conference, as designated on the assignment sheet. The direction-giving conference is dominated primarily by the leader's giving instructions to the group in preparation for the completion of individual and group assignments. Time is limited; therefore the leader must impart the necessary information to the members quickly and well. Following are behavioral objectives a nurse leader may follow to ensure a successful direction-giving conference:

1. Prepare thoroughly before meeting with the nursing personnel.
   a. Prepare a detailed worksheet that (1) contains all known pertinent information; (2) indicates areas of priority, special concerns, and need for additional information; and (3) allows space for updating data as necessary (refer to sample worksheet provided in Figure 7-2).
   b. Receive report from those who have had prior responsibility for patient/client services; update worksheet.
   c. Check pertinent data, such as tests, preoperative orders, and special treatments, or confer with head nurse or physician as needed; update worksheet.
   d. Visit all patients/clients briefly for individual assessment; make necessary notations on worksheet.
   e. Make patient/client care assignments according to criteria for effective assignment making.
2. Organize conference activity for efficiency and conservation of time.
   a. Keep to the same time schedule for at least a week at a time if possible. Begin and end the meeting according to schedule. This provides for continuity of work and gives all members opportunity to develop a routine.
   b. Seat all members to provide for comfort and to encourage recording of information on individual worksheets.
   c. Introduce self and group members to one another as needed. Composition of nursing groups changes frequently in some settings, and giving names and role identification in a warm, friendly atmosphere promotes group morale and facilitates comprehension.
   d. Ask that each member record relevant information pertaining to *all* patients/clients assigned to the team, not just that pertaining to her individual assignment, to allow for informed coverage for all other members. It is very helpful to have worksheets containing basic information (name, age, diagnosis, physician, diet, and activity) ready for nursing personnel when they report for duty. These sheets may be prepared by computer services or by clerical staff on the previous shift. Having basic information available reduces the amount of time spent in recording and enables the members to listen better and to clarify directions, thus reducing the high possibility of error when many people transcribe directions at one time.
   e. Use the procedure and pace that are right for the purpose and nurses. Use direct, simple language. The more accurately words and phrases are tailored to the level of the receivers, the more effective communication is likely to be. A certain amount of redundancy may be necessary in direction giving. If a message is very important or complicated, it is probably necessary to repeat it in a different way, possibly adding the reason for the procedure. Unnecessary repetition should be avoided, because it will dull the receiver's attention. Speak clearly, adjusting the pace to the receivers' preference and needs, allowing accurate recording of necessary information. Directions should proceed systematically. For example, it is most effective to offer information according to the format of the worksheet (e.g., name, age, physician, diagnosis, diet, activity, intake and output IVs, and so on) with instructions and explanations given after each item as needed. Irregularity in presentation increases the time spent in recording and also increases the probability of transcribing misinformation.
   f. Include all information necessary for individual and group members to hear. The direction giver does not need to repeat all information already known or provided on the worksheet, as time is better spent in reviewing items that require reinforcement or elaboration. Documented, well-written nursing care plans provide detailed information on who, what, when, where, and how. However, enough information should be included to help the group understand what is needed to function together with purpose and harmony.

g. Use feedback, looking for verbal and nonverbal cues from receivers. The more complex the information, the more essential it is that receivers are encouraged to ask questions and indicate areas of confusion. For example, the direction-giving process breaks down when the team leader instructs, "Give Buerger's exercises to Mr. Fletcher for 15 minutes at 10 and 2," and the caregiver duly records the order on the worksheet without understanding it. If time is limited or certain items are not relevant to the total group, the leader may note items needing clarification and attend to these matters later with individual staff members.

h. Leave group members with the belief that the leader is available to them for assistance. This allows members to address uncertainties about their assignments with assurance that support and help will be forthcoming if needed.

Informal direction giving by the nurse leader for patients/clients assigned to the group is necessary from time to time. As the delivery of nursing care proceeds, matters arise that may not have been anticipated in time for the direction-giving conference, or they may simply have been overlooked. Nursing staff members should expect some interruptions in completion of assignments. Give additional tasks to the staff member assigned to the area in which the action is to occur. For example, if a new treatment is ordered, the nurse assigned to care for the patient/client will be asked to administer it, or if a patient needs more assistance than one nurse can provide and there is no double coverage assigned to that patient, the leader will ask the nurse nearest to that locale to provide assistance, keeping in mind other factors of assignment making, such as overassignment versus underassignment.

Using a management control process that assesses the quality of care given and evaluates individual and group performance given by nursing personnel. Management control is the continuous process through which nurse managers assure that actual activities conform to planned activities. This definition points to the close link between planning and controlling individual and group activities. In the planning process the fundamental standards and objectives of the overall organization and separate nursing units and the method for obtaining them are established. Such standards and objectives can be in the form of quality measures, quantity, time, cost, and performance. They identify and assess specific conditions, behaviors, the environment in which nursing activities occur, and the criteria of acceptable conditions and behavior. The control process measures progress toward those standards and objectives, enabling managers to detect deviations from the plan so that they can take whatever remedial action is necessary, including a change in plan. Chapter 10 discusses the control process for nursing care and performance of workers in greater detail.

SUMMARY

1. Direction is the connecting link between organizing for work and work accomplishment.
2. Directing is issuing assignments, orders, and instructions that permit the worker to know what is expected of him or her and guiding and overseeing the work.
3. Work flow, equipment, and techniques and procedures used to complete work assignments are the technical aspects of directing.
4. At the lower or first-level of management, the number of people who report directly to a manager represents the managerial span of control. The larger the span of control, the greater the hierarchy; with a lesser span of control, there is greater decentralization.
5. The span of management depends on standards of care, kinds of patients/clients, numbers and kinds of nursing staff needed, capabilities of the nurse leader, and the leader's responsibilities.
6. The physical support system includes space, equipment, and physical environment provided. There is great variation among health care facilities. A nurse manager's task is to work with prevailing circumstances toward desired adaptations and changes.
7. Delegation of responsibilities includes the

regulation of activities, correction of problems, prevention of problems, and promotion of quality care through growth and development of nursing personnel.

8. Delegating well-defined tasks and responsibilities to staff members frees managers to give time to other important activities and also serves as a helpful management training and developmental tool. Lack of delegation can stifle initiative.

9. Barriers to delegation include lack of trust in others; low self-confidence; vague job descriptions; and fear of competition, risk taking, and relinquishing control.

10. Effective delegation of activities considers goals of the agency, gives first priority to needs and problems of the patients/clients, and provides for coordination and efficiency among departments that provide support services.

11. Direction giving is best handled by one person for one group, with the leader having authority to act.

12. In the functional nursing system the charge nurse makes assignments and gives direction to all nursing personnel assigned to the nursing unit. The primary purpose is to accomplish tasks with the greatest efficiency, making personal attention to patient/client needs difficult.

13. Team nursing provides a mechanism in which the charge nurse relinquishes responsibility for assignment making and direction giving to team leaders whose primary purpose is to match the staff members to patients/clients according to their needs and problems.

14. In primary nursing an RN or LPN/LVN is delegated responsibility and accountability for planning, giving, and communicating all phases of care for a patient or group of patients from the time of admission through discharge.

15. Modular nursing is a modification of team and primary nursing. The system differs from team nursing in that the registered nurse provides direct care to assigned patients with the assistance of nurses' aide(s).

16. In case management, delegation of responsibilities extend beyond the traditional nursing unit or shift-specific boundaries by focusing on the patient's entire episode of illness, from before admission, through the hospital stay, to care following dismissal.

17. Case managers develop a critical path, which reviews step-by-step the care the patient receives and its cost, and compares this with predetermined standards for that treatment.

18. Determination of patient/client needs and problems is accomplished through current nursing care plans, the patient/client, people of significance to the patient, physician, records, reports, and caregivers.

19. Preparation of a comprehensive worksheet provides data for assignment making and guidelines for activities of the nursing team.

20. Effective assignments assure continuous coverage for all nursing staff (RNs, LPNs/LVNs, nurse assistants), with specific guidelines for all absences from work (coffee and lunch breaks, conferences, and so on).

21. Nursing personnel should not be required to engage in nonnursing activities, such as cleaning the kitchen and utility rooms; however, the supportive systems that are required should be assigned on a rotational basis. Protocol is established for response to incidental requests.

22. All nursing assignments consider safety standards, regulations, mechanism for handling emergency situations, and the need of patients/clients to have continuous care given by the same nursing staff as much as possible.

23. Variety in assignments enables nurse members to identify needs and interests and develop their potential, thus becoming versatile and valuable staff members.

24. Directions for work accomplishment for a group of patients/clients by a group of nursing personnel are managed through the mechanisms of one-to-one instructions, tape-recorded reports, in-person reports, and formal conferences.

25. For all direction giving the leader is to be well prepared, organized, and friendly; should present information in a clear, con-

cise manner; elicit feedback; and leave the receivers with a feeling of confidence in themselves and in the leader's availability to provide necessary assistance.

26. Control of nursing care and work perfor-

mance is a continuous process through which nurse managers assure that actual activities conform to planned activities. Activities and behaviors are measured against predetermined criteria.

Questions for Study and Discussion

1. If you were a nurse manager, would a small or large scope of responsibility appeal to you? Why?
2. If you were asked the question, "What is the right span of control?" how would you respond?
3. Explain the differences between regulatory, corrective, and preventive managerial responsibilities.
4. The department manager feels insecure in preparing the departmental budget and so delegates the procedure to the assistant manager, who understands the hospital system and enjoys working with figures. Do you agree with the department manager's decision? Explain your response.
5. Of the reasons given by managers for not delegating as much responsibility as they

should, with which of them do you identify? What procedure might you follow to overcome the difficulty?
6. Select one of the systems used for delivery of nursing care. Explain its basic structure and use of nursing personnel.
7. Which nursing care delivery system appeals to you? Why?
8. Which of the nursing care delivery systems is least attractive to you? Why?
9. As team leader for 12 patients, you arrive to work one-half hour late. You decide to catch up by giving only the absolutely necessary information to your team members for work accomplishment. Your rationale is that they are all experienced workers and will know what to do. Do you think this is an appropriate choice of action? Why?

REFERENCES

1. Kreitner R: Management, ed 4, Boston, 1987, Houghton Mifflin Co.
2. Grove A: High output management, New York, 1983, Random House.
3. Hellriegel D and Slocum J: Management, ed 5, Reading, Mass, 1989, Addison-Wesley Publishing Co.
4. Longest B: Management practices for the health professional, ed 4, Norwalk, Conn, 1990, Appleton & Lange.
5. Robbins S: Organization theory: structure, design, and applications, Englewood Cliffs, NJ, 1990, Prentice-Hall.
6. Wake M: Nursing care delivery systems: status and vision, JONA 20(5):47-51, 1990.
7. Christensen P and Kenney J: The nursing process: application of theories, frameworks and models, ed 3, St Louis, 1990, Mosby–Year Book, Inc.
8. Tappen M: Nursing leadership and management: concepts and practice, ed 2, Philadelphia, 1989, FA Davis Co.
9. Bennett M and Hylton J: Modular nursing: partners in professional practice, Nurs Man 21(3):20-24, 1990.
10. Weil M: Historical origins and recent developments: case management in human services practice, San Francisco, 1985, Jossey-Bass.
11. Salmond S: In-hospital case management, Orthop Nurs 9(1):39, 1990.
12. McKenzie C, Torkelson N, and Holt M: Care and cost: nursing case management improves both, Nurs Man 20(19):30-34, 1989.
13. Distasio C: How to delegate effectively, Health Care Supervisor 3(4):69, 1985.
14. McGregor D: The human side of enterprise, New York, 1960, McGraw-Hill Book Co.

SUGGESTED READINGS

Adams C: Leadership behavior of chief nurse executives (delegation) Nurs Man 21(8):36-39, 1990.

Berry J: How many crises can a good nurse conquer?
Nurs Man 21(9):29-30, 1990.

Bice-Stephens N: 7 ways to sharpen your leadership
skills, Nursing 89 19(10):130-135, 1989.

Coker E and Schrieber R: The nurse's role in a team
conference, Nurs Man 21(3):46-48, 1990.

Donnelly L, Yarbrough D, and Jaffe H: Organizational management systems decrease nursing costs
(shift change report), Nurs Man 20(7):20-21, 1989.

Manthey M: Trust: essential for delegation, Nurs
Man 21(11):28-31, 1990.

Murphy J and Burke L: Charting by exception: a
more efficient way to document, Nursing 90
20(5):65-69, 1990.

Potect G: Nursing administration and delegation,
Nurs Admin Q 13(3):23-32, 1989.

Practice briefs: Making yourself perfectly clear,
Nursing 90 20(2):86-87, 1990.

Short B: Making the most of your time. . . by involving others, Nursing 90 20(1):99-104, 1990.

Undermanaging, overmanaging and managing that's
just right, J Nurs 90(7):18A-18E, 1990.

8

Communication Process

_____ **BEHAVIORAL OBJECTIVES** _____

On completion of this chapter the student will be prepared to:

☐ Differentiate between interpersonal and organizational communication and indicate the importance of the communication process.
☐ Diagram and define the steps in an effective communication model.
☐ Offer guidelines that promote effective feedback.
☐ Identify barriers to effective communication in nursing service and describe ways to overcome them.
☐ Define the informal or "grapevine" channel of communication and recognize positive and negative features of the system.
☐ Describe the channels of communication in management.
☐ Explain the impact of computers on contemporary nursing and the prospects for computer uses in the future.

Leadership and management are achieved through effective communication. Just because managers spend most of their time communicating does not necessarily mean they are effective communicators. Eric Skopec, director of the Southern California School of Business Administration, records words from an experienced manager: "Over the years, I've seen lots of bright young men and women move into management. That step always demands growth and it is never an easy one. . . . I know from experience that some make it and some don't. The one thing that seems to make a difference is how well a new manager gets along with his or her people. If the relationship is good, they learn whatever they have to. If the relationship is bad, no amount of technical skill can make up the difference."[1]

Communication is the process whereby a message is passed from sender to receiver with the hope that the information exchanged will be understood as the sender intended. One difficulty with the communication process is that people are seldom totally effective in transmitting their intended meanings to others, frequently sending messages not intended. Medication and treatment errors and policy infractions are often the result of ineffective communication. Unfortunately, the action taken to resolve these errors usually centers on resolution of the error, with no attempt to study the faulty communication process that exists in the clinical setting. The goal of communication is to narrow the gap between the intended message and the received message. Nurse managers can accomplish this goal by understanding the communication process, which will enable them to identify, define, and resolve communication problems.

Communication is the key process that enables the nurse in a middle management position to serve as a role model of exemplary care to clients, direct subordinates, challenge peers to produce, and support higher management. In its broadest sense the purpose of communication is to effect change and to influence action toward the welfare of the clinical setting.

Nurse managers are involved in two kinds of communication: interpersonal and organizational. *Interpersonal communication* is the process of exchanging information and meaning either from one person to another, or in small groups of people. *Organizational communication* is the process whereby managers use the established communication system to receive and relay information to people within the organization as well as to relevant individuals and groups outside the organization. A nurse manager works toward creating an environment that promotes ease in communication among individuals and groups within the formal and informal communication systems.

This chapter considers the importance of the communication process in organizations and in the nurse manager's role. Models of interpersonal communication are presented, followed by barriers to effective communication and suggested ways these barriers can be overcome. The informal channel of communication in organizations is discussed, emphasizing positive and negative features. Management functions and communications are explored from the downward, upward, and horizontal perspectives. Computerized data processing is introduced, with emphasis on the nurse manager's role now and in the future.

IMPORTANCE OF THE COMMUNICATION PROCESS

The communication process is the foundation on which nursing management achieves organizational objectives. Since managers carry out their responsibilities through others, all management functions of planning, organizing, directing, and controlling must pass through the communication channel. The communication channel can be used by nurse managers as a basis for planning and delegating. Organization requires communication with nursing personnel about job assignments. Directing requires nurse managers to communicate with workers for individual and group goal achievement. Written or verbal communications are an essential part of controlling and evaluating the nurse's delivery of care. In short, nurse managers do not manage in isolation; they carry out all management functions by constantly interacting and communicating with others.

Nurse managers spend most of their time communicating. Managers spend most of their work time communicating, giving information, and implementing decisions.[2] Nurse managers are rarely alone while thinking, planning, or contemplating action. In fact, a large amount of the nurse manager's time is spent in face-to-face communication with nursing personnel, physicians, supervisors, people in supportive services, or patients/clients. When not conferring with others, nurse managers may be recording information, monitoring the development of nursing care plans, preparing schedules and reports, or reading orders, memorandums, and reports. Even in those few periods when nurse managers are alone, they are frequently interrupted by communication from others.

Good communication motivates staff members. Staff participation and interest is positively influenced by good communication. Sharing information of mutual interest and benefit to the group gives vital support to an employee's sense of belonging. Nurse managers can enhance motivation by explaining plans and reasons for their actions, and by asking for feedback in the form of questions, clarification, or suggestions.

For example: The nurse manager says to a nurse on her staff, "Jennifer, I have been asked to select someone from our department to serve on the case manager committee. This would be a new system in delivery of nursing care for many patients. The role would be broader in scope than the primary care system we use. The case manager would not replace primary nurses, but would work with them to conserve costs and to improve the quality of care. Would you be interested in serving on this committee?"

Jennifer is given information regarding the possible creation of the case manager position in advance of other staff, as well as the opportunity to accept a challenging role on the committee responsible for developing the position. This timely communication may motivate Jennifer to respond affirmatively.

Communication leads to influence and power. When nurse managers share information with individuals and groups and communicate that information effectively, they are more apt to be viewed as individuals who exert influence. Nursing has a great deal of potential to effect changes in health care. Yet because nursing is primarily a women's profession, attempts to use this potential can lead to power struggles. The traditional role for the nurse has been one of subservience and of service to others. Nurses need to learn to develop effective communication skills so that they are able to articulate their ideas, control their environment, and achieve results. These accomplishments will, in turn, increase their self-esteem and, consequently, the esteem of the profession.

Because nurse managers are in a central location within the communication network, they are able to acquire vast amounts of information, to use that information to achieve organizational goals and objectives, and to provide opportunity for workers to grow personally and professionally. There is direct relationship between power and position; that is, persons in a central position with high status in the communication system can receive and give more messages and exert greater influence than can people with lower status. For example, the director of nursing services can influence the board of directors to open a new wing of the hospital or to achieve an across-the-board increase in nurses' salaries. The lower- or first-level nurse manager can exert influence to institute a treatment or to change the entire direction of the nursing care plan. Through effective communication the nurse manager can influence nursing supervisors to adopt a different system for delivery of care or to add another member to the nursing staff.

Communication of power can result in a chain reaction. The nurse manager who feels secure in personal skills and abilities will be likely to release power to others through work delegation, thus creating an atmosphere in which staff members feel secure and capable of assuming responsibility for their work. As a result, productivity will rise and more goals will be achieved.

GUIDELINES FOR EFFECTIVE COMMUNICATION
Communication Model

It is easy to tell people that they should be good communicators; it is much more difficult to tell them *how* to be good communicators. Figure 8-1 reflects the basic elements of the communication process: sender, receiver, message, encoding, transmitting, decoding, action, and feedback.[3]

Sender and receiver. The sender is the source of information and the initiator of the communication process. The sender tries to choose the type of message and channel (such as computer, telephone, written memo) that will be most effective to meet the needs of the receiver. The receiver is the person who receives the sender's message and translates it into a form that has meaning.

Message. Senders must have something to say before they send a message. The first step for the sender is to choose a fact, concept, idea, or feeling to communicate. This is the content of communication; it is the basis of a *message*. In an organization the nurse manager is a person with needs, feelings, information, and a purpose for communicating them. A nurse manager wishes to communicate information about patients/clients or organizational matters for the purpose of informing or motivating other members of the nursing team. Without a reason or goal, the sender has no need to begin the communication process.

For example: During a staff meeting, the nurse manager presents a new concept: "As you may know, our agency is investigating the pros and cons of using case managers throughout the hospital." (The manager knows that information travels quickly. She wants the staff to receive a correct message, that a final decision has

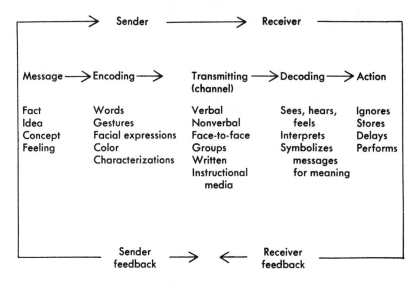

Figure 8-1. The communication process.

not yet been made.) "I have asked Jennifer to serve on the planning committee; she will serve as the liaison between you and the planning committee."

Encoding. The second step, *encoding,* means translating the message into words, gestures, facial expression, and other symbols that will communicate the intended meaning to the receivers. Words have many meanings. It has been pointed out that each of the 500 most often used words in the English language has approximately 28 different meanings. The meanings of words are determined not only by dictionary definitions, but also by the way they are used in a sentence and by the context and setting in which they are used. All communication uses symbols to represent persons or things.

It must be kept in mind that only the symbols are transmitted. The meaning received depends upon the receiver's interpretation of those symbols. For example, the cross has special meaning to Christian people, just as the Star of David has to Jewish people. To some, the color red symbolizes happiness; to others, it is a color linked with prostitution. Black is a symbol of conservatism to many; to others it is equated with death. Words, gestures, facial expressions, and all other symbols are learned through the influence of parents, culture, school, religious

affiliation, friends, and employment. Communication is never perfect because none of the symbols used in communication has universal meaning.

Encoding the message requires decisions not only about what will be said, but how, when, and where it will be said. Encoding may also involve decisions about expressing or concealing emotion. Effective communication depends on the appropriate degree of intensity for the message. The nurse manager may, for example, decide not to show fear or frustration and to communicate in a matter-of-fact, unemotional manner while working in an emergency or situation of crisis. The manager may ultimately decide to talk with patients/clients and nursing personnel later, tailoring the message to the circumstances of each, communicating with them informally or formally as the appropriate occasion arises.

The following concepts should be understood by nurses who want to encode messages well: (1) words mean different things to different people, (2) the message should be encoded in the simplest terms, (3) if complex, the message should be expressed in several ways, and (4) the language used should reflect the personality, culture, and values of the receiver.[4] Effective encoding depends on a clear message delivered at the right pace and phrased in such a way as to attract the receiver's attention. Encoding may occur within a few seconds, as when one person greets another with a "Hi" rather than with a more formal greeting. Regardless of the time required and the degree of conscious planning, the transmission of a message depends on proper encoding.

For example: The nurse manager presents information regarding case management in a positive tone of voice: "Case management, if used in this hospital, will mean that nurses who have at least a bachelor's degree and who receive the necessary training will be responsible for managing care of patients in selected DRG categories from the time of their admission through at least 2 weeks of care. The case manager will work closely with the primary nurses, some of whom will become associate case managers, a function very similar to that of the associate primary nurse, but with an expanded role. I believe the system would benefit the hospital in that costs would be more carefully controlled and we would give more efficient nursing care."

Transmitting. As shown in Figure 8-1, *transmitting* is the channel used to communicate a message, that is, what form it will take. A manager would certainly use different language in a phone call than in a formal report. The number of receivers to be addressed is also important. Usually, the greater the number of receivers, the more formal the language should be. The message may be in any form that can be experienced and understood by one or more of the receiver's senses—speech may be heard, written words may be read, and gestures or facial expressions may be seen or felt. A touch of the hand may communicate messages ranging from love and comfort to anger and hate. A wave of the hand can communicate widely diverse messages, depending on the position ("Come here!" or "Get lost!"). Nonverbal messages are often more honest or meaningful than verbal or written exchanges. For instance, the patient or client who smiles and laughs while saying, "I have an unbearable headache" and the staff member who frowns and is uncooperative while saying "Everything is fine" are transmitting nonverbal messages that are different from the spoken word.

In addition to verbal and nonverbal messages, instructional media can be used effectively to transmit information. Client records, charts, computer printouts, articles, books, slides, overhead transparencies, videocassette tapes, and films are resources often used.

For example: For staff meetings the nurse prepares visual materials, explaining, "I have brought an organizational chart to show how case managers might function throughout our hospital and community and what our roles would be in the new system. I have also brought copies of articles on how the case manager system works in similar hospitals. I'll leave them in this room for you to read. After you have read and talked about case management with one another, bring your reactions and questions to Jennifer or me and come to our next meeting prepared to talk about it further. Be thinking about whether or not you would be interested in becoming a case manager or an associate case manager."

Decoding. In the *decoding* step of the communication process, the initiative transfers from the sender to the receiver, who perceives and interprets or decodes the sender's message into information that has meaning. Ideally, the information communicated consists of what the sender believes the receiver should know and what the receiver wants to know. Understanding is the key to the decoding process. Words and symbols have multiple meanings, and there is no assurance that the intended meanings of the sender have been encoded to mean the same thing to the receiver who decodes or interprets them.

The decoding process is affected by the receiver's experiences, personal interpretations of the symbols used, expectations, and mutuality of meaning with the sender. Normally, receivers make a genuine attempt to understand the intended message. Even with the best of intentions, however, a receiver may not understand the intended message because perceptions of the two people are different. As shown in Figure 8-2, the more experiences the sender and receiver have in common, the more likely it is that the sender's intended meaning will be communicated. In order for people with different experiences to communicate they must have a shared language. Nurse managers who aspire to

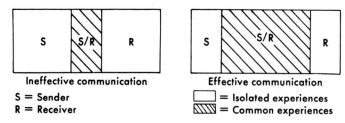

Figure 8-2. Effectiveness of communication depends on commonality of experiences.

communicate with members of the nursing staff with varied fields of preparation and experience must learn how they think, feel, and respond in a variety of nursing situations. By applying such knowledge, nurse managers are usually able to predict with acceptable accuracy how a given message will be decoded.

For example: Following the group meeting and before the nursing staff has read the articles, several nurses express fear: "Those of us who don't have bachelor's degrees are going to lose our jobs"; "I don't see why we need to change; we are getting along fine with primary nursing"; "They must not think we are doing a good job." Jennifer helps to allay fears: "The way I see it, we will all have a chance to do more for our patients. We'll know more about them and we will be able to contribute toward cutting costs by identifying duplication of services and instances when the patient might benefit from other services, or by going home sooner to the care of other professionals and / or family members. We could learn a lot from case managers since they will be clinical specialists in our area of care. I realize that this potential change may be frightening. Reading the articles may help reduce your concerns. After you've read them, we'll talk more."

Action. *Action,* the next step in the communication process, is the behavior taken by the receiver as a result of the message sent, received, and perceived. Action is the process of doing or performing something; it is behaving or functioning in a certain way. The sender of a message has no guarantee that what has been heard and decoded will be put into the action intended. The receiver may listen but may or may not choose to act on the message. Many nurse managers overlook this important fact when giving instructions or explanations. They assume that merely giving a staff member a message ensures that the intended action will take place. Communication is not successful until the message received has been understood and acted upon appropriately.

Several options are available to the receiver once a message has been received: (1) ignore the information and fail to act, (2) store it as reference material until choosing to respond, (3) respond by saying one thing and doing another (credibility gap), or (4) respond to the message according to the receiver's interpretation.

For example: Five of the six staff nurses heed Jennifer's suggestion to read the articles. The sixth goes about her work disconsolately, expressing negative feelings about the proposed change of delivery system.

Feedback. The communication process is not complete until the last step, *feedback,* occurs. Feedback is an integral part of the communication process whereby senders and receivers exchange information and clarify the meanings of the message sent. Two-way rather than one-way communication allows both sender and receiver to search for verbal and nonverbal cues. Effective two-way communication occurs when a receiver acknowledges a message and then sends meaningful feedback to the sender. The more complex the information the nurse manager is trying to communicate, the more essential it is to encourage receivers to ask questions and to indicate areas of confusion throughout the entire communication process.

Feedback may be in direct and indirect forms, both verbal and nonverbal. Behaviors such as recording information in a direction-giving conference, nods of acknowledgement, smiles, and movements to accomplish the given task offer one kind of feedback. On the other hand, actions such as a blank stare, lack of motion to respond, or a frown provide quite different feedback. For nurse managers, feedback serves as a control measure. In most organizational communications, the greater the feedback, the more effective the communication is likely to be. For example, early feedback will enable a nurse team leader to know whether the instructions given team members have been understood and accepted. Without such feedback the nurse manager might not know until it is too late whether the instructions given were accurately received and carried out.

For example: In the process of reviewing the articles on case management in other hospitals, and in discussing their reactions with one another, Jennifer and the unit managers, most nurses become convinced that case management is worth trying. They ask Jennifer to seek clarification regarding just how the primary nurse will relate with the case manager, and if the primary nurse will be stripped of her authority. The sixth nurse is drawn reluctantly into the discussion.

Characteristics of effective feedback. The following guidelines are offered as means to ensure that feedback between managers and staff is effective.[5]

1. *Feedback should be well timed.* Feedback is most effective when it closely follows the behavior on which it is focused. Giving feedback to a nurse at a departmental party is altogether different from giving feedback in a private setting.

Poor timing. At a party, the department manager laughs in the presence of others and says, "Mary you sure goofed up today when you went off to lunch at the wrong time. We had no coverage for you—we had to scramble."

Good timing. After Mary returns from lunch, the department manager takes her aside and asks, "Mary, did you misunderstand the schedule?" Together they explore the situation and identify ways to prevent it from recurring.

2. *Feedback should be targeted to specific behaviors.* A description of what was noted, given without overtones of personal judgment, may help an individual to respond without anger or resentment. Feedback should always be related to performance goals, not personality traits.

Inappropriate targeting. "Mary, the staff members are angry with you because of your thoughtlessness, and I agree with them."

Appropriate targeting. "Mary, you took your lunch hour at a time that was not scheduled. Was there a misunderstanding?"

3. *Feedback should be tactful.* Messages that take into consideration the feelings of another are more likely to be heard than those that are abrasive and accusing.

Tactless feedback. "Mary, how could you have put us in such a spot? You were thinking only of yourself when you went off to lunch at the wrong time."

Tactful feedback. "Mary, it is not like you to leave us in a jam. Was there a mixup in the schedule?"

BARRIERS TO EFFECTIVE COMMUNICATION

Communication in an organization is a difficult process because of the many organizational and interpersonal aspects that must be considered. Comprehending barriers common to communicating in health care facilities and taking steps to minimize them improves a nurse manager's ability to communicate effectively. There are three broad types of barriers occurring in nursing services: (1) physical, (2) social-psychologic, and (3) interpretation of meanings, or semantics.[6]

Physical Barriers

Physical barriers are environmental factors that prevent or reduce opportunities for the communication process to occur. Some examples include physical space or distance, temperature and ventilation, structural or equipment problems, and distracting noise. As mentioned previously, face-to-face communication offers the best means for confirmation that the message has been received as intended. A greater space or distance between the sender and receiver reduces opportunity to clarify intention. Conversation in close proximity to the persons involved increases the probability that the message will be received correctly. Room temperature has an impact upon communication. Extreme cold or heat may be distracting and affect communication. The presence or absence of walls and equipment influences the kind of communication possible. Most of these barriers are relatively easy to correct or adapt to should they exist.

Noise. Noise is an integral part of the communication process and may influence the process at any or all points. Noise is any disturbance, especially a random and personal disturbance, that obscures or reduces clarity or quality of a message. Static on a telephone line causing a message to be garbled, commotion in the halls, unusual noises caused by maintenance or construction workers, screams or moans from patients, angry exchanges, the sounds of many people moving about and talking or asking questions at the same time, and the loud ringing of telephones are examples. Noise can be minimized by foreseeing and neutralizing potential sources of interference (e.g., limiting the nursing unit system or central area to strictly business, requesting that repair work or refurbishing be done in the nursing unit at times other than peak hours, reducing the volume of the ring of the telephone, and attending to patient needs quickly).

System overload. Members of a health team are limited in their capacity to send and receive messages; unless controlled, a system overload occurs. When an individual is confronted with messages and expectations from a number of sources that cannot be heard well or completed within the given time and according to established standards of quality, a system overload occurs. Dilemmas like this are a constant part of the nurse manager's position.

A nurse manager can never expect to respond to every sound or gesture, even if it is possible to be aware of all of them. Lower or first-level managers who receive more messages than they can handle can reduce the system overload by isolating the most important messages and attending to them. The nurse manager uses the problem-solving process in relation to priority setting to differentiate between relevant and irrelevant messages. Often the process is rapid, based on accumulated information, experience, and judgment. For example, life-threatening situations such as respiratory and cardiac failure or natural disasters demand immediate response, whereas a request for a walker for re-

habilitative purposes could be attended to when convenient. Similarly, a staff member's request for help in computing a drug dosage would take precedence over another member's request to discuss special privileges regarding vacation time.

Managers can learn a variety of time-saving techniques such as recording and combining messages rather than interrupting other individuals with a number of details. Again, judgment enters into each decision. Although skills commonly improve with practice, ability to cope well with all noises and other sensory overload may not be physically possible. Critically important information may be lost in the volume of input. Options need to be considered, such as adding staff support, technical equipment, or changing or modifying the system of delivery of nursing care in order to reduce the number and kinds of noises as well as the number of communication contacts. For example, changing from functional nursing to team or primary care nursing can automatically reduce these problems.

Social-Psychologic Barriers

Social-psychologic barriers are blocks or inhibitors in communication that arise from the judgments, emotions, and social values of people. Just as physical interferences may create barriers between people, psychologic and social distance can develop, which may prevent communication or cause a misinterpretation. Messages may not be given or received accurately while the communicators are experiencing stress. Life experiences and emotions act as filters in nearly all communication. Individuals see and hear what they are emotionally tuned in to see and hear; thus communication cannot be separated from personality and social implications.

Barriers can confront both sender and receiver. The dominating emotion (eagerness, anticipation, trust, lethargy, fear, defensiveness) affects the communication process. Positive emotions indicate the process is open and receptive, while negative emotions indicate the presence of a barrier.

Lack of trust in the nurse leader / manager by those led is a major barrier to communication. Trust is a firm reliance in the integrity and ability of another to the extent that there is confidence in that person. Team members, for example, commit guidance of their activities into the care of a nurse manager, believing that manager will maintain their trust. Relying on a person also implies a decision to accept the consequences of actions taken, whether they are successes or failures. Openness in communication is important to a free flow of information throughout an organization. The relationship between openness and trust has been emphasized since the 1930s when it was recognized by human relations advocates that authoritarian practices created secretiveness and fear.

A climate favorable to openness rests on a foundation of mutual trust. A study of employees in four organizations showed that the higher the trust in their manager, the more they believed that information received from the manager was accurate.[7]

There are three major barriers to the development of trust: (1) insincerity, when managers ask for feedback and do not value their members' opinions; (2) time, when the demands of task accomplishment preclude devoting time to hearing what the workers want to say; and (3) defensiveness, when the manager's ego is threatened by an open climate, which may have generated from a variety of causes such as inadequate knowledge and skill or low self-image.[8]

Defensiveness can be aroused early in the sender or receiver if certain characteristics are present: evaluation (judgment), control (rules and regulations), strategy (manipulation), neutrality (noncaring), superiority, and certainty (dogmatic). Conversely, communication was found to be enhanced if defenses were reduced. Establishing a supportive climate helped individuals concentrate more on the content and cognitive meaning of the message, rather than spending time searching for hidden meanings and innuendos. Supportive behaviors include: description (presentation of message that gives facts without value judgment), problem orientation (a desire to collaborate), spontaneity (free of deception), empathy (caring), equality (mutual trust and respect), and provisionalism (willing to experiment and investigate).[7]

Communication between nurses and doctors can be positive or negative. This author once worked with a patient who had multiple and serious problems. The attending physician bounded into the room, noted that I was new to the case, and began barking orders and criticizing treatment given. My first reaction was to retaliate angrily; however, I waited until we were alone in the chart room. Then I said, "Doctor Lee, when you spoke to me as you did in Mrs. Fine's room, I felt very angry. I am a competent nurse, fully capable of meeting Mrs. Fine's needs. I felt you criticized me because you don't know me and I perhaps have different ways of doing things. Am I correct in my assessment?" (I used a nondefensive tone and attitude, simply stating facts and feelings.) This strategy caught the usually abrasive doctor off guard. He looked at me as if for the first time, then responded, "I didn't realize that I came across that way. Please accept my apology." The use of defusing tactics helped. Being in an area away from patients and distractions and using open, forthright communication helped to resolve the situation.

Semantics

The interpretation of messages through signs and symbols is often referred to as semantics. The importance of encoding and decoding messages with understanding has been emphasized because information that is not clearly comprehended (*misinterpretation of meaning*) becomes a barrier in the communication process. Barriers to the interpretation procedure include defects in the communication skills of verbalizing, listening, telephoning, writing, and reading.

The ability to speak effectively (*verbal communication*) is a requisite for nurse managers. Oral communication requires one-to-one or face-to-face exchanges, fosters a cooperative spirit, and encourages feedback. The lower- or first-level nurse manager must develop verbal skill in one-to-one relationships, as well as skill in leading small groups. This is in keeping with the high value placed on group or participatory decision making.

A barrier in the communication process occurs when the manager experiences difficulty in exercising verbal skills. A constant challenge in communicating is to develop a delivery that is inviting to hear, and one that avoids talking too much or too little. Some members "tune out" when they hear unpleasant, confusing, or even too many messages (sensory overload). Others are left without enough information to perform well. Both extremes should be avoided.

The following suggestions may improve a nurse manager's verbal communication skills: (1) clarify ideas before speaking; (2) consider the physical and human setting (time, place, and emotions); (3) use a tone of voice and choice of language that makes the desired impact; (4) speak clearly and to the point, using as little time as necessary for the communication to be effective; (5) repeat the key concepts of the message; (6) restate difficult messages; (7) recycle ideas wherever feedback indicates they are weak or misunderstood; and (8) use synonyms for the key words in an attempt to clarify.

Listening is "tuning in" or giving heed to something. It involves hearing, but also includes thought processes. Eugene Raudsepp, Ph.D., president of Princeton Creative Research, Inc.,[8] believes that most people develop poor listening habits over the years. Instead of listening, we allow our minds to wander while people are talking to us, thinking of what we are going to say next before the other person finishes talking. Such poor listening habits can cause misunderstandings on a busy nursing unit. Consider April, a staff nurse, who approaches the busy nursing manager with a request. "Will you tell Dr. Fox when he comes that Mrs. Frazier needs a change of pain medication? I'll be busy in Room 402." "Uh-huh," the department manager replies, returning to her work. Dr. Fox comes and goes without receiving the message. April is angry, the patient's need is not served, and the department manager is upset with herself for not following through. Communication had broken down because the department manager did not hear what was said. Had she really listened, she would have taken into consideration that she, too, might be busy when Dr. Fox arrived and would have requested April to leave a note for Dr. Fox in the patient's record. Dr. Raudsepp offers seven fundamental listening skills:[8]

1. *Take time to listen.* Many people experience difficulty in expressing what they want to say, making careful listening essential for the receiver. If possible, set aside what you are doing and establish eye contact with the communicator. Provide cues that you un-

derstand the message by nodding, or ask questions as needed for clarification.

2. *Teach yourself to concentrate.* It is often easy to fix our gaze on someone who is speaking, yet think about other things at the same time. One reason for this is that the thinking process is three to four times faster than a person's rate of talking. Pace your thinking process with the speaker's rate of speech; keep analyzing what he or she is saying.

3. *Do not interrupt.* The point of anticipating and summarizing the speaker's message is to help us concentrate on what he or she is saying, not to jump to a conclusion. Do not finish sentences for another person, as this is a most effective way to break down communication. Apologize every time you finish a sentence for another person, as this will help to break the habit.

4. *Listen to what a person is saying, not how he or she is saying it.* Poor grammar, disorganized thought patterns, and slow speech can inhibit the listener from understanding the message. Instead of concentrating on delivery problems, ask yourself, "What is he saying that I need to know?"

5. *Suspend judgment.* When ideas are presented that do not match our own ideas and beliefs, we tend to tune them out, as most of us are convinced that we are correct in our thinking. For example, staff nurse Carol says, "Patients in this unit should be able to monitor their own oral medications. We should leave the medications in their rooms with instructions and simply record each day what they say they have taken." Fern believes differently. With such a system she envisions danger and loss of control. Fern does not hear Carol speak of establishing standards of safety with dangerous drugs, educating patients before the use of the system, and documenting information on a medication flow chart. Unless we listen very carefully, we tend to hear what we want to hear or are expecting to hear.

6. *Listen between the lines.* People often speak of other things to hide the real message. For example, before each of the last three consecutive staff nurse meetings, Darrel has reported to the department manager that he could not attend. He had a head-

ache, an emergency came up, and he was tied up in traffic. The department manager observed that Darrel was rarely late or absent from work or any other required function. She discussed the issue with the staff nurse and discovered that he was fearful of being asked to serve on a committee or to contribute his views, because he felt uncomfortable in speaking in a formal setting. Understanding the underlying cause helped the department manager to handle the problem.

7. *Listen with your eyes.* Facial expressions often communicate more than words. The department manager may say, "I'm glad you will be working with us," but her averted eyes and fixed expression belie her words. Look directly at the person who is speaking to you, indicating that you are ready and willing to hear what is being said.

INFORMAL COMMUNICATION—THE GRAPEVINE

Informal or casual groups emerge whenever people come together and interact regularly. This type of communication is commonly called the "grapevine," a term that was coined during the Civil War when intelligence telegraph lines were strung loosely from tree to tree in the manner of a grapevine. The messages were often garbled.[7] Grapevines occur when an informed group member appears to be more informed than others in the group about what is going on in the formal organization and those uninformed seek to obtain the information through informal channels. Through this means, false as well as accurate information can easily spread. The grapevine is direct, fast, and flexible; yet it does not have access to official information sources.

Process

Keith Davis, one of the foremost authorities on informal communication, has written some pertinent information about the grapevine process.[9,pp.438-444]

1. The grapevine is a social interaction, fulfilling people's needs for communication and recognition. Therefore it is as varied as the people who communicate within the grapevine.

2. The grapevine is based on a natural motivation to exchange information—so much so that if members of a work team do not talk about their work and the people involved informally, they are probably disinterested.

3. The grapevine occurs at all levels in an organization in horizontal, vertical, and diagonal patterns.

4. The grapevine is extremely influential, shaping persons' attitudes and having the capacity to carry information both helpful and harmful to the organization.

5. The grapevine has an unusual ability to find out even the most tightly guarded organizational secrets.

6. Employees become active in the grapevine when they have news that is fresh and "hot."

7. The grapevine can become active when information is of high interest to the individual and the messages regarding that interest are vague or unclear. If a subject has no interest to a person, then that person has no cause to rumor about it. And if enough facts are known to satisfy the individual, there is no need to set rumor in motion.

8. The source of information directly affects the strength and duration of the grapevine, as does the believability of the information passed along. The greater the believability, the more legitimate the grapevine becomes.

9. In organizations the grapevine is more a product of a situation than of personality. The grapevine flourishes wherever anticipation or fear becomes dominant within an organization, for example, when a major change in the agency's management causes fear of transfer, dismissal, or uncertainty regarding wages and benefits. The grapevine can also thrive when an individual member becomes known for some achievement, good or bad.

Utilization of the Grapevine

According to Davis, the accuracy of the grapevine in normal situations tends to be about 75%.[9] Serious problems may arise with the inaccurate information transmitted. Often the whole story is not shared. Managers sometimes hope the grapevine in an agency will go away, but it will not. Informal communication chan-

nels will emerge whether or not managers encourage them. If suppressed, the grapevine will
emerge in another place or in another form. The
best approach for managers is to use the grapevine to help the organization as much as possible
to offset a negative impact. Following are methods a nurse manager can use:
1. Keep staff as well informed as possible concerning work-related issues that have relevance to them.
2. Maintain an open communication system
   that encourages feedback.
3. Listen and learn from the grapevine. Learn
   who the leaders are, how the grapevine operates, and what information it carries. The
   object is to determine what is important to
   nursing staff members. Omissions in information or false messages can be identified;
   then strategies can be developed to heighten
   areas of satisfaction and reduce anxiety, conflict, and misunderstanding.
4. Try to influence the grapevine by giving relevant information to liaison or key people.
   This is especially necessary when the grapevine has been spreading incomplete or inaccurate information such as possible layoffs,
   transfers, or mandatory rotation of shifts.
   In management the nurse leader will dis-
courage the development and use of grapevines
for work-related matters and will promote the
use of formal communication channels. The effective nurse manager will recognize the need
for informal communication by the staff and
will use the grapevine to enhance organizational
goals.

MANAGEMENT FUNCTIONS AND COMMUNICATIONS

Leaders and managers determine the work climate and influence the attitudes of staff members. Authority figures must communicate with
staff and vice versa. Figure 8-3 illustrates the
roles of communication in the managerial process. There are three forms of necessary managerial communication: downward, upward,
and horizontal.

Downward Communication

Downward communication flows from people
at top management levels to those at lower levels
in the organizational hierarchy. Media used for
downward oral communication include instructions, speeches, meetings, telephone, loud-
speakers, and the grapevine. Examples of written communication are memorandums, letters,
handbooks, pamphlets, posters, policies, and
procedures.

Upward Communication

Upward communication travels from staff and
lower- and middle-management personnel and
continues up the organizational hierarchy.

Horizontal Communication

This is communication that flows between functional units, such as a nursing department manager, nurse case manager, nursing team, or primary care unit. Horizontal channels connect
people on the same level. Messages usually relate to coordinating activities, sharing information, and solving problems.

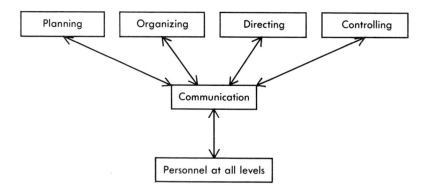

Figure 8-3. Management functions and communications.

ASSESSING ORGANIZATIONAL COMMUNICATION

Nursing literature frequently addresses communication problems within organizations. Job dissatisfaction is often associated with communication problems. Researcher Pincus identified three components of organizational communication systems related to job satisfaction: (1) positive communication atmosphere, (2) positive communication between staff nurses and their immediate superiors, and (3) personal feedback on job performance.[10] (See Figure 8-4.)

Farley, another researcher, has developed a communication assessment questionnaire (Figure 8-5) that can be used by nurse managers to obtain information from the nursing staff.[11] Farley suggests that from an administrative perspective, there are at least six areas of critical importance. Questions should be included from all six categories.

1. *Accessibility of information.* All personnel should have access to such resources as procedure manuals for caregiving, work schedules, special requests, and personnel policies.
2. *Communication channels.* Both formal channels (organizational chart) and informal channels (grapevine) should be explored on the unit and administrative levels. Where and how information is received is also important.
3. *Clarity of messages.* Both written and unwritten messages should be clear to all staff members. Administrators should know whether what they write and say is clearly understood.
4. *Span of control.* Span of control refers to the number of people for whom a nurse is responsible. Questions should address the degree to which nurses are satisfied with the type and frequency of communication between staff and managers.
5. *Flow control and communication load. Flow control* refers to the ability of managers to determine what information and to what extent that information is passed on to staff nurses. *Communication load* refers to the amount of information received by a person within a given period of time. When too much information is disseminated, staff tend to ignore it, thus missing important items. When too little is forthcoming, staff become uneasy and distrustful. To give only verbal messages may cause serious problems because of people's inability to retain everything that is heard as well as personal differences in understanding.
6. *Communicator effectiveness.* Effectiveness relates to how well the communication process is used (message, encoding, transmitting, decoding, action, and feedback). Questions should address staff members' per-

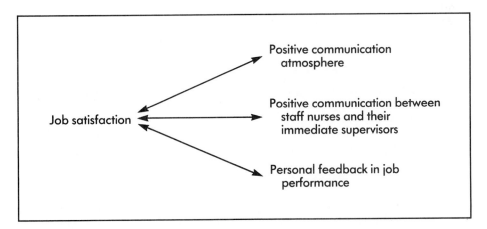

Figure 8-4. Components of organizational communication systems related to job satisfaction. *Adapted from Pincus J: Communication: key contributor to effectiveness—the research, JONA 16(9):19, 1986.*

Please circle the number representing the extent to which you
believe the statement is true for you in your work environment.

    1 = the statement is not at all accurate

    5 = the statement is completely accurate

1. I have the information I need in order to do my job in the most effective and efficient manner.   1 2 3 4 5
2. I know where I can get the information I need in order to do my job well.   1 2 3 4 5
3. I receive information about my job from
   - a) my immediate supervisor   1 2 3 4 5
   - b) my co-workers   1 2 3 4 5
   - c) notices posted on bulletin boards   1 2 3 4 5
   - d) personnel from departments other than nursing   1 2 3 4 5
4. I receive the information about any changes that might affect my job in a timely manner.   1 2 3 4 5
5. The communications I receive are clear and understandable.   1 2 3 4 5
6. I am satisfied with the frequency of communications I have with my immediate superior.   1 2 3 4 5
7. I receive too little information about things that are happening in this organization.   1 2 3 4 5
8. I believe that nursing administration shares critical and pertinent information with nursing personnel.   1 2 3 4 5
9. People in administration effectively communicate with employees.   1 2 3 4 5

Figure 8-5. Sample of a communication assessment questionnaire. *From Farley M: Assessing communication in organizations, JONA 19(12):28, 1989.*

ceptions of nurse managers' ability to communicate.

INFORMATION MANAGEMENT

To ensure quality care and control costs, nurse managers must be able to identify, secure, and interpret data pertinent to controlling operations within their scope of management, and they must do so in a timely manner.[12] The volume of data nurse managers must deal with can be overwhelming at times. Alvin Toffler[13] believes that one revolutionary source for change in the area of information management is the use of the computer, because the computer can:

- remember and interrelate large numbers of causal forces

- help cope with problems at a deeper than customary level
- sift vast masses of data to find subtle patterns
- assemble parts into meaningful wholes
- trace the consequences of alternate decisions
- suggest imaginative solutions through analyzing relationships among the data

Nurse Utilization of Computers

Because the functions of various hospital departments are so diverse, each nursing department needs a unique configuration of data to control activities effectively. Examples of types of systems that are useful to nurses are[14]:

1. Allocation and distribution of staffing based on patient classification
2. Patient data management
3. Infection control surveillance
4. Quality control
5. Productivity and management reporting
6. Time record keeping
7. Employee data management
8. Contracted services utilization
9. Budgeting

These types of data can be used to organize and monitor daily and periodic operations that help first-line managers account for unit productivity.

Once the purposes and potential uses of the computer are determined, a system can be designed and installed to meet these needs. Coordination among departments and disciplines within the agency is vital. Extensive committee work is necessary before final decisions can be made.

Introducing Nurses to Computers

Kathleen Herrick and Sandra McCullough, information systems analysts at Sharp Health Care in San Diego, California, say that educating nurses in the use of computers doesn't sound so difficult until one takes into account a multihospital environment with varying nursing structures and a mandatory implementation period.[15] Acceptance of computers, proper utilization by all users, and coordination between nursing and all concerned in provision of health care are vital to successful implementation of the system. Most large health agencies begin to orient their nursing staffs at least 1 year in advance of activating a computer system. Because many nurses do not have computer skills, most educational departments use commercially available programs to teach the basics, then rely on experienced staff for hands-on training. Time is needed to learn new systems. Computers are strange and threatening to some people. Without adequate preparation, the computer system may fail, resulting in great expense and lost potential. For example, in a large hospital where nurses are expected to be on-line with a new computer system in about 6 months, nurse managers are meeting regularly and learning the system. The next step will be to orient the nursing staff, through the nursing education department, then to introduce the system one nursing unit at a time.

Computers and the Future

After consulting many experts, Patricia Nornhold offered some key trends and developments that we can expect to see in the 1990s regarding computers in health care.[16]

1. More hospitals will merge to form coalitions that will require new methods of communication, including the interface of computer systems.
2. There will be a general trend toward noninvasive technology; information from bedside equipment such as cardiac monitors, IV pumps, and ventilators will be transferred automatically to a computer, which should help to reduce time spent in documenting.
3. Hospitals, and nurses in particular, will use computers more effectively and creatively. For example, computers will be used in tracking patients' progress before, during, and after hospitalization.
4. Nurses will use voice-activated computers to record their notes (e.g., the nurse will enter a password and speak into the headset or handset attached to the computer, which will record all that is said). Physicians will also use this method to order treatments.
5. Computers will be designed to read physicians' handwriting through use of a special recording pad with built-in safeguards to prevent errors.
6. Computers will help nurses spend less time talking and transcribing orders. Most physicians' offices and nursing units will have a facsimile (FAX) machine or computer terminal for transferring orders and other patient information electronically.
7. A computerized universal chart will be used for each patient. Stored on a microchip and put in a laminated card that can be carried in a wallet or purse, it will be possible to call up the information on a computer screen.
8. Computers will isolate nurses from one another as they spend most of their time in the patients' rooms. Computers will also create problems involving patient confidentiality.

Whatever the future brings, nurse managers will play a key role in designing computer systems and programs to better meet their own needs and the needs of their staff and patients during the 1990s. This is an exciting and challenging opportunity.

SUMMARY

1. Interpersonal communication is a process of passing a message from one person to another, or within a small group of people, with the intention that the message sent will be received and understood as intended.

2. Effective communication is accomplished when clarity and accuracy are sufficient to influence desired action toward the welfare of the enterprise.

3. The communication process serves as the foundation used by the nurse manager to achieve organizational objectives. Effective communication between nurse-nurse, nurse-physician, and all others, leads to influence and power.

4. An effective communication model consists of sender, receiver, message, encoding, transmitting, decoding, action, and continuous feedback.

5. The nurse manager's message should have a reason or goal consisting of a fact, idea, or feeling.

6. Encoding means translating a message into verbal and nonverbal symbols that will communicate the intended meaning to the receiver(s).

7. Transmitting involves the channel used to communicate the message, including speech, written word, electronic media, and action.

8. Decoding is the process whereby the receiver perceives and interprets the sender's message into information that has meaning. The effectiveness of the communication process depends greatly on commonality of experiences.

9. Action is the behavior taken by the receiver as a result of the message sent, received, and perceived. Communication is not successful until the message received has been understood and acted upon appropriately.

10. Feedback is a continuous two-way process wherein sender(s) and receiver(s) exchange information and clarify meanings of the message sent. The greater the complexity of information, the greater the need for feedback.

11. Accurate feedback is achieved best with face-to-face communication, use of simple and direct language, and sensitivity to the individual's values, needs, attitudes, and expectations.

12. Effective feedback between managers and staff is characterized by proper timing, focusing on specific behaviors, and tact.

13. Three types of barriers to effective communication occur in nursing services: physical, social-psychologic, and interpretation of meanings, or semantics.

14. Physical barriers consist of environmental factors such as space or distance, temperature and ventilation, structure and equipment, and distracting noises.

15. Noise that obscures or reduces clarity or quality of a message interferes with the communication process and must be corrected.

16. Social-psychologic barriers are those blocks that arise from judgments, emotions, and social values of people. Communication cannot be separated from personality and social implications, as whatever emotion dominates a person at the time affects the communication process.

17. A major barrier to communication in the nursing management process is lack of trust in the leader/manager. Distrust results when the manager is insincere, fails to devote enough time to the members, and is defensive in attitude.

18. Establishing supportive climates with behaviors such as description, problem orientation, spontaneity, empathy, equality, and provisionalism motivates members to participate in the work assignments.

19. Interpretation of meaning, or semantics, occurs in the encoding and decoding process. Barriers arise when there are defects in the skills of verbalizing and listening.

20. Fundamental listening skills include taking time to listen, concentrating on the mes-

senger, not interrupting, listening to *what* is being said, not *how* it is said, suspending judgment, listening between the lines, and listening with one's eyes.

21. Informal or casual communication, commonly called the "grapevine," is a social interaction occurring outside established organizational channels.

22. The grapevine fulfills individuals' needs and develops anywhere there are people, and at all levels, becoming a powerful force producing both positive and negative effects.

23. The source and believability of information passed along directly affects the strength and duration of the grapevine. Grapevine information is usually about 75% accurate.

24. The effective nurse manager uses the grapevine advantageously by maintaining an open and trusting relationship through the use of formal communication channels and by giving pertinent information to liaison or key people.

25. In management, three forms of communication occur: downward (flows from top management down), upward (travels from staff, lower- and middle-management up), and horizontal (flows between people on the same level).

26. Job satisfaction is directly related to positive communication atmosphere, positive communication between staff nurses and their immediate supervisors, and personal feedback in job performance.

27. To ensure quality care and control, nurse managers must be able to identify, secure, and interpret data pertinent to controlling operations within their scope of management, and they must do so in a timely manner.

28. Information management is enhanced and accelerated through the use of computers, which can store and produce data in many different forms.

29. Each nursing department needs a configuration of data unique to its departmental activities in order to control its departmental activities effectively.

30. Acceptance of computers, proper utilization by all nurses, coordination among nursing staff and all persons concerned in provision of health care, and sufficient lead time are vital to successful implementation of a computer system.

Questions for Study and Discussion

1. Describe in your own words what comprises an effective interpersonal communication system.

2. Diagram an effective communication model from memory.

3. You have just attended a morning team conference and are mulling over one of the instructions for care. Which part of the communication process is in effect? If you do not understand what to do, which part of the communication model should you use?

4. In your daily face-to-face contact with others, which link in the communication process tends to be weakest? Why? What corrective action could you take?

5. Think of a situation that could be a serious communication problem for a nurse manager.

6. What kinds of communication barriers can block the transfer of understanding in the classroom? Can any of your responses apply to a nursing unit? Explain.

7. You feel hurried, yet you need to hear what your supervisor is saying. What can you do to help yourself to understand the message?

8. How can a nurse manager best utilize the grapevine?

9. What sort of experiences have you had with computers in the workplace? Summarize the positive and negative aspects of your experience.

10. Some nurses believe that use of computers for the development of nursing care plans and for documentation is too depersonalized. What is your opinion? Explain your rationale.

REFERENCES

1. Skopec E: Communicate for success: how to manage, motivate, and lead your people, Reading, Mass, 1990, Addison-Wesley Publishing Co.
2. Kreitner R: Management, ed 4, Boston, 1989, Addison-Wesley Publishing Co.
3. Huseman R, Lahiff J, and Hatfield J: Business communications: strategies and skills, ed 3, Hinsdale, Ill, 1988, Dryden Press.
4. Hellriegel D and Slocum J: Management, ed 5, Reading, Mass, 1989, Addison-Wesley Publishing Co.
5. Blankenship P and Woodward-Smith M: Feedback . . . to a "T," Nursing 90(4):32Q, 1990.
6. Raudsepp E: 7 ways to cure communications breakdown, Nursing 90(4):132, 134, 137-138, 142, 1990.
7. Landy F: Psychology of work behavior, ed 4, Pacific Grove, Calif, 1989, Brooks/Cole Publishing Co.
8. Raudsepp E: 7 ways to cure communications breakdown, Nursing 90(4):132, 134, 137-138, 142, 1990.
9. Davis K and Newstrom K: Human behavior at work: organizational behavior, ed 7, New York, 1985, McGraw-Hill Book Co.
10. Pincus J: Communication: key contributor to effectiveness, J Nurs Admin 16(19):1925, 1986.
11. Farley M: Assessing communication in organizations, JONA 19(12):27-31, 1989.
12. Johantgen M and Parrinello K: Microcomputers: turning the database into unit management information, Nurs Man 18(2):30-38, 1987.
13. Toffler A: The third wave, New York, 1980, Bantam.
14. Grobe S: Computer primer and resource guide for nurses, Philadelphia, 1984, JB Lippincott.
15. Herrick K and McCullough S: Introducing nurses to computers in a multi-hospital environment, Nurs Man 20(7):31, 1989.
16. Nornhold P: Changing health care industry, Nursing 90(1):35-41, 1990.

SUGGESTED READINGS

Adamson G and Ernswiller T: Communicating the vision, Healthcare Forum J 34(1):12-15, 1991.

Franks J and Hayden M: Establishing a permanent charge nurse support group, Nurs Man 21(6):46-48, 1990.

Grensing L: A formula to avoid miscommunicating, Nursing 90 20(9):122-125, 1990.

Kim K and Michelman J: An examination of factors for the strategic use of information systems in the health care industry, Management Information Systems (MIS) 14(2):201-215, June 1990.

Iyer P: New trends in charting, Nursing 91 21(1):48-50, 1991.

Juhl N: Watch your memo manners! Nurs Man 20(10):88N-88P, 1990.

Leebov W: Getting along with co-workers better, Nursing 91 21(1):113-114, 1991.

Manthey M: Vulnerable no more, Nurs Man 20(4):26, 1989.

Olson S: Walk a day in my shoes, Nurs Man 22(1):31, 1991.

Pinto M: Gaining cooperation among members of hospital project teams, Hospital Topics 68(1):15-21, 1990.

Practice briefs: Making yourself perfectly clear, Nursing 90 20(2):86-87, 1990.

Quillen T: How to help foreign nurses adapt, Nursing 90 20(11):131-133, 1990.

Simpson R: Closing the gap between school and service, Nurs Man 21(11):16-17, 1990.

Wiseman J: Get with it (computing), Community Outlook Feb, 11-12, 1990.

9

Conflict Resolution

_____ **BEHAVIORAL OBJECTIVES** _____
On completion of this chapter the student will be prepared to:

☐ Define conflict as applied to organizations.
☐ Define intrapersonal conflict and explain how it affects the nurse manager.
☐ Differentiate between conflict between health organizations and conflict within health organizations, interpersonal and intergroup.
☐ Discuss the positive and negative consequences of conflict.
☐ State five responses used in resolving conflict, and identify which response is most appropriate for given situations.
☐ Differentiate between assertive and aggressive behavior.

Conflict is an inevitable by-product of interpersonal dealings. Conflict exists when an inner or outer struggle occurs regarding ideas, feelings, or actions. Intrapersonal, interpersonal, or intergroup conflicts may cause organizational dysfunction because of the vast differences among people in background, point of view, values, and needs. Most health care organizations experience a substantial amount of conflict, because a complex organizational structure requires its members to engage in numerous and varied interdependent relationships. For example, more and more patients / clients are becoming aware of their rights, and nurses are learning ways to serve as their advocates.

Nurses and other health agency personnel are also learning ways to promote their work-related interests through such means as negotiation, strikes, or integrative decision making. Administrators, physicians, and nurses are experiencing conflict as they attempt to understand and meet the expectations of others.

Margaret Collyer believes that a manager's leadership style sets the strategy for conflict resolution.[1] She also believes that how nurse managers approach workplace conflicts is an example of how they approach all other organizational and leadership functions.

Management of conflict is a high-priority issue for nurse managers. Conflict in itself is neither functional (beneficial) nor dysfunctional (harmful). Conflict can threaten the harmony and balance of an organization, but it can also be desirable and useful in improving organizational performance, depending on how it is managed.[2] The task of the nurse manager is to identify the source of conflict and to understand the points of friction. The nurse manager can then proceed with the process of conflict resolution, striving to see that all participants are left with a feeling of self-worth because their views, feelings, and behaviors were treated with respect and value. This section will consider attitudes toward conflict; the kinds of conflict; the consequences of conflict; conflict resolution; and passive, aggressive, and assertive behaviors.

ATTITUDES TOWARD CONFLICT

Views about conflict influence the choice of management system for an organizational setting. Chapter 3 compares the bureaucratic approach with the human relations approach, pointing out that rarely is one system practiced alone, but that changes and adaptations are made according to specific situations.

Bureaucratic or *conservative managers* believe that conflict is unnecessary, harmful, and reflects a failure of planning and control. They equate conflict with a fight, an unpleasant argument, trouble, anger, pain, and tension. Bureaucrats are convinced that if the principles of scientific management were applied, conflict between labor and management would disappear. They propose that conflict be suppressed and eliminated. Strategies or methods used by bureaucratic managers include establishing a repressive, disapproving climate in which acknowledgment of reactions is discouraged or penalties are assigned for creating conflict, such as overtime, unpleasant jobs, transfer, or even dismissal. Other methods used are bargaining, persuasion, and confrontation with an "I win, you lose" approach.

Human relations theorists take a liberal approach to conflict, contending that it is a normal, frequent occurrence because human beings often have needs that clash. Nurse managers of different departments, for example, may have conflicts over priorities of allocation of personnel or supplies. Staff members may argue with their leaders over their work assignments. The liberal, progressive approach is that some conflict is desirable, because the search for solutions may lead to greater effectiveness. This view still suggests that much conflict is dysfunctional and can harm individuals or can impede attainment of goals. The progressive-minded manager is concerned with human communications that will not suppress or resolve all conflict but will recognize and manage conflict so as to minimize its harmful aspects and maximize its benefits.

Human relations supporters believe it is possible for people to experience conflict and cooperate at the same time.[3] For example, two nurses may agree on goals for implementing nursing care, but disagree strongly on how to attain those goals. Through communication the manager tries to find the most effective balance between conflict and cooperation. Methods employed by human relations managers for resolving conflict are confrontation and problem solving, helping to reach a decision that integrates the thinking and feelings of all parties so that each person feels he or she has "won."

KINDS OF CONFLICT

There are various kinds of conflict: (1) conflict within the individual, (2) conflict between organizations, and (3) conflict within organizations (interpersonal and intergroup).

Conflict within an Individual

Intrapersonal conflict in a nurse manager occurs when the leader is confronted with two or more incompatible demands. Inner conflicts that are fairly common in health organizations occur (1) when there is uncertainty about the work expectations because of insufficient or unclear information; (2) when the nurse is confronted with an ethical issue and is torn between loyalty to personal convictions and loyalty to the organization; (3) when there is a role conflict, as when the nurse manager is trying to meet job demands in addition to the demands of the roles of spouse and parent; (4) when the nurse feels there is work overload and expectations from a number of sources cannot be completed within the given time and quality limits; (5) when the nurse feels divided between a desire for personal independence and feels committed to conform to the demands of the organization; or (6) when expectations exceed capability, and the nurse is confronted with making decisions about whether to "bluff" the situation through while learning the job or risk the consequences of revealing incompetence for the role.

Intrapersonal conflicts in the nurse manager cause the body to respond in helpful or harmful ways. Hans Selye[4] labeled all things that create "wear and tear" on the body as "stressors," and all responses to that wear and tear as "stress." Selye maintains that stress responses have three phases: (1) the excitement phase (or the "fight-or-flight" response), (2) the resistance phase, and (3) the exhaustion phase.

In the excitement phase the person experiencing stress prepares for fighting or running with an increase in epinephrine, faster breathing to increase the oxygen supply to the brain, and a quickened heartbeat to pump more blood through the system. A moderate amount of stress by excitement may improve performance. For example, the nervous tension that a nurse manager experiences while in conflict about what exactly should be done in a situation of crisis may have a helpful, energizing effect.

The resistance phase is that period when the body mobilizes its resources to fight stressors. This is often the stage in which diseases are manifested. The physiologic overactivity that accompanies constant strain or use of maladaptive ways to cope with strain, such as smoothing and avoidance, can cause the body to develop headaches, hypertension, ulcers, heart disease, and other serious illnesses.

The exhaustion phase occurs after an accumulation of stress over a long period of time, which causes depletion of the individual's physical and emotional resources.

Exposure to stressful events is an intrinsic part of management. Stress cannot be eliminated from the workplace. However, health care facilities can diminish the amount of stress in the workplace by selecting confident, able individuals as managers.[5] Nurse managers need to begin early in their careers to identify those inner conflicts that create stress and to deal with them through constructive methods for conflict resolution and appropriate preventive measures. For example, nurse managers can obtain as much information as possible about each new assignment initially and continuously so that they will not experience excessive role uncertainties as their careers progress.

Conflict between Health Organizations

Conflict between health organizations is usually restricted to issues pertaining to competition for buildings, types of facilities, funding, and business. Today an increasing number of satellite health centers are springing up, each competing for the same health care dollar, causing tensions to rise and conflicts to emerge among providers.

In American society, this form of conflict is considered desirable, because it can lead to the development of new and better services.[6] Lower- or first-level nurse managers may become involved in interagency conflict when information is needed to justify new or expanded services or when data are needed on use of methods, time, or resources. They may also offer their views relating to organizational issues at public and professional gatherings.

Conflict within Health Organizations— Interpersonal and Intergroup

The major sources of organizational conflict in health agencies include (1) differences between management and staff, (2) the need to share resources, (3) the interdependence of work activities in the organization, and (4) differences in values and goals among departments and personnel regarding the delivery of nursing care.

Differences between management and staff. One of the most common forms of organizational conflict is the conflict between staff members and personnel in charge of them. The root of the conflict lies in the fact that staff members (for example, nursing assistants, LPNs/LVNs, and staff nurses) view one another and their roles in the organization from a perspective different from that of supervisory or management personnel (for example, head or charge nurse, supervisor, and nursing director). Staff members' orientations are usually geared to the "here and now," concentrating on accomplishing their respective tasks effectively, whereas management people share this concern but are also attending to broader horizons in terms of time and accomplishments. Issues that concern staff members center on complaints about staffing, blocks or barriers in communication, wages, benefits, and other concerns. Conflicts between management and staff may arise as a result of staff going beyond their lines of authority, lack of dedication to the job, or lack of understanding of the management process and position regarding issues.

Shared resources. An effective nurse manager works through the established system to obtain what is needed. The manager needs to be aware of the source of supply, method of allocation, and procedure for requests of resources. Sharing resources in a health organization frequently leads to conflict because vital resources are limited. If every department had access to unlimited amounts of manpower, space, supplies, and equipment, the problem of how to share these resources would hardly arise. These resources must be allocated, with the inevitable result that some groups will get less than they want or need. Lack of cooperation or even direct conflict can result when people seek to satisfy only their own wants and needs. The lower- or first-level nurse manager in a hospital is often confronted with the problem of acquiring enough linen, wheelchairs, lifts, scales, hardware and software, and other equipment. Further, the leader may be asked to cooperate by sharing a staff member with another department for a few hours or a day. A conflict may occur when the team leader determines the needs of the team are so great that the member cannot be spared. It is these kinds of problems that call for the nurse manager to acquire sufficient knowledge and understanding about available resources.

Work interdependence. Work interdependence exists when two or more departments or subunits or individuals depend on each other to complete their respective tasks. For example, nursing departments must relate with many other groups, such as admitting, discharge, x-ray, laboratory, pharmacy, dietary, and many others. There exists the potential for a high degree of conflict or cooperativeness, depending on how the situation is managed. Sometimes conflict occurs when groups have too much to do. Conflict may flare if one individual or group is perceived by another to be shirking responsibilities. Potential for conflict is greatest when one department or individual is unable to begin work until the other unit or individual completes a job ("How can we serve breakfast if the lab doesn't take the fasting specimens?" or "How can I complete my assignment on time if I have to wait until X is ready to help me?").

Differences in goals and values. Differences in goals and values among departments and personnel regarding the delivery of nursing care frequently lead to conflict of interest or priorities, even when the overall goals of the organization are agreed on. As an agency becomes departmentalized and specialized, each subunit develops its own goals, tasks, and problems that may not be in harmony with the goals of all other departments. The maternity department, for example, might want to discharge infants and mothers at times most convenient to the family members, whereas the business office insists on holding to a specified time of discharge. Each department may express concern for the family, but they are in conflict as to how best to serve their respective interests.

The differences in goals among members of the various departments in an organization are influenced by differences in attitudes, values, and perceptions that may be another source of conflict. Lower- or first-level nurse managers may be stressed as a result of the nursing team's being asked to accomplish too great a work load. The manager is told to "just do the best you can—we'll talk about it later." Issues of safety and poor quality care plague the leader until conflict erupts. Interpersonal conflicts are also common in nursing practice among personnel and between nursing personnel and patients/clients. Attitudes, values, and perceptions play a major role in these relationships. Because each individual is unique, it is often difficult to resolve conflict amicably without exercising good communication skills.

CONSEQUENCES OF CONFLICT

The conflict process can lead to positive or negative results. Two or more people are involved in a relationship, and the outcome of their social exchange depends on the communication process used. Following are some possible consequences of conflict:

1. *Issues are recognized and brought out in the open.* Suppression of feelings within an organiza-

tion leads to trouble. When conflict arises, it should be identified and dealt with. Recognition of conflict by management sanctions open communication between the individuals or group members, the first step in the process of conflict resolution.

2. *There is a rise in group cohesion and performance.* As a rule, group members in an intergroup conflict situation close ranks and put aside former disagreements. (For example, during conflict the group follows its chosen leader, who may or may not be the leader appointed by management). The heightened closeness of the group can be positive (the staff can choose to pull together to accomplish the work load while negotiating with management) or negative (the team may choose to accomplish only that which they believe feasible, or they may engage in a work slow-down to emphasize the problem).

3. *Poor performance.* Extremely low levels of conflict may result in poor performance. Passive people who are afraid to "rock the boat" rather than try to find new and better ways of getting things done repress their feelings of conflict and accept things the way they are. Individuals and group members drift along, tolerating each other's weaknesses and lack of performance, building up tension and stress.

4. *Constructive or destructive results.* Moderate conflict may produce resolution of problems in constructive, problem-solving ways, whereas high levels of conflict almost always produce results destructive to the organization. High levels of conflict may also lead to distortion of perception. In situations of conflict there is a tendency to regard individual and group ideas irrationally ("Management thinks we are machines." "Those staff members just do not want to work"). Negative stereotypes are apt to be developed as each side belittles the other's views and ideas. Competitive struggle adversely affects the rivals' ability to grasp and think accurately about their respective positions. Strong group identification, heightened by fear of defeat, blinds both sides to the similarities in their views that, if recognized, could make conflict resolution possible.

5. *There may be a rise of leaders.* When conflict occurs, individuals in a group may emerge as leaders, whose talents might not otherwise have been recognized.

CONFLICT RESOLUTION

The organizational structure and climate influence how beneficial conflict resolution is likely to be. Conflict can call attention to the problem areas of an organization and can lead to better ways of getting things done. However, if an organization or an individual or group rigidly resists change, the situations of conflict may never be relieved. Tensions will continue to mount, and each new conflict will split the parties involved farther apart. Unresolved conflict can adversely affect subgroups (for example, nursing teams) in which there is a great deal of dependence on one another for information to accomplish goals.

Many nurses have developed ineffective responses to conflict. As a result, frustration is created and feelings of helplessness and low self-esteem are generated.[7] Basically, there are five responses that are used in resolving conflict: (1) competition and power, (2) smoothing, (3) avoidance, (4) compromise, and (5) collaboration.[8] Figure 9-1 demonstrates how Collyer applies nurse leadership styles to Blake and Mouton's Managerial Grid® for resolving conflicts.[1]

The conflict resolution style used to solve each conflict will depend on the nurse manager's values regarding work production and human relationships.[9] The following situation will serve as the basis for discussing the five approaches to conflict resolution mentioned:

Nurse manager Dolores is faced with a serious and persistent staffing shortage, as well as economic pressures to keep costs within budget. Employing registry nurses is more costly than employing regular staff. Consequently, there are fewer replacements from the registry than are needed. Dolores has felt it necessary to assign the more complicated patients to nurses familiar with the unit and to give them heavier assignments to accommodate new personnel's need for orientation. She is sitting in her office one afternoon grappling with a budget problem. Her concentration is suddenly interrupted by a loud knock

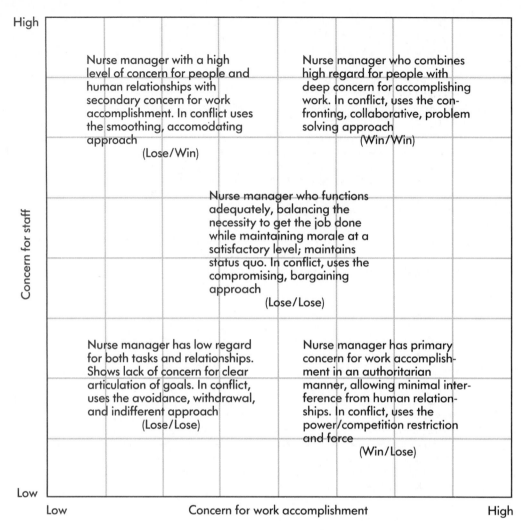

Figure 9-1. Leadership styles and conflict resolution. *Adapted from Blake R and Mouton J: The managerial grid: the key to leadership excellence, Houston, 1985, Gulf Publishing Company; and Collyer M: Resolving conflicts: leadership style sets the strategy, Nurs Man 20(9):77-80, 1989.*

on the door. Without waiting for an invitation to enter, three of the hospital nursing staff burst into the office. They are obviously upset and angry. They slam the door and one nurse speaks: "We've just about had it! If you are trying to get us to quit, you are doing all the right things!" Taken aback, Dolores asks the reason for their anger. "You should know—you take advantage of us every day by overloading us without a break. We never get a chance to relax. You'd better do something about this situation or we'll quit!"

Competition/Power

As Figure 9-1 indicates, when the nurse manager's primary concern is for work accomplishment, with minimal regard for staff relationships, the strategy will be to exercise power, restriction, and coercion. There is an all-out effort to win, regardless of the cost.

Dolores responds to the three nurses, "I am in charge here and I'm doing what I think best for all concerned *(power)*. Surely you can hang in there until this crisis is over *(coercion)*. If you choose to quit, I'll see to it that your lack of co-operation goes on your record" *(restriction)*.

The nurse manager "wins" because the nurses return to work as they do not wish to transfer or resign under negative circumstances. The staff nurses "lose," and their resentment, hostility, anger, and frustration will build.[8] Later, these feelings may be actualized in other ways, such as in poor performance, absenteeism, and undermining the nurse manager in her relationship with their peers, or by taking their problem to a grievance committee.

Smoothing

Smoothing behavior is a more diplomatic way of suppressing conflict. The nurse manager who has a high concern for relationships, and a secondary concern for work accomplishment, might use the smoothing, accommodating approach (Figure 9-1). Smoothing is accomplished by complimenting, down-playing differences, and focusing on minor areas of agreement, as if little disagreement exists.

Dolores jumps up from her chair and asks the nurses to join her for a Coke, "on me" *(accommodating)*. She tells them, "I know just how you feel—I would feel the same way if I were in your shoes" *(agreement)*. I've given you the complicated assignments because you are the best nurses I have and I know you are concerned with giving high quality care *(complimentary)*. This situation is rough but it won't last long. We'll be getting new nurses soon and won't need to use as many people from the registry *(down-playing the issue)*. I will get an additional nurse from the registry to ease your load" *(accommodating)*.

Approaching conflict this way sets up a lose-win situation. Dolores is accommodating the nurses at her own expense—she will exceed her budget, be forced to cut back, and will demonstrate lack of competency to her superiors and lack of trust to her staff. The nurses win in that they were listened to and are promised a more equitable number of nursing staff. Smoothing tactics are never satisfactory as they are only surface measures, and another eruption is likely to occur.

Avoidance

The nurse manager who uses avoiding strategies has low regard for both workers' output and

relationships. Shunning or avoiding a problem means not taking a position regarding the conflict. The nurse manager reasons, "If we don't talk about the problem, it will go away."

Dolores responds to the irate nurses, "I'm sorry, but I don't have time to discuss this now—later perhaps." This is a lose-lose situation. The avoidance response does nothing but create a higher degree of frustration and anger on the part of the staff nurses. The problem will accelerate, eventually forcing the nurse manager to address the ever-increasing conflict.

Compromise

Compromise is a means of settling differences in which each side makes concessions. Concession-making behavior is moderately assertive and cooperative; however, it produces a lose-lose situation, as each party gives up something in order to gain something and neither gets what he or she wants. Compromise is sometimes the only choice, as when a decision must be made immediately, or when the two parties in conflict have equal power. From a management point of view, compromise is a weak resolution method because the process usually fails to reach a solution that will best help the organization to reach its goals.

After hearing the angry nurses' complaints, Dolores responds, "I see we have a bigger problem here than I imagined. Sit down and we'll see what can be worked out." She explains that a staff increase is out of the question, but agrees to assign patients equitably among the nurses on duty, regular staff and registry personnel alike. "The registry people will have to understand how it is and dig in a bit harder. Will you promise to help them get oriented as much as you can?"

The nurse manager, in an effort to balance the necessity for adequate nurse coverage, while maintaining regularly employed nurses' morale at a satisfactory level, agrees to a situation in which both parties lose. The nurse manager compromises her commitment to provide quality nursing care by lowering her standards in making assignments. The regularly employed nurses lose in that they will not be satisfied to see patients receive less than the best care, and they will feel put upon if they have to frequently interrupt their caregiving to assist the registry nurses. The registry nurses, on the other hand, will feel equal dissatisfaction, as they may be given assignments beyond their ability. This solution will soon fail, and the organization is not helped to reach its goals.

Collaboration

Collaborative problem solving is a constructive process in which the parties involved recognize that conflict exists, confront the issue, and openly try to solve the problem that has arisen between them. Instead of using dominating, suppressing, or compromising behaviors, the individuals look for a resolution they all will want to accept. The outcome is integrative problem solving, in which all members and groups involved in the conflict work together toward a common goal in an atmosphere of open and free exchange of ideas, stressing the benefits of finding the best solution.

The collaborative approach to conflict resolution requires (1) problem identification, (2) clear definition of values, purpose, and goals,

(3) open and honest communication of facts and feelings, (4) a sense of responsibility of all who participate, and (5) an environment of trust and commitment of all to the success of the process.[10] A constructive plan for the nurse manager to follow when conflict is present or anticipated is to designate a specific time for meeting all persons involved in the disagreement, allowing enough time to discuss the issue and providing coverage for the group while it is in session.

Figure 9-2 presents a model for effective conflict resolution. Leadership through the conflict resolution procedure is important. First the persons in conflict must be helped to state their values, purposes, and goals; then they must be guided toward a solution that is acceptable to all parties. Of course, it is impossible to meet goals that are absolutely incompatible, but if all parties are committed to the process, many established ideas can be changed.

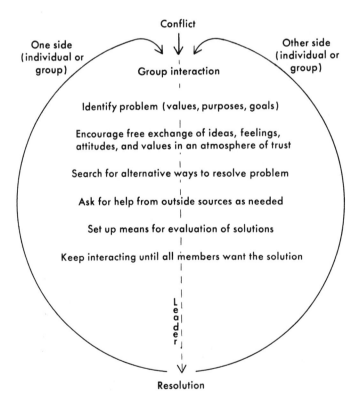

Figure 9-2. Model for conflict resolution.

All members should be encouraged to share both positive and negative thoughts in an atmosphere of acceptance. The leader discourages behaviors that are destructive to the process. One behavior is apologizing prematurely: "OK, you're right, I'm sorry." This kind of comment stops the process. Another unhelpful behavior is refusing to take the conflict seriously: "Oh, you shouldn't feel that way. Ha, ha, ha. . . ." These are repressive, dehumanizing responses. The silent treatment of withdrawal is another dead-end behavior. Distraction or addressing unrelated issues is a tool used by some, making it difficult for members to focus on the problem.

Constructive behaviors that a leader should encourage include full expression of positive and negative feelings, with the knowledge that as the positive comments increase, the negative will decrease. In conflict resolution the leader does not stop the disagreement. The effort is to hear what individuals are thinking and feeling.

A paraphrasing ground rule should be established, whereby one person cannot respond to another until the first person is satisfied that his or her feelings have been heard and understood. Phrases such as "Are you saying . . .?" and "Tell me in another way" promote clarification. After two or three exchanges it is frequently discovered that there really is no conflict of goals; the problem was a matter of semantics, or how to reach the goal.

Nurse manager Dolores recognizes that she is confronted with a problem: the conflict has reached a state of crisis and some immediate action must be taken. She allows the nurses to confront her, then responds, "I can see this is a serious matter *(respect for the nurses' opinions)*. We do not have time to work it out now, but I will give the matter serious thought and we will discuss the problem at staff meeting this afternoon" *(accommodation)*. When the group convenes, Dolores has a chart pad set up, ready to record the proceedings. She begins the discussion by saying, "I value your opinions and I want to hear what you have to say, whether positive or negative *(open, honest, and trusting)*. We must get at the problem." She asks for a volunteer to record the messages *(participation)*:
"We're overworked."
"We never have time to be together."
"I resent always having the heavy assignments."
"Registry nurses do less and get paid more."

"The hospital should have more nurses."
"You play favorites."
"I'm afraid I'm going to make a mistake."
"My family life is going to pot."
"I hate to come to work and I used to love to."
After making certain all have had their say, Dolores asks the group to identify what it is they want:
"We want an equitable patient assignment that we can comfortably manage."
"We want to feel our patients are being cared for."
"We want registry nurses to be able to carry their load."
"We want to feel you (nurse manager) care enough about us to meet our needs."
Dolores asks, "From the discussion thus far, how would you identify the problem?" After discussion the group agrees on:
"Continuous pressure as a result of overassignments and a feeling of lack of support from the department manager."
From this point, Dolores moves on to a search for alternate ways to solve the problem. Again, the responses are recorded:
"Department manager fights for our rights."
"Hire more nurses."
"Stage a few 'sick-outs' to show administration we are serious."
"Take the problem to the grievance committee."
"Train the registry nurses better."
Dolores concludes, "You have helped to clarify the issues. I ask that you give me a week to see what can be done. I realize the problem is real and serious, and I will do what I can to resolve the matter." From here, Dolores will meet with her supervisor and plan strategies that address the problem. The department manager and supervisor will go through the decision-making process of weighing actions against risks and will come to a decision.

The reader is asked to use the problem-solving process to develop possible answers to the problem.

PASSIVE, AGGRESSIVE, AND ASSERTIVE BEHAVIORS

Deciding which style of behavior to exhibit while communicating in the role of manager is often difficult for nurses. Even when a decision is made as to the best approach, the nurse may hesitate to act. There is no one right way to respond all of the time—the nurse behaves in a specific manner according to circumstances. Imposing one style of behavior on others indicates a desire for the members to respond in kind, with all participants in the communication process becoming victims every time circumstances change and alternate behaviors are warranted. There are three common styles of behavior used by leaders/managers: passive, aggressive, and assertive. The effective nurse manager learns the process used in each, as well as their advantages and disadvantages.

Passive Behavior

Passive behavior is submissively accepting whatever circumstances are in force, without resistance or complaint. The passive individual has low self-esteem and is unable to initiate contact with others and to stand up for individual rights or the rights of patients/clients and staff. Very often, passive nurses see themselves as second-class employees, unable to exert influence and power in strategic circumstances, rather than as peers or equals with the right to act on their own convictions. Behaviors characteristic of the passive person are apologetic speech ("You're right, I'm wrong, I'm sorry." "I don't really know, but . . ."), avoidance or withdrawal, hedging when asked to make a decision, and giving of self unstintingly. The passive nurse manager avoids direct confrontation, thus allowing people and circumstances to dominate the situation. Unable to articulate thoughts or feelings in an assertive manner, this kind of leader experiences feelings of helplessness and powerlessness, which leads to failure in accomplishing the managerial role.

A usual behavioral pattern of the passive nurse is to engage in self-pity, self-righteousness, and superiority, telling others (usually those outside the work scene) of the oppressive conditions caused by the bureaucracy, the charge nurse, or any other scapegoat. Periodically the typical passive person will reach a breaking point and have an emotional outburst of aggressive behavior (for example, shouting, crying, blaming). Immediately afterward the nurse feels guilty and ashamed and quietly returns to the passive routine. Passive individuals have not learned that each individual is responsible for his or her reactions to circumstances, and they continue to allow others to manipulate them.

Aggressive Behavior

An aggressive individual acts in a bold, attacking, and hostile manner, often accomplishing purposes at the expense of others, with injurious and destructive results. Aggression is disagreeing by being unpleasant and cantankerous. Examples of aggressive means of communication are blaming, shaming, refusing to take "no" for an answer, belittling remarks, humiliating or embarrassing another in the presence of others, stomping feet, banging doors, cursing, slamming the receiver down, and crying.

Assertive Behavior

In the discussion of leadership styles and conflict resolution, specific behaviors used by nurse managers to cope with different interpersonal relationships were addressed. In a "win-win" resolution, the nurse manager uses the confronting, collaborative, and problem-solving approach, each of which requires assertiveness.

Assertive behavior is maintaining a balance between passive and aggressive behavior. As Table 7 illustrates, assertiveness means expressing one's positive and negative beliefs and reactions openly without infringing on the rights of others. The assertive person makes choices about how, when, where, who, and why actions are taken. This may include choosing whether to be assertive. Assertiveness means being in control of what happens to oneself, of making requests and having needs met, and being able to refuse compliance with unrealistic demands or requests. Assertiveness helps the individual initiate and terminate conversations with confidence. Assertive behavior allows the nurse manager to act in the best interests of self, patients/clients, and members of the health care team by expressing honest feelings comfortably and without undue anxiety.

Marie Manthey urges nurses to develop a professional mind-set that lets clients, co-workers and the public view nurses as responsible individuals who can take care of their own needs. In so doing, nurses become more capable of taking care of the needs of others.[11] She lists nine ways to be assertive:

1. Learn to say what you think. People can have different opinions without drawing sides of "right" or "wrong."
2. Admit that it is possible you can be wrong.

◇ **Table 7.** Comparison of behaviors exhibited by passive, assertive, and aggressive nurses

PASSIVE	ASSERTIVE	AGGRESSIVE
Low self-esteem	High self-esteem	High-low self-esteem
Feels self-pity	Feels self-worth	Mixed feelings of worth
Shy, withdrawn	Forthright	Forward and attacking
Apologetic	Open and honest	Hostile, manipulative
Denies rights and needs of self and patients / clients	Acts in best interest of self, patients / clients	Demands needs be gratified for self and others
Feels victimized	Feels self to be on peer level	Feels must fight for rights
Allows situation to control rather than controlling situation	Controls situation	Attacks situation

3. Do not accept persuasion, coercion, manipulation or guilt unless you choose to.

4. Set limits as to how far you will go. Learn to say, "This is what I will do; I expect this much from you."

5. Expect healthy interpersonal relationships within all work groups and promote whatever is necessary to achieve them (support groups; free, open, and honest communication).

6. Show concern and compassion without trying to "rescue" the person in trouble. "What do you need from me?" is an appropriate question.

7. Discuss your feelings and problems as you wish, but do not expect others to rescue you—just expect them to listen.

8. Think of talking as a tool and a pleasure, as talking helps in understanding oneself and others.

9. Take responsibility for your communication. Be honest, direct, and open. Be firm, or gentle and loving, when appropriate. Give first priority to being who you are and saying what you need to say.

SUMMARY

1. Conflict is present when an inner or outer struggle occurs regarding ideas, feelings, or actions. Intrapersonal, interpersonal, and intergroup conflicts may cause organizational dysfunction.

2. How nurse managers approach workplace conflicts is an example of how they approach all other organizational and leadership functions.

3. Bureaucratic managers believe conflict is unnecessary and harmful, reflecting poor planning and control.

4. Human relations theorists take a liberal attitude toward conflict, contending that it is a normal, frequent occurrence, some of which is desirable, because the resolution may lead to greater effectiveness.

5. Inner conflict within a nurse manager (intrapersonal) occurs when the leader is confronted with two or more demands, such as uncertainty about expectations, ethical dilemma, role conflict, and work overload, all of which cause the body to respond in helpful or harmful ways.

6. Selye's theory offers three phases to stress response: excitement (when the individual goes into a "fight or flight" stance), resistance (when the body mobilizes its resources to combat stress, often manifested by illness), and the exhaustion stage (when the individual gives up).

7. Conflict between organizations is usually restricted to broad issues such as competition for buildings, grounds, and facilities. Lower- or first-level nurse managers usually play a secondary role in this kind of conflict.

8. Conflict within health organizations occurs between people (intrapersonal) and groups (intergroup). The major sources of conflict include differences between management and staff, shared resources, interdependence among departments, and values and goals regarding delivery of nursing care.

9. Possible consequences of organizational conflict include the following: (1) issues are recognized; (2) there is a rise in group cohesion and performance; (3) constructive problem solving can be employed in moderate levels of conflict; (4) incorrect information or distortion of perception may lead to destructive or dysfunctional actions; and (5) leaders may emerge who might not otherwise have been recognized.

10. Methods used in resolving conflict are competition and power, smoothing, avoidance, compromise, and collaboration. All methods may be used at some time by managers, but the collaborative approach offers the most constructive way to resolve conflict.

11. The collaborative approach to conflict resolution requires clear definition of values, purposes, and goals; open and honest communication; responsibility; and trust.

12. A model for conflict resolution consists of an effective leader who brings together the individuals or groups in conflict and facilitates identification of the problem; free exchange of ideas, feelings, attitudes, and values; and a search for alternate ways to solve the problem. This also involves getting help from outside sources as needed and establishing a plan for evaluation of the proposed solutions and of the solution finally decided on.

13. Assertive behavior is maintaining a balance between passive and aggressive behavior. The assertive person chooses which behavior to use and expresses positive and negative beliefs and reactions without infringing on the rights of others. Assertive behavior allows the nurse manager to act in the best interests of self, patients / clients, and members of the health care team by expressing honest feelings comfortably and without undue anxiety.

14. Nurses need to develop a professional mind-set that allows clients, co-workers and the public to view nurses as responsible individuals who can take care of their own needs; hence they will be better able to take care of the needs of others.

15. Ways to be assertive include learning to say what you think, admitting that it is possible you can be wrong, not accepting pressure from others unless it is your choice, setting limits as to how far you will go, expecting healthy interpersonal relationships within all work groups and promoting them. Assertiveness also means showing concern and compassion without trying to "rescue" the person in trouble, discussing your feelings and problems with others and expecting to be listened to, thinking of talking as a pleasure and a tool, taking responsibility for your own communication, and giving first priority to being who you are and saying what you need to say.

Questions for Study and Discussion

1. Are there any positive outcomes of conflict? Explain.
2. Why is it naive to think that dysfunctional on-the-job conflict can be completely avoided?
3. A staff member approaches you, her manager, with the complaint "You always give me the most disagreeable assignments, and I'm not going to take it anymore!" How would you respond to the staff member? Which of the five interpersonal conflict-management styles have you used?
4. Think of the most recent employer you have had (or present employer). How would you describe that person's relative use of the five interpersonal conflict-management styles? Give an example.

REFERENCES

1. Collyer M: Resolving conflicts: leadership style sets the strategy, Nurs Man 20(9):77-80, 1989.
2. Longest B: Management practices for the health professional, ed 4, Norwalk, Conn, 1990, Appleton & Lange.
3. Landy F: Psychology of work behavior, Pacific Grove, Calif, 1989, Brook / Cole Publishing Co.
4. Selye H: The stress of life, ed 2, New York, 1976, McGraw-Hill.
5. Westman M: The relationship between stress and

performance: the moderating effect of hardiness, Hum Perf 3(3):141-155, 1990.
6. Kreitner R: Management, ed 4, Boston, 1989, Houghton-Mifflin Co.
7. Beaubien J and Caesar B: How to handle criticism, Nursing 89(10):95-98, 1989.
8. Jones M, Bushardt S, and Cadenhead G: A paradigm for effective resolution of interpersonal conflict, Nurs Man 21(2):64B-64L, 1990.

9. Wolfe D and Bushardt S: Interpersonal conflict: strategies and guidelines for resolution, J Am Med Rec Assoc 56(2):18-22, 1985.
10. Hellriegel D and Slocum J: Management, ed 5, Reading, Mass, 1989, Addison-Wesley Publishing Co.
11. Manthey M: Vulnerable no more, Nurs Man 20(4):26, 1989.

SUGGESTED READINGS

Cauthorne-Lindstrom C and Hrabe D: Co-dependent behaviors in managers: a script for failure, Nurs Man 21(2):34-35, 1990.
Grensing L: How to deal with anger, Nursing 90 20(7):100, 1990.
Guntzelman J: Making frustration work for you, Nursing 90 20(12):85-89, 1990.
Kaye G and Burke E: Your grievance procedures alone will not protect you, Nurs Man 21(2):24-27, 1990.
Morgan K and Miller J: Non-professional nursing staff attitudes about AIDS, Nurs Man 21(10):84-87, 1990.
Wilson C, Hamilton C, and Murphy E: Union dynamics in nursing, JONA 20(2):35-39, 1990.

10

Control

On completion of this chapter the student will be prepared to:

☐ Define the control process and the steps necessary for its successful implementation.

☐ Explain the impact of third-party control on nursing.

☐ Discuss how the decentralized budget process for middle-level nurse managers is utilized.

☐ Differentiate between operating, capital expenditure, and personnel budgets.

☐ Define the process used to prepare a budget in a decentralized system.

☐ Identify the basic steps used in a nursing services control system.

☐ Differentiate between task analysis and quality control of nursing care.

☐ Define performance appraisal and explain its use.

☐ Describe the components of an effective nursing appraisal system and recognize problems and pitfalls associated with personnel appraisal.

☐ Relate methods used for measurement of performance to their usefulness in nursing.

☐ Give the purpose of a nursing performance review session and list guidelines for an effective session.

☐ Review the process for managing the problem employee.

The managerial function of control consists of measuring and correcting the activities of people and equipment in an organization to make sure that objectives and plans are accomplished. Control is a function of all managers on all levels. The word *control* sometimes carries a negative connotation. People tend to think of control as surveillance, correction, or even reproach. However, control, when used effectively, is a normal, positive, and pervasive process. It can guide behavior as well as set into motion plans for the future.

THE IMPACT OF THIRD-PARTY CONTROL ON NURSING

Just a few years ago, most hospitals were reimbursed either on the basis of itemization of charges or on the full cost of services by the vast majority of third-party payers such as Blue Cross, Blue Shield, Medicare, and Medicaid. Because of changes in Medicare reimbursement and the increasing number of Health Maintenance Organization (HMO) and Preferred Provider Organization (PPO) contracts, most hospitals must now assume some financial risk for providing care to 50% to 70% of their patients.[1] The former system encouraged hospitals to promote extended hospital stays. Long hospital stays resulted in high reimbursement from third-party payers, which increased hospital profits. The costs of these long stays were passed on to the consumer in the form of increased insurance rates. The purpose of prospective reimbursement was to establish, in advance, the amount that would be paid for inpatient hospital care in each Diagnosis Related Group (DRG) category. Hospitals now have an incentive to control costs, because if their costs are below the amount set by prospective payment guidelines, they may keep the "difference"; if their costs are higher, hospitals stand to lose money.

Accordingly, nurse managers are influenced strongly to conform their nursing care to the patient length of stay (LOS) established by the DRG. Research studies indicate that nursing care hours (NCH) prescribed by the JCAHO, by state nursing practice acts for safe nurse practice, and by those preassigned to DRG categories, have a mean average of about 64%, a rather high degree of similarity.[2,3]

Still, several questions must be addressed in the near future to assure that safe, quality care is given to *all* recipients of care. Care for those DRG patients that does not correlate closely with the established LOS and NCHs must be examined closely. Attention must be given to factors such as (1) care for patients who require a higher or lower intensity of care than that allotted per DRG category, (2) the level of preparation of nurses and the patient care delivery system utilized, and (3) the relationship of NCH per DRG category to the mortality rate.[4,5] The study of these factors can help to determine how the preparation of the nurse and the nursing care hours employed significantly affect patient LOS and outcome.

Any cost containment effort must begin with an understanding of the interacting components of (e.g., patient age, primary diagnosis, medical treatment, nursing diagnosis, and the means necessary to meet all patient needs), a means of measuring productivity, and a way to measure changes in output against resource consumption. Cost containment and quality health care are not compatible.[6] The nurse manager's role is to seek ways to learn the budgeting and control process to establish harmony between costs and provision of care.

CONTROL PROCESS

Control is the process by which managers attempt to see that actual activities conform to planned activities. As evidenced in this definition, there is a close link between planning and controlling. In the planning process the fundamental goals of the organization (and the subunits within that organization) and the methods for obtaining them are established (see Chapter 6). In the control process, progress made toward achievement of these goals is measured. For example, if some part of the nursing activity is assessed as weak or wrong, or if there is a gross discrepancy in some part of the budget, the manager tries to identify deviations from the plan so that remedial action can be taken. Although the functions of planning and controlling should be kept distinct, the control process would be meaningless without a plan.[7]

A well-designed nursing control system (1) establishes trust and commitment to the system by all personnel concerned through use of an effective communication system; (2) clarifies organization and individual objectives; (3) presents uniform and fair standards with precise definitions of each standard, goal, and objective; (4) compares expectancy with performance; and (5) improves organization development by providing information for decision making on staffing, system for delivery of care, and quality of care; and (6) promotes growth and development of personnel. A combination of standards, well-planned objectives, strong organizational support, and capable direction has a high probability for success when an adequate system of control is in effect.

Financial Control System

A financial control system is implemented by a *budget,* which is defined as a tool for planning, monitoring, and controlling cost, or a systematic plan for meeting expenses. A statement of estimated future expenditures is prepared each year based on previous records and educated predictions of future needs. The purpose of the budget is allow the organization to stay on top of the changes in the health care system; to maintain quality care while containing costs.[8] The budget can be a powerful instrument, since it serves as a guide for nursing performance and allocation of personnel, supplies, support services, and facilities.

An effective budget system (1) has enough sources to supply sufficient funds, (2) allocates financial resources to specific units or departments based on certain criteria, and (3) conducts a controlling system that shows how effectively financial resources are being used. Budgets form the link in the management process that began with goals and strategies; they are the most detailed management practice used to ensure that an organization's goals are achieved.

CENTRALIZED BUDGETING

Some organizational budgets are centralized: the budgets are developed and imposed by the controller, administrator of the hospital, and the director of nursing services, with little or no consultation with lower-level managers. The formal organizations of most hospital nursing departments distribute responsibilities along bureaucratic lines and enforce accountability for

carrying them out through hierarchical channels. Nurse managers are expected to use all hospital information systems, but they have relatively little input into the selection, implementation, and evaluation of those systems.[9] This top-down approach leaves the implementors of the budget without autonomy or the right to appropriate or control expenses.

DECENTRALIZED BUDGETING

More and more health agencies are recognizing the value of having budgets prepared by those who must implement them. With decentralization the middle-level manager (head nurse or department manager) becomes actively involved in the planning and budgeting process; autonomy, accountability, and authority are placed at the practitioner level.[8] Top-level managers still attend to overall forecasting needs for the new fiscal year, looking at past experiences and records, considering any changes, such as closing or opening of facilities or services, studying anticipated population changes, and taking account of any regulating changes that might result in policy change or legislation. The middle-level nurses are given the authority to develop and monitor the budget for their respective units for each year. This decentralized approach, or bottom-up budgeting, has five distinct advantages:

1. Head nurses or department managers have a more intimate view of their needs than do those at the top.
2. Middle-level managers can provide a more realistic breakdown to support their requests.
3. There is less likelihood of overlooking vital needs.
4. Morale and satisfaction are usually higher when individuals participate actively in the making of decisions that will affect them.
5. There is room for more flexibility and quicker action.

Decentralized budgeting is believed by the author to be the most effective approach.

TYPES OF BUDGETS

The budget types most commonly managed by nurses in institutions are *operating budgets, capital expenditure budgets,* and *personnel budgets.*

Operating Budget

As shown in Figure 10-1, an operating budget includes services to be provided and goods the unit expects to consume or use during the budget period. For a nursing unit this covers the cost of supplies, small equipment, and other miscellaneous items.

The operating budget relies on the patient-day forecast. Most health institutions provide managers with a medical supplies stock list, a linen supplies list, and a stationary stock list from which to order. In some institutions, the movement of supplies throughout the organization is so closely monitored that decreases in any item to a preestablished critical level triggers issuance of a computerized order for that item from outside vendors tied into the system.[10]

What is included in the nursing department's operating budget varies among institutions. Utilities, housekeeping, and engineering services, for example, are usually considered indirect expenses and are not direct budget items. For these services a portion of the total cost is assigned to the unit by top-level management after hospital cost studies have been made.

Capital Expenditure Budget

A *capital expenditure budget* consists of an itemized list of current capital assets (usually items over $500) and enumerates each piece of capital equipment together with its serial number, current value, and physical location. If a new item is intended to replace an outmoded piece of equipment, the older piece of equipment and its serial number should be removed from the capital equipment inventory to prevent confusion in later monitoring of equipment.[10]

Capital items are usually requested on a special form that requires a statement of justification. Capital costs consider long-term goals and must complement the agency's objectives.

Personnel Budget

The personnel budget consists of the numbers of various nursing and support personnel required to operate a nursing unit, and the monies allocated for that personnel. The personnel budget is an especially important part of the budgeting process as it can account for as much as 90% of the total nursing service budget. Factors that influence staff projection include[7]:

1. The delivery system in effect (e.g., total care, modular, team, primary nursing, or case management)
2. The mix of nursing personnel (e.g., RNs, including clinical specialists, LPNs, LVNs, nurses' aides)
3. The acuity level of nursing service given
4. The health care facility's occupancy rate

Classification system. Patient census and patient acuity are used in a patient classification system (PCS) to determine the number and mix of nursing personnel needed. Refer to Chapter 5 for a discussion of the PCS process.

Full-time equivalent positions (FTEs). A position is allotted to each person employed by the health agency. For example, a nurse who works 80 hours per 2-week pay period is assigned a 1.0

Operational budget	Capital budget	Personnel budget

Supplies
Services
Small equipment
Miscellaneous items
	Large equipment (usually in excess of $500)
	Physical changes
	Physical additions to the unit
		Number of personnel
		Salaries
		   Working days
		   Time off
		   Fringe benefits

Figure 10-1. Example of items usually included in a nursing operating, capital, and personnel budget.

FTE, and a second nurse who works 40 hours in a 2-week pay period is assigned a 0.5 FTE. The nurse manager cannot exceed the number of FTEs approved by nursing administration for the fiscal year, but can use ingenuity in filling the positions. For example, one FTE position could be shared by three nurses, two working 2 days each and one working a single day. When nurses are on paid leave, sick time, or vacation, their FTE positions are not available for full-time replacement, as their salaries are being paid. For these occasions, temporary replacement by nurses "on call" are utilized as needed. In the budgeting process, the department manager takes these matters into account and determines the number of FTEs needed for a year, based on past records. The department manager uses an electronic spread sheet to track positions, shift by shift, which can provide a summary of filled and vacant positions budgeted for each job category, as well as an itemized account of times when census or patient acuity was low and the full complement of anticipated staff was not needed.[11]

Case managers and economic control. Harper Hospital in Detroit, Michigan, reports that the case management system has saved the hospital thousands of dollars by expediting care and minimizing duplication of services.[12] This hospital employs only masters'-prepared nurses as case managers, believing the roles of clinician, educator, collaborator, and researcher, with the added management focus, require at least this level of preparation. Its case managers are accountable for the management of both clinical and financial outcomes. They are given appropriate institutional power and control to achieve the desired goals, which are designed to link quality and economic concepts. The case manager uses preprinted standard patient care plans to determine the needs of each patient and to monitor patient progress throughout his or her stay. (Review Chapter 5 for a more detailed account of case manager activity.) Case managers have access to a computerized cost management system that assists in tracking the activities and costs incurred for each patient. With this tool they can look for duplication of services or inadequate progress.

PREPARATION OF THE BUDGET

Preparation of the budget begins several months before the end of each fiscal year to allow time for careful preparation. Figure 10-2 diagrams the budgetary process in a decentralized system: (1) participants review agency policies, standards, and objectives, (2) top-level administrators project for the future and prepare guidelines, (3) middle-level nurse managers prepare the annual budget, (4) administrator of nursing services and controller review the budget, (5) the budget is accepted or modified, and (6) the budget is implemented and evaluated on a regular basis.

Participants Review Agency Policies, Standards, and Objectives

Because all types of budgets are projections or plans of future events, they provide managers with standards for control. Before preparing a budget, a review of policies is important, as *policies are broad guidelines for making all decisions.* Policies made at the top level are interpreted and implemented through each division's own standards and objectives. For example, one agency's policy might be to provide care for all people regardless of their ability to pay. Another policy might be to include education and research as an integral part of all organizational operations. A more common policy is that enough income must be generated to offset all expenditures.[13]

Standards are established levels of quality or quantity used to guide performance: they constitute the norm or standard of activity that is acceptable in an institution (for example, standards for admission and dismissal of patients, and standards of nursing practice). *Objectives state how the policies and standards will be carried out.* Review of policies, standards, and objectives at the top level focus on the broad picture. Then from the top-level down, all budget deliberations consider the agency's broad policies, standards, and objectives, which are then reflected in budgeting appropriations.

Top-Level Projections and Guidelines

Those who prepare budgets must exercise judgment in using historical data and forecasts of changing conditions and costs. The principal focus of making projections and

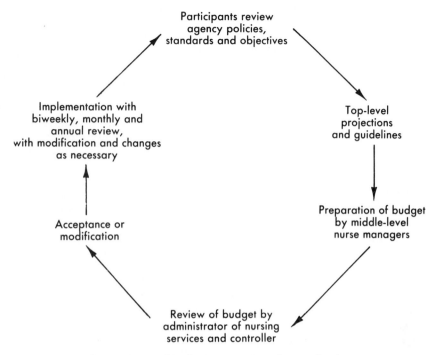

Figure 10-2. Model of budget process in a decentralized system.

establishing guidelines is to maximize efficiency and productivity. Again, top-level administrators project and guide in broad terms, and these projections are used as guides by all administrators. Examples of broad *projections* might be to increase patient census by one tenth in the next fiscal year and to add a new wing to the hospital in the next 2 years. Examples of broad *guidelines* might be to explore ways to utilize labor more productively, to upgrade the existing facilities, to maintain a work environment that nourishes people and rewards their accomplishments, and to give first priority to the needs of patients.[8]

Preparation of Budget by Middle-Level Managers

The key to controlling a budget begins with preparation of the annual budget. Middle-level managers (head nurses or department managers) prepare the budget for their units based on past expenditures and predictions for the coming year, provided by the chief fiscal officer

within the framework formulated by top-level management. Department managers communicate with other department managers and their supervisors, whose operations are related and interdependent. In decentralized budgeting, coordination is important; otherwise each department might operate without regard to what any other department is doing or consideration for the organization's overall goals. Computer printouts of the master operating budget and related departments' past budgets are shared and used in projecting budgets for the upcoming year.[14]

Costing out nursing services

Hospitals. Hospitals' attempts to separate nursing costs from room rates have been under way for at least 10 years. With the development of DRGs, concern has increased. The phrase *costing out nursing services* means simply determining cost of services provided by nurses. The goal, in relation to DRGs, is to identify the cost of nursing for a specific patient so that nursing costs can be reflected as a separate charge on the patient's bill. The box below gives reasons that hospital directors would support efforts to determine costs of nursing services. To evaluate nursing costs, the following issues must be explored[15]:

1. The cost of nursing time per DRG per acuity level in a particular institution
2. Direct (hands-on) versus indirect (other) costs of nursing
3. Comparison of nursing costs with total hospital cost
4. Comparison of nursing costs with other departments
5. Comparison of nursing costs at one institution with nursing costs at other institutions.

It is believed that identifying costs for specific nursing interventions or services will allow evaluation of the cost of nursing care, such as what nursing diagnoses are associated with what medical diagnoses (DRGs), and what nursing interventions provide the best outcome for specific nursing diagnoses.[15]

Community health agencies and nursing homes. Community health nursing agencies have kept cost records based on nursing cost per visit for many years; however, this cost analysis has included all costs of the agency (operative and capital expenditure budgets) without any attempt to identify only nursing costs. What is needed is cost per diagnosis or nursing treatment.

With regard to nursing homes, some states have prepared a list of nursing services based on an assumed provider (usually an LPN/LVN or nurses' aide) along with the average amount of time needed to deliver those services, based on time-and-motion studies and expert opinion. Generally speaking, costs for nursing are treated the same as hospital costs, with little effort given to determining the costs of specific nursing services. Until this is done, nurses cannot justify the numbers or levels of nurses needed to provide care for a specific unit or agency.[16]

Skilled and intermediate care facilities (SNF/ICF). Before passage of the Omnibus Budget Reconciliation Act, skilled nursing facilities were required to provide adequate nursing services as regulated by the state. As of October 1, 1990, a skilled nursing facility or an intermediate care facility must have sufficient nursing staff to pro-

---

Reasons Why Hospital Directors Would Support Efforts to Determine the Costs of Nursing Services

1. Efforts will result in knowledge about cost of nursing care now hidden in room cost.
2. Nursing care is the largest product of any hospital. While costs of other products are known, nursing costs remain obscure.
3. Knowing the cost of nursing will allow for accurate billing of nursing services, contracting with HMOs and PPOs for nursing services and better determination of cost of providing a new service.
4. Knowledge of nursing cost does *not* mean higher healthcare costs. It opens the door to cost reduction in nursing, through design of more effective delivery methods.
5. If costing out nursing services should lead to the conclusion that nursing is being unfairly compensated or that nursing is subsidizing other services, the hospital administrator should be the first to have this information in order to promote a more equitable allocation of reimbursement among providers.
6. Knowing the type, quality and cost of services of all healthcare providers allows consumers and managers a safe substitution of cheaper alternatives. Increased competition in the healthcare arena will reduce costs for the consumer.
7. Efforts to cost out nursing services are consistent with the values of hospital directors to promote quality care in a cost-effective manner.
8. Local efforts to cost out nursing services are in line with the national trend. Hospital and nurse directors either can take a proactive role in defining and collecting their own data or can wait passively until it is done by others, who may not collect or use the data appropriately.

From McCloskey J: Implications of costing out nursing services for reimbursement, Nurs Man 20(1):49, 1989.

vide nursing *and related services* so that the facility can "attain or maintain the highest practical physical, mental, and psyco-social well-being of each resident, as determined by [its] assessments of individual plans of care."[17] Compliance will be costly, with intermediate care facilities without skilled nursing beds tending to bear the largest cost increases.

To satisfy the "sufficient nurse staff" requirement, skilled and intermediate care facilities must have a registered nurse on duty at least 8 consecutive hours a day, 7 days a week, and a full-time RN must serve as director of nursing. Nurse managers are in a position to estimate new costs stemming from the new rules. This is important, as Medicare and Medicaid are directed in the new law to pay their share of reasonable costs of the new requirements. In preparing a budget for staff members, especially for new categories such as occupational therapist or a psychologist, full justification must be included.

Review of Budget by Administrator of Nursing Services and Controller

Budgets from each unit are received by the administrator of nursing services and the controller or chief financial officer, who reviews and compares them with past budgets, budgets of all other nursing departments, and the amount of revenue that can reasonably be expected in the coming year. Some administrators require written justification for budget requests.[18]

Acceptance or Modification

Budgets often have to be reduced or modified to balance expected costs and revenues. Generally, items of lowest priority are cut first, although when revenue is very limited, even high-priority items must be eliminated. Once accepted, the budget is approved by the administrator and governing board and sent to each department or unit to serve as the financial guide for the coming year.[8]

Implementation with Biweekly, Monthly, and Annual Review, with Modification and Changes as Necessary

Ongoing surveillance of the budget is vital to its success. The most effective system is to have a two-way flow of information between middle and top management with a utilization report issued every 2 weeks or monthly. Figure 10-3 illustrates how budgetary responsibilities can be analyzed. The nurse manager is regularly provided with a computerized statement from the controller, indicating the items for which she is responsible, the current period of budget, and how much has been spent, with an indication of variance (the amount spent over or under the budget). By comparing what is actually spent with what was budgeted, the nurse manager is able to check on unit operation. Variations from the projected budget will show excess supply costs, too many or too few of the wrong kinds of personnel, and overuse or underuse of the nursing unit.[10] The manager is also given the year-end data analysis and a comparison of the previous year's budget.

In addition to the biweekly or monthly scrutiny, there is a quarterly evaluation. Projections and actual occurrences are compared, and minor modifications can be made. No major changes are made without going through the entire budgetary process. With sufficient information the nurse manager can see what is working satisfactorily and identify problem areas and unfavorable trends to initiate corrective action when necessary.

NURSING SERVICES CONTROL SYSTEM

The definition of control provides the intention of control; that is, activities conform to plans. It does not tell the manager how to establish and implement a process that will lead to desired results. The control process may be divided into: the following basic components: (1) establishing standards, objectives, and methods for measuring performance; (2) measuring actual performance; (3) comparing results of performance with standards and objectives and identifying strengths and areas for correction; and (4) acting to reinforce strengths or successes and taking corrective action as necessary (Figure 10-4).

Establishing Standards for Measuring Performance

The meaning of standards must be clear to those who are controlling them. Standards may be stated in terms of the highest or optimal level

Monthly responsibility summary
[computer printout]

	Area of service		Month		Year		Nurse manager				
Items budgeted	Current period			Year-to-date			Prior year				
	Actual	Budget	Variance	Actual	Budget	Variance	Actual	Budget	Variance		
Salaries											
Management											
R.N.											
L.V.N.											
Aides											
Orderlies											
Clerical											
Total wages											
F.I.C.A. taxes											
Vacation pay											
Group health insurance											
Group life insurance											
Pension and retirement											
Workmen's comp. insur											
Holiday pay											
Sick leave											
Surgical packs; CSS sterilizer											
Surgical supplies, general											
IV solutions											
Pharmaceuticals											
Other medical care supplies											
Office/administration supplies											
Instruments/minor equipment											
Repairs and maintenance											
Depreciation/equipment											
Equipment rental											
Telephone											
Training sessions; books											
Travel											
Dues and subscriptions											
Other expense											
TOTAL EXPENSE											

Figure 10-3. Example of a form in which monthly expenditures for an area of responsibility can be logged.

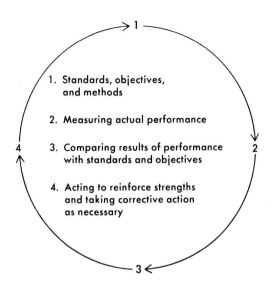

1. Standards, objectives, and methods

2. Measuring actual performance

3. Comparing results of performance with standards and objectives

4. Acting to reinforce strengths and taking corrective action as necessary

Figure 10-4. Basic steps in the control process.

of attainment desired, the minimal or baseline level, or any level in between (similar to a grading system of A, B, C, and so on). Those using the standards must understand the meaning and agree on the standards chosen. As discussed previously, standards may be official or voluntary. A universal standard that health agencies must adhere to is the requirements for licensure, accreditation, and certification for employees and the agency. In addition, they may want to develop standards that exceed requirements of outside interests, or they may wish to develop standards that are not vested in regulations but that uniquely apply to them.

Standards are formulated at all levels, from top to middle to lower or first levels. They are used to provide guidance to all personal and impersonal functions in the agency. There are three types of standards: structure, process, and outcome.[7] *Structure* standards are those that focus on the structure or management system used by an agency to organize and deliver care, including the number and categories of personnel who provide that care. In evaluation of structure, the conditions under which nursing care will be given are assessed, not the quality or inner workings of those conditions. For example, a structure sample might be: "A team leader is responsible for no more than 20 patients / clients with no fewer than three team

members to provide care." *Process* standards refer to actual nursing procedures—those activities engaged in by nurses to administer care. The nursing process is individualized, occurring between the nurse and the patient / client. The process standard would read: "Determination of the nurse-patient ratio takes into consideration the physical, psychologic, social, and spiritual needs of the patients / clients."[19] *Outcome* standards are designed for measuring the results of nursing care. Responses or changes in the patients / clients are compared with patient / client objectives. Continuing with the staffing illustration, an outcome standard for the results of nursing care could be: "The patient's / client's needs identified in the physical, psychologic, social, and spiritual classifications were met according to established standards and objectives for care."[19]

Establishing Methods for Measuring Performance

For process and outcome to be evaluated within a structure, measurable criteria or objectives specific to giving nursing care must be developed. This is difficult, as nursing care is delivered within a framework of interdependent relationships with physicians and a multiplicity of other health care personnel. Until more progress is made, the best approach is to select tools for measurement that are easy to use and that will provide as understandable and valid assessment as possible and to select evaluators who are familiar with the evaluation process. The most commonly used methods for measurement of nursing care are task analysis and quality control.

Measuring Actual Performance

Like all aspects of control, measurement of performance is an ongoing, repetitive process with the actual frequency dependent on the type of activity being measured. For example, safety factors may be continuously monitored, whereas a formal appraisal of performance may occur only once or twice a year. Measurements may be scheduled in advance, may be done at periodic but unannounced intervals, or may occur at random. Use of all methods provides a more comprehensive assessment. One should not confuse measurement of tasks with quality nor allow too long a time to pass between measurements. It is much better to clarify the purpose of the measurement and to measure performance on a continuous basis. In this way the manager and staff can be alerted to those tasks and levels of care that need attention, rather than waiting until remedial action is necessary or impossible and the problem is costly in time, money, and emotional involvement.

Comparing Results of Performance with Standards and Objectives

Comparison of nursing tasks and quality of nursing practice is made in the organization and can serve as a basis for comparison of nursing from one institution to another. The pivotal question addressed is: "Does the performance match the standards and objectives?" In some ways comparison is the easiest step in the control process. The standards, objectives, and methods of measurement have been set; now it is a matter of comparing measured results with them. If performance matches standards and objectives, managers may assume that things are under control; if performance is contrary to standards and objectives, action is necessary.

Reinforcing Strengths or Successes and Taking Corrective Action as Necessary

One part of the control process often overlooked is identifying those areas that have contributed to successful accomplishment of goals. Positive aspects need to be identified so that they may be translated into encouragement and motivation for the nursing members involved. Corrective action may need only minor changes because of temporary circumstances; however, there may be a real flaw in the plan, necessitating changes in standards or objectives. Unless managers see the control process through to its conclusion, they are merely monitoring performance, not exercising control. The emphasis should always be on finding constructive ways to improve performance, rather than on merely placing blame or looking for areas to criticize.

TASK ANALYSIS AND QUALITY CONTROL OF NURSING CARE

Goal achievement in nursing is assessed through measurement of task performance and quality of care. In *task analysis* actions and procedures

such as written guides, schedules, rules, records, and budgets are inspected. In *quality control* the level of nursing care provided and its effects on the patient/client are assessed. A study of task analysis and quality control is necessary, because they indicate both process and outcome of nursing activity. The lower or first-level nursing manager has an important role in each.

Task Analysis

Task-oriented measurements consider the actual process of giving nursing care using such tools as time studies and checklists. Task analysis studies are used to determine issues such as how long it takes a nurse to give a bath or perform a procedure or how many staff members are needed to care for a specific number of patients/clients. One problem in evaluating the tasks involved in the nursing process is that there are few tangible, identifiable, and fixed "returns on investment" to study; the physical, psychologic, social, and spiritual factors are closely interrelated. Task analyses have serious drawbacks, because they fail to measure needs other than physical support and they always deal with the present situation rather than the ideal. In addition, the delivery of nursing care and the effects of that care fluctuate greatly according to the patient/client, caregivers, type of agency, and the kind of service rendered. Resistance is another deterrent to task analysis. Like all workers, nurses may become comfortable in their niches and routines and may be hesitant about or even resistant to inspection and change.

Quality Control

Quality control is the responsibility of all employees within an organization. It is achieved through a variety of preventive and corrective methods that are intended to ensure compliance with established standards. Quality control generally focuses on measuring inputs, organizational functions, and outputs. The results of these measurements enable management to make decisions about products or services rendered.[20]

In nursing, quality assurance is both official and voluntary. Every agency must meet minimal requirement for quality control, but may carry the issue as far as they wish. With the expansion of government control on healthcare organizations and the broadening of professional nursing practice, the issue of accountability has increased in importance.

The evolution of quality assurance in the nursing profession has been greatly affected by several fundamental sources: (1) the Nurse Practice Act and Medical Practice Act of each state and (2) the development of standards by which to evaluate the delivery of health care. The Social Security Amendments of 1972 mandating Professional Standards Review Organizations (PRSOs) provided the impetus to the JCAHO to stipulate that "there shall be evidence of a well-defined, organized program designed to enhance patient care through ongoing objective assessment of important aspects of patient care and correction of identified problems.[21]

The American Nurses' Association model for quality control of nursing care. The American Nurses' Association (ANA) suggests that Standards of Nursing Practice set forth by the ANA Divisions on Practice can be applied to nursing practice in any clinical situation and therefore can serve well as a model for quality assurance.[22] The ANA-approved model for quality assurance through implementation of standards is presented in Figure 10-5. This model is a more explicit adaptation of the basic functions of the control function (standards, measurement, correction) and is geared directly toward control of nursing care.

In the ANA model *value identification* looks at such issues as patient/client philosophy; needs and rights from an economic, social, psychologic, and spiritual perspective; and values of the health care organization and the providers of nursing services.

Identification of the kind of structure, process, and standards in existence in an institution providing health services offers a framework for the review process. Examples of structure are the in-

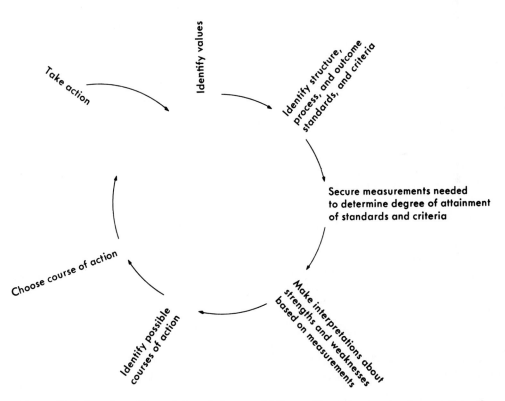

Figure 10-5. American Nurses' Association model for quality assurance; implementation of standards.

stitution's status in relation to requirements of licensing boards, the JCAHO, and medical and nursing groups.

Process describes the nature and sequence of activities undertaken by nurses in the care of patients/clients (what they do, how they do it, and in what order). *Standards* refer to the agreed-on level of nursing care that is to be provided. *Criteria* are the characteristics or behaviors used to measure the level of care (e.g., "A nursing team provides care from nursing care plans that are updated at least once every 8 hours." "The patients/clients are protected from accident and injury."). *Outcome standards and criteria* reveal the end results of nursing care. For example, outcome measures may focus on what the patient/client has learned as a result of nurse contact, based on items chosen to measure end results.

Measurements are those tools used to gather information or data, determined by the selection of standards and criteria. Audits and appraisals of cost, quality, and accountability are mandated by the JCAHO. They are accomplished by individuals, physicians, nursing staff, patients/clients, community, and other health disciplines. A standard rating scale is an example of a method used for quality control. Standards are listed, then checked off by an evaluator as to their degree or level of accomplishment. Other methods used are questionnaires, observations, peer review, and tabulations of patient/client records or patient care audit.

The nursing audit provides an opportunity for nurses to have a voice in the control of nursing practice. The director of nursing services or an appointed representative (such as patient care coordinator) is responsible for initiating and maintaining a nursing audit program, using methods decided on within nursing (including established standards and criteria, measurement of actual practice against standards and criteria, evaluation of results) and for taking actions to reinforce strengths and correct deficiencies in nursing service. Nursing audits consider the past or the present, documenting compliance with standards for nursing care as established by the agency; the nursing department; and the professional, governmental, and accrediting groups.[23]

A retrospective or closed chart audit is an inspection of a patient's/client's chart after he or she has been discharged. Retrospective audits provide an objective way of assessing accountability for care given to a representative sampling of patients/clients who have been hospitalized.[23] A current or open chart audit is an evaluation of the record of a patient/client still receiving care in the hospital or agency. Measuring quality of care through inspection of the nursing process in a variety of ways allows an auditing procedure that will protect against overlooking relevant information.

Interpretations of conclusions about strengths and weaknesses in the delivery of nursing care are made after the information has been analyzed. Possible courses of action are identified. *A course of action is chosen* by using the problem-solving method, by weighing the options, then following through with a well-thought-out plan. Finally, *a course of action is taken,* and the assessment procedure is completed.

The control processes as proposed by management authorities and the ANA's model are similar, as shown in Figure 10-6. The ANA model can be helpful to nurse managers, as the steps proposed directly apply to evaluation and control of the Standards of Nursing Practice.

Peer review. Peer review is the examining and evaluating, by associates, of another nurse's practice. Preestablished standards, objectives, and methods are used as a basis for judgment. A new head nurse at the University of Michigan Hospital in Ann Arbor, Michigan, discovered that the staff of the diabetes unit to which she was assigned did not fully understand documentation standards.[23] A staff program of peer review of closed charts was initiated to improve documentation and to develop peer review skills within the group. A chart audit worksheet was developed (see Figure 10-7 for a sample) to be used by all staff, after an orientation to the system, including a demonstration of how to audit the chart. The Ann Arbor staff audited charts of recently dismissed patients in small groups (retrospective or closed audit), as the head nurse felt this small group interaction encouraged constructive communication. Through the process, nurses gained increased insight into areas that needed improvement and set about making constructive changes in their nursing practice and helping their peers to grow as well. Documentation markedly improved over a period of several months, as noted in Figure 10-8,

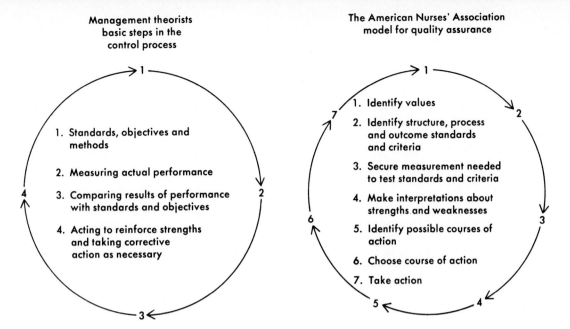

Management theorists
basic steps in the
control process

1. Standards, objectives and methods

2. Measuring actual performance

3. Comparing results of performance with standards and objectives

4. Acting to reinforce strengths and taking corrective action as necessary

The American Nurses' Association
model for quality assurance

1. Identify values

2. Identify structure, process and outcome standards and criteria

3. Secure measurement needed to test standards and criteria

4. Make interpretations about strengths and weaknesses

5. Identify possible courses of action

6. Choose course of action

7. Take action

Figure 10-6. Comparison of management theorists' basic steps in the control process with the American Nurses' Association model for quality assurance.

1. Mechanisms for coping with stress
   How does the patient react to stress?
   What does the patient do to cope with stress?
   e.g., Eats more or stops eating when under stress
   Nursing assessment _____
   Nursing progress note _____
   Other _____
   Absent _____
2. Literacy
   Can the patient read and write?
   What level of education has the patient reached?
   Nursing assessment _____
   Top of data base form _____
   Other _____
   Absent _____
3. Foot Condition
   Is there a description of the patient's foot condition?
   Nursing assessment _____
   Nursing progress note _____
   Other _____
   Absent _____

Criteria	Audit results—first 6 months % of criteria achieved		
	April	July	September
1. Mechanisms used to cope with stress	25	75	83
2. Literacy	87	100	100
3. Foot condition	75	75	90

Figure 10-8. Audit results of the first 6 months percentage of selected criteria achieved in peer auditing. *Christensen M: Peer auditing, Nurs Man 21(1):52, 1990.*

Figure 10-7. Sample of a chart audit worksheet used in peer audition. *From Christensen M: Peer auditing, Nurs Man 21(1):50, 1990.*

which tracks the audit results of three nonrelated items. An added benefit to peer review was that staff nurses have become more comfortable with other types of peer review and with each other. When they see the need for additions to be made on a current or open chart, they feel free to leave a note on the chart or to communicate with the nurse. The overall improvement in documentation has more than met the head nurses' objectives.

Problem-focused quality assurance program. The JCAHO mandates a written plan and a comprehensive approach to quality assurance (QA).[24] In planning for their next visit from the JCAHO, the Veterans Administration Medical Center in San Diego, California, renovated their existing QA program and developed a revision based on the goal to "provide an ongoing objective assessment and correction of those problematic aspects of nursing care which have the greatest impact on patients."[25] Each major nursing service, every clinical unit, and all special care units participated, shifting the focus of quality assurance activities to problem-focused patient care evaluation studies. Figure 10-9 provides guidelines for writing a problem-focused patient care evaluation summary. Note that after problems have been identified, a correction plan is developed to resolve them, along with a reassessment plan and time frame. The San Diego VA reports positive results from its QA program and invites all nursing services who so wish to use these guidelines.[25]

PERFORMANCE APPRAISAL

Performance appraisal is a method of acquiring and processing information needed to improve the individual worker's performance and accomplishments. Performance appraisal consists of setting standards and objectives against determined standards and objectives; reviewing progress; having ongoing feedback between the appraiser and the one who is being appraised; and planning for reinforcement, deletion, or correction of identified behaviors as necessary.[20] Performance appraisal of staff nurses and assistants is one of the most important tasks a nurse manager must accomplish, for an organization depends on its nursing personnel to provide the

prescribed level of nursing care at reasonable cost and in a satisfactory environment. Yet the assessment procedure is one that most nurse managers have difficulty handling adequately. It is not easy to judge a nurse's performance accurately, and it is often harder still to convey that judgment to the worker in a comfortable or helpful manner.

Nurse Manager's Responsibility

In hospitals and other health care agencies the usual practice is for supervisors to review the performance of head nurses (or charge nurses). In turn, head nurses assume responsibility for preparation of appraisal forms and conduction of formal interview of nursing personnel assigned to their respective departments or subunits. Lower or first-level nurse managers participate in the procedure by preparing the initial evaluation of each nursing staff member assigned to them, since they are best equipped to assess activities of the team members on a day-to-day basis. Assessments made by the team leader or primary nurse are reviewed with each worker, followed by a conference between the team leader and immediate supervisor. This process assures a clear, complete, and fair report.

Historical Events in the Development of Performance Appraisal[22]

The first recording of a performance appraisal system was made about 1800 by Owens of Scotland, who devised a plan using different-colored blocks to represent various levels of performance. Each day workers would find a colored block of wood at their place that best corresponded with Owens's assessment of their work for the previous day. Other time-and-motion studies were developed until World War I highlighted the need for a tool to identify and evaluate military leaders. Business and industry assumed the task of studying appraisal of managers. Many forms became available, which still focused primarily on time and motion. During this period rating scales were introduced. Individuals' performance was graphed on a scale from "poor" or "unsatisfactory" to "good" or "excellent."

Quality Assurance

Nursing service quality assurance program, San Diego VAMC
Guidelines: writing the problem-focused patient care evaluation summary

The purpose of the *problem-focused patient care evaluation summary* is to provide a written account of specific elements which are derived from the evaluative QA studies that nurses on your unit have conducted.

The specific elements on the *problem-focused patient care evaluation summary* are: 1) Topic, 2) Sample and Time of Review, 3) Basis for Problem Selection, 4) Preestablished Clinically Valid Criteria, 5) Objectives, 6) Data Collection, 7) Results, 8) Corrective Action Plan and Time Frame and 9) Reassessment Plan and Time Frame.

In the section to follow each of the nine topics above is discussed separately and an example(s) is provided to assist you in writing each section.

Topic	*Topic* refers to what you wrote on your initial QA topic statement form that was submitted to the QA Committee. All you need do is repeat what you said on that form. For example, your topic may have been *Patient Anxiety,* or *Patient Falls* or *Heparin Lock Use.* Do not write your topic as a complete sentence. As you can see in the example, a few words or word will identify your topic.
Sample	*Sample* refers to 1) the number of elements in your QA Study, e.g., 15, 25 patient records or procedures, e.g., code blues, arterial catheterizations or personnel, e.g., nurses, doctors or patients or staff interviewed or surveyed, and, 2) when these elements were measured. For example, *retrospectively* (in the past), *concurrently* (in the present), or *prospectively* (in the future, e.g., forecast of patient care needs at a future point in time). Hence, your entry in this section may appear as: 25 Patient Records; reviewed retrospectively / 46 I&O Slips; reviewed retrospectively. Another example might be: 10 SICU patients; interviewed concurrently / 12 RNs; surveyed concurrently / 100 code blues; reviewed concurrently
Basis for problem selection	*Basis for problem selection* refers to those factors which indicated that the topic you selected for QA Review was problematic. This statement has been written on your topic sheet that you submitted several months ago to the QA Committee. For example: 1) Nurses on the Oncology ward do not have current information on the potential complications of chemotherapeutic agents. This has negative consequences for oncology patient care. 2 Nurses in the Mental Health Clinic have observed low follow through from the Psychiatric inpatient service and are concerned about problems in exchange of pertinent, timely patient information.
Preestablished clinicially valid criteria	*Preestablished Clinically Valid Criteria* refers to specific elements against which you may measure your problem. The source of these specific elements may be: 1) standards of practice, 2) published nursing research, 3) policies and procedures, 4) experts in the field and/or 5) VA guides. For example, the following are critical criteria elements derived from a VAMC Blood Transfusion Protocol:

Continued.

Figure 10-9. Guidelines developed for use in a nursing service quality assurance program, San Diego VAMC. *From Harris S, Kreger S, and Davis M: A problem-focused quality assurance program, Nurs Man 20(2):57-58, 1989.*

◇   ◇

Quality Assurance—continued

Preestablished clinically valid criteria—continued

CRITICAL CRITERIA ELEMENT	STANDARD	EXCEPTION
1. Baseline vital signs obtained prior to administration.	1. 100%	1. None
2. Blood initiated within 30 minutes from time of arrival on ward.	2. 100%	2. None
3. Line clamped immediately with reaction.	3. 100%	3. None
4. Blood absorbed within 2 hours.	4. 100%	4. MD specifies otherwise

One criterion may suffice or you may need to cite several criteria. There is no requirement that a specific number be used.

Objectives

Objectives refers to what you want to find out about the problems you selected for your QA Study. Your objectives have already been written on the topic sheet you submitted to the QA Committee. So all you need to do is rewrite in this section what you had written. Examples:
1. To determine the incidence of patient falls occurring on 3 North.
2. To identify patterns about when patients falls occur most frequently on 3 North.
3. To find out what factors may be causing or contributing to patient falls on 3 North.
   You will probably have more than one objective. There is no specified number. Remember, statements of your objectives should always begin with the word "to" . . . to find out, to determine, to assess, etc.

Data collection

Data collection refers to the tool(s) and/or method(s) which you have used to collect information about the problem you studied. If a tool was used, simply say (see attached tool). Again, this should be an easy task since you have already indicated on your topic sheet your method and/or tool for collecting your data. All you need do is repeat in this section what you have written. For example:
   Random audit of patient records.
   Patient questionnaire and interviews. (See attached tool.)
   Observation of team conferences. (See attached tool.)
   Review of incident reports, patient records and tabulation of incidence patterns of medication errors.
   Random audit of patient records and tabulation of no show appointment in MHC.
   A copy of the tool should be attached to the Summary Sheet.

Results

Results refers to what you found out, e.g., the findings, from your data collection.
   In this section, write about your results first. Then, if you have any table(s) which summarize that data, refer the reader to them. The table(s) should be attached to the Summary Sheet.
   The results section should be limited to one brief, factual paragraph which can be confined to the space provided on the Summary Sheet.
   To begin the Results section, simply complete the following sentence or a variation of it. "Analysis of the data revealed that. . . ."
   Analysis of the data revealed that eight (8) medication errors occurred during the period of review. Four (4) errors were made by RNs and four (4) errors were made by LVNs. Six (6) errors were made during the night tour.
   These errors consisted of:
   a) Medication given to the wrong person (3).
   b) Medication not given (2).
   c) Incorrect dosage administered (1).
   d) Topical medication applied to wrong site, and
   e) Medication given at wrong time (1).

Figure 10-9, continued.

Quality Assurance—continued

Corrective action plan and time frame

Corrective action plan refers to your plan for resolving the problem. When describing your plan, state exactly *what* you plan to do to correct the problem by listing each step of your plan separately.

Time frame refers to *when* you plan to implement your corrective action and *who* will be responsible for implementation.

For example, let's say you studied the incidence of pressure sores on your ward for a two-month period and found out that you had an unacceptable level of occurrence. Your objective is to detect skin problems in your patients at the earliest possible time to prevent their occurrence and to heal pressure sores as quickly as possible, should they occur.

An example of your plan might be:
1. Present results of study to staff.
2. Conduct an inservice program on prevention and management of pressure sores.
3. Develop a screening tool which will rapidly identify skin-compromised patients on admission and on a daily basis during hospitalization.
5. Delineate staff assignments to match skills of nursing personnel with skin care needs of patients.
6. Educate patients in skin care.

After you have stated your corrective action plan, indicate who will be responsible for implementation and the target date(s) of implementation. For example:

Mary Jones, RN   *September 1-October 31, 1981*
Responsible Person(s)   Target Date(s)

Reassessment plan and time frame

Reassessment plan and time frame refers to *what* you plan to do to see if the problem has been corrected and *when* you plan to do this. Describe in your plan *what* your reassessment plan is, e.g., what method you will use to reassess; *who* will be responsible for the reassessment; and *when* you plan to reassess. Examples:
1. Readminister patient questionnaire to patients in the clinic following program changes.
   Susan Smith, RN   *January 1-31, 1982*
   Responsible Person(s)   Target Date(s)
2. Review incident reports every four months for medication errors.
   Mary Brown, RN   *April 30, 1981*
   Helen Carr, RN   *August 31, 1981*
                                      December 31, 1981
   Responsible Person(s)   Target Date(s)
3. Observe treatment team in action once a month for 3 months using the "Interaction Flow Sheet" tool.
   Robert Johnson, RN   *October 15, 1981*
                                      November 19, 1981
                                      December 17, 1981
   Responsible Person(s)   Target Date(s)

Figure 10-9, continued.

In the 1930s and 1940s appraisal forms concentrated on personality and behavioral characteristics, in keeping with a surge of interest in human relations. By 1950 available tools included both work-related activities and human elements. During this decade management by objectives (MBO) was introduced. Emphasis was on determination of objectives for both the organization and its managers, and the measurement of performance against these objectives.

Appraisal of performance has now become a legal matter, with a U.S. Supreme Court decision in 1970 *(Griggs vs Duke Power Company),* and thus has increased significance for the nurse manager. This decision mandated that any type of testing procedure for a particular job must relate directly to the job duties to be performed. Soon after this ultimatum the Equal Employment Opportunity Commission (EEOC) developed guidelines that reinforced the Supreme Court decision, stating "when used as tools for selection, promotion or transfer, performance appraisals are considered tests and the Supreme Court decision applies."[26] The effective nurse manager is aware of governmental controls when developing and working with performance appraisal. These controls are made known to nursing management personnel through the designated channels of communication of the organization. For example, under centralized control the personnel office would advise the director of nursing services, who in turn would pass the information along to supervisors, then to head nurses, and on to lower- or first-level nurse managers.

Components of an Effective Nursing Performance Appraisal System

The effective nurse manager knows the controlling process is used to promote positive and favorable activity. Nurse managers have responsibility for securing the common purposes of the total enterprise, but they also have responsibility for maintaining a climate in the health organization in which nursing personnel who work toward these common purposes obtain job satisfaction. One way to assess progress made by nursing personnel in realizing these purposes is through performance appraisal.

A number of factors contribute to a successful nursing performance appraisal system[27]:

1. *There is compatibility between criteria for individual evaluation and organizational goals.* To be realistic and workable, the appraisal procedure has been agreed on at each level of management. Elements in the appraisal process reflect the combined aspirations of all individuals and groups under consideration. Involvement of personnel in all phases of the evaluatory process increases belief in the fairness and accuracy of the evaluation, establishes a commitment to the evaluation, and increases motivation to utilize the results.[27]

2. *The nursing performance rated applies directly to the performance standards and objectives expected of the worker.* Before evaluation of service

begins, predetermination of roles for each member of the health team and goals in the form of behavioral objectives and success criteria (e.g., job descriptions and procedure manuals) are clearly established. When nursing roles and job descriptions are stated in terms of relevance of each item to nursing practice, there is an objective way to determine whether goals have been reached. If the job description is vague or ends with "and such other duties as may be required," the staff member will not know what direction to take or what goals and objectives will be considered most significant when outcomes are surveyed.

3. *Behavioral expectations have been developed or mutually agreed on by the nurse appraiser and the individual being evaluated.* The MBO system provides an excellent example of how behaviors are formulated and tested. Employees who participate in formulating goals for delivery of nursing care are more zealous in seeing them accomplished than are those who are merely given goals for fulfillment.

4. *The nurse appraiser understands the appraisal process and uses the procedure effectively.* All nurses who hold positions of leadership are expected to competently evaluate themselves and others as a part of the management process. Not all nurses are prepared to assess competencies of nursing staff members, but this does not relieve them of responsibility for acquiring evaluative skills. Provisions can be made by the employing agency for adequate training in the appraisal process through on-the-job activity or inservice education. The nurse manager may wish to complete one of the many courses offered on the subject of appraisal sponsored by professional organizations and groups.

5. *Each individual is rated by her immediate supervisor.* This system is by far the most commonly used in management. Although nurse managers rely in part on the views of a number of people, such as patients/clients, other nursing personnel, and contacts, appraisals are most accurate when the data are gathered and processed by one supervisor who is knowledgeable about the individual being evaluated.

6. *The performance appraisal concentrates on areas of strength, as well as notes weaknesses, in the individual to improve performance.* Reinforcing strong performance breeds more strong performance.[27] Placing a premium on what an individual does well pays off for management. No one is strong in every area; all are subject to shortcomings. Weaknesses should be noted only if they are perceived as a threat to safety or if they provide a significant deterrent to goal accomplishment.

7. *The appraisal process encourages feedback from nursing members about their performance, needs, and interests.* Through daily contact the nurse manager attempts to gain understanding of each staff member. This is accomplished through observation, questioning, and listening. When it is time for preparation of a formal appraisal, the nurse manager is better equipped to accurately reflect the profile of the worker. Even after recording, staff members are given opportunity to verify or discredit anything that is written about them.

8. *Provision is made for initiating preventive and corrective actions and making adjustments to improve the worker's performance.* Performance appraisal can become a positive vehicle when approached from a constructive point of view of self-improvement, with agency assistance through such means as orientation, ongoing coaching, and staff development programs. Emphasis is placed on the individual's assuming responsibility for her own growth, with help from management or other nursing staff as needed.[27]

Performance appraisal is a difficult task at best, but it can be made easier by following these guidelines, which contribute to a successful procedure.

Methods of Measuring Performance

Informing nurses of how well they are doing in their work occurs both informally and formally. *Informal appraisal* occurs on a routine basis and may consist of (1) observation of work performance while engaged in individual or group functions; (2) incidental face-to-face confrontation and collaboration with the worker; (3) responses offered by the worker during a conference; (4) noting the reaction to the worker of an involved person, such as a patient/client,

family member, or staff person; or (5) noting the effects of a worker's actions on patients/clients, families, personnel, or environment. During informal appraisal the nurse manager may spontaneously mention to the worker that a particular activity was performed well or poorly, or the staff member may ask what effect her action had on the patient/client. Because of the close connection between the behavior and the feedback, informal appraisal quickly encourages desirable performance and discourages undesirable action before it becomes habitual.

A further benefit of the informal appraisal method is that if behavior noted on an informal basis is recorded with some regularity, the data can provide valid information for compilation of a formal report. The nurse manager can note significant behavior on the daily worksheet (Figure 10-10) or on separate paper or cards and keep these notes for reference.

Formal appraisal is best accomplished by regularly and methodically collecting objective facts that can then be calculated to tell the difference between what was expected and what actually occurred. Once suitable standards and objectives have been set, a method for formal performance appraisal is selected. There is no one approach that applies to every work setting. To be effective, methods used should be (1) accurate, (2) timely, (3) objective, (4) focused on the level of worker's performance in every worker category (e.g., nursing assistant, LPN/LVN, other staff nurses), (5) addressed to major roles expected of the worker (job description), (6) economically realistic, (7) appropriate for the organizational structure, and (8) acceptable to the members involved. If the method used meets these criteria, there will be positive cooperation in the collection of data.

A number of methods are used to record and report formal evaluation. The following discussion presents those methods most commonly used in nursing: the checklist and the criterion rating scale.

Checklist. A checklist contains a compilation of all nursing performances expected of the worker. The appraiser's task is to respond to what is noted by placing a mark in the "yes" or "no" column in accordance with the worker's

Staff member	Room no.	Patient's name	Information pertaining to administration of care	Needs and problems
Bea Kindall	66	Roy Snell	Ca Lung	11 A.M. Bea completed her assignment early and helped Vici.
Vici Wilson	70a	Elaine Metz	Ca Colon	12:30 P.M. Vici changed her lunch hr. 3 sanction — no coverage for pt.

Figure 10-10. Sample of personnel appraisal notations made on a nurse manager's worksheet.

behavior. The checklist is a simple means of covering items considered important and is an efficient way of assessing technical procedures and handling large number of employees. The checklist may or may not have space provided for comments. The checklist fails to address the issue of frequency of behavior or the degree to which the behavior occurs.

Criterion rating scale. A criterion rating scale is the most commonly used method in nursing appraisal. It is one way to provide for measurement of present practice and for planning for professional growth that is directly related to job description. A criterion is one way of describing success. For example, the criterion in a college course might be the grade. A criterion for a salesperson might be the dollar volume of sales in a 1-month period.[28]

A criterion rating scale for nursing performance appraisal generally includes categories that pertain to delivery of patient/client care, with an assessment of how well the steps in the nursing process are used: assessing, goal setting, implementing, and evaluating. Usually behaviors relating to communication and interpersonal relations, supervision, and

teaching are included as appropriate to each worker.

There is often a problem for the appraiser in determining the level of performance, particularly those behaviors that are considered above or below the satisfactory level. It is suggested that space be provided by each category of performance to allow for notations that illustrate or explain the rationale behind the decision.

When personnel appraisal is weighed against criteria that have been agreed on by the nurse manager and the staff member, then all that must be done is to determine whether the worker has lived up to them. The rationale for this approach is that "satisfactory" performance in nursing is demanding and consistent with personnel departments' standards and/or unions' specifications. Maslow's and Drucker's theories are applied with the belief that only individuals themselves can make themselves give more to a job than they must. For achievements to reach beyond the satisfactory level, the nurse manager must create a climate that motivates staff members to reach their highest potential. Clues for accomplishing this goal are provided in this discussion and throughout this book.

PERFORMANCE REVIEW SESSION
Purpose

The final step in the formal appraisal process is the review session between the nurse manager and the individual being appraised. The review session is a crucial aspect of evaluation and must be treated accordingly. Primary purposes of a performance review are to increase the effectiveness of the nursing staff member in the health care setting and to promote worker satisfaction. The formal performance appraisal provides a "physical conversation piece," as there is tangible evidence for the evaluator and staff member to see and discuss. During the interview the immediate supervisor and worker discuss the progress of the worker through (1) clarification of goals and objectives of the agency and area to which the worker is assigned, (2) identification of job related strengths and weaknesses, (3) promotion of a feeling of satisfaction about the work and the individual's part in work accomplishment, and (4) establishment of new goals.

Process

A key element in the review session is maintenance of an open, two-way communication system in which give-and-take can occur. The principles of effective communication apply to the review process; however, there is a uniqueness about this process. Any time an individual meets with a supervisor to review work progress there is a certain amount of nervousness and apprehension. This is particularly true if the individual feels that job performance is questionable or inadequate and that the job is in jeopardy. The situation can be eased by adhering to the following guidelines.

1. Provide a comfortable, private environment. Arrange seating side by side so the written forms can be reviewed by both parties.
2. Assure freedom from work assignment. Arrange for coverage during the time of meeting; begin and end the session on time.
3. Establish rapport. Indicate to the staff member the appraiser's concern for sharing the manager's evaluation with the member. A few brief exchanges of chitchat are advisable, but the appraiser should move right on to the business at hand.

4. Indicate that the appraisal is tentative, pending feedback from the individual. Without a response from the worker, the nurse manager does not know what that person has heard or her reaction to the information.
5. Begin the session on positive terms. Establish as positive a relationship as possible. The appraiser must be sincere; if the message is untrue, trust will be destroyed.
6. Include all important issues. The degree of attention that is given to individual items or issues during the appraisal session depends on the time factor and the significance of the matter to the job situation. Preplan the session to allow for appropriate emphasis. The appraiser makes certain the member being evaluated understands the rules of the conference: standards and objectives for the particular worker are used to assess the worker (job description, objectives), and feedback is encouraged. Broad categories can be covered with a single statement, such as "You function well in these areas," giving a few examples to confirm the assessment. Persons under appraisal need to know that their entire performance is considered, not just a few isolated incidents. Remember that most people respond readily to positive feedback and thereby are motivated to improve their performance.
7. Present criticism sparingly and carefully. The purpose of criticism is to effect constructive behavioral change, not to reduce the individual to tears or to cause anger and hostility. Negative reactions to criticism of work cannot be avoided, but they can be made mild enough so that the worker will seriously consider the criticism rather than withdrawing or attacking the appraiser. Before recording and offering criticism during an appraisal conference, the appraiser should consider whether the behavior is critical and affects job performance.
8. The nurse manager and worker sign the formal appraisal form. After the review session is completed and necessary adjustments made, signatures of both parties should be affixed to the form. This act simply indicates that the appraiser and individual being evaluated have met and reviewed the assessment. A space should always be reserved for the

comments of both parties. This provides an opportunity to react to the content or process of the review session. Unresolved differences can be mentioned, giving the next supervisor to receive the report as much input as possible.

9. Establish new goals for modifying or improving behavior. If the nurse manager accepts the concept that human resources are the greatest asset to goal accomplishment, that each individual is unique, and that each person has potential for improvement, then efforts will be made to understand and help individuals meet their needs. A nurse manager can greatly affect the quality of performance of the worker by using the review session as a means for planning for change. Simply stating that new goals are needed does not make them materialize. But too much structure can lead to undesirable outcomes. The effective nurse manager maintains a balance between too much and too little control. As already suggested, nurse managers need to develop a managerial style that considers people, resources, and environment. This is true with the degree of control exercised. In detecting important deviations and in guiding behavior in the desired direction, some structure and limits are necessary. As illustrated in Figure 10-11, too much control causes workers to feel over-controlled, and the environmental climate becomes stifling, inhibiting, and unsatisfying. With too little control the environment becomes chaotic, and people become disorganized and ineffective in achieving goals. The nurse manager works toward maintaining a balance of control by allowing enough freedom to exercise individual judgment and initiative and yet provides structure by having enough check points to assure goal-oriented activity.

Before the review session with the staff member, the nurse manager will have planned methods to assist the worker in professional growth and development. At the close of the conference the manager and worker will agree on a plan that best suits the individual's needs and organizational interests.

CONTROLLING THE PROBLEM EMPLOYEE

The problem employee is one who exhibits chronic disruptive behavior. This person can wreak havoc on the unit's productivity and cause peers to feel anger and resentment toward the troublesome worker. The behavior of the problem employee is characterized by absenteeism; arriving late for work; personality conflicts; excessive griping; and display of dissatisfaction, resentment, pessimism, or indifference.

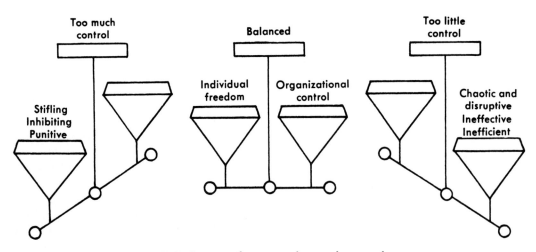

Figure 10-11. Impact of managerial control on employees.

An even more serious problem employee is the substance abuser. People with alcohol or other drug addiction often have personality changes, gradually moving from being productive, cooperative workers to workers whose efficiency level drops. They become erratic in attendance and adherence to schedule and have an increasing number of accidents.

The chronically disruptive employee is far more common that the substance abuser. Irrespective of cause, all behaviors that create problems with effective control are to be managed.

Progressive Discipline Policy and Procedure

It is customary for agencies to have a progressive discipline policy prepared from broad representation of the work force.[29] Such a policy specifies that certain steps will be taken if an employee's behavior becomes chronically disruptive. Disruptive behavior is documented, and the documentation is witnessed by the head nurse (or her designee) and the disruptive employee. If the employee refuses to witness the documentation, another person, such as the assistant head nurse or team leader, is asked to witness the fact that the conference was held and the employee refused to sign. The nurse conducting the conference is not to act as a therapist; instead, dialogue occurs, observations are made, and recommendations are given. Following is an example of disciplinary procedure:

1. *Gather the facts.* Meet the problem employee in a private area, such as the head nurse's office, and state the reason for the conference:

   Head nurse: Mary, I am concerned about your behaviors this month. I have noted several of them for us to discuss. (Note that dates and times are included.)

11/1	Added 20 minutes to morning break (10:30 A.M. to 11:00 A.M.)
11/2	Left unit without notice for 30 minutes (1:30 P.M. to 2:00 P.M.)
11/3	Forty minutes late for work (arrived at 7:40 A.M.)
11/4	Called in sick; told peer (JL) she was too tired to come to work
11/5	Talked on phone with friend for 25 minutes (11:00 A.M. to 11:25 A.M.)

   Mary: I didn't realize I'd broken the rules so many times. Since my husband left, I've been sort of crazy. I can't sleep, and when I do, I don't hear the alarm. I go out at night to get out of the house, and then I'm too tired to go to work. I need to talk with someone. I won't do these things again.

2. *Develop a written plan with the employee for a change in behavior.* Record what behaviors are expected. If the employee will not participate, document that fact.

   Head nurse: Mary, I'm sorry that you're upset about your home life. My responsibility is to the unit here in the hospital. We have standards and policies to follow for the benefit of the patients. You are breaking some of them and creating serious problems. Let's review each behavior and decide on necessary changes.

   1. Will abide by time allotment for breaks
   2. Will ask for coverage if there is a valid reason for leaving the unit
   3. Will arrive for work on time
   4. Will not be absent unless ill or there is an emergency
   5. Will restrict personal phone calls to no more than one per day, not to exceed 3 minutes

   Mary, I suggest that you seek counseling from hospital services or a therapist of your choice. Whatever you do, please know that these changes in behavior are mandatory. We'll meet in 2 weeks. In the meantime, I'll be observing your behavior.

3. *Obtain signatures and schedule a meeting for 2 weeks later.* The signature means only that the employee was present, not that she agreed with the statements. The employee is free to record comments about the content or process of the conference.

4. *Document significant behaviors during the ensuing 2 weeks, both positive and negative.*

5. *Hold a second meeting.* If only positive behaviors are recorded, give positive reinforcement to the employee and do not meet again to discuss the disciplinary matters. Record the change in behavior on the disciplinary form. If conditions were not met or only partially met, review the accounts.

   Head nurse: Mary, in the past 2 weeks you have improved. You were late to work two times, however (stipulate when and how much), and you left work 1 hour early last Tuesday without letting me know.

Mary: Well, I did do better. It's hard to change all at once. Something came up last Tuesday that I didn't want to talk about. I just had to leave.

Head nurse: You are choosing to let your private affairs interfere with your professional responsibility. According to our policy, you have one more period of 2 weeks to change your behavior. If you fail this time, you will be dismissed.

Mary: You can count on me.

6. *Repeat step 3.*
7. *Meet with the employee again.* Refer to documented activity.

Head nurse: Mary, your behaviors are such that I am forced to dismiss you. (Itemize the absences, latenesses, and leaving the unit without coverage.) Please get your things and leave the department.

Note that no specific reference was made to peer relationships or the impact Mary had on others, nor did the head nurse resort to recriminating statements such as "How could you do this to us or to yourself?" Conversations are to be kept as objective as possible, concentrating on facts. The key to the entire process is good documentation. When disciplinary procedure is followed, the head nurse and hospital are protected against legal action should the nurse decide to challenge the decision.[29]

SUMMARY

1. Managerial control consists of measuring and correcting the activities of people and things in an organization to ensure that objectives and the plans made to attain them are accomplished.
2. Because of the impact of third-party control on nursing, health care agencies have an incentive to control costs.
3. A well-designed nursing control system establishes trust and commitment by all personnel involved, clarifies objectives, operates fairly, compares expectancy to performance, provides the organization with necessary information on staffing and quality of care, and promotes growth and development of personnel.

4. An effective budget system has enough resources to supply sufficient funds, allocates funds based on criteria, and conducts a controlling system that shows how resources are being used.
5. Top-down budgeting is centralized; bottom-up budgeting is decentralized.
6. Decentralized budgeting allows those most familiar with circumstances to plan for their needs and promotes greater satisfaction among the managers.
7. The budget types most frequently managed by nurses are operational (supplies and services) and capital (large equipment, physical changes or additions to the facilities), and personnel (number, salaries, working days, time off, and fringe benefits).
8. The budgetary process consists of review of policies, standards, and goals; top-level projections and guidelines; preparation of the budget by middle-level managers; review of budget by top-level managers; acceptance or modification; implementation; and evaluation, with changes as necessary.
9. "Costing out" nursing services means determining costs of services provided by nurses.
10. Basic steps in the control process are establishing standards, objectives, and methods for measuring performance; measuring actual performance; comparing results of performance with standards and objectives (expectations); and acting to reinforce strengths and taking corrective action as necessary.
11. Goal achievement in nursing is measured through analyzing task performance and determining quality of care.
12. In task analysis motions, actions, and procedures used in the actual process of giving nursing care are inspected, using such methods as time studies and checklists. Although this method provides worthwhile information, it fails to consider many important intangible aspects of nursing.
13. Quality control is the responsibility of all employees and is concerned with assessment of the level of nursing care provided and its effects on the patient / client through process (studying the nature and sequence of activities undertaken by nurses in the care

of patients / clients) and outcome (studying the end results of nursing care). Methods used to gather information include rating scales, questionnaires, observations, peer reviews, and audits of open and closed records.

14. Accountability for quality care is both voluntary and official.

15. The American Nurses' Association offers a model for quality assurance using standards of nursing care that can be applied to nursing practice in any clinical setting. The model is compatible with processes of control proposed by management theorists.

16. Peer review is the examining and evaluating, by associates, of another nurse's practice.

17. The JCAHO mandates a written plan and comprehensive approach to quality assurance.

18. Performance appraisal is a method of acquiring and processing information needed to improve the individual worker's performance and accomplishments.

19. Performance appraisal consists of setting standards and objectives; reviewing progress; maintaining ongoing feedback between the appraiser and subject; and planning for reinforcement, deletion, or correction of identified behaviors.

20. Lower- or first-level nurse managers participate in performance appraisal by preparing the initial evaluation of each nursing staff member assigned to them, reviewing the appraisal with the worker, and passing it on to the next immediate supervisor.

21. The first formal performance appraisal was recorded about 1800. Emphasis was placed on time-and-motion studies until the 1930s and 1940s, when personality and behavioral characteristics were added. By 1950 task analysis was combined with human elements. In the 1950s management by objectives (MBO) was introduced as a means of measuring performance against specific objectives at all levels in the organization.

22. In 1970 appraisal of performance became a legal matter, requiring that any testing procedure for a particular job must relate directly to the job duties to be performed.

23. An effective nursing performance appraisal system applies directly to standards and objectives of the worker, is compatible with organizations and individual goals, contains expectations that have been mutually agreed on by the appraiser and the subject of evaluation, is conducted by an appraiser who understands and uses the appraisal process effectively, assures that each individual rating is performed by the worker's immediate supervisor, encourages feedback, and gives nurturance and preventive or corrective actions as appropriate.

24. There are two kinds of methods for measuring performance: (1) *informal,* occurring on a day-to-day basis through observation; incidental face-to-face confrontation and collaboration; responses of workers during conferences; and reactions noted in contacts with involved persons, such as patients / clients or other staff members, and (2) *formal,* consisting of regular and methodical collection of objective data.

25. Methods used to acquire information on the performance of a worker must be accurate, timely, objective, and focused on the worker's role and performance, economically realistic, fit within the organization structure, and be acceptable to the members involved in the appraisal process.

26. Methods most commonly used to appraise nursing performance are the checklist and criterion rating scale. The criterion rating scale is the most commonly used.

27. Performance review sessions are conducted to increase the effectiveness of the nursing staff member in the health care setting and to promote worker satisfaction.

28. A key element in the performance review session is maintenance of an open, two-way communication system by providing a comfortable environment and freedom from work responsibilities, supplying ground rules for the conference, beginning the session on positive terms, including all important issues, accentuating the positive, and offering criticism sparingly.

29. New goals for the worker are established after the personnel review session. Successful implementation of goals depends on a reciprocal relationship of trust and security

between worker and manager, the individual's motivation to change, realistic goals using principles of learning, handling only one or two problems at a time, and planning for feedback and reinforcement.

30. The problem employee is one who exhibits chronic disruptive behavior. Behavioral change is facilitated through progressive disciplinary policy.

 Questions for Study and Discussion

1. Control has been defined by some as a negative force dominating the work life of his or her staff. Discuss this statement in light of what you know about the control function.
2. How do the planning and control functions work together?
3. Describe the impact of government control on health care agencies.
4. In observing a nursing unit, what symptoms of inadequate control might you detect in services and personnel?
5. As nurse manager, it is your job to stay within the designated number of FTEs. Several of your RN staff want more flexibility in their schedules (e.g., long weekends, extra days off). What are some options within the allotted FTEs for meeting staff wishes?
6. What has been your experience with performance appraisals (including student evaluations of teacher effectiveness)? Would the instrument(s) you have used constitute a defensible criterion reference tool?

REFERENCES

1. Pointer J and Pointer R: Case-based prospective reimbursement, Nurs Man 20(4):30-34, 1989.
2. Trofino J: A study of the consistency of nursing care hours and patient length of stay per DRG category in selected Joint Commission on Accreditation of Health Care Organizations as measured by diverse classification systems, doctoral dissertation, New York, 1988, Teacher's College, Columbia University.
3. Cromwell J and Price K: The sensitizing of DRG weights to variation in nursing intensity, Nurs Econ 6(1):18-26, 1988.
4. Trofino J: JCAHO nursing standards: nursing care hours and LOS per DRG. I. Nurs Man 20(1):29-32, 1989.
5. Trofino J: JACHO nursing standards: nursing care hours and LOS per DRG. II. Nurs Man 20(1):33-35, 1989.
6. Omachonu V and Nanda R: Measuring productivity: outcome vs output, Nurs Man 20(4):35-40, 1989.
7. Longest B: Management practices for the health professional, ed 4, Norwalk, Conn, 1990, Appleton and Lange.
8. Wheelen T and Hunger J: Strategic management, ed 3, Reading Mass, 1990, Addison-Wesley Publishing Co.
9. O'Grady T: Nursing administration: changing organizational structures, vol 2, Product-line management for nursing: a new framework for nursing, Redwood City, Calif, 1989, Addison-Wesley Publishing Co, pp 129-137.
10. Martin K: Controlling the budgetary plan, Nurs Man 20(10):64, 1989.
11. McCabe J and Hartnack J: FTE reports and fiscal management, Nurs Man 20(11):46-48, 1989.
12. Cronin C and Maklebust J: Case-managed care: capitalizing on the CNS, Nurs Man 20(3):38-47, 1989.
13. Robbins S: Organization theory: structure, design and applications, Englewood Cliffs, NJ, 1990, Prentice-Hall.
14. Francisco P: Flexible budgeting and variance analysis. Nurs Man 20(11):40-43, 1989.
15. McCloskey J: Implications of costing out nursing services for reimbursement, Nurs Man 20(1):44-49, 1989.
16. Bullough B and Bullough V: Nursing in the community, St Louis, 1990, Times Mirror/Mosby College Publishing.
17. Grimaldi P: New SNF/ICF requirements will push nursing costs up, Nurs Man 20(6):18-20, 1989.
18. Tappen R: Nursing leadership and management: concepts and practice, ed 2, Philadelphia, 1989, FA Davis Co.

19. Drake University Hospital Nursing Services: Guidelines for nursing care: process and outcome, Philadelphia, 1983, JB Lippincott.

20. Hellriegel D and Slocum J: Management, ed 5, Reading, Massachusetts, 1989, Addison-Wesley Publishing Co.

21. The Joint Commission of Accreditation of Healthcare Organizations: Accreditation manual for hospitals, Chicago, 1990, The Commission.

22. American Nurses' Association: ANA standards, Kansas City, MO, 1986, The Association.

23. Christensen M: Peer auditing, Nurs Man 21(1):50-52, 1990.

24. The Joint Commission of Accreditation of Hospitals: The QA guide: a resource for hospital quality assurance, Chicago, 1988, The Commission.

25. Harris S, Kreger S, and Davis M: A problem-focused quality assurance program, Nurs Man 20(2):55, 1989.

26. Equal Employment Opportunity Commission: Guidelines of employment and selection procedure. Federal Register 35(149):12333-12336, 1970.

27. Pardue W: Writing effective appraisal reports, The Appraisal J, 58(1):16-23, 1990.

28. Landy F: Psychology of work behavior, Pacific Grove, Calif, 1989, Brooks/Cole Publishing Co.

29. Brooke P: Firing for cause, JONA 20(9):45-49, 1990.

SUGGESTED READINGS

Abramczyk M and Forrester T: Utilization review: a psychiatric perspective, Nurs Man 20(2):46-48, 1989.

Barnett G and Winickoff R: Quality assurance and computer based patient records, Am J Public Health 80(5):527-528, 1990.

Davidbizar R and Giger J: When subordinates go over your head: the manipulative employee, JONA 20(9):29-34, 1990.

Dubnicki C and Williams J: Getting peak performance in the knowledge-based organization, Healthcare Forum J 34(1):33-36, 1991.

Dyer C: Health care economics: AHA margins uncertain; inflation offsets gains, Hospitals 63(21):66-67, 1990.

Fagin C: Cost effectiveness: nursing value proves itself, Am J Nurs 90(10):17-30, 1990.

Franks-Joiner G: Perspectives used for gaining approval of budgets, JONA 20(1):34-38, 1990.

Glandon G, Colbert K, and Thomasma M: Nursing delivery models and RN mix: cost implications, Nurs Man 20(5):30-33, 1989.

Jones R: Taking the "guesstimates" out of FTE budgeting, Nurs Man 20(2):65-73, 1989.

Koska M: Quality—thy name is nursing care, CEOs say, Hospitals 63(3):32, 1989.

Linder C: Work measurement and nursing time standards, Nurs Man 20(10):44-49, 1989.

Mailbot C, Binger J, and Slezak L: Managing operating room budget variances, JONA 20(5):19-26, 1990.

Manthey M: Discipline without punishment. II. Nurs Man 20(11):23, 1989.

Metzger N: Evaluating supplemental professional nurses, Nurs Man 21(1):54-59, 1990.

Mitchell M: The power of standards (nursing homes), Nurs Health Care 10(6):307-309, 1990.

New N: Quality measurement: quick, easy and unit-based, Nurs Man 20(10):50-51, 1989.

Omachonu V and Nanda R: Measuring productivity: outcome vs output, Nurs Man 20(4):35-40, 1989.

Preziosi P: Long-term care: the cost/quality debate continues, Nurs Health Care 10(3):118-120, 1990.

II

Staff Training and Development

_____ **BEHAVIORAL OBJECTIVES** _____

On completion of this chapter the student will be prepared to:

☐ Differentiate among technical, human, conceptual, and diagnostic skills.

☐ Demonstrate how leadership and management skills are acquired.

☐ Identify staff nurses who need training and development and give rationale for their need.

☐ Define role clarification and differentiate among role expectation, role conception, and role congruence.

☐ Define the adult learner and describe the teaching-learning process as applied to nurses.

☐ Define a work group and identify factors that influence work productivity.

☐ Explain the change process and forces that influence change.

☐ Identify the key factors of programs designed for orientation of new employees and the new graduate, and for preceptor training.

☐ Describe on-the-job development through self-learning.

IMPORTANCE OF TRAINING AND DEVELOPMENT

In today's complex and dynamic environment, it is no longer necessary to debate whether training and development activities are luxuries in which only the largest organizations can indulge in prosperous times. Most organizations, large and small, have come to realize that the development of an effective work force is no more a luxury than having a housekeeping or accounting department. It is an accepted fact that training and development are necessary for the spirit, survival, and performance of an organization and that workers must be developed to manage the organization effectively now and in the years to come. This is particularly important in agencies that undergo changes in technology. Changes through the implementation of computerized care planning and the use of intricate machines, for example, are better received when nurses feel they will be capable of handling the new systems.

Effective managers recognize that training and development are ongoing, continuous processes, not one-time activities. New problems, new procedures and equipment, new discoveries, and new jobs are constantly creating the need for employee instruction.

TRAINING AND DEVELOPMENT FUNCTION

For the individual learner, the function of training and development needs to be one of providing an environment and resources that facilitate a learning and maturing process in each person.[1] The goal of staff education is to enable the staff member to learn under conditions that foster changing behavior, attitudes, or opinions. As learning takes place, personal experiences are translated into new and different ways of behaving.[2]

The training and development function in an organization involves a multifaceted purpose and definition.[3] *Training* is an activity that is primarily directed at improving an employee's current job performance. It generally involves the acquisition of technical and some human skills by both nonmanagerial and managerial personnel. Learning to do procedures or the right way to conduct a performance evaluation are examples.

Individual *development* refers to any action or program undertaken by the organization to provide opportunities for employees to learn and develop skills. Development involves two equally important components. First is management and leadership development, which is concerned with the question, "What kinds of leaders and managers does the organization need now, and what kind will be needed tomorrow to achieve its goals in a changing environment?" In management and leadership development, the age and skills as well as the role of the managerial staff are considered. Second, development is concerned with the structure of the or-

ganization and the types of managers and leaders required to function in this structure.

To be successful, any program needs *administrative support*. Training and development programs must evolve from a planned, purposeful approach by top nursing administration to the preparation of competent managers and leaders. The nurturance of a supportive climate allows for the attainment of competency and performance of functions that fulfill the philosophy and goals of patient care for nursing and the health agency.[4]

This chapter begins with a discussion of skills needed by the nurse to lead and to manage, how these skills are acquired, the nurse population in need of training and development, and knowledge important to the success of training and development programs. It concludes with examples of training and development programs at staff nurse levels.

MANAGEMENT SKILLS NEEDED BY STAFF NURSES

At lower levels of management, the major need is for technical and human skills. At higher levels, the administrator's effectiveness depends largely on human and conceptual skills. At the top, conceptual skill becomes the most important of all for successful administration.[5]

Most successful nurses have acquired a certain set of skills during their working lives that has had a strong impact on their levels of achievement. Four specific managerial skills are needed by all nurses: (1) technical, (2) human, (3) conceptual, and (4) diagnostic[5] (Figure 11-1).

Technical Skill

Technical skill pertains to *what* is done and to working with *things* and one's ability to use technology to perform an organizational task.

The ability to use tools, techniques, procedures, or approaches in a specialized manner is referred to as *technical skill*. Nurses are expected to have or to acquire proficiency in a broad variety of skills that relate to every part of the human being. Nurses with technical skills are recognized as experts at what they do. Nurse managers are expected to have developed expertise in their areas of professional practice. Technical skills are usually the easiest to acquire

Technical expertise	Human skills		Conceptual skills	Diagnostic skills	Coach and mentor skills

Tools
Techniques
Procedures
	Select
	Motivate
	Work with
	Lead
		Self
		and
		others
			See total picture
			Link own work
			  with that of others
				Plan
				Organize
				Direct
				Evaluate/Control
					"Hands-on" process
					Plan mutually
					  acceptable action
					Create supportive
					  and helpful climate

what...things	how...people		why...whole picture	why...whole picture	how..people

Figure 11-1. Leadership and management skills necessary for nursing practice at any level.

because they can be taught through educational and training activities.

Human Skill

Human skill pertains to *how* something is done, to working with *people,* and to one's ability to work with others in the achievement of goals.

Nurse managers need the ability to select, motivate, work with, and lead employees, either individually or in groups. Human skills are much more difficult to acquire, because interpersonal relations involve consideration of the differences in attitudes, emotions, and cultural characteristics of many individuals and groups. Nurse leaders, workers under their supervision, and supervisors and other administrators to whom they are responsible are examples. These characteristics vary with different employees, and their impact on performance is difficult to predict.

Conceptual Skill

Conceptual skill pertains to *why* something is done, to one's view of the organization as a *whole* picture, and to one's ability to understand the complexities of the organization as it affects and is affected by its environment.

The nurse manager must be able to link the work of the group with the work of other people (physicians, clergy, social workers, and so on) and other departments (radiology, laboratory, dietary, therapy, and so on).

Diagnostic Skill

Diagnostic skill includes the ability to determine, by analysis and examination, the nature and the circumstances of a particular condition or situation. It is the ability to specify *why* something occurred and to cut through unimportant aspects and quickly get to the heart of a problem. For example, many nurse managers have a problem with workers' poor use of time. Overtime is accrued, which means increased costs, and frustration and anger are generated because nurses cannot get home to their families or attend to other obligations on time; incoming workers experience delay in getting their work started. The nurse manager who can quickly assess the problem and solve it to the satisfaction of both administration and employees has used diagnostic skill effectively. Conversely, the nurse who is unable to choose a plan of action is on the road to failure. All too often nurses fall into a state of paralysis because they are not able to resolve the doubts in their own minds. President Truman used to lament that when he asked his economists for recommendations, they would answer, "On the one hand . . . and on the other hand . . . " Exasperated, President Truman said, "Oh, for a one-armed economist!"[6]

Conceptual and diagnostic skills are interchangeable and the most difficult to acquire, mainly because they involve time and a certain level of intellectual ability. Conceptual and diagnostic skill development depends, to a certain extent, on the degree to which technical and human skills have been acquired and mastered. In essence, conceptual and diagnostic skills are mature skills that require a capacity to learn and a level of experience in observing and practicing acceptable behaviors.

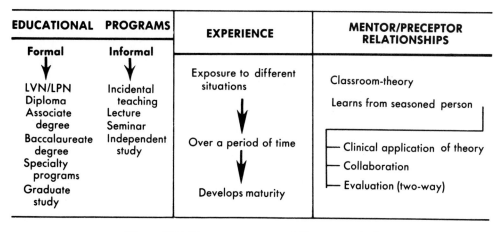

EDUCATIONAL PROGRAMS		EXPERIENCE	MENTOR/PRECEPTOR RELATIONSHIPS
Formal	**Informal**	Exposure to different situations	Classroom-theory
LVN/LPN	Incidental	↓	Learns from seasoned person
Diploma	teaching		
Associate	Lecture		
degree	Seminar	Over a period of time	— Clinical application of theory
Baccalaureate	Independent	↓	— Collaboration
degree	study		— Evaluation (two-way)
Specialty		Develops maturity	
programs			
Graduate			
study			

Figure 11-2. How management skills are acquired.

Coach and Mentor Skill

Staff members, particularly early in their careers, are fortunate when they have a manager who knows how to coach and guide, and to teach them along the way. Coaching is a day-by-day, hands-on process that helps employees to recognize opportunities and ways to improve their performance and capabilities. Coaching resembles on-the-job training, but it requires managers to have skills beyond those of trainer, such as planning mutually acceptable action, creating a supportive and helping climate, and influencing employees to change their behavior. By helping staff members expand their capabilities and improve their performance, managers can gain more time for self-improvement. Managers who are most effective at developing employees have incorporated the skill of coaching into their management style.[7]

HOW MANAGEMENT SKILLS ARE ACQUIRED

There are at least three mechanisms that facilitate the acquisition of managerial skills: (1) education and training, (2) experience, and (3) a preceptor/mentor relationship with a higher-level person (Figure 11-2).

Education

Training and development of managerial skills are carried out in nursing schools according to their mission and goals (see Chapter 4). LVNs/LPNs are trained to manage their own work load under RN supervision and to be effective team members. Diploma and associate degree nurses are educated to serve as managers of nursing care for a group of patients/clients with common, well-defined health problems within structured settings. Baccalaureate degree graduates are to be accountable for their own nursing practice, qualified to provide nursing care through others, serve as advocates for patients/clients, and apply interpersonal and leadership skills in working with other health professionals. Many other formal and informal programs for the development of leadership and management are available through on-the-job training, workshops, seminars, independent study, and graduate study.

Experience

"Experience is the best teacher" is an old saying that contains much truth for managerial success. Three factors are necessary to gain experience in management. First, experience is the *exposure* to a variety of situations, problems, and demands. For example, a nurse may have worked in several hospitals or other health agencies in divergent roles, necessitating the use of some managerial and leadership skills in each setting. Exposure is "learning the ropes" by being an integral part of various organizational activities. The head nurse may allow the staff nurse who is judged to have leadership and management potential to make work assignments, take shift report for the entire unit, prepare a time schedule for the month, or attend a midlevel planning meeting. In these situations, learning takes place by *doing*. Second, gaining experience involves *time,* which is necessary to allow enough exposure to various managerial situations. Finally, with experience it is expected that a level of *maturity* will emerge, which is the philosophical attitude or belief of the individual at work. It is the ability to resist panic in crises, using rational and analytical reasoning instead. The prepared and experienced nurse has the ability to look beyond trivial matters to the cause of a problem, a crucial managerial quality that comes from exposure to a variety of situations over time.

Mentor or Preceptor Relationships

The terms *mentor* and *preceptor* may be used interchangeably. A *mentor* is "a wise and trusted counselor or teacher, a guide, a trainer, or preceptor." A *preceptor* is an "instructor, teacher, tutor, trainer, monitor and director."[8] Because of the similarity in definitions, and because most nursing professionals use this term in the literature, *preceptor* will be used throughout this chapter. In simple terms *precepting occurs when an inexperienced person learns a set of managerial skills from observing, working with, and relating to a more experienced person.* Precepting can be a formal or informal activity: the novice can be taught through a formal preceptor training program with didatic and practical training, or a more experienced nurse can share knowledge and expertise with a protégé on an incidental basis.

Much may be gained from a preceptor relationship. For the protégé it provides not only an opportunity to learn technical skills from an experienced clinician, but it also affords a learning experience on how to relate to people (human skills) and how to approach various problems faced by the nurse in the managerial role (conceptual and diagnostic skills.) More than this, it is an opportunity for the protégé to acquire some career direction and a mechanism to develop a personal philosophy of management and the invaluable quality of self-confidence in managerial ability.

Preceptor matching. Three variables seem to make a difference in preceptor relationships: (1) past experiences (e.g., if past life has been dom-

inated by authority figures, one tends to bond with authority figures), (2) mode of learning (e.g., some need almost constant supervision, while others need only see or hear something to be fully capable of carrying on), and (3) stage of professional development (e.g., if a person is in the early stages of a career, almost everything about the job needs to be learned).[8] Left to his or her own choosing, a person tends to seek preceptors who make him or her feel most comfortable. This is not always beneficial to growth. Matching the learner with the right preceptor is crucial to optimal professional development.

NURSE POPULATION IN NEED OF TRAINING AND DEVELOPMENT

All nurses are in need of training and development, irrespective of their positions in the agency. If such are not forthcoming, the worker becomes stagnant and functions far below capability. Three categories of nurses in need of leadership and managerial training and development are selected for discussion in this chapter: (1) the new graduate, (2) the experienced nurse new to a health agency, and (3) the staff nurse in need of additional preparation to fulfill the leadership/management role of preceptor.

The New Graduate

Current literature identifies serious difficulties faced by the novice entering the work force.[1] Studies have shown that new graduates feel anxiety when they first enter an organization. New rules, regulations, policies, and procedures are introduced. Novice nurses worry about how they will remember all of the new information, much less follow it. They feel inadequate compared with more experienced nurses, and they are concerned about how well they will get along with their co-workers.

Early job experiences play a very critical role in the nurse's career in an organization. It is during these experiences that the individual's and the organization's expectations confront each other. If their expectations are not compatible, dissatisfaction will result. For these reasons effective orientation programs are aimed at reducing the anxiety of new employees.

Unfortunately, for most new graduates, orientation programs designed for all new employees are not sufficient training to bridge the gap between education and service. Role transition for the new graduate becomes a significant problem for nursing service and nursing education and must be addressed realistically.

The New Employee

Orientation programs are designed to provide the information a new employee needs to function comfortably and effectively within an organization. Typically, induction and orientation will convey to the new employee three types of information: (1) a review of the organization's physical facilities, history, mission, and goals and how the employee's job contributes to the organization's needs; (2) presentation of the organization's policies, work rules, and employee benefits; and (3) general and specific information about role expectations and the daily work routine. Co-workers are introduced, and questions by new employees are encouraged. Orientation explains the who, what, when, where, and why specific to an agency.

Staff Nurses

Staff training and development programs are designed for nurses who need additional preparation to fulfill job requirements and to advance to positions in leadership and management. The American Nurses' Association (ANA) states that "Continuing education in nursing consists of planned learning experiences beyond a basic nursing education program. Those experiences are designed to promote the development of knowledge, skills, and attitudes for the enhancement of nursing practice, thus improving health care to the public.[9,p.32]

Continuing education for staff development should provide personnel with the opportunity to acquire new knowledge and skills based on changes in health care practices, and investigative new approaches to the delivery of health care; strengthen their clinical competencies; and assist them to become self-directed in their own learning.

Each component of nursing practice, regardless of level, requires leadership and management to some degree. Assessment, gathering data, planning nursing interventions, and evaluating effects of nursing care delivered are integral parts of the leadership / management pro-

cess. Every individual needs impetus to increase knowledge and skills. Sometimes the desire comes from within the person; other times the person is motivated by external forces. A head nurse, for example, may see something in a staff member that evidences a special ability and may offer the nurse opportunity to take on added responsibility, such as precepting a new graduate or becoming an assistant. With this offer comes the responsibility of the agency to prepare the staff member adequately for the new role.

There is increasing recognition of the fact that people differ in ability, experience, and personality and there is a need for creativity in preparing learning experiences.[10] Thus training and development programs are becoming more tailored to fit the unique requirements of those attending.

CONCEPTS IMPORTANT TO THE SUCCESS OF ALL TRAINING AND DEVELOPMENT PROGRAMS

Training and development mean changing behavior patterns—always a difficult task. An individual's method of doing a job, the skills employed, the energy and thought applied, and the amount of checking and coordinating with other people that is undertaken all partly reflect the individual's personality. Since new work methods or a change in work structure may be a threat to the nurse, the psychological needs for security and a sense of accomplishment must be emphasized. Educators and trainers of staff nurses have a particular need for understanding basic concepts of role clarification, teaching and learning, group dynamics, and change.

Role Clarification

A role may be defined as a set of prescriptions for behavior. A role indicates the kind of behavior that is appropriate for an individual who has a specific position within a group[11] (see Chapter 6). Assuming the role of nurse involves the process of integrating role expectations and role conception. Role integration proceeds most smoothly when the nurse is clear about the expected behaviors and the new or added responsibilities for which she is being trained. Three significant factors constitute any role: (1) role expectation, (2) role conception, and (3) role congruence and performance[12] (Figure 11-3).

Role expectation. Role expectation originates from two sources: the provider of services and the recipient of services. The employing agency establishes a formal set of behaviors expected of the employee and in turn agrees to certain employee rights and privileges. The employer has job descriptions requiring specific preparation and skills for each category of worker, with stipulated protocol for performance. For example, first-level staff nurses must have proper certification if they aspire to employment in an intensive care unit (they must have successfully completed an advanced course in the subject and have had some clinical experience in the area); the nurse who wants to be head nurse or department manager must have at least a bachelor of science degree and management training. The agency may also spell out behaviors expected of the nurse, such as those that relate to communications, punctuality, flexibility in time schedules, or ethics.

In turn, the administration agrees to certain rights and privileges. Nurses may be given the right to negotiate work contracts with the agency through their professional representative, they may have the right to earn advancement in the organization and to earn fringe benefits, or they may have the privilege of a stipulated amount of paid educational leave per year.

The patient/client brings a different set of expectations, less formal and binding, yet their fulfillment forms the very crux of nursing. The patient's/client's role concept for the nurse focuses primarily on himself or herself and significant others. The patient/client wants his or her needs and the needs of the family approached from a holistic frame of reference; that is, from a physical, psychological, social, and spiritual approach. The recipient of nursing services wants quality care provided in an environment that is safe, supportive, and nurturing.

The American Hospital Association issued a Patient's Bill of Rights in 1972 that incorporates the components of quality care in the expectation that they will be supported by the hospital on behalf of its patients as an integral part of the healing process. The ANA adopted a Code for Nurses in 1950 and revised it in 1976. It is intended to guide the nurse in the practice of nursing consistent with ethical principles. These

ROLE EXPECTATIONS		ROLE CONCEPTION
Set by employing agency	**Set by patient**	**Set by nurse**
Duties (job descriptions) Preparation Skills Habits Flexibility Ethics Rights and privileges	Personal needs: Physical Psychological Social Spiritual Significant others' needs: Information Support Participative	Dependent upon: Cultural and environmental contacts Past and present experiences Interests Needs Desires

ROLE CONGRUENCE AND PERFORMANCE

Integration of role expectation, patient expectation, and self-concept of role

Figure 11-3. Factors that determine role performance. *Modified from Rheiner N, Nurs Man 13(3):20-22, 1982.*

documents in themselves are not legally binding; however, they can be persuasive in court proceedings arising from breakdowns in patient/client care.[13]

Role conception. Pressures from the employer, the patient/client, and self have a direct influence on the nurse's conception or analysis of her role. Another influencing stimulus is the nursing profession itself. Both as a group and as individuals, nursing professionals influence each other in many ways as they develop their role conception. Another important factor in role conception is self-identification—becoming clear about who one is. People cannot escape the common heritage of their culture; the self places limits on how the individual will perceive and act in any given role. Individuals think or act in unique ways because of their personalities, abilities, and attitudes and the motives, needs, and ambitions that govern their lives. People cannot escape their heritage, but as they mature they can modify that inheritance through their personal perception and make use of it.

Role congruence and performance. The role the nurse adopts depends on the person's knowledge of *who she is in relation to others.* A person who has moved through normal developmental process will be able to differentiate between primary and secondary roles in life. The nurse may fulfill roles such as friend, spouse, parent, student, activist, and so on, but professionally attention is given over to the role that brings the nurse into contact with the health care system in which a specialized body of knowledge and intervention skills can be used to maintain or restore health and prevent illness.

Role ambiguity and role conflict occurs when there has been a failure to communicate role expectations or there is contradiction between expectations and compliance.[14] Continuous working toward common understanding in roles will help to reduce the distance that may lie between any of the principles involved. Training and development programs help to serve this purpose.

Teaching and Learning Process

The role of the nurse as teacher and trainer is basic to professional practice. Not only must nurses learn how to teach and train others, they must learn to do it well.[15]

Nurses as effective teachers. Nurses teach health to people and in so doing prevent disease, maintain health, facilitate coping, and enable individuals to learn to reestablish healthful living patterns. Further, all nurses lead in one way or another and, in so doing, teach others indirectly or directly. Effective teaching strategies can help members to grow and develop, thereby improving quality of patient care. A teacher is also a catalyst who brings knowledge and the learner together and stimulates a reaction, which can either be positive or negative, depending on the teacher's skill and the learner's receptiveness.

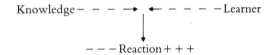

All nurses as teachers. Nurses teach patients, families, ancillary personnel, and one another. Teaching is inherent in the nurse role whether or not the nurse consciously cultivates and exhibits teaching behaviors. Effective teaching is a learner process. Mastery of teaching requires knowledgeable, careful planning and continuous practice, for it is the *teaching process, not the teacher,* that is the key to learning. It is not what teachers are *like* but what they *do* that determines the outcome of the instruction and how the learners feel about themselves. The nurse serves as teacher in a wide variety of everyday activities:

1. In one-to-one activities for solving nursing problems, learning procedure or policies
2. In preplanning and teaching small or large groups, using either an informal or formal structure
3. In role modeling, directly as a preceptor or indirectly through example

Factors that influence learning capacities. Human beings can *develop their aptitudes* into abilities needed for the job. In general, individuals have different learning capacities, learn at different rates, and learn in different ways at various stages in life. Learning begins at birth and can continue until death. Psychologists such as William James, Abraham Maslow, and Carl Rogers believe human beings use only 5% to 10% of their capacity. Furthermore, all persons are not equally motivated to learn. But it is possible, with proper motivation, to transform latent talents into tangible skills and competencies.

An individual's development is influenced by the *stage of life* he or she is in. Erikson presents eight life stages he believes are normal for individuals to experience.[16] Each person is faced with the task of developing these senses:

1. *Sense of trust* (first year). Trust is formed by a set of satisfying experiences of finding biologic and emotional need taken care of consistently without pain or harm.
2. *Sense of autonomy* (12 months to 3 or 4 years). Independence, or asserting and concluding that one is an individual with the freedom to make some choices and be responsible for his or her own actions, comes by allowing the child to make some decisions and to accept the consequences of those decisions.
3. *Sense of initiative* (4 to 6 years). The child finds out what he or she can do by incessant questioning, locomotion, physical attack, and vigorous learning.
4. *Sense of industry and accomplishment* (6 to 12 years). The child becomes engrossed in real, worthwhile, and socially useful tasks that can be completed correctly and well. This age individual is a "joiner," very aware of causes that are "right" and "just."
5. *Sense of identity* (12 to 15 years). In this early adolescent stage individuals struggle to clarify who they are, what their role in the world will be, and to what group or groups they belong. They are trying to determine their state of dependence versus independence, child or adult.
6. *Sense of intimacy* (15 to 20 years). In the middle to late adolescent years friendship and companionship with peers, needs for warmth, close bonds with others, and even for an inner feeling of fusion with others become uppermost priority.
7. *Sense of generativity* (adulthood). Individuals are deeply engrossed in producing and caring for their children or are functioning in nurturing roles.
8. *Sense of integrity* (maturity). Healthy persons accept their life, limitations, people, group, and time period, knowing with some realism their potential for the future.

It is reasonable to assume that individuals do not proceed in discrete stages as described, but rather progress in a slow, continuous fashion. No task is mutually exclusive of other tasks, and most tasks overlap and are repeated in subsequent stages of development. Development usually proceeds at the rate at which it starts. For example, a child who learns to walk and talk at a very early age is likely to be a fast learner as an adult.[16,17]

Glueck, a management consultant, compiled the findings of several pshychiatrists and psychologists into developmental stages that concentrate on adult life, believing this knowledge bears great significance to management[18]:

1. *Leaving the family* (16 to 22 years). Fantasies of life begin to meet reality. The family ceases to be the primary influence and is replaced by peers who have equal standing with the individual, as with age and job. Peers impose group beliefs, and friendships with them are made and broken easily, usually with feelings of betrayal. Emotions are camouflaged to protect the person's feelings of insecurity. Nurse managers who have young employees can recognize these behaviors as normal and deal with them accordingly.
2. *Reaching out* (23 to 28 years). During this period the individual becomes more stable, attempting to discover personal identity, which includes trying to understand the meaning of work. Deep relationships are formed, with the person looking to an older, more experienced individual to serve as a role model. For the nurse staff, this role model is often the nurse manager.
3. *Questioning period* (29 to 34 years). This is a period of crisis when individuals begin to wonder what life is all about and to question their personal and work relationships. Needs such as freedom from restraint versus upward mobility come into conflict. By this time most nurses are married and may be having children. At the same time many are trying to be successful in the professional

marketplace. Some are feeling a need for educational advancement. During these turbulent years individuals begin to feel that if they do not make the right choices and moves, they may never become the persons they hope to be. A significant point for the nurse manager to know is that if a person does not begin to settle down by age 34, the chances of forming a reasonably satisfying life structure are small.

4. *Unstable period* (35 to 43 years). During this period an individual becomes aware that his or her life may be half over or more. These years are sometimes labeled second adolescence. Parents are blamed for unresolved personality problems. At work the person no longer seeks role models but instead seeks to become a role model or counselor to someone else.

5. *Settling in* (44 to 50 years). Most persons realize that major career decisions are settled and must be lived with. This does not negate their natural thirst for more learning and greater self-development. It means that usually they have attained the highest level of advancement in the work setting they are apt to achieve. (There are many exceptions to this statement, particularly with persons in the highest positions.) Economic interest becomes less predominant; the individual looks to family and a few close friends as sources of social fulfillment and support.

6. *Mellowing* (50 years and over). This is the period when a person settles into a quiet pace, giving attention to the satisfactions, irritations, joys, and sorrows of each day. Parents are no longer blamed for personal problems, and the individual looks for opportunities to nurture others. Little attention is given to the past, but rather to the future. Persons in this age group are intensely interested in a retirement plan whereby security for life is assured. They are usually very dependable and stable workers, unencumbered by the problems of young families. The person over age 50 is intent on leaving a good record and acquiring as many benefits as posssible.

Knowledge and understanding of developmental patterns and human behavior and its impact on individuals and groups in the work setting can provide the nurse leader/manager with general and practical implications for action. The reader is invited to explore other theories of human behavior that add to this brief presentation.

Learning patterns. Nurse teachers need some understanding of the pattern in which new skills are learned.[5] When a person first begins to learn a new skill, he or she is likely to be usually clumsy or inept—"all thumbs." This can be very discouraging, especially to persons who pride themselves on their ability. The situation requires the teacher to offer sufficient training, provide for enough return demonstrations, and give support throughout the learning process (Figure 11-4). After this period the typical learning rate is rapid. This is the stage of increasing returns, in which small additional amounts of practice by the trainee produce substantial increases in task proficiency. During this second period the learner's confidence and satisfaction rise.

After more practice time has elapsed, a plateau develops. During this time additional training or monitoring results in the same level of performance. Both the teacher and the learner may be deceived into thinking that maximal proficiency has been attained. The plateau in learning may occur because of a lack of further motivation or the need to devote time and energy to the development of other new skills.

For continued skill proficiency, overlearning needs to take place, which means that the reflex sequences relating to muscular responses and sensory stimuli become more deeply ingrained when the individual continues to practice, even after reaching top performance. This is demonstrated by considering what happens if a swimmer or a typist has not swum or typed for years; yet when the person resumes the skill, proficiency returns after minimal practice.

Implications for the nurse teacher are important. First, the learning curve is not the same for all people; there are profound differences in ability to synchronize muscular movement, to effect eye-hand coordinations, and to sense subtle differences in tactile and muscular responses. When these differences are added to differences

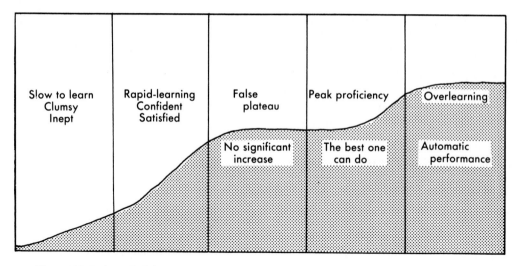

Figure 11-4. A typical learning curve. *Modified from Strauss G and Sayles L: Personnel: the human problems of management, ed 3, Englewood Cliffs, NJ, 1972, Prentice-Hall, Inc, 451.*

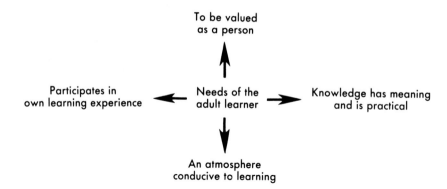

Figure 11-5. Four things an adult learner wants from a teacher. *Modified from Sanford N: J Contin Educ Nurs 10(6):5, 1979.*

in motivation, morale, and knowledge base, they result in wide disparities in learning rates. In teaching the nurse must assess the person's readiness for learning, the areas of knowledge and skill deficit, and the best training for the person.

Adult learners. Teachers of adults should be concerned with philosophical inquiry into the nature, value, and meaning of adult education, as well as the practical aspects of learning. The adult learner wants and expects the following

from the individual who is serving as teacher (Figure 11-5).

1. *The learner is valued as a person, knowledgeable and worthy of teacher time, effort, and commitment.* Learning involves the feelings as well as the intellect. Facilitation of significant learning rests on a positive, trusting relationship between the teacher and the learner. The nurse teacher is committed to teaching the student, and the student in turn is committed to focusing on the task at hand.[19]

2. *The learner is presented with material and strategies that are practical and have meaning for the learner.* Significant learning takes place when the learner perceives the subject relevant to his or her own purposes. Learning with understanding is more permanent and transferable than rote learning. A nurse is far more likely to concentrate on learning or refining skills or neurologic assessment, for example, if these skills will need to be performed on the unit to which she is assigned. Strategies used for teaching and learning will be selected with the adult learner in mind. Small group participation and problem-solving exercises work very well, along with opportunities for independent study and activity. These methods will be discussed in more detail later in this chapter. The important point to remember is that whatever strategy is used, the learning process of *input* (subject and content), *operations* (activities to facilitate learning the subject and content), and *feedback* (verification of progress, feelings, and learning between the teacher and the learner) occur.

3. *The learner participates in his or her own learning experience.* Significant learning is acquired when the adult learner participates responsibly and actively in the learning process. When adult students are free to determine what they will learn according to their prevalent life needs, most will invest more of themselves, work harder, and retain and use more of what they have learned. (The author has first-hand knowledge of this, having conducted and taught RN refresher programs for mature women who wished to reenter the work arena. These nurses were given the opportunity to identify their needs and to participate in planning their curriculum. The results were gratifying: motivation was high, and learning occurred rapidly.)

Goal-setting is a concept central to adult learning.[20] Adults tend to focus on immediate problems, on activities that they can use now. The teacher serves as provider of necessary knowledge and experiences, resource person, facilitator, validator, conferee, and consultant *within a structure that promotes security and trust.* The learner has opportunity for an ongoing two-way evalua-

tion of learning experiences. The fact that the teacher has taught something does not mean that learning has taken place. When progress is assessed in relation to established goals, both persons involved in the learning experience know where they stand. Tools such as interviews, job descriptions, a list of skills for assessment, and problem-solving exercises can assist the learner in determining where needs lie.

The pace of learning is also a very important factor for consideration. Increasing the difficulty of learning material in small increments promotes learning success. For example, the learner should not attempt to master the effect on the body of all fluids and electrolytes, as well as the acid-base balance system, in one sitting. Instead, if given the opportunity, the learner should study one increment at a time. He or she will surely be more successful if the subject is divided into subcategories, each concept learned is applied to clinical practice, and knowledge and activity are validated before proceeding to the next step.

4. *An atmosphere conducive to learning is established and nurtured.* A basic concern of nurse managers is to arrange a motivating atmosphere for learning to take place. This is an endeavor that not only requires an understanding of people, their roles, and the adult as a learner, but also knowledge of how to design, organize, and arrange the work environment to provide channels for learning. A motivating environment is one which provides opportunities for personnel to (a) express and satisfy their own motives in a way which, at the same time, allows them to (b) contribute to the achievement of organizational goals.[21]

Group Dynamics

The study of groups is important to the nurse manager for a number of reasons: (1) groups serve as the focal point of social life, providing a means for understanding social values and norms; (2) through participation in groups individuals may satisfy needs for belonging, status, and security; and (3) groups provide a major mechanism for the achievement of organizational goals. Groups organized for the purpose of achieving work goals will be the focus of this discussion. Please review Chapters 8 and 9 on communication and conflict resolution for greater detail. In addition, group process is addressed through the text as it applies to each subject being presented.

Definition of a work group. In this chapter a group is considered a collection of two or more people who are interdependent and who interact with one another for the purpose of performing to achieve a common goal.[3] The main characteristics of this definition—that goals lead to interactions, which lead to performance—are critical to management effectiveness. These characteristics also distinguish a working group from a collection of people who congregate together to see a play or a sporting event. Groups of existing health care workers in an agency might include such combinations as nurse–physician, nurse–immediate supervisor, nurse–nursing team, nurse–patient / client and family, and so on.

Purpose of an organized working group. Formal groups exist in organizations to carry out the purposes and goals of the organization. In health care this means providing quality care according to clearly defined standards. Nursing work groups have different reasons for forming: to hear shift reports, impart assignments, conduct direction-giving sessions, solve institutional or patient / client problems, engage in committee or task-force activities, or simply for a one-to-one session.

Group development. The ability of a group to work well together develops over time. Group members must (1) get to know and accept one another; (2) agree on their purpose for meeting; and (3) be willing to establish structure, rules, and procedures for accomplishing their goals. Some groups never reach the second or third stages, for a number of reasons. Some may reach them but revert back to the first or second stage. Many times the leader is at fault, because he or she is not well versed in group dynamics and therefore fails to note the signs as they occur.

Group norms and conformity. A *norm* is a measure or standard of behavior or performance. For

example, norms for a member of a nursing team might be to check for coverage with another team member before leaving the unit, to assist other group members when his or her assignment is completed, or to check the procedure book before beginning a special task. Group *conformity* is following and adhering to the established norms. For example, a new nursing team member might decide she wants to spend her "free" time sitting at the desk observing others. In all probability group members will attempt to enforce adherence to group norms on the nonadhering member. Generally, in such a case a three-phase reaction occurs. First, the new member will be reminded by another member of the norm, who will suggest that it be followed. If the comment is ignored by the new worker, the group becomes less friendly. More members may attempt to persuade the new person. If their efforts fail, the new person is ostracized—no one will talk to her unless absolutely necessary, eat at the same table, or provide help with heavy duties unless forced to do so. It is incumbent on the nurse leader to recognize when such a situation is occurring and to understand whether the enforced group norm is actually beneficial to the organization.

Status in groups. Status is a social ranking in a group given to persons because of their position in the organization. The director of nursing services holds greater status than the nurses' aide. Another important factor is seniority and / or expertise. For example, the oldest nurse in a medical unit might enjoy high status in the group because of age, tenure, or expertise. Like norms, status symbols have positive and negative aspects. The positive aspects are the clarification of relationships, authority, and responsibility. On the other hand, overemphasis on status can reduce both the frequency of interaction among members and the level of communication. The team leader who never lets the members forget who is boss or the team member who reminds the group frequently, "I have been here the longest and I should have first preference," creates conflict, and group activity is diverted toward resolving the conflict.

Group member roles. The main managerial roles of a nurse are interpersonal (to relate well with others), information (to provide clear directions), and decisional (to make sound decisions based on the use of nursing process). Membership roles are also multiple, depending on each person's rank and assignment. They too must maintain a system that leads to *group cohesiveness,* in which the factors acting on group members to remain and participate in the group are greater than those acting on the members to leave it.[3]

Team building for special tasks. Team building is a process for developing work group maturity and effectiveness; it is the most widely used human resource development technique in the business world.[22] Team building emphasizes interactive group processes, or the "how" of effective group behavior. Team builders (1) set goals and/or priorities, (2) analyze or allocate how work is performed, (3) examine the way a group is working, considering such factors as norms, decision making, and communication, and (4) examine relationships among the people doing the work. It is important for the group itself to achieve these purposes by relying on its own leadership to solve real-life problems. A consultant or group facilitator may help to get the group headed in the right direction and may coach as necessary along the way.[3]

In nursing, team building is used to prepare groups of people to accomplish particular tasks. A team may be formed to design a new nursing care delivery system or to introduce the use of computerized equipment throughout the health care agency. Often these teams consist of individuals who have specific areas of expertise (e.g., nurse specialists, social workers, or business managers) but no allegiance to or even familiarity with each other. Team-building techniques are geared toward developing an appreciation among team members for what the task is, what roles must be filled, and who will fill them. In the process, individual strengths are highlighted as they pertain to the tasks, and group cohesion is developed.[22]

CHANGE PROCESS

No one can escape change, particularly managers in health care settings. Their environment includes community, government, patients/clients, families, nurses, ancillary staff, physicians, and myriad other workers who contribute to health care and maintenance. What affects one part of the environment affects all; therefore change is ever-present. Nurses must acquire skills that bring about *planned change,* rather than chaos, in whatever their areas of service. Nurses are facilitators of change and need to promote this image to their staff.[1]

Change means substituting one thing for another, experiencing a shift in circumstances that cause differences, or becoming different than before. The causes and effects of change will be addressed in this section, as well as a process that may be used to bring about desired changes.

Forces That Influence Change

Forces can be external or internal. *External forces* on an institution are generally those happenings that influence the organization as a whole or the top admininstrators. Examples are:
1. Population explosion, which may influence or accelerate plans to add a new wing to the maternal-child health department (need to add to staffing, cope with transition period, and plan for the future of the department)
2. Legislation that restricts certain patients from being admitted to the hospital (need to find alternatives for the patients, possibly fight legislation or reduce staffing)
3. Economic forces that demand accountability from nursing services (nursing inservice or nursing services need to demonstrate that education, training, and delivery of nursing care contribute to cost containment and improvements in the quality of patient/client care services provided by the health agency personnel)
4. A breakthrough in research that alters the kind of care given to certain patients, such as those with peptic ulcers or carcinoma (need to change focus of care, update knowledge, teach new skills)

Internal forces originate primarily from inside operations or are the result of external changes. (Refer to the "need to's" in the section above.) A number of internal factors are involved in anticipated changes in an organizational work force:
1. Composition of staffing patterns can change, such as all RNs or a reduction in numbers of RNs and an increase in the numbers of LPN/LVNs and nurses' aides (need for phasing out of some RNs, orientation of

new workers; need to plan for additional roles and responsibilities of RNs and to cope with their reactions: may need to develop strategies to combat the change in staffing pattern).

2. Productivity may need to be increased, as when top administration decides the nurse-patient ratio is to be changed from 1:4 to 1:6 (need to acquaint staff with the dictum and train them in establishing different priorities of care).

3. Quality of working life may need to be improved. There is a growing popularity of the concept that the time spent at work should be satisfying and that basic needs should be fulfilled, as well as provide for self-actualization, leading to a feeling of challenge and excitement about the job. People spend a high proportion of their time in activities associated with their work, and they want and expect conditions that are pleasant and productive. Given the broad title of "quality of working life," the focus of nurses' interest has centered on such issues as:

   a. Provision of quality nursing care
   b. The need for sufficient numbers of nurses who are qualified to provide care
   c. Staff development programs
   d. Budget limitations that do not provide for realistic personnel requirements (salaries, fringe benefits, equipment and supplies, promotions, and so on)
   e. Absenteeism among staff
   f. Time spent by nursing personnel performing nonnursing duties
   g. Improper use of personnel
   h. Instability and inflexibility of staff
   i. Work schedule problems (too many weekends and holidays worked, time schedules not posted far enough in advance, little leeway for change, no provision for other options than the 8-hour day, 5 days a week)
   j. Lack of communication among either the nursing unit to which assigned or the different levels of personnel
   k. The need for formal nurse-employee representation to negotiate work contracts (professional organization versus a union)

Change Process: a Planned Procedure

The process of change is change with a purpose, devised to solve problems affecting nurses and their work. The process of change deals with making alterations by choice and deliberation, rather than by indoctrination, coercion, natural growth, or accident.[23]

Douglass and Bevis suggest the need to establish basic ground rules for change, including[24]:

1. Try to avoid surprises. Keep everyone informed in advance of plans that will have impact on them. People like to be informed and resent being ostracized.
2. Allow people to vent their feelings. This will give valuable input to the decision makers and make staff members feel as though they are part of the change.
3. Try to arrange for alternative actions if the change fails. Plan for implementation one piece at a time, if possible.
4. Set up times for progress reports and meetings; these encourage the feedback necessary to the success of any change.

Steps in Change Process

The process of planned change involves a number of distinct steps or subprocesses. Application of the problem-solving process is central to successful change and step-by-step procedures and analysis provide an orderly way to proceed.[25] Figure 11-6 illustrates how the process operates while effecting change.

The following is a situation requiring change. A step-by-step analysis of the application of the change process accompanies it:

Under a decentralized organizational system, the staff nurses on the sixth-floor oncology unit are disgruntled because they believe there is inequity in assignments of nurses employed by the hospital. Their particular concern lies with assignments for weekends and holidays. Some of the nurses' friends, fiancés, spouses, and families are pressuring the nurses to rebel.

Step 1: *Perceive a need for change.* The head nurse of the oncology unit senses unrest among nurses, demonstrated by angry comments about the time schedule: "I have weekend duty again, and you guessed it! Joan has the time off; this makes three weekends in a row for her.

1. Nurse perceives a need for change

2. Group interaction
    a. Identify internal and external forces
    b. State the problem
    c. Identify constraints
    d. List change strategies or possible approaches to the problem
    e. Select the best change strategy or strategies
    f. Develop plan for implementation
    g. Select or develop tools for evaluation

3. Implement plan one step at a time, if possible
   Conduct evaluation sessions as changes are in progress

4. Evaluate overall results of the change
   Retain as is, alter, delete parts, or decide to discontinue the plan

Figure 11-6. The change process.

Man, is that unfair. You'll see! When Thanksgiving and Christmas come around, Joan will be off and I'll be right here! I hear it's like that all over the hospital." Several other staff nurses nod their heads, indicating confirmation. Passive-aggressive actions are occurring: staff nurses arrive for work late, there is an excess of absences, and it is difficult to get a nurse to volunteer for helping services.

Step 2. *Initiate group interaction.* Two or more nurses may gather together for discussion of any perceived work-related problem. A variety of techniques are employed: an informal discussion group, a committee or task-force group, or a general meeting to explore a situation. The method used depends on the power or status of the nurse (administrative or staff person) and availability of resources for meeting and action. In this situation the head nurse posts an invitation to all nursing staff of the oncology unit to attend one of two meetings scheduled at times so that all shifts can attend. She posts the subject for the meeting and time schedules and

asks members who attend to select a secretary to transcribe the remarks, encouraging each member to participate in the discussion. During the meeting:
a. *Identify external and internal forces for change.* The group gathers, and the head nurse presents her perception of dissatisfaction among some staff members because of work schedules. She defines external and internal forces, then asks the secretary to use a chart pad to log responses *without judgment or comment.* Use of a chart allows for a written record of actual proceedings (Figure 11-7). The head nurse may or may not leave, depending on the mix of the group. If the members express their feelings freely with the head nurse present, she stays; if they are hesitant, she leaves and receives the minutes of the meeting.
b. *State the problem.* This is a critical step in the change process. The external and internal forces are examined; the basic questions of who, what, when, where, and why are addressed; and a clear statement of the problem

External forces	Internal forces
Negative reaction from: Boyfriends Fiancees Husbands Families	Unfairness in scheduling Head Nurse plays favorites One person (Joan works very few weekends or holidays) The same thing happens in other nursing units in the hospital. It makes me feel like not reporting to work on time. I stay home on a holiday I'm scheduled whenever I think I can get away with it.

Figure 11-7. Chart pad.

is formulated: *dissatisfaction among staff nurses on sixth-floor oncology unit about time schedule for weekends and holidays, with the belief that the problem exists on all other nursing units in the hospital.*

c. *Identify constraints.* A constraint is something that restricts, limits, or regulates a person and activities. Constraints present in leadership may be leadership climate or style (authoritarian versus participative); organizational climate (centralized versus decentralized); individual characteristics (attitudes, such as unwillingness to change); or a general fear of repercussions to change. Given the situation, the group will list their perception of constraints that might effect a change, again using a chart pad. A staff member takes notes to allow for freedom of expression (Figure 11-8).

d. *List change strategies or possible approaches to solving the problem.* Allow sufficient time for dialogue to occur. Again, the head nurse may or may not be present. Remember that two sessions of staff members are being held to address the same issues. Also, the process of planning for change may cover several meetings over time, in consideration of time constraints and to allow assimilation and reflection. Continue with a group-designated staff member transcribing feedback from the participants. Promote a free, open, and receptive climate; make no comments about responses (Figure 11-9). Continue the discussion until all possible solutions are exhausted. Invite the members to include other alternatives for consideration at the next meeting.

e. *Select the best change strategy or strategies.* The group leader should be someone other than the head nurse in this situation, because she is a focal point of the problem. She may be asked to withdraw from the group at any stage of the change process to allow complete freedom of expression. The members may wish to invite an outside person, such as the staff development educator, who has the oncology unit as part of her responsibilities. Care must be taken not to invite people who are not skilled in the art of facilitating, otherwise they may take matters into their own hands or tell the group what to do.

Constraints

My husband won't let me work on holidays and weekends. (Jane)

I find it hard to talk to our H.N.

⊤⊦⊦ //   (Six others concur)

I feel that our Head Nurse has the power to do whatever she wants with the time schedule and we have to take it.

            (One other member agreed)

Figure 11-8. Constraints.

Possible approaches to solving the problem

---

1. Talk to the Director of Nurses.

2. Let's join a union!

3. Seek help from the professional association who bargains for our contracts.

4. Let's stage a sick-out; all stay home for one Saturday, Sunday, or holiday.

5. See if we can talk this out with our Head Nurse.

6. Conduct a survey of all staff nurses to see if the problem is hospital-wide.

7. Ask H.N. to insist that Jane take her fair share of weekends and holidays; if she refuses, transfer or dismiss her.

8. Report the problem to Supervisor or Coordinator.

Figure 11-9. Possible approaches to solving the problem.

In the situation given, the group decided on the following priorities:

PRIORITY	NUMBER OF ALTERNATIVE	RATIONALE
1	Item 5: Talk with head nurse	Perhaps she has been unaware of the extent of the problem and will be amenable to change without any further action.
2	Item 7: Problem with Jane	Resolution of priority #1 might also resolve this problem, but make the priority known.
3	Item 8: Report to supervisor or coordinator	It is wise to follow lines of authority in an agency. In the decentralized system the supervisor is the next person in authority.
4	Item 6: Conduct a survey	If satisfactory resolution has not occurred, poll other nurses in the hospital.
5	Item 3: Seek help from professional association	This step may occur before or after the survery, depending on the group's ability.
6	Item 1: See director of nurses	By this time data will have been collected and professional advice given as to procedure.
7	Item 2: Join a union	Give the professional association a chance first.
8	Item 4: Sick-out	Unprofessional action; harmful to clients.

Add alternatives and engage in the priority exercise. In so doing, another answer might be selected as the clue to success.

f. *Formulate plan for implementation.* Priority #1 is to talk with the head nurse. Before the meeting the group decides on the following strategy:

1. Select representatives of the group who are to meet with the head nurse. Choose those members with the best interpersonal skills.
2. Make an outline of the group's position and request.
3. Conduct a simulated setting in which one person plays the part of the head nurse and those selected to represent the group make the presentation.
4. Ask for feedback and suggestions from the remaining group members.
5. Make changes as decided.
6. Contact the head nurse and arrange for a meeting. Tell her what it is about.
7. Arrive on time; make the presentation. Depending on outcome, either consider the change process completed or yet in process.
8. If necessary to carry the problem further, follow similar strategies of being prepared with data and using effective communication techniques.

g. *Develop or select tools for evaluation.* In this situation the criterion can be that the step taken was successful or unsuccessful. If, however, there is need to conduct a survey, then tools already developed may be used, or one may be designed by the group or associate. In situations that involve standards of care or other protocol, these would be the basis for the evaluation, checking each factor item by item.

Step 3. *Implement the change one step at a time, if possible.* In the situation given the change would probably occur at once; however, if major changes were to be made, implementation by stages would be better. *Hold evaluation sessions with persons involved as changes are in progress.* In the work-schedule situation it would be advisable for the head nurse to meet with her staff periodically to hear their reactions. If the change process was taken further than the first step, then each phase would be evaluated in the same careful manner. It is much easier to handle problems in the formative stages rather than to wait until the problem seems insurmountable.

Step 4. *Evaluate the overall results of the change and make adjustments as necessary: retain, alter, delete parts, or discontinue the process.* In the situation given, the head nurse would assess the general satisfaction level of the group through group meetings or by asking for anonymous comments in a suggestion box. Group discussion is preferable, as unsigned comments may reinforce passive-aggressive behavior.

Other situations are presented below. Use the change process to find optimal answers to the problems listed:
1. A nurses' aide on a surgical unit is creating conflict among the other nurses by pitting one against the other.
2. The quality control committee of a community hospital recognizes a need for more consistent documentation of nursing care on patients' records to comply with JCAHO standards.
3. The turnover of nurses is high on a neurologic unit. Exit interviews reveal that new employees are treated coolly by the staff and are expected to prove themselves with little help from the stable staff.
4. You are one of the nurses in a clinical area who wants to change the pattern of nursing care from team nursing to primary nursing.
5. A preceptor assesses herself as one who enjoys the beginning of precepting, when the novice is very dependent on her for learning; however, she does not like relinquishing her role to the new person, even when the two agree that the novice is ready to manage the assignment. She wants to continue precepting.

EXAMPLES OF ORIENTATION AND STAFF DEVELOPMENT PROGRAMS

In this section a description of several staff nurse programs are offered for review: a general orientation program, a nurse internship for the new graduate, a preceptor training workshop, and self-directed learning. For each category the overall purpose, objectives, and length of the program are given, along with comments. Adapt the programs to meet needs of a specific work environment. Information specific to the organization is available through agency documents. Other content for the workshops may be found in this chapter, as well as in other sections of the book. The suggested readings at the end of each chapter supply other references that may be used as resources.

General Orientation Program

Overall purpose. To provide experienced nurses and others new to the organization with orientation to practice nursing in keeping with the hospital's mission and goals to meet JCAHO standards and Medicare criteria.

Length of program. Fifteen days, followed by a probationary period to total 3 months.

Instructors. Members of the staff development department (inservice) and representatives from administration (hospital and nursing), personnel, quality assurance, infection control, and other departments as appropriate.

Objectives. On completion of the program each participant is expected to be able to do the following regarding the hospital in general and the nursing service in particular:

Hospital
1. Recognize the overall physical setting of the hospital and specify the work area to which she is assigned.
2. Review the mission, goals, and policies of the hospital.
3. Describe the organizational structure of the hospital.
4. Describe the communication process in effect interdepartmentally and intradepartmentally (computer, intercommunication systems, forms, notices, and so on).
5. Identify the functions of departments other than nursing and the nurse's relationship with them.

Nursing service
1. Read the overall philosophy, goals, and standard of nursing care adopted by nursing service as the criteria for determining quality care.
2. Review nursing organizational structure, with primary focus on staff nurse levels (e.g., levels 1, 2, 3, 4) and conditions for advancement.
3. State the purpose of the hospital staff development department (or inservice department) and ways in which the staff nurse can be served by its offerings.
4. Identify hospital committees on which staff nurses can become members; recognize the conditions for membership.
5. Complete nursing skills inventory by the end of the 15-day orientation period or make arrangements with the staff development instructor for a time extension.

6. Demonstrate acquisition of baseline level of understanding and skill in content and procedures common to nursing practice in the specified area of practice. (This objective may be accomplished by classroom instruction, demonstration, and/or use of modules for independent study.) Many of the components of orientation are often transcribed on videotape prepared by the staff development department. Examples of content and procedures:
   a. Nursing process adopted for hospital-wide use
   b. Documentation system (charting)
   c. Discharge planning
   d. Team nursing and/or primary nursing
   e. Pharmacology (drugs used most commonly in the specified area of practice, computation of dosages; these tests need to be developed according to areas of service, such as intensive care, cardiovascular, medical, surgical, pediatrics, maternal-neonatal, oncology, and so on)
   f. Intravenous therapy, blood therapy, central lines, monitoring of equipment
   g. Infection control
   h. Quality assurance program
   i. Life support systems (cardiopulmonary resuscitation, advanced life support systems)

Up to this point, all nurse orientees may be oriented and tested together. For induction into the clinical area to which she is assigned, the experienced nurse new to the hospital is assigned to the care of a trained preceptor. The goal of this plan is for the new employee to ease into the job with as much help as needed, the expectation being that the experienced nurse will be able to function in the role assigned fairly independently by the end of the 15-day orientation period. The new employee is encouraged to return to the staff development department for review of any part of the orientation offerings that are yet unclear.

Nurse Internship for the New Graduate

The example presented here is the result of a nurse intern study group charged by the nursing administrators of the Association Hospitals and the California Nurses' Association, Region 10,

to develop goals and objectives for an internship program for the new graduate. The group was further charged to develop levels of practice within the internship program and to recommend a time frame for the program.

Good Samaritan Hospital of Santa Clara Valley, California, was one of five participating hospitals selected to conduct a pilot group. The author developed the program. The program was implemented with 23 new graduates from five different educational programs and was evaluated as successful. Only the major highlights are given.

Overall purpose. To supplement the clinical and leadership skills of the new graduate nurse to facilitate professional and social integration into the health care team.

Length of program. Three months; however, a second program, 9 weeks long, was conducted. A comparative analysis revealed that 9 weeks was sufficient for an internship program.

Instructors. Staff development personnel, head nurses.

Other participants. Preceptors, nursing staff, and members from other departments, as appropriate.

Objectives. Overall goals are given for the four levels, with specific objectives for level IV, as this final phase of the program outlines ultimate expectations of its graduates.

Level I. Basic nursing skills. At the completion of level I the intern functions as a team member or associate nurse to the preceptor and delivers nursing care to patients with a varity of uncomplicated health problems.

Level II. At the completion of level II the intern functions as a team member or associate nurse and delivers nursing care to patients with a variety of moderate to complicated health problems.

Level III. At the completion of level III the intern functions as a team leader or primary nurse with dependence on the preceptor and directs and/or delivers nursing care to patients with a variety of learning needs. The intern recognizes, develops, and uses teaching and learning strategies to meet patient/client and family needs and staff learning needs.

Level IV. At the completion of level IV the intern functions as team leader or primary nurse fairly independently, uses resource persons appropriately, demonstrates a consistent pattern of leadership skills needed for problem solving and priority setting, and meets frequently with preceptor to discuss progress in the following areas:

a. Uses data obtained from other disciplines and own assessment to establish priorities of patient care and nursing activities (examples are provided the intern)

b. Demonstrates ability to reorganize priorities based on changing patient care needs

c. Makes rounds with physician, as necessary, and collaborates in plan of care to meet patient needs

d. Provides direction, consultation, and when appropriate (as team leader) supervision of the nursing team on a routine basis

e. Evaluates information from appropriate sources and incorporates into patient care plan

f. Evaluates own documentation or charting and that of others, when appropriate, for evidence of care given and patient progress

g. Evaluates activities of self and others for adherence to hospital policy and procedures; takes appropriate action

The interns were assigned a combination of classroom and clinical activities, with opportunity to come to the nursing education department (staff development) for review or instruction when necessary.

Each intern was assigned to a trained preceptor. The intern and preceptor conferred formally and informally through each level of the program. Other conference participants included the head nurse, the clinical instructor, and others as considered appropriate.

An evaluation form was prepared for each level of the program. Competency at the level in question was indicated by successful completion of skills (Figure 11-10). Documentation of competency was required by the preceptor or instructor at least once as determined by the critical nature of the skill.

Among other assessment tools was a six-dimension scale for evaluation of nursing behaviors. The box on p. 232 shows an excerpt. The list contains only a sample of activities in which nurses engage. The actual tool should list the usual behaviors exhibited by the nurse under each category (e.g., leadership, critical care, teaching, and collaboration, etc.) for the intern,

Skill performed by nurse intern	Supervised/ assisted by	Validation of successful completion No. 1	Validation of successful completion No. 2
A. Uses data obtained from other disciplines and own assessment to establish priorities of patient care and nursing activities	Remarks: *Followed procedure — weak on responses. Suggest review.* Date: 4/8/84 Sig.: *L. Douglass, Instr*	Remarks: *Has reviewed theory and skills in skills lab. Demonstrated ability to recognize rales and rhonchi.* Date: 4/12/84 Sig.: *D. Gamberg, Preceptor*	Remarks: *Completed admittance of new patient thoroughly and well. Excellent rapport with pt/family* Date: 4/20/84 Sig.: *D. Gamberg, Preceptor*
B. Continue on with objectives for level IV	Remarks: Date: Sig.:	Remarks: Date: Sig.:	Remarks: Date: Sig.:

Figure 11-10. Sample of a tool used to assess competencies based on predetermined criteria. *Courtesy of The Good Samaritan Hospital, Santa Clara Valley, San Jose, California.*

Performance of Nursing Behaviors

Instructions: This tool contains a list of activities in which nurses engage with varying degrees of frequency and skill. Please indicate how well you believe you perform or how well you believe the intern can perform the activities by using numbers from the following key:

KEY TO SUBSCALES

1—Not very well	L —Leadership
2—Satisfactorily	CC—Critical care
3—Well	TC —Teaching and collaboration
4—Very well	PE —Planning and evaluation
	IPR—Interpersonal relationships
	PD —Professional development

TC _____ Teach a patient's/client's family members about the patient's/client's needs.
PE _____ Coordinate the plan of nursing care with the medical plan of care.
L _____ Give praise and recognition for achievement to those under her direction.
TC _____ Teach preventive health measures to patients/clients and families.
IPR _____ Promote the inclusion of the patient's/client's decisions and desires concerning care.
CC _____ Perform technical procedures (e.g., oral suctioning, tracheostomy care).
PD _____ Attend quality assurance committee meeting.

The intern, preceptor, and the head nurse evaluate the intern's performance toward the end of the program to validate successful achievement and to identify areas that need further attention.

---

preceptor, and head nurse to evaluate separately and collaboratively.

Preceptor Workshop

Overall purpose. To prepare qualified nurses to serve as preceptor, role model, and resource person to new graduates or new employees and to create a supportive, unstressful orientation period.

Objectives. On completion of the 2-day workshop, each participant is expected to:
1. Serve as a mentor, role model, and resource person for trainee.
2. Use effective communication skills with trainee.
3. Keep within the designated time frame for preparation of trainee.
4. Complete necessary reports regarding trainee progress.
5. Consult with educational staff regarding concerns or problems that relate to trainee.

Length of program. Two days.

Qualifications of preceptor candidate. The interested nurse should:
1. Be permanent, full-time (nurses with exceptional ability and interest may be considered if their status is three-fifths or four-fifths time)
2. Demonstrate proficiency in technical, intellectual, and interpersonal skills
3. Exhibit an interest in teaching new graduates and new employees
4. Desire to work in a close one-to-one relationship with a new employee
5. Agree to attend preceptor training workshop and acquire as much knowledge and skill from the sessions as possible

Suggested content. Suggested content for a preceptor training workshop includes:
1. Review of hospital's orientation program and tools for assessment of comprehension
2. Roles of head nurse, preceptor, instructor, new graduate, and new employee
3. The adult learner, the teaching-learning process, development and use of behavioral objectives, coaching the learner

4. Communication process in a one-to-one relationship
5. Group process: working with small groups
6. The change process applied to the preceptor role
7. The evaluation process as it applies to the preceptor role

The preceptor and intern are provided a day-by-day activity manual with tools for assessment of accomplishment. The content relates specifically to the objectives listed for the particular program (e.g., new employee, 15-day program, or new graduate, 3-month or less program). The key to success of the preceptor program lies in the application of principles of effective leadership and management.

Self-Learning Programs

Overall purpose. To meet self-learning needs of nursing personnel in health agencies.

Objectives. Program objectives include:
1. To provide programs that address the identified development needs of the nursing staff
2. To have 15- to 20-minute learning programs readily accessible in the workplace available whenever the nurse's workload permits
3. To provide a learning resource center, available to all nursing staff, containing resources that address the developmental needs of the nursing agency's entire staff.
4. To allow the staff nurse to be in control of scheduling her own learning programs
5. To identify nurses in the agency who are specialists in their fields who can serve as resource persons when inquiries are made

Length of programs. From 15 to 20 minutes in the workplace and 30 minutes to 1 hour or more in a learning resource center.

Suggested format for self-learning in the workplace

Modules. For each subject the staff development department or designated person(s) prepares a module contained in a folder. Included are extracts from available literature and other media information. The following is a suggested format and examples:

Format	Example
Subject	Protective measures needed by a nurse caring for a patient with AIDS
Objective	To protect the nurse from contracting AIDS
Content	Facts on how AIDS is transmitted, research, conclusions
Summary	Meaning for the nurse. (There is no need to use isolation procedures, except for transmission of blood or body fluids.)
Quiz	True or false statements about the main points

The information is capsulized and customized for the learner. The content is approved by an inservice educator, head nurse, or designated person. The advantages of the modular system are that the modules are economical to prepare, do not require hardware, are portable, and are easily produced. A nurse can review the module anytime the work load allows or during coffee or lunch break. Disadvantages are that it is time consuming to prepare the modules, and they do not lend themselves well to procedures when demonstration and practice are required.

Bulletin boards. Large fixed or portable bulletin boards can become learning centers. They provide a graphic or pictorial account of a subject pertinent to the nursing staff. Bulletin boards can be placed in the chart room and rest areas or any other place where nurses gather. Brief narrations can be printed or typed on 5 × 8 file cards and mounted on attractive colored paper. Anatomical diagrams, graphs, pictures of rashes, wounds, positions, and so on are appropriate for this format.

Bulletin boards need to be changed frequently; once the information is absorbed, staff tend to ignore the board. Staff members may wish to prepare or assist in the preparation of a display.

Resource material in the nursing unit or department. Information can be acquired quickly from resources available in a work area. Each department should have on hand a current *Physician's Desk Reference*, a text or texts covering the areas that the department services (e.g., pediatrics, medical/surgical, cardiovascular, psychiatric), and policy and procedure manuals. Providing nursing periodicals in the nurses' lounge is another excellent means of assisting the staff in self-directed learning.

Portable media. Health agencies are wise to provide each nursing unit with a *slide/filmstrip* projector, along with teaching media selected by the staff. Slides and filmstrips are commonly used to illustrate real-life situations, such as "Communication with a Sexually Abused Child," and nursing procedures. Commercially prepared filmstrips on many subjects are readily available at minimal cost. Slides and filmstrips can be changed with ease and can be viewed almost anywhere—a wall or other blank surface reflects the pictures adequately.

The videocassette recorder (VCR) allows any agency, large or small, to have benefit of the finest presentations at minimal cost. Further, staff members can view the cassettes at their own time and pace. The VCR is probably the most cost-effective media available for staff development, considering the quality of content and the number of people who can be served collectively and individually. Two types of presentations are common: those discussing interpersonal relations and psychosocial-religious issues and those demonstrating and explaining procedures. Whatever the presentation, each one should include statements of overall and specific purpose (e.g., "to gain an understanding of arterial bypass surgery," "implications for the nurse in the first 24 hours after the procedure"). Each presentation should be followed by a written quiz to help the nurse assess whether the objectives have been met and to verify completion of the program if continuing education units or some other form of credits are being earned. Since most VCR programs are 30 minutes to 1 hour or more long, the nurse usually goes to the agency's resource center for viewing. Some agencies, particularly during the afternoon and night shifts, roll a VCR to the nursing department, where nurses can view the program as time permits. Another method is to allow the nurse to sign out the cassettes from the resource center to view at home. A marked disadvantage to the use of the VCR is the lack of opportunity to communicate with the presenter(s). When possible, a staff development person should be on hand to respond to inquiries and conduct follow-up discussion.

Computers. Terminals are becoming increasingly common in health care agencies, with videodiscs incorporating all types of media—slides, motion, audio, and print, in black and white and color. Holographic techniques make it possible to produce three-dimensional images at different magnifications. However, there is a delay in preparation of quality instructional materials. Given time and expertise, a nurse will be able to obtain immediate data on any subject relevant to nursing practice and will be able to tap into previously unavailable resources quickly through a computer. Typically, the computer used for staff development presents cases, medication computation problems, or conversion tables for consideration. The nurse requests information, responds, interviews, and receives feedback about the consequences of decisions made.

Resource persons. Use of existing personnel is an efficient means of improving and upgrading employee performance. The self-directed nurse can contact the hospitalwide staff development department (or the appropriate person) to identify expert staff members who are willing to share their skill and knowledge with another. Arrangements can be made for responding to the needs of the individual. The response may be a simple telephone call or a meeting for demonstration, practice, or dialogue.

SUMMARY

1. The function of training and development is to provide an environment and resources that facilitate a learning and maturing process in each person.
2. Managerial skills needed by all nurses are technical, human, conceptual, diagnostic, and those of coach and mentor.
3. Management skills are acquired through education and training, experience, and preceptor relationships.
4. All nurses are in need of training and development, irrespective of their position in the agency.
5. In addition to content already presented in this text, knowledge important to the success of training and development programs includes concepts of role clarification: role expectations, role conception, and role congruence and performance.

6. Every nurse has the responsibility to be an effective teacher. Teaching and learning always stimulate a reaction, either positive or negative. It is the teaching process, not the teacher, that is the key to learning.

7. Human beings are affected by their stage in life and their learning patterns. Adult learners expect to be valued as knowledgeable persons, to have practical and meaningful learning experiences, to participate in the learning experience, and to learn in an atmosphere conducive to learning.

8. Work groups fulfill purposes and goals of the organization through goal establishment, interaction, and performance. Group norms, conformity, status, and roles influence group productivity.

9. Team building is a process for developing group maturity and effectiveness with emphasis on goals and group process.

10. Any nurse can effect change. Change is influenced by external and internal forces. The process of change is change with a purpose, devised to solve problems affecting nurses and their work. Steps involved in the change process are to (a) perceive a need;

(b) engage in group interaction to identify internal and external forces, state the problem, identify constraints, list strategies and select the best one(s), formulate a plan, and develop tools for evaluation; (c) implement and evaluate the changes one step at a time; and (d) make final assessment of the change, making adaptations as necessary.

11. Three staff development programs are offered by many hospitals: organization programs for all personnel new to the hospital, nurse internships for new graduates, and preceptor training programs for qualified nursing staff. These and other training and development programs, including provision for meeting continuing education requirements, are commonly offered by the staff development or inservice department of the institution.

12. A nurse interested in on-the-job, self-directed learning has many avenues to pursue: modules, bulletin boards, resource materials in the department, slide / filmstrips, videocassettes, computers, the resource learning center, and resource persons.

Questions for Study and Discussion

1. Your job is to establish a staff development center for nursing staff. What is your major function?

2. Give an example of a conceptual or diagnostic skill required of a nurse manager.

3. Describe the characteristics of a preceptor you would like to have on your first job. Now list them in order of priority and explain your rationale.

4. Explain why role analysis and team building are useful to nurse managers.

5. Decide where you are in relation to Glueck's developmental stages for adults. Does the position you identified relate to the ages given for the category? If age and category

do not correlate, is this a negative factor? Why or why not?

6. Assume you must learn a nursing procedure new to you. What is the best approach to learning for you? What would you do first, second, and so on? Does your plan relate to the "norm" for teaching and learning? If it is unusual, why do you think you learn differently?

7. You have been a staff nurse for 4 years and believe strongly that the authoritarian structure of the unit needs to be changed to allow for more staff input and participation. What could you do to bring about the desired change?

REFERENCES

1. Davis A: Managing the education function, J Healthcare Educ Train 5(1):33, 1990.

2. Pankan J: Refocusing healthcare education, Healthcare Forum J 4(1):20-23, 1989.

3. Kreitner R: Management, ed 4, Boston, 1989, Houghton Mifflin Co.

4. Longest B: Management practices for the health professional, Norwalk, Conn, 1990, Appleton and Lange.

.5. Wheelen T and Hunger J: Strategic management, ed 3, Reading Mass, 1990, Addison-Wesley Publishing Co.

6. Levenstein A: Avoiding responsibility, Nurs Man 14(2):28-30, 1983.

7. Orth C, Wilkinson H, and Benfari R: The manager's role as coach and mentor, JONA 20(9): 11-15, 1990.

8. Sayles L: Leadership: managing in real organizations, ed 2, New York, 1989, McGraw-Hill Book Co.

9. American Nurses' Association: ANA nursing standards, Kansas City, Mo, 1986, The Association.

10. Geyer K and Korte P: Creativity in nursing staff development, J Nurs Staff Development 6(3):112-117, May/June, 1990.

11. Tappen R: Nursing leadership and management: concepts and practice, ed 2, 1989, Philadelphia, FA Davis Co.

12. Rheiner N: Role theory: framework for change, Nurs Man 13(3):20-22, 1982.

13. Potter D, editor: Nurses reference library, Springhouse, Pa, 1984, Springhouse Corporation, 77, 448.

14. Gillies D: Nursing management: a systems approach, ed 2, Philadelphia, 1989, WB Saunders Co.

15. Broadwell M: The new supervisor, ed 4, Reading, Mass, 1990, Addison-Wesley Publishing Co.

16. Erikson, E: Childhood and society, ed 2, New York, 1963, WW Norton and Co, Inc.

17. Phillips J: The origins of intellect: Piaget's theory, San Francisco, 1969, WH Freeman and Co, Publishers.

18. Glueck W: Business policy and strategies management, ed 3, New York, 1980, McGraw-Hill Book Company.

19. Skopec E: Communicate for success: how to manage, motivate, and lead your people, Menlo Park, Calif, 1990, Addison-Wesley Publishing Co.

20. Hellriegel D and Slocum J: Management, ed 5, Reading, Mass, 1989, Addison-Wesley Publishing Co.

21. Robbins S: Organization theory: structure, design, and applications, Englewood Cliffs, NJ, 1990, Prentice-Hall.

22. Dyer W: Team building and issues and alternatives, ed 2, Reading, Mass, 1987, Addison-Wesley Publishing Co.

23. Landy F: Psychology of work behavior, ed 4, Pacific Grove, Calif, 1989, Brooks/Cole Publishing Co.

24. Douglass L, and Bevis E: Nursing management and leadership in action, ed 4, St Louis, 1983, The CV Mosby Co.

25. Sullivan E and Decker P: Effective management in nursing, ed 2, Menlo Park, Calif, 1988, Addison-Wesley Publishing Co.

SUGGESTED READINGS

Barrett C and others: Nurses' perceptions of their health educator role, J Nurs Staff Development 6(6):283-286, Nov/Dec 1990.

Beck S: Developing a primary nursing performance appraisal tool, Nurs Man 21(1):36-42, 1990.

Benedum E, Kalup M, and Freed D: A competency achievement program for direct caregivers, Nurs Man 21(5):32-34, 1990.

Casebeer L: Personnel decisions: "wheeling" toward better performance, Nurs Man 21(8):42-44, 1990.

Davee P and Tranbarger R: A hospital-based program for recovering chemically-dependent nurses, Nurs Man 21(10):33-35, 1990.

Davis L and Barham P: Get the most from your preceptor program, Nurs Outlook 37(4):167-171, 1989.

Davishizar R: The best approach is doing "nothing," Nurs Man 21(3):42-44, 1990.

Dubnicki C and Williams J: Selecting and developing outstanding performers, Healthcare Forum J 33(6):28-34, 1990.

Dunne R, Ehrlich S, and Mitchell B: A management development program for middle level nurse managers, JONA 18(5):11-16, 1988 (a CE program).

Fine E: Community hospital merger: the challenge to nursing management, Nurs Man 20(12):30-33, 1989.

Geber B: Goodbye classrooms, Training 27(1):27-35, 1990.

Gilmore T: Effective leadership during organizational transitions, Nurs Econ 8(3):135-141, 1990.

Heilig S: Teaching for quality, Training 27(3):49-51, July/Aug 1990.

Hendrickson J: Training in context, Training 27(3):65-70, 1990.

Koszalka M: Preparing nursing leaders, Nurs Man 21(7):23, 1990.

Lee J: A hospital-based learning center, Nurs Man 20(2):74-78, 1989.

Leftridge D: RUGs: implications for staff development, Nurs Man 21(1):63-64, 1990 (long-term facility).

Madden T: Bridging the gap for new nurses, Nursing 89 19(6):44-45, 1989.

Martin B: A successful approach to absenteeism, Nurs Man 21(10):45-48, 1990.

McGregor R: Advancing staff nurse competencies from novice to expert, J Nurs Staff Development 6(6):287-290, Nov/Dec, 1990.

Quillen T: Preparing for staff development sessions, Nursing 90 20(12):90-96, 1990.

Sanniti K and others: Selection, promotion and development of employees, Nurs Man 21(1):30-34, 1990.

Thompson V: How to get promoted, Nursing 90 20(5):164-168, 1990.

Werkheiser L and others: New nurse managers. I. Orientation for the 1990s, Nurs Man 21(11):56-62, 1990.

Werkheiser L and others: The nurse manager resource peer. II. Nurs Man 21(12):30-33, 1990.

12

Legal and Ethical Issues

☐ Define legal terms important to nursing practice.

☐ Differentiate between common law and common practice and permissive licensure and mandatory licensure.

☐ Identify five common areas of control of a nurse practice act.

☐ List the four most common causes for nurse disciplinary procedure.

☐ Explain the difference between employer and personal malpractice insurance.

☐ Indicate protective measures the nurse can take to prevent personal lawsuits.

☐ State two roles of the nurse as a witness in court and describe responsibilities.

☐ Explain how to best defend oneself if sued.

☐ Define formal, express, written express, and implied contracts.

☐ Respond appropriately to selected ethical issues.

LEGAL ISSUES
Importance of Law to the Nurse

Times are changing; contemporary nurses have much more responsibility than they used to. Over the years nurses have moved from subsidiary roles into roles of leadership and management. No longer do nurses depend on the employing agency and physicians for protection. The expanded roles of the nurse require a higher level of education, knowledge, skill, and decision-making capabilities. Professional nurses also assume accountability for their own acts. But nurses do not function alone; they have guidance and protection from legal forces. Nurses must recognize the law as an essential component of nursing practice, there to assist in the decision-making process, and there to protect in times of need. There are often gray areas of practice in which the nurse is uncertain of grounds for practice. The risk of liability is ever present. It behooves the nurse to become aware of the laws and regulations of the profession, so that professional responsibility can be defined and appropriate resources can be used in times of need. The many ethical and professional problems that may emerge are solved with greater confidence if the nurse has a sound basis of theory and facts on legal and ethical issues.

Definitions. *Law* is a rule or standard of human conduct established and enforced by authority, society, or custom. It is a set of rules or customs governing a discrete field or activity. Law is a socially oriented discipline, committed to the welfare of society. Laws tell us what we can and cannot do. However, laws are not static; they move with the times. What was once law may now be extinct, such as the law of prohibition.

Nursing law is not a separate entity. Instead, it draws on general laws and rules and regulations of federal and state as a basis for defining and governing nursing practice. Law and nursing share many societal similarities. Each considers a state of wellness as the sought-for optimal condition for both the individual and social group. Each intervenes when there is an interruption in the state of wellness that is manifested by altered conduct. When this occurs, each takes steps to restore individual or social equilibrium. Each turns to the social and behavioral sciences to understand conduct and to guide remedial action.[1]

There are certain types of laws that create rights and responsibilities for nurses:

Statutary law is a law passed by federal or state legislature declaring, commanding, or prohibiting something.

Public law determines an individual's relationship to the federal government and the states. It consists of constitutional law, administrative law, and criminal law. Private law or civil law determines one's relationship to other individuals, such as the nurse to the patient/client.

Tort law is private law concerning any wrongful act, damage, or injury done willfully, negligently, or in circumstances involving strict liability, but not involving breach of contract, for which a civil suit can be brought. Nurses are most closely associated with this type of law, since actions of malpractice fall into this category.

Criminal law refers to action harmful to the public and the individual and stipulates punishment for offenders. Examples of criminal acts are gross negligence, such as not attending to the vital needs of a patient/client, improper use of narcotics, or illegal practice of medicine. Nurses can be witnesses in criminal cases if they provide care to victims of such acts as child abuse, rape, or assault.

Liability is legal responsibility for acts or failure to act according to standards, resulting in another person's harm.

Malpractice is improper or unethical conduct by a professional, resulting in harm to another person.

Scope of practice is the range of activities a nurse may perform as stipulated in each state's nurse practice act.

Law in the Practice of Nursing

Common law and common practice. *Common law* is the cumulative result of many court decisions over the years. *Common practice* is that which falls within both the legal scope and the profession's definition of nursing practice. It is determined by statutes, regulations, basic nursing curricula, specialty nursing curricula, standards of practice, court cases, attorney general opinions, and professional associations' policy position.[2] Just because a nursing function is legal or even common practice does not mean that every nurse should engage in it. Consider this example:

> All staff nurses employed in the hospital have had some basic nursing education and training working with infants and children. A nurse from pediatrics was asked by her head nurse to relieve for lunch breaks in the neonatal ICU. She had not worked with newborns for 10 years, but agreed to cover if the head nurse believed she was able. The critically ill newborn "went sour" and died in spite of the desperate efforts of the pediatric nurse.

A review of common law and common practice would support the precept that a nurse can work with gravely ill neonatals, but only if that nurse has acquired the technical skill and knowledge necessary to safely administer that care. The staff nurse can be held liable, as well as the head nurse who sent her to cover for lunch break. The neonatal nurse has to bear responsibility for her actions in leaving the critically ill infant in the care of an inexperienced nurse.

Nurse Licensure

Permissive licensure implies that one can practice without a license as long as she does not use the title RN or claim to be licensed.[3] The danger of permissive licensing is that anyone who is not licensed can practice nursing in any form without threat of malpractice. The American Nurses' Association (ANA) became concerned with this problem at the turn of the century and was instrumental in seeing that governmental control was placed on nursing practice early in the 1900s. North Carolina was the first state to enact a nursing practice law in 1903. New Jersey, New York, and Virginia followed suit in the same year. Maryland was the only state to pass a nursing law in 1904, but by 1917 45 states and the District of Columbia had nurse practice acts. In 1952 all states and territories had such laws. In all states the original law was permissive; that is, the state had a mechanism for licensure in place, but no one was required to follow the plan. The nurse practice acts confined their content to stating minimal education standards, with little reference to the practice of nursing. Nursing titles, such as graduate, trained, or licensed, were assigned. The danger of this type of permissive licensing was that schools of nursing could produce nurses without adherence to state regulations, making it impossible to determine whether a nurse seeking licensure had met even minimal standards for education set by the state board.

Mandatory licensure means that everyone who practices nursing for compensation must be licensed. As the years passed it became apparent that for nursing to be better regulated, there had to be a definition of nursing. In 1958 the ANA published a model nurse practice act (see Chapter 4), defining the scope of nursing practice. This model facilitated progress by providing a basis for setting basic practices.

Requirements for licensure. Certain requirements must be met to obtain licensure. The applicant must:

1. Have completed the content necessary for nursing in a state board-approved school of nursing (All states require graduation, except California; military corpsmen with certain experience and preparation may take the examination for licensure in California and West Virginia.)
2. Pay a fee, determined by the state
3. Pass an examination with a score established by the state, prepared by the National Council of State Boards of Nursing (NCSBN). (The NCSBN suggests a passing score of 1600. Examinations are given twice a year throughout the nation on the same day. Since 1982 the examination has been based on nursing process and application of knowledge. Also included are basic concepts of leadership and management, accountability, life cycle, and client environment.[4])

Good physical and mental health and moral character are optional requirements, as these are difficult to document. A certain age, citizenship, and residence are no longer required. A temporary license may be issued to the applicant pending results of the first licensure examination. However, this practice may not be in the applicant's best interest. The unlicensed graduate who is hired by a health care agency to work under the supervision of a preceptor may become quite excited, only to be devastated if she fails the examination (in some areas the failure rate is high). It may be wiser for the new graduate to wait 6 or 8 weeks to hear from the board.

Renewal of license. A nurse's license is renewed every 2 years. In almost all states renewal requires a fee and completion of a designed number of hours of board-approved continuing education. The new graduate is exempt from continuing education requirements for the first 2 years after graduation and initial licensure.

The Nurse Practice Act

Composition and control. Nurse practice acts are designed for each state in accordance with their needs. The profession of nursing and the state share responsibility for development of a nurse practice act. Concern is for the health, safety, and welfare of the public. Laws are developed that are realistic, control nursing practice, and provide for flexibility as changes occur. Separate boards are established for the RN and the LPN/ LVN. Most nurse practice acts contain (1) a definition of nursing, (2) requirements for licensure, (3) exemption from licensure, (4) conditions for revocation of license, (5) provisions for endorsement or reciprocity for persons licensed in other states, (6) description of how a board of nurse examiners is created, (7) board responsibilities, and (8) penalties for practicing without a license.[3]

Control under one board. In 1976 the ANA recommended there be only one nursing practice law for each state, with provisions for licensing all practitioners of nursing under one board. The recommendation differentiated between RN and LPN/LVN roles, clearly identifying independent functions of the RN and dependent functions of the LPN/LVN. In 1980 the ANA introduced as suggested legislation principles considered essential in nurse licensure legislation. The NCSBN published the Model Nursing Practice Act in 1982 based on research on critical requirements for safe and effective nursing practice.[5] The NCSBN model is considerably broader in scope than that of the ANA, although both support a broad definition of nursing. Most states have grappled with revisions of their practice acts, but to date one board for licensing RNs and LPNs/LVNs has not been established. Nursing process (assessment, diagnosis, planning, intervention, and evaluation) is most commonly used to define nursing.

Advanced or expanded nursing practice. Advanced or expanded nursing practice is dealt with by three general means by state legislatures.[5]

1. *Nonamended statutes.* A few states have made no changes from the 1958 ANA model and allow for liberal interpretation of the law by its board members.
2. *Administrative statutes.* Most widely used by nursing boards, these are regulations drawn up under the direction of the board of nursing examiners by nurses and members of other overlapping professions (e.g., medicine, pharmacy, and physical therapy). In some cases, such as with nurse practitioners or nurse-midwives, joint agreements are drawn up between members of more than one discipline. Less than half the states have such arrangements.
3. *Authorization.* This is the least applied category of nursing definitions. This law permits the performance of basic health care procedures according to *standardized procedures,* later defined as policies and protocols. Standardized procedures in New York in 1972 and California in 1977 spearheaded the way for a higher level of independent nursing practice.

This author served on standardized procedure committees in California, which made it possible for qualified nurses to establish independent practice in cities and suburban and rural areas. One of the most gratifying experiences occurred at a state hearing to determine if qualified nurses could practice midwifery independently in rural areas. One physician from a rural area appeared, pleading for prepared nurses to be allowed to practice independently in his area. He told of lives that could be saved and educational benefits that could be derived from nursing efforts. The expanded role has not been strongly supported, or supported at all, in some states by physicians. Always, the degree of support rests on the perceived need for the nurse's services and any threat that might be felt by another professional.

With the sharp change in economic conditions, which has resulted in health care agencies competing for patients/clients, nurses are being viewed in a new light. Their knowledge, skill, and expertise are being considered an economic advantage to the agency. Concomitantly, administrators of health care facilities, physicians, and other involved professionals meet with nurses to develop policies and protocols for nursing actions that exceed the state's nurse practice act. For example, nurses are playing a greater role in giving glucose tolerance tests, intubation, administering chemotherapy, physical examinations, diagnosis, and treatment.

EXAMPLE: Joan is a nurse practitioner working in a family-practice HMO in Indiana. Recently one of her colleagues told her that NPs are held to the same standard of care as the physicians she works with. That concerned her. She asked for legal advice and was told that she certainly is held to a higher standard of care than an RN, even if the nursing board hasn't established separate regulations for nurse practitioners. The court of appeals in her state has ruled that a nurse practitioner is a specialist who should meet a standard of care appropriate to her level of knowledge and skill, even if she is working under a physician's standing orders. In fact, the court said the standard could be the same as that applied to the physician, depending on what the nurse practitioner does.

Board of Nurse Examiners

Membership. The name of the state administrative agency varies from state to state, as does the number and composition of members. Until recently, the board was made up entirely of nurses. In most states the governor appoints the members from a list of names submitted by the state professional nursing association. The number of members ranges from 5 to 19. In recent years membership has changed to include people from a variety of nursing disciplines (e.g., nursing education, nursing administration, and nursing practice), physicians, and consumers or laypersons. Having diverse interests represented on a nursing board can be an advantage to nursing. As members become educated and aware of the problems of the profession, support is generated. Danger exists when nonnurse membership exceeds nurse membership. The author of this text served as a member and president of the California Board of Registed Nursing for 4 years. Membership consisted of four nurses, one physician, one businessman, and one layperson active in community affairs. The mix was excellent, and much was accomplished. During this period the nurse practice act was revised to more accurately reflect current practice and standardized procedures written for the expanded role of the nurse. The ANA at national and state levels provided invaluable input through its publications, along with representatives from state nurse professional organizations and groups. Nonnurse members of the board raised relevant and pertinent issues and questions.

Responsibilities. The major responsibility of the board is to ensure that the nurse practice act is carried out. Members of the board generally engage in the following activities:
1. Review the nurse practice act regularly and refine or amend as necessary.
2. Establish rules and regulations to implement the broad terms of the law.
3. Set minimal standards of practice.
4. Establish standards for nurses engaged in an expanded role.
5. Approve nursing education programs and develop criteria for approval of such things as curriculum, faculty, and facilities.
6. Evaluate applicants seeking licensure.
7. Conduct examinations for licensure.
8. Issue licenses to qualified applicants.
9. Discipline those who violate the law or are found to be unfit to practice nursing.

As deemed appropriate, the board may conduct or sponsor workships or hold hearings throughout the state on a given subject to provide information and elicit input. The board may also conduct research (e.g., differentiating between the role of the associate degree and baccalaureate degree nurse). Board members are provided a staff of professional and support personnel to conduct routine business.

Disciplinary procedures. Most nurses practice their profession year in and year out within the scope of practice designated by their respective state boards of nurse examiners. There are a few nurses, however, who endanger a patient's health, safety, and welfare. When this occurs, a state board has the right to take action. It can (1) issue a formal reprimand, (2) place the nurse on probation, (3) deny renewal of license, (4) suspend the license, or (5) revoke the license.

The most common reasons for nurse review by a board are (1) practicing nursing while under the influence of alcohol or drugs, (2) addiction or dependency on alcohol or other habit-forming drugs, (3) incompetent or negligent practice, and (4) practicing beyond the state-designated scope of nursing practice. Other reasons are obtaining a license fradulently, allowing another person use of the nurse's license, moral turpitude (harming a patient), practicing while the license is suspended or revoked, and unprofessional conduct or committing immoral acts as defined by the board. In most cases nurses lose their licenses because of drug abuse or drug theft.

Of the many hearings over which the author of this text has presided, all but two cases dealt with the results of alcohol and/or chemical addiction. No pattern of age, race, or area of practice could be established. The problems appeared to generate within the individual. Almost all tried to justify their stealing drugs from patients (e.g., "I didn't take from patients who really needed the drug," "I just watered the drug down a bit is all"), forging the narcotic records, and taking drugs while on duty (e.g., "I couldn't go on without the medication, my legs hurt too badly," "I work better with my nerves calmed"). The sad part of the judicial procedure is the high rate of recidivism. Many nurses have broken their promises to desist and reform and have returned to their deviant practices.

Typical steps for the board of nurse examiners in disciplinary proceedings are to (1) receive a sworn complaint from a health care agency, health care organization, or an individual; (2) send a paid staff member of the board to investigate the complaint; and (3) conduct a formal hearing, if sufficient evidence is found, after which a decision is made. The nurse has the right to challenge the board's decision through court appeal.[6] The appellate court will examine the board's process and decision to see if they were proper. If not proper, the court can grant the defendent a new trial. In the author's experience very few cases went beyond the state board. Most first offenders charged with drug and/or alcohol abuse were placed on 2 years probation, with definite stipulations, depending on individual circumstances. Usually the offender was required to have no physical contact with narcotic administration, to enroll in and complete a state-approved drug or alcohol rehabilitation program, and to report to her assigned state board staff member at designated periods. Repeat offenders usually had their licenses suspended or revoked. Nurses who have had their licenses suspended may apply for reinstatement according to the state's nurse practice act. In most cases at least 1 year must pass before the petition will be considered. Usually, a hearing is held to review the case. The burden of proof of rehabilitation lies solely with the defendant. If a nurse's license is revoked, the decision is probably final.

NURSING RISK MANAGEMENT

Risk is the possibility of suffering harm, loss, or danger. Risk management entails defining the probability that certain incidents will occur if conditions are not corrected; then taking the steps necessary to prevent them from occurring.

Today the health care system and health workers are faced with a burgeoning number of malpractice suits. Nurses are considered fair game for such lawsuits. Nurses have promoted themselves through increased expertise, specialization, accountability, and autonomy in their professional practice. As such, they have opened the door to liability for their actions. The increase in nursing malpractice suits can be attributed to such factors as (1) increased and often unrealistic consumer expectations of nursing services, (2) lack of client understanding of treatments and technology, (3) impersonal delivery of care, and (4) more exposure among the general population to health care today than in the past.[7]

For self-protection, nurses should become aware of the set of standards of care that courts expect from nursing and the most common causes of lawsuits. This knowledge can give health care agencies the tools to begin a risk-management program in order to minimize the occurrence of lawsuits. In malpractice suits against nurses, courts commonly refer to the ANA Standards of Care, JCAHO nursing care standards, and the standards of the American Association of Critical Care Nurses, as well as the standards established by the agency being sued.[7]

Some of the most common causes of lawsuits against nurses have been identified as (1) failure to perform treatments correctly, (2) patients' falls, (3) failure to remove foreign objects (as in surgery), (4) burns, (5) failure to observe and report changes, (6) mistaken patient identification, (7) errors by certified RN anesthetists, (8) use of defective equipment, (9) failure to assess patients and take adequate histories, (10) failure to document pertinent information, and (11) failure to report known or suspected deviations from accepted practice.[8]

Risk-management teams or committees can promote educational programs to provide nursing staff with the knowledge required to ensure quality patient care and to practice preventive nursing. This is especially important, as nurses form the first line of defense in preventing malpractice suits.

NURSE LIABILITY FOR SHORT-STAFFING SITUATIONS[9]

To understand the nurse's liability where there is a nursing shortage, one must understand the framework of the hospital's liability. The hospital that fails to maintain the level of nursing care required to provide safe, quality treatment may be held liable for any patient injuries that result under the legal theory of *respondeat superior* (vicarious liability), which means that an employer can be held responsible for the employees' negligence while on the job. Nurse managers can be held accountable for staffing shortages if they have the power to control the situation but fail to do so. If they do not have the power, they should not be held accountable. The individual staff nurse, on the other hand, does not have the ability to solve the hospital's short-staffing problem. The individual nurse's legal duty should be satisfied as long as the nurse fulfills the duty of communicating the short-staffing problem to his or her immediate superior.

MALPRACTICE INSURANCE FOR NURSES

Malpractice suits are on the increase. The majority of suits are settled out of court between the plaintiff's lawyer and the agency. However, many nurses have found themselves in court because of plaintiff's dreams of huge monetary awards or because they believe they have been wronged by the nurse and demand public recourse. Being named in a lawsuit could destroy a nurse financially; therefore insurance protection is imperative.

Employer Coverage

The nurse's employer is obligated to carry malpractice insurance on its employees. The nurse must know what is covered by that employer's policy. An employer is liable for the nurse's actions while on duty because of the principle of *respondeat superior*. Each professional liability has a maximal dollar coverage limit. Most hospitals have a deductible provision that makes the employer responsible for damages under a certain figure. The nurse employee should know this limit, as the employer can settle a claim against the nurse's name without benefit of defense. This could harm the nurse's reputation. The nurse who is named in a suit should keep abreast of the proceedings and know what decisions are being considered.[10]

Nurse Coverage

Every registered nurse should carry personal malpractice insurance. Policies are available through the professional nurses' association, Nurses' Services Organization, and independent insurance agents. The usual malpractice policy covers the nurse with (1) 1 million dollars for each occurrence or 2 million dollars annually, if a malpractice suit is lost; (2) legal defense; and (3) lost wages. Some policies cover incidences occurring in or around the home. The cost of these policies is relatively inexpensive—under $100 per year.

Statute of Limitations

A *statute of limitations* is a law that specifies a limited number of years when one person can seek damages from another. The statute of limitations is specified in each state's medical malpractice law (usually 1 to 3 years), depending on the statute set; however, a nurse can be sued for malpractice many years after the nursing care was provided, as the court sometimes extends the limitation in favor of the plaintiff. When the statute of limitations begins is an important issue also. Some begin on the date of the plaintiff's injury; others being when that injury is discovered. For example, a patient/client may fall and think he is uninjured, only to discover 6 months later that he has back trouble and difficulty in walking. Accurate and complete documentation of all nursing care can provide invaluable assistance in this instance. As the years pass, recall becomes dim. Patient records are official and therefore admissible in a court of law. The records become the first line of defense.

The ANA Code for nurses requires registered nurses to take definite action to safeguard both patient and public against "incompetent, unethical or illegal practice of any person."[2] In this case, neither the institution nor the patient has incurred negligible risks. The charge nurse reported the incident to the Board of Nurse Examiners, placed the nurse on 2 weeks without pay, then on probation for 1 year with the promise of dismissal should any other legal infraction occur.

THE NURSE AS A WITNESS

A nurse called as a witness to court serves one of two capacities: (1) as a witness to the conditions or circumstances present in the issue in question or (2) as an expert witness to give an opinion from the facts presented. Nurses who are summoned to serve as witnesses may or may not be the persons charged. They report what they saw, what they were told, or what they overheard. Witnesses must give only facts based on direct knowledge.[15]

The Nurse as an Expert Witness

Before the early 1970s, physicians often served as expert witnesses for nursing care. This practice continues today, but there is a gradual shift to having nurses serve as experts of nursing care. When nurses represent nurses, professional self-regulation and professional accountability are demonstrated.

Qualifications of an expert witness.[15] For a nurse to give expert testimony, certain criteria must be met. The nurse must have:

1. Familiarity with nurse standards (ANA Code of Ethics, state nurse practice act, ANA Standards of Practice, specific overall standards of the agency employing the defendant, and specialty standards applicable to the clinical area in question)
2. Clinical expertise and past experience, usually a minimum of 5 years
3. Effective communication skills; the ability to offer clear, decisive responses to questions while on the stand
4. General knowledge of the components of malpractice liability
5. Ability to represent nursing well, demon-

strating professional commitment and ethical standards (e.g., membership in professional association, continuing education participation, and professional activities)

Responsibilities of an expert witness. Much is required of the expert witness. The nurse (1) meets with the attorney to get a general idea of the types of reports wanted; (2) reviews documents (medical records, depositions, interrogatories, and other expert reports); (3) decides whether the defendant's action or inaction was the cause of the injury, compares the situation with behavior expected of a "reasonably prudent nurse" in a similar situation, according to standards; and (4) gives a verbal expert opinion to the attorney based on the analysis of the case. If asked, the nurse also writes an opinion; attends depositions (testimony under oath) before the trial; and testifies in court, remembering not to volunteer additional information.

A case in Missouri provides a valuable nurse-expert opinion.[16]

> A 1-year-old child developed tachycardia following heart surgery and was given 0.1 mg of digitalis, with two follow-up doses of 0.55 mg. The child died after receiving the overdose. Suit was brought against the physician, the ICU nurses, and the hospital pharmacist. The plaintiff used a nurse–expert to review the case and offer an opinion on the ICU nurses' actions. The nurse expert proved that (1) nursing curricula teaches how to calculate infant dosages, (2) digitalis is commonly given by ICU nurses, and (3) children are weighed specifically to determine drug dosages. With this knowledge, the attorney proved that any nurse should have picked up the error at the transcription stage. The suit was settled before it went to court.

How to become known as an expert witness. Many state nurses' associations have resource banks of nurse-expert witnesses. Nurses who wish to be included submit the necesary information for consideration. Advertising may be placed in the state law journal, journal of the state nurses' association, or legal publications that focus on litigation. The nurse should be very specific about the area of specialization. Nurses who serve as expert witnesses are paid well for their services (usually by the hour) and have the satisfaction of helping to protect consumers' rights to quality care and upholding the standards of nursing practice.

GOOD SAMARITAN LAWS

The enactment of Good Samaritan laws in many states exempts physicians and nurses from civil liability when they give emergency care "in good faith" with "due care" and without "gross negligence," outside the workplace. In 1959 California was the first state to pass such a law; by 1979 all states and the District of Columbia had Good Samaritan laws. However, not all include nursing.[3]

Victims rarely sue Good Samaritans. Nurses have never had to invoke a Good Samaritan act as a defense; the common law serves as a deterrent.

NURSES' RESPONSIBILITY IN AN EMERGENCY

When a nurse encounters an emergency, such as someone drowning, bleeding profusely, clutching his or her chest and moaning, thrown from a car, or trapped in a vehicle, three choices of action are available: (1) the nurse can stop and assist the victim(s), (2) the nurse can pass the scene and call from the nearest phone for authorized assistance, or (3) the nurse can pass the scene and do nothing.[10] The victim of an accident or injury is not the nurse's patient; he or she is a stranger and therefore has no right to make any claims on the nurse, *unless* the nurse stops at the scene and makes an appearance. Once this is done, a nurse-patient relationship is established, and the nurse must take care of the victim(s) with treatment that meets the standard of care of a reasonably prudent nurse who exercises good judgment and common sense. The nurse must stay with the victim(s) until skilled personnel arrive to assume care.[10]

Breach of Duty

The nurse is at minimal risk when actions are conducted according to standard as much as is possible in a given situation. If the victim's condition was worsened as a result of the nurse's action, the court considers the degree of harm. Measurable harm would have to be proved for the nurse to be considered negligent. Further,

the victim must prove that the probability is better than 50% that the nurse who stopped to help caused his or her injuries.[10]

GUIDELINES FOR NURSES WHO ARE SUED

A nurse can never know if she will be sued, or even what circumstances provide the highest risk. Receiving a summons naming a nurse as defendant can shock the nurse into actions that might be regretted later. Knowing what actions to take in the event of being named in a suit can save the nurse much pain and loss. *Nursing 84*, on legal risks, offers good advice. The nurse who is sued is advised to take action immediately by following a specific plan.[10] The nurse should:

1. Contact legal services administrators at work and follow their directions.
2. Telephone the representative of her own professional liability insurance. Document the date, time, representative's name, and instructions given. Hand deliver or send by certified mail the lawsuit papers. Get a receipt, as the insurance company can refuse coverage unless the company representative is contacted within a specific time period.
3. Never try to defend herself. The odds are definitely against the nurse who is inexperienced in legal matters or closely involved with the suit.

The insurance company will:

1. Appoint an attorney of record, which means the attorney's name appears on the legal records.
2. Obtain copies of all relevant documents.
3. Quiz the plaintiff in the presence of a court reporter.
4. Hire a physician not involved with the case to examine the plaintiff.
5. Prepare the nurse to testify.

Marc Mandell, lawyer and editor of a legal newsletter for physicians, prepared a list of commandments for nurses who are sued:[17]

    I. *Don't discuss the case at your hospital with anyone other than the risk manager.* Talking with others in the workplace will harm you. Others may even construe your comments as admissions of guilt.

    II. *Don't discuss the case with the plaintiff.* Talking with the plaintiff does not work. His or her mind is set, and he or she might even take what is said to be more incriminating evidence.

III. *Don't discuss the case with the plaintiff's lawyer.* Don't give in to the urge to talk to the plaintiff's lawyer. The lawyer's code of ethics forbids it, unless the defendant's lawyer gives consent. However, an unscrupulous lawyer might listen, hoping the nurse will say something to help the plaintiff's case.

IV. *Don't discuss the case with anyone testifying for the plaintiff.* These people have already decided that the defendant is guilty, or they would not be testifying. If the judge or jury suspects the defendant was trying to convince somebody to change his or her testimony, the case will be harmed.

V. *Don't discuss the case with reporters.* Say, "I choose not to speak about this." Any remark can be distorted, misquoted, or taken out of context.

VI. *Don't alter the patient's/client's records.* This is illegal. Tampering with a chart is the worst mistake a nurse can make. The defense is gone. The jurors will never forget that a patient's/client's record was altered.

VII. *Don't hide any information from your lawyer.* The lawyer needs to know every detail, no matter how unimportant or self-incriminating it seems. He or she needs to know the weak aspects of the case as well as the strong ones.

VIII. *Don't go on the witness stand unprepared.* Years can pass between the occurrence of the alleged malpractice and the resulting trial. All records need to be reviewed carefully, especially those involving you.

IX. *Don't be discourteous on the witness stand.* Remain polite and composed, even though the plaintiff's lawyer may address you rudely and abrasively. Generally, jurors respond favorably to nurses, because they come across as honest and sincere. Good manners count.

X. *Don't volunteer any information.* Answer only the questions asked and keep answers short. Whenever possible, answer with a simple "yes" or "no." Long, thoughtful answers only provide ammunition for the plaintiff's lawyer.

DOCTRINE OF SOVEREIGN IMMUNITY

The statute of sovereign immunity provides government employees with special legal protection. Unless the sovereign (government employer) agrees, a government employee cannot be sued for on-the-job mistakes. Some states have felt that this law is unfair to the patient/client who has no recourse if injury occurs, and have passed laws that allow patients/clients to sue public hospitals and other government agencies. Some states have set dollar limits on the amount a patient/client can receive if he or she wins the suit.

CONTRACTS FOR NURSES

Fewer problems occur when the nurse and employer understands each other's rights and responsibilities. Understandably, the nurse is nervous when going for an interview. The position desired may be a "plum"; the nurse may feel like doing almost anything to get the job. Or the nurse may already be employed and is seeking a promotion or expanded role. In these stressful situations, a cool head is needed. Papers signed or verbal agreements made without careful consideration may cause trouble later.

Types of Contracts

A *formal contract* is an agreement between two or more parties that is written and enforceable by law. A contract is valid when the nurse (1) meets specifications for the job, such as having current licensure and being of age and sound mind; (2) agrees to perform specified services; (3) agrees to abide by the employer's terms; and (4) receives remuneration for services. The formal contract may be an individual contract between the employer and nurse, or it may be a collective contract with a labor organization, such as a union has negotiated with the employer for the employees.

An *express contract* may be written or oral. A nurse may talk with her head nurse about her need to grow professionally. The head nurse may offer the new position of patient advocate, being created in 2 months. If the nurse agrees to take the position, she has entered into an *oral express contract.* When she signs papers indicating that she has the position, she has participated in a *written express contract.*

An *implied contract* is an agreement between two or more persons involving matters that are understood but not clearly or openly expressed. Many contracts contain implied conditions. For example, the employer assumes that the nurse will maintain proper decorum and will practice nursing safely; conversely, the nurse assumes the employer will provide facilities and maintain an environment conducive to effectively carrying out nursing duties.

Breach of Contract

A *breach* is any failure to keep the law or to fulfill one's duties without justification. A nurse breaches her contract when all or any part of the contract is not kept. Employers are loathe to seek an injunction against a nurse for failing to live up to the agreement, as it is a very costly procedure. An injunction keeps the nurse from working for another employer. Instead, the employer may reprimand the nurse and demand compliance or discharge the nurse. In any event the nurse's reputation is damaged. The nurse should understand the terms of the contract before agreeing to employment, then hold to that agreement or resign in good stead.

ETHICAL ISSUES

An *ethic* is a principle of right or good conduct. Professional organizations often choose to establish rules or standards governing the conduct of members of their profession. Individuals in the profession observe these standards by exercising critical, rational judgment and by applying the ethical precepts to life situations. The ANA first suggested a code of ethics in 1926, and adopted an official code in 1950. Revisions were made in 1956, 1960, and 1968. The fourth revision in 1976 is the current Code of Ethics for Nurses (see box on p. 251). The ANA published a guide in 1985 designed to help the nurse carry out nursing responsibilities consistent with quality in nursing care and ethical obligations of the profession.[18]

The ANA code addresses human dignity, nondiscrimination, and protection of the patient/client. The independent role of the nurse and participation in activities that promote high standards and quality of nursing care are em-

phasized. The ANA Code of Ethics, like other professional codes, does not have legal power as state nurse practice acts do; however, it can be used as a guideline for professional conduct in a malpractice lawsuit. The Code of Ethics exceeds the minimal standards set by a state board and therefore provides a more realistic guide to expected practice.

Patients' Rights

Most patient rights are established in common law; however, many health care organizations feel the need to identify patient rights more specifically. In 1959 the National League for Nursing (NLN) was the first professional group to publish a statement on patients' rights. This professional organization titled its document "What People Can Expect of Modern Service," proposing the patient be a partner in health care, participating as much as possible. The American Hospital Association (AHA) prepared a Patient's Bill of Rights in 1972, recognizing that legal precedent has established that the institution itself also has a responsibility to the patient/client (see box on p. 252). Most hospitals develop their own bills of rights, using the AHA bill as a guideline.

President John F. Kennedy summarized the four basic consumer rights in his 1962 message to Congress: (1) the right to safety, (2) the right to be informed, (3) the right to choose, and (4) the right to be heard. Patients' bills of rights, either adopted or developed by major health care providers and consumer groups across the country, have made today's patients very much aware of what is being done to and for them. There are a few states, such as Minnesota and Pennsylvania, that have incorporated the patient's bill of rights into their law.

Ethics Committees

Establishment of an ethics committee in hospitals is sporadic in the United States. Ethics panels are more likely to be in force in large hospitals where high-risk issues are prevalent. The membership of an ethics committee is important, as the members need to command the respect of top management, physicians, and board members. A survey conducted by the American Hospital Association estimated the number of hospitals in the United States with

American Nurses' Association Code of Ethics for Nurses

Preamble

The Code of Ethics for Nurses is based on belief about the nature of individuals, nursing, health, and society. Recipients and providers of nursing services are viewed as individuals and groups who possess basic rights and responsibilities and whose values and circumstances command respect at all times. Nursing encompasses the promotion and restoration of health, the prevention of illness, and the alleviation of suffering. The statements of the Code and their interpretations provide guidance for conduct and relationships in carrying out nursing responsibilities consistent with the ethical obligations of the profession and quality in nursing care.

Code for nurses

1. The nurse provides services with respect for human dignity and the uniqueness of the client unrestricted by considerations of social or economic status, personal attributes, or the nature of health problems.
2. The nurse safeguards the client's right to privacy by judiciously protecting information of a confidential nature.
3. The nurse acts to safeguard the client and the public when health care and safety are affected by the incompetent, unethical, or illegal practice of any person.

4. The nurse assumes the responsibility and accountability for individual nursing judgments and actions.
5. The nurse maintains competence in nursing.
6. The nurse exercises informed judgment and uses individual competence and qualifications as criteria in seeking consultation, accepting responsibilities, and delegating nursing activities to others.
7. The nurse participates in activities that contribute to the ongoing development of the profession's efforts to implement and improve standards of nursing.
8. The nurse participates in the profession's efforts to improve standards of nursing.
9. The nurse participates in the profession's efforts to establish and maintain conditions of employment conducive to high quality nursing care.
10. The nurse participates in the profession's effort to protect the public from misinformation and misrepresentation and to maintain the integrity of nursing.
11. The nurse collaborates with members of the health professions and other citizens in promoting community and national efforts to meet the health needs of the public.

Reprinted with permission from the American Hospital Association.

---

ethics committees to be 60%. A group of nurses surveyed 121 hospitals in the five boroughs of New York City and found that 58% had ethics committees, which is consistent with the AHA survey.[1]

Ideally an ethics committee discusses actual situations as they happen and is concerned with issues that directly relate to the institution. For instance, if the hospital is in a community with a high concentration of elderly people, the ethics committee should spend more time considering problems that arise when treating the elderly.

Common ethical problems include the question of when to remove life support systems; whether to inform a patient/client that he or she is dying; abortion; transfusions; restraining an unwilling patient/client; performing needed cosmetic surgery on patients/clients who are

unable to pay; and determining, in times of shortage, who will get the best care. An ethics committee can listen, teach, and make suggestions based on a multidisciplinary approach to the problem. As the ethics committee becomes more established, it can review hospital policies and help develop policies on issues such as caring for handicapped infants and providing transplants to the needy.

The ANA has sponsored a committee on ethics since 1983 and has published position statements and guidelines for such issues as withdrawing or withholding food and fluid and risk versus responsibility in providing nursing care.[2]

Wills: the Nurse's Responsibility

A *will* is a declaration of how a person wishes his or her possessions to be disposed of after his

◇   ◇

American Hospital Association's Patient's Bill of Rights

1. The patient has the right to considerate and respectful care.
2. The patient has the right to obtain from his physician complete current information about his diagnosis, treatment, and prognosis in terms the patient can be reasonably expected to understand. When it is not medically advisable to give such information to the patient, it should be made available to an appropriate person in his behalf. He has the right to know, by name, the physician responsible for coordinating his care.
3. The patient has the right to receive from his physician information necessary to give informed consent prior to the start of any procedure and/or treatment. Except in emergencies, such information for informed consent should include but not necessarily be limited to the specific procedure and/or treatment, the medically significant risks involved, and the probable duration of incapacitation. Where medically significant alternatives for care or treatment exist, or when the patient requests information concerning medical alternatives, the patient has the right to such information. The patient has the right to know the name of the person responsible for the procedures and/or treatment.
4. The patient has the right to refuse treatment to the extent permitted by law and to be informed of the medical consequences of his action.
5. The patient has the right to every consideration of his privacy concerning his own medical care program. Case discussion, consultation, examination, and treatment are confidential and should be conducted discreetly. Those not directly involved in his care must have the permission of the patient to be present.
6. The patient has the right to expect that all communications and records pertaining to his care should be treated as confidential.
7. The patient has the right to expect that within its capacity a hospital must make reasonable response to the request of a patient for services. The hospital must provide evaluation, service, and/or referral as indicated by the urgency of the case. When medically permissible, a patient may be transferred to another facility only after he has received complete information and explanation concerning the needs for and alternatives to such a transfer. The institution to which the patient is to be transferred must first have accepted the patient for transfer.
8. The patient has the right to obtain information as to any relationship of his hospital to other health-care and educational institutions insofar as his care is concerned. The patient has the right to obtain information as to the existence of any professional relationships among individuals, by means, who are treating him.
9. The patient has the right to be advised if the hospital proposes to engage in or perform human experimentation affecting his care or treatment. The patient has the right to refuse to participate in such research projects.
10. The patient has the right to expect reasonable continuity of care. He has the right to know in advance what appointment times and physicians are available and where. The patient has the right to expect that the hospital will provide a mechanism whereby he is informed by his physician or a delegate of the physician of the patient's continuing health-care requirements following discharge.
11. The patient has the right to examine and receive an explanation of his bill, regardless of source of payment.
12. The patient has the right to know what hospital rules and regulations apply to his conduct as a patient.

Reprinted with permission from the American Hospital Association.

or her death. A will becomes legal when the testator or person making the will (1) is mentally competent (testamentary capacity), (2) is of legal age for making a will (varies with the state), (3) makes a written declaration that the instrument is a will, and (4) has the proper number of witnesses present (usually two). The witnesses sign the will in the presence of each other and the testator and cannot be beneficiaries.

It is not advisable for a nurse to prepare wills for patients/clients. If the nurse were to perform such a service regularly, she could be prosecuted for practicing law without a license. When asked to witness a will, the nurse should attempt to find another person to do so, such as the agency's legal advisor or representative. If none is available, the nurse, before signing, (1) notifies her immediate supervisor and (2) notifies the patient's/client's physician. If sanction is received from both parties, the nurse may serve as a witness without comment on the content of the will. The procedure is thoroughly documented in the nurse's notes.

Policy Considerations Related to AIDS[19]

AIDS is a life-threatening disease and a major public health issue. Because of this fact, nurse managers have a responsibility to prepare and guide nursing staff to care for patients with AIDS diligently.

The foremost legal obligation of nurse managers is to ensure that staff do not abandon patients. Nurses may be held liable for abandonment if they make a decision to sever the nurse-patient relationship with AIDS' patients. There is no fault if the nurse and the AIDS patients mutually agree to terminate the relationship. Prejudicial attitudes and discriminatory behavior are also subject to disciplinary action. Nurses who refuse to care for patients out of fear or moral indignation fall into this category.

The American Nurses' Association[2] and The American Hospital Association[20] have prepared useful resources addressing obligation for care of and protection of AIDS patients and health care workers. In addition, information and training opportunities are available for nurse managers and their staff through federally funded regional AIDS Education and Training centers across the country.[21]

Protection of Civil Rights: Defamation of Character

The nurse is responsible for guarding the reputation of patients/clients, physicians, and colleagues as well as she would her own. A casual negative remark, such as "I wouldn't go to that doctor for any amount of money—he's a butcher," or "If that nurse were assigned to me, I would jump out the window," supply the ingredients for a lawsuit for defamation of character. Conversely, a nurse has the civil right to protect her own good name. One nurse in Texas

filed suit against a physician for making false statements about her.[22] The physician declared that the nurse had rearranged laboratory slips to cover up a mistake. The nurse had to prove that the physician was well aware that the statements he made were probably false. In this case the nurse was awarded $250,000, as the wrong seemed decidedly intentional. Happily, a suit is not filed each time a defaming remark is made. However, it is wise to be careful about what one says and to refrain from making negative statements about another.

Ethical Dilemmas in Nursing Practice

Every day nurses are confronted by situations that impinge on patients'/clients' rights. Nurses must adhere to the minimal standards set by their nurse practice acts and at the same time consider the ethical issues of the situation.

Advocacy. An effective leader/manager is always an advocate for his or her group. An *advocate* supports or defends someone or something and recommends or pleads in another's behalf. The leader/advocate works to change the power structure so that a situation will be improved. A head nurse, for example, might work for an increase in the number of nursing staff so that the quality of nursing care can be improved. A primary care nurse might discuss communication with an employee who was perceived by a patient/client to be rude. Or a team leader might recognize that team members are avoiding a "difficult" patient/client and hold a team conference on behalf of that patient/client.

Nurses have long been concerned with acting on behalf of their patients/clients. The AHA's Patient's Bill of Rights in 1972 and the ANA's Code for Nurses in 1976 have given credence to patient/client advocacy and have accentuated the need for nurses to assume the role of patient/client rights advocate. Nurses should carefully review their employing agency's policies on employee handling of patients' rights so that parameters for action can be identified.

There is no one way for a nurse to achieve the role of advocate. Each situation has different conditions and circumstances and therefore must be judged on its own merit. Each nurse must accept responsibility for studying background information, considering ethical and legal issues, determining possible courses of action, considering risks, and deciding what action to take. Advocacy often requires assertiveness and noncompliance with others. It also may be that the nurse does not totally agree with the patient/client or family but feels a responsibility to support them in their belief or decision.[23]

Following are some ethical issues that call for the nurse to act as an advocate. Consider each situation and determine what you would do in the patient's/client's behalf. Such situations have actually occurred. References are given so that you may see how the issues were resolved and the reasoning processes that led to the decisions:

1. You are to discharge a client from a short procedure unit with teaching about the dangers of lifting any heavy object. The client replies that she has to lift her 20-pound child.[24]
2. You are one of the nurses to care for a profoundly retarded, blind, and deaf infant with multiple physiologic problems, including lack of temperature control, diabetes mellitus, and inability to swallow or digest food well. The infant is not expected to live beyond a few weeks or months. She is a ward of the court, and you have been instructed to act in the infant's best interest. You must decide how aggressive to be in caring for the infant, particularly in feeding.[25]
3. You are assigned to a patient who is told by her physician that she is dying of leukemia and that chemotherapy is her only hope of survival. The procedure is life threatening and has undesirable side effects. You believe that alternative treatments may benefit the patient, including the use of Laetrile, and that a particular clinic accessible to the patient could help her.[26,27]

SUMMARY

1. Laws are rules or standards of human conduct established and enforced by authority for the benefit of society.
2. Tort law is law concerning any wrongful act, damage, or injury done willfully, negligently, but not involving breach of contract, for which a civil suit can be brought.

Most malpractice suits against nurses are treated under tort law.
3. Common law is the culmination of many court decisions over the years. Common practice is that which falls within the definition of nursing and the legal scope of nursing practice.
4. Permissive licensure implies that one can practice nursing without a license, providing the RN title is not claimed or used. Mandatory licensure means that all who practice nursing for compensation must be licensed.
5. Nurse practice acts are designed for each state. Most nurse practice acts contain a definition of nursing requirements for licensure, exemption from licensure, conditions for revocation of license, provisions for endorsement or reciprocity for persons licensed in other states, description of how a board of nurse examiners is created, board responsibilities, and penalties for practicing without a license.
6. The major responsibility of a board of nurse examiners is to see that the nurse practice act is carried out, to set minimal standards of practice, to establish standards for nurses in the expanded role, to approve and monitor nursing education programs, to manage nurse licensure, and to discipline nurses who violate the law or are found to be unfit to practice nursing.
7. The most common reasons for nurse review by a board of nurse examiners is practicing nursing while under the influence of alcohol or drugs, addiction or dependency on alcohol or other habit-forming drugs, incompetent or negligent practice, or practicing beyond the state-prescribed scope of nursing practice.
8. Increased expertise, specialization, accountability, and autonomy in professional practice places nurses in high-risk situations. Some common causes of lawsuits against nurses include failure to perform treatments correctly; patients' falls; and failure to observe and report changes, to assess patients, to take adequate histories, or to document pertinent information.
9. Nurse managers can be held accountable for staffing shortages if they have the power to

control the situation but fail to do so. The individual staff nurse's legal duty should be satisfied as long as the nurse fulfills the duty of communicating the short-staffing problem to her immediate supervisor.

10. Accountability rests on the integrity, competence, and reliability of the health care agency and personnel.

11. A nurse's employer in most agencies is obligated to carry malpractice insurance on its employees. An employer is liable for the nurse's actions while on duty because of the principle of *respondeat superior*. The nurse should know the extent of coverage and be appraised of any lawsuits or claims against her. Every nurse should carry personal malpractice insurance, as the agency's policy does not cover the nurse in all situations, particularly those away from the job.

12. A statute of limitations specifies a limited number of years when one person can seek damages from another. From 1 to 3 years is the usual limit.

13. The best way for one to avoid a lawsuit is to practice nursing within established nursing standards and the ANA Code of Ethics and to be accountable for one's actions. Proper documentation, care in transcribing orders, and caution in accepting oral or telephone orders are examples of precautionary behavior.

14. Nurses are called to court as eyewitnesses or expert witnesses to give an opinion from the facts presented. Expert witnesses should be familiar with ANA nursing standards, the ANA Code of Ethics, the state nurse practice act, and the employer's standards, particularly for the clinical area in question. Also expected are clinical expertise, effective communication skills, general knowledge of the components of malpractice liability, and ability to represent the nursing profession well.

15. Good Samaritan laws in force in most states protect physicians and nurses from civil liability when they give emergency care in good faith, with due care, and without gross negligence. Once a nurse stops and makes an appearance at the scene of an emergency, a nurse-patient relationship is established, and the nurse cannot leave the scene until skilled personnel arrive to assume care. Measurable harm has to be proved for the nurse to be charged with breach of duty.

16. If a nurse is sued, the employer's legal representative and the nurse's personal malpractice representative are consulted, and all facts are gathered, including copies of relevant documents. Conversations about the case should be limited to the nurse's legal representative and a trusted friend. No record should be altered, and all testimony should be honest, respectful, and limited to answering the questions posed.

17. The doctrine of *sovereign immunity* provides federal employees with special legal protection. Unless the sovereign agrees, a government employee cannot be sued for on-the-job mistakes. In recent years some states have altered this law to some degree, placing a limit on the amount of money the government would pay if the employee is found guilty.

18. There are formal, express, and implied contracts. A formal contract is an agreement between two or more parties that is written and enforceable by law. A contract is valid when the nurse meets specifications for the job, agrees to perform specified services, agrees to abide by the employer's terms, and receives remuneration for services. An express contract may be written or oral. It is an agreement between two or more people but does not become a written express contract until placed in documental form. Implied contracts occur between two or more people when terms are understood but not stated verbally or in writing.

19. An ethic is a principle of right or good conduct. The American Nurses' Association has developed a Code for Nurses to abide by, and the American Hospital Association has developed a Patient's Bill of Rights for the protection of the public. Some agencies have developed ethics committees to consider ethical problems that concern the agency and surrounding community.

20. A will becomes legal when the person making the will is mentally competent, is of legal age for making a will, makes written declaration that the instrument is a will, and

has the proper number of witnesses present. It is not advisable for a nurse to prepare wills for patients/clients or to serve as a witness if legal representatives from the agency are available. If the nurse does serve as a witness, before signing she contacts the patient's/client's physician and her immediate supervisor for sanction.

21. The foremost obligation of nurse managers regarding AIDS patients is to ensure that staff do not abandon these patients. Nurses may be held liable for abandonment if they sever the nurse-patient relationship without the patient's consent. There is no fault if the nurse and AIDS patient mutually agree to terminate the relationship.

22. A nurse is responsible for guarding the reputation of patients/clients, physicians, and colleagues as well as she would her own.

23. An advocate supports or defends someone or something and recommends or pleads in another's behalf. An effective leader and manager is always an advocate for his or her group. Advocacy often requires assertiveness and noncompliance with orders.

 Questions for Study and Discussion

1. What are the similarities between the rules or customs of public law and the rules or customs of nursing?

2. With which type of law is the nurse most closely associated? Give two examples.

3. Outline the steps required to obtain nurse licensure.

4. Assume that you are about to become a nurse practitioner in a rural area. Beyond RN licensure, what measures do you need to take to protect yourself from legal liability?

5. What is your attitude toward legal accountability and risk management in terms of your career aspirations and expectations? How does this compare with your concept of nursing upon entry into the nursing education program?

6. What insurance protection can a nurse expect from his or her employer? Is additional insurance by the nurse advisable? Explain.

7. You, an RN, witnessed the resuscitation procedure of a patient who subsequently died. You believe that the attending nurse went through the proper procedure but that her heart was not in it, as she later shared with you that she felt that the patient, if he had lived, would have become a "vegetable." The family is suing the attending nurse for liability. You have been summoned to give testimony as a witness. What would you say?

8. As the nurse assigned to a patient who fell out of bed during your term of duty, you are being sued for malpractice. A family member telephones you and asks you to fill her in on the details so she will be better able to understand the situation. How will you respond?

REFERENCES

1. Scanlon C and Fleming C: Confronting ethical issues: a nursing survey, Nurs Man 21(5):63-65, 1990.

2. American Nurses' Association: Ethics in nursing: position statements and guidelines, Pub No. G-175, Kansas City, Mo, 1988, The Association.

3. Kelly L: Dimensions of professional nursing, ed 5, New York, 1985, Macmillan Publishing Co.

4. The American Nurses' Association: Enforcement of the Nursing Practice Act, pub no. D-89, Kansas City, Mo, 1986, The Association.

5. National Council of State Boards of Nursing: The model practice act, Chicago, 1982, The Council.

6. The American Nurses' Association: Suggested state legislation: nursing practice act, nursing disciplinary act, prescriptive authority act, pub no. NP-78, Kansas City, Mo, 1990, The Association.

7. Luquire R: Nursing risk management, Nurs Man 20(10):56-58, 1989.

8. Bernzweig E: The nurse's liability for malpractice: a programmed course, ed 5, St Louis, 1990, Mosby–Year Book, Inc.

9. Fiesta J: The nursing shortage: whose liability problem? I. Nurs Man 21(1):24-25, 1990.

10. Nurses' Reference Library: Practices: legal risks, ethics, human relations, career management,

Nursing 84, Springhouse, Pa, 1984, Springhouse Corp.

11. Creighton H: Law for the nurse manager, Nurs Man 17(7):11, 1986.
12. Wagner M, editorial director: How to avoid lawsuits, Nurs Life 6(4):57-58, 1986.
13. Rabinow J: When a doctor gives a medication order over the phone, Nurs Life 6(4):57-58, 1986.
14. Pinch W: Nursing ethics: is "covering-up" ever "harmless"? Nurs Man 21(9):60-62, 1990.
15. Salmond S: Serving as an expert witness, Nurs Econ 4(5):236-239, 1986.
16. Cushing M: *Brosseau v Children's Mercy Hospital*, Am J Nurs 86(10):1107, 1986.
17. Mandell M: Ten legal commandments for nurses who get sued, Life 6(3):18-21, May-June 1986.
18. American Nurses' Association: Code for nurses with interpretive statements, pub no. G-56, Kansas City, Mo, 1985, The Association.
19. Sullivan A and Mills M: Policy considerations related to AIDS, JONA 20(1):12-17, 1990.
20. American Hospital Association: AHA Special Committee on AIDS/HIV infection: recommendations for healthcare practices and public policy, AHA catalog no. C-094691, Chicago, Ill, 1988, The Association.
21. Education and training centers for AIDS management, JONA, 19(4):15, 1989.
22. Fiesta J: You have the right to protect your civil rights, Nursing 86 16(9):57, Sept 1986.
23. McCloskey H and Grace H: Current issues in nursing, ed 2, Boston, 1985, Blackwell Scientific Publications, Inc.
24. Rabinow J: Avoiding legal rights in the SPU short procedure unit, Nurs Life 6(1):25, 1986.
25. Mitchell C: Code gray: ethical dilemmas in nursing, Nurs Life 6(1):19-23, 1986.
26. Creighton H: RN advocate and the law, Nurs Man 15(12):14, 16-17, 1984.
27. Haston L, clinical editor: Nurses' legal handbook, Springhouse, Pa, 1985, Springhouse Corp.

SUGGESTED READINGS

Brent N: The legalities of home care: confidentiality and HIV status: accidental exposure to patient blood and bodily fluids, Home Healthcare Nurse 8(4):5-6, 1990.

Brown P: How to state your case, Nurs Times 86(38):52-54, Sept 19, 1990.

Calfee B: Confidentiality and disclosure of medical information, Nurs Man 20(12):20-23, 1989.

Cohen A: The management rights clause in collective bargaining, Nurs Man 20(11):24-34, 1989.

Cook A: Comparable worth: an economic issue, Nurs Man 21(2):28-30, 1990.

Cushing M: Law and orders, Am J Nurs 90(5):29-32, 1990.

Feutz S: Do you need professional liability insurance? Nursing 91 21(1):56-57, 1991.

Fiesta J: Informed consent—whose legal duty? Nurs Man 22(1):17-18, 1991.

Johnson L: Preparing for a deposition, Nursing 90 20(7):44-47, 1990.

Johnson N and Wroblewski M: Litigation stress in nurses, Nurs Man 20(10):23-25, 1989.

Lacombe D: Avoiding a malpractice nightmare, Nursing 90 20(6):42-43, 1990.

Luquire R: Nursing risk management, Nurs Man 20(10):56-58, 1989.

Manthey M: What nurses value, Nurs Man 20(12):12-13, 1989.

Nokes K: Rethinking moral reasoning theory, Image 21(3):172-175, 1989.

Northrop C: How good samaritan laws do protect you, Nursing 90 20(2):50-51, 1990.

Quinley K: Twelve tips for defending yourself in a malpractice suit, Am J Nurs 90(1):37-40, 1990.

Reilly D: Ethics and values in nursing: are we opening Pandora's box? Nurs Health Care 10(2):91-95, 1990.

Supples J: "My colleague, my friend": the impaired nurse, Nurs Man 21(8):48I-48P, 1990.

Glossary

ability possession of skills, proficiency, or expertness; can accomplish a purpose

accountability liability for one's actions; willing to be judged against performance expectations; willing to live with the results of one's actions and be able to determine whether those results were successful and how they need change or modification

accreditation to supply with credentials or authority to function as a supplier of health services, occurring at municipal, state, and national levels

action the process of performing in a certain way; the behavior adopted by an individual as a result of a message sent, received, and perceived; putting thoughts into observable behaviors

advocate one who supports or defends someone or something and recommends or pleads on another's behalf

American Hospital Association (AHA) professional association made up of U.S. hospitals

American Nurses' Association (ANA) national professional association of registered nurses in the United States; founded in 1896

ancillary nursing personnel individuals who provide supportive nursing services to the registered nurse; may be nurses' aides, orderlies, nursing assistants, attendants, or practical/vocational nurses who provide such services as comfort, personal hygiene, and protection of patients

anthropology (cultural) study of effects of culture on human behavior

aptitude a natural or acquired talent or the degree of quickness in learning and understanding

assessment data collected from tangible and intangible elements that is classified, analyzed, placed in order of priority, and translated into a diagnosis or need

assistive nursing personnel (nurse aides, nurse assistants, orderlies, and attendants) perform designated nursing and support services for patients that do not require RN/LPN licensure

authority (formal) official or positional sanction to take actions to carry out managerial functions of the position held

authority (functional) the right to act derived from personal qualifications of the leader in professional competency, experience, technical expertise, and knowledge of managerial functions and human relations

authority (general) the power and right to take action; sanction to act

autonomy independence or freedom to make choices

behavior (aggressive) acting in a bold, attacking, and hostile manner, often accomplishing purposes at the expense of others with injurious and destructive results

behavior (assertive) maintaining a balance between passive and aggressive behavior; expressing positive and negative beliefs and reactions and needs openly without infringing on the rights of others

behavior (general) the actions or manner in which one responds to stimuli under specified circumstances

behavior (passive) submissively accepting any circumstance without resistance or complaint

behavior modification changes in the behavior of an individual that result from certain conditions or behavior control techniques

behavioral science approach incorporation of the sciences of psychology, sociology, and cultural anthropology

breach of contract failure to perform all or part of the contract without justification

budget a tool for planning, monitoring, and controlling cost; a systematic plan for meeting expenses

bureaucratic a technical and scientific hierarchical structure based on legalized, formal authority guided by rules and regulation, work specialization, appointment by merit, and an impersonal climate

centralization a hierarchical system with control emanating from the top down

characteristics (leader) personality traits or distinguishing features about a person

classification system (patient) a method of grouping patients according to the amount and complexity of their nursing care requirements

client individual, family, group, community, or agency who receives nursing services in any setting; person(s) dependent on the services of another or others; synonymous with patient

clinical nurse specialist (CNS) registered nurse with education and clinical practice beyond licensure in a specialty area; expands the scope of nursing practice by providing patient care with greater comprehensiveness, continuity, and coordination of patient services

cognitive the mental process of thinking, reasoning, feeling, and perceiving

common law the cumulative result of many court decisions over the years

common practice that which falls within both the definition of nursing and the legal scope of nursing practice

communication (grapevine) an informal communication system of social interaction focusing on personal and group interests

communication (grapevine, cluster chain) information communicated selectively according to interest in the subject

communication (grapevine, gossip chain) one person seeking out and giving everyone information indiscriminately

communication (grapevine, probability chain) information imparted to individuals at random

communication (grapevine, single chain) a system in which one person transmits a message to another, that person tells another, and so on

communication (interpersonal) the process of exchanging information and meaning from sender to receiver with the hope that the message sent will be received and understood as the sender intended

communication (organizational) the formal process by which managers use the established organizational channels to receive and relay information to people within the organization and to relevant individuals and groups outside it

community health nursing a synthesis of nursing practice and public health practice applied to promoting and preserving the health care of individuals, families and groups in a community

conflict (general) an inner or outer struggle about ideas, feelings, or actions

conflict (organizational) struggles relating to differences between management and staff, sharing of resources, interdependence of work activities in the organization, and values and goals among department and personnel regarding delivery of nursing care

contract an agreement between two or more parties that is written and enforceable by law

control the ongoing and continuous process through which managers assure that actual individual or group activities conform to plan; a check to make sure that what is done is what is intended

control process a system of establishing standards, objectives, and methods; measuring actual performance; comparing results of performance with standards and objectives; acting to reinforce strengths; taking corrective action as necessary

criminal law punishment stipulated for those who commit acts harmful to the public and individual

data processing assembles, sorts, stores, correlates, or otherwise processes and/or prints information derived from predetermined sources

decentralization a top-down management system in which each department is on a par with all other departments

decision making the process of developing a commitment to some course of action

decoding interpretation of messages for meaning

Diagnosis Related Group (DRG) a prospective reimbursement system whereby the most common diseases are placed in groups and a set fee is established for services rendered during hospitalization

direction issuance of assignments, orders, and instructions that permit individuals or group(s) to understand what is expected of them and the guidance and overseeing of workers so they can contribute effectively and efficiently to the attainment of organizational objectives

documentation preparation or assembly of written records

encoding translating a message into words, gestures, facial expression, and other symbols that will communicate the intended meaning to the receiver(s)

ethics beliefs about moral principles and standards governing the conduct of workers in a profession

expanded role expansion of the nurse role beyond the traditional limits of nurse practice acts; common roles are primary nurse and nurse practitioner, necessitating legal coverage through establishment of standardized procedures or amendments or changes in nurse practice acts

expert a person with a high degree of skill in or knowledge of a certain subject

express contract (written or oral) agreement between two or more people to do or not to do something

family persons who are related by blood or marriage; members of a household; a group of people with like interests

feedback a process whereby senders and receivers exchange information to clarify the meanings of the message sent

follower an individual or group who is willing to be led

functional nursing a centralized pattern or system of nursing care that is task and activity oriented

goal the purpose toward which an endeavor is directed; things an individual, group, or organization wishes or strives to achieve

Good Samaritan law protects the professional from liability for damages for alleged injuries or death after rendering first aid or emergency treatment in an emergency away from proper medical equipment, unless there is proved gross negligence

gross negligence flagrant disregard for duty; failure to act in a reasonable manner; reckless disregard of consequences

health agency (government) official bodies that provide health services to the public under the support and direction of the voting public

health agency (proprietary) an organization that operates for profit, serving people who can pay for services, directly or indirectly

health agency (voluntary) a nonprofit organization designed to meet religious, ethnic, economic, or special interest health needs of the public

health care system the resources (money, people, physical plant, and technology) and the organizational configurations necessary to transform these resources into health services

Health Maintenance Organization (HMO) an organized system providing a comprehensive range of health care to a voluntarily enrolled consumer population

hierarchy a body of persons or things organized or classified in pyramidal or vertical fashion according to work, capacity, or authority

home health care the provision of health services such as nursing, therapy, and health-related homemaker or social services in the patient's home

hospital an institution designed for the care of the sick and well; depending on agency goals, emphasis is on administering patient care, educating health agency personnel and the public, research, and protection of the health of the public

human relations approach to management a participative, democratic structure with concern for work effectiveness and human satisfaction

induction formal procedures an employee follows immediately after employment, such as getting on the payroll, learning about benefits, and completing records

influence (managerial) any attempt by an individual to change the behavior of others

injunction a court order prohibiting a party from a specific course of action

input any information fed into a communication system, such as thinking or reasoning, facts, theory, or instruction

intangible elements cognitive ability or knowledge to think and to problem solve; feelings, emotions, and attitudes

interpersonal relationships verbal or nonverbal communication or actions between two or more persons

intrapersonal inner thoughts and feelings

intuitive approach to decision making relies on personal perceptions, hunches, biases, and personal values

job descriptions a written account of roles, activities, and responsibilities expected of a staff member

law a rule or standard of human conduct established and enforced by authority, society, or custom

leader one who influences others toward goal achievement, either formally or informally, with power to enforce decisions as long as followers are willing to be led

leadership the ability to influence others to the attainment of goals

leadership (authoritarian) a closed system ranging from rigid to benevolent practice demonstrating a high concern for task accomplishment and low concern for people

leadership (democratic) a people-oriented approach to work, with participation and collaboration between manager and personnel

leadership (participative) an open, democratic environment with mutual responsibility to meet work-related goals

leadership (permissive) a general climate of ultra-liberalism or laissez-faire management with workers given free reign to function

leadership style the way in which an individual uses personal and interpersonal influences to achieve goals

liability legal responsibility for acts or failure to act according to standards, resulting in another person's harm

listening   to give heed to something through hearing and thought processes

magnet hospitals   urban, medium-to-large community hospitals or medical centers that have a reputation for higher rates of retention of nurses and for excellence in nursing practice

malpractice   improper or negligent treatment of a patient, resulting in damage or injury

management by objectives (MBO)   a system of management in which every person or group in a work setting has specific, attainable, and measurable objectives that are in harmony with those of the organization

management process   achievement of organizational objectives through planning, organizing, directing, and controlling human and physical resources and technology

manager   one who carries out predetermined policies, rules, and regulations with official sanction to act

manager, nurse (lower or first level)   one who has responsibility for administering direct nursing care to a small group of patients; common titles are team leader and primary care nurse

manager, nurse (middle level)   one who directs activities of other nurse managers that lead to implementation of the broad operating policies of the organization; common titles are supervisor and head nurse

manager, nurse (top level)   one who has broad and general responsibility for establishing overall policies and goals for the management of the organization; responsibility for all activities of the facility that require nursing services; common title is director of nursing services

mandatory licensure   stipulates that everyone who practices nursing for compensation must be licensed

Maslow's motivation theory   a study of human needs and their influence on behavior, based on the premise that people have physiologic, security, social, ego, and self-actualization needs, depending on their individuality

matrix system   a system using the benefits of both centralized and decentralized control

mentor   a trusted counselor and teacher

merger   incorporation of groups of hospitals, nursing home, psychiatric facilities, HMOs, and home care agencies into multiunit systems

message   a concept, fact, idea, or feeling transmitted by spoken or written words, signals, or other means from one person or group to another

modular nursing   a modification of team and primary nursing; a geographic assignment that encourages continuity of care by organizing a group of staff to work with a group of patients

motivation   an incentive, inducement, emotion, desire, physiologic need, or similar impulse providing desire to act

National Council of State Boards of Nursing (NCSBN)   comprised of membership from 59 boards of nursing; organized in 1978; chief function is to develop and evaluate licensing examinations for RNs and LPNs/LVNs

nurse (assistant)   see ancillary nursing personnel

nurse (associate degree)   a graduate of a community college nursing program who uses the nursing process to assess, plan, implement, and evaluate individualized nursing care and who is prepared to communicate with others, teach clients, manage within structured settings, and assume responsibility for professional activities and development

nurse (baccalaureate degree)   a graduate of a baccalaureate program in a senior college or university prepared as a generalist able to provide, within the health care system, comprehensive services that assess, promote, and maintain health of individuals and groups; accountable for own practice; can serve in leadership and managerial roles in a variety of hospital and community settings

nurse case management   the nurse assesses patient and family needs, establishes nursing diagnoses, develops nursing care plans, delegates nursing care to associates, activates interventions, coordinates and collaborates with interdisciplinary team, and evaluates outcomes prior to admission and through at least 2 weeks after discharge

nurse (diploma)   a graduate of a diploma program, sometimes affiliated with an associate degree program; skills equivalent to the associate degree nurse

nurse midwife   a nurse who follows the birthing process from inception through delivery

nurse (practical, LPN)   a nurse who is licensed to practice within the definition and roles specified by the nurse practice acts of the state(s) to which requirements have been met; sometimes called vocational nurse (LVN); accountable to registered nurses in employing agency

nurse practitioners (NP)   a select group of nurses who have special preparation beyond that required for nurse licensure in medical history taking, physical assessment, and patient management; also known as family nurse practitioner (FNP), obstetric-gynecologic nurse practitioner (OGNP), and psychiatric-mental health nurse practitioner (PNP)

nurse (registered, RN)   a nurse who is licensed to practice in one or more states within the definition and roles specified by the nurse practice acts of the states; may be a graduate of a diploma program, community college, or a baccalaureate program

objectives specific, measurable aims or purposes that address the questions of who, what, where, when, and why

Occupational Health Nurse (OHN) or Industrial Nurse a nurse who provides consultive services, assesses environmental hazards, conducts preemployment history and physical exams, provides health teaching, and is available to employees for their health needs

Omnibus Budget Reconciliation Act (OBRA) an annual process in which health care spending that is not controlled through the regular congressional appropriations process is brought into conformity with the annual budget resolution

organization an institution or functional group, such as a hospital or health department, that arranges and allocates the people and resources so that goals of that enterprise can be achieved

organizational chart a formal diagram in which each department, position, and function is outlined and the relationships between them shown

organizational structure a mechanism through which work is arranged and distributed among members of the organization so the goals of the organization can logically be achieved; the process by which a group is formed, its channels of authority, span of control, and lines of communication

organizing putting together people and resources in an orderly, systematic manner

orientation the formal process of apprising a new employee about the organization and the individual's place within the structure

patient the recipient of nursing care, including the prevention of illness or the promotion of care; individual, group, family, significant others, community, or agency that receives nursing services

pattern of nursing care that system used for the delivery of nursing care to patients, such as total, primary, functional, team nursing, and case management

peer review examining and evaluating, by associates, another nurse's practice

performance appraisal (formal) the process of regular and methodical collection of objective data through setting standards and objectives, reviewing progress, providing ongoing feedback; planning for reinforcement, deletion, or correction of identified behaviors as necessary

performance appraisal (informal) incidental observation and/or recording of work performance

permissive licensure nursing can be practiced without a license as long as the title "RN" is not used and licensure is not claimed

philosophy (nursing) an intentionally chosen set of values or purposes that serve as the basis for choosing the means to accomplish nursing objectives

philosophy (organizational) the sense of purpose and reasoning behind organizational structure and goals

plaintiff the party that institutes a suit in a court

planning (general) a continuous intellectual process of assessing, establishing goals and objectives, implementing, and evaluating, subject to change as new information is known; knowing what should be done and determining how to do it

planning (organizational) a continuous process of assessing, establishing goals and implementing and controlling them to ensure that decisions on the use of people, resources, and environment help achieve agency goals for the present and future

power the ability to perform effectively, exercise authority, and control through personal, organizational, and social strength

pragmatic approach to decision making deals with actual facts or occurrences using the problem-solving approach

Preferred Provider Organization (PPO) a health financing and delivery arrangement in which a group of health care providers (e.g., hospitals and physicians) offers its services on a predetermined financial basis to health care purchasers (e.g., employers of large numbers of people)

primary nursing a continuous and coordinated process in which a primary nurse provides the initial patient care assessment and assumes accountability for planning comprehensive, 24-hour care for individual patients for the length of hospitalization or duration of care needed; patient-oriented rather than physician-oriented care

priority actions established in order of importance or urgency to the welfare or purposes of the organization, patient, or other person at a given time

private or civil law determines one's relationship to other individuals, such as the nurse to the patient

Prospective Payment System (PPS) payment levels set on services before they are provided

public health services acts that are intended to maintain or improve health (e.g., communicable disease control, environmental health services, and personal health services)

public law determines an individual's relationship to federal government and the states

quality control examination of the actual process of providing care and the outcome of care for the protection of the public

recruitment the process of seeking nursing personnel to fill open job positions

reinforcement (negative) an unpleasant or punishing consequence that discourages repetition of a behavior

reinforcement (positive) a favorable consequence that encourages repetition of a behavior

respondeat superior   stipulates that an employer has legal responsibility for an employee's wrongful acts resulting in harm to a patient

responsibility   a trustworthy performance in caring for the welfare of patients and in working with others; a feeling of obligation to perform activities and assigned tasks efficiently

retrospective payment system   reimbursement for services already provided

risk management   protecting nursing practice by being aware of the standard of care expected from nursing by the state, the employing agency, and the courts

role   an organized set of behaviors that are attributed to a specific office or position

school nurse   supports the educational process by helping students maintain health and by teaching students and teachers preventive health practices

scientific approach to decision making   utilizes one's intelligence to consider the designs and possible courses of action to make an educated choice

scope   the breadth or opportunity to function; how far a manager can go in developing plans for self and others

scope of practice   the range of activities a nurse can perform as stipulated in each state's nurse practice act

sociology   study of group behavior in modern society

sovereign immunity   provides government employees with special legal protection—the government employee cannot be sued for on-the-job mistakes

span of management   the number of persons who report directly to the manager and the territory to be supervised

staffing   the process of assigning competent people to fill the nursing roles designed for the organizational structure through recruitment, selection, and placement of personnel

staffing (centralized)   a system whereby a master plan for staffing for all nursing personnel is developed at the top level

staffing (cyclical)   a system in which days for work and time off are regularly repeated for a designated number of week periods, such as 4, 6, and 12 weeks

statute of limitations   a law that specifies a limit on the number of years a person can seek damages from another

stressors   all things that create wear and tear on the body

system overload   inability to cope with messages and expectations from a number of sources that cannot be heard well, understood, or completed within the given time and according to established standards of quality.

tangible elements   things that can be seen or touched, such as buildings and grounds, equipment, rules, charts, and records

team nursing   a decentralized system of care in which a qualified RN leads a group of health care personnel in providing for the nursing needs of an individual or group of people through participative effort

third party payers   payment for health care services is received from a source such as private insurance, government programs, or charitable organizations rather than directly from the individual who received the care

tort law   a legal wrong independent of a contract liability action brought in civil court

total care   the assignment of one nurse to one patient for the provision of total nursing care

trait theory   focuses on personality traits or distinguishing features of an individual, such as intelligence, shyness, aggressiveness, ambition, or laziness

transactional analysis (TA)   a method of examining how people relate with others through the study of ego states of parent, child, and adult

transmitting   the channel used to communicate a message, either verbal or nonverbal

trust   confidence in the integrity, ability, or character of a person or thing

values   principles, standards, and qualities that are considered worthwhile, important, useful, or desirable

witness   one who has seen or heard something; one who furnishes evidence

Index

f indicates figure; *t* indicates table.

A

Ability, 4, 13
  definition of, 5
  relationship with authority and power, 5*f*
Accountability
  identification of, 131-142
  and malpractice, 245
  in staffing shortages, 254-255
Accreditation, 55
  of home health care, 42
  organizations for, 42-43
Action (communication), 156, 166
Adult nurse practitioners, 70
Advocacy, 253-254, 256
Aggressive behavior, 178, 179*t,* 180
AIDS
  ethical liability related to, 256
  policy considerations related to, 253
Alternative courses of action, development of, 119
Alternative solutions, generation of, 114, 122
American Association of Critical Care Nurses
      (AACCN), 68
American Association of Critical Nurses (AACN),
      67
American Association of Homes for the Aging
      (AAHA), accreditation by, 43
American Association of Occupational Health
      Nurses (AAOHN), 71
American Association of Operating Room Nurses
      (AAORN), 68
American College of Physicians (ACP),
      accreditation by, 43
American Hospital Association (AHA), 35, 55
  accreditation by, 43
  guidelines of, 35
  Patient's Bill of Rights of, 250, 252, 255
American Medical Association (AMA),
      accreditation by, 43
American Nurses' Association (ANA), 55
  accreditation by, 43
  certification program of, 66, 70
  Code of Ethics of, 245, 250, 251, 255
  quality control model of, 193-194
American Nursing Home Association (ANHA),
      accreditation by, 43
Appeal, upward, 4
Aptitudes, 217
Argyris, Chris, 51-52
Argyris structure, 51-52
Arizona model, 98
Assertive behavior, 3, 84, 178-179, 180
Assistive nursing personnel, 72, 75

Associate degree (AD), 65, 73
Attitudes, of followers, 30
Authoritarian leadership style, 20-21, 31
Authority, 13
  definition of, 4
  in functional nursing facility, 92*f*
  in organizational structures, 56
  and power, 4-6
  in primary nursing, 95*f*
  in team nursing system, 94*f*
  in typical total health care facility, 91*f*
Autocratic leaders, attitudes of, 20-21
Avoidance behavior, 175, 180

B

Bachelor of science in nursing (BSN), 65, 73
Behavior
  learned, 20
  power and, 4
Behavioral science
  applied to nursing management, 9-11, 13
  approach of to management, 9, 13
Behavioral styles, 18-20, 177-179, 180
  comparison of, 179*t*
Bennis, Warren, traits of successful leaders, 17, 18*f*
Blake, Robert, Managerial Grid of, 19-20
Blocking, 4
Breach of duty, 248
Breaks, coverage for, 136
Budget, 206
  centralized, 184
  decentralized, 184
  preparation of, 186-189
  projections of, 186-187
  standards and objectives of, 186
  types of, 184-186
Bureaucracy, 56
Bureaucratic management approach, 48
  compared with human relations approach, 54*t*
  rules and regulations in, 48-50
  specialization and division of labor in, 50
  view of conflict from, 179

C

Capital expenditure budget, 185
Case management system, 96-98
  direction in, 148
  identifying responsibility and accountability in,
      138-142

Case management system—cont'd
models of, 98, 100
monitoring systems in, 138-139
patient care monitoring in, 139-142
sample care plan form for, 140-142f
Case managers, and economic control, 186
Centralized budgeting, 184
Centralized organization, 45-46, 55-56
advantages of, 45
disadvantages of, 45-46
significance of organizational charts in, 46-48
Certification, 73
Certification programs, 66
Change process, 223, 235
attention to need for, 9
forces that influence, 223-224
identifying constraints on, 226
identifying forces for, 225
implementation plan for, 228
as planned procedure, 224
steps in, 224-229
strategies for, 226
Characteristic theory, 17-18
Charisma, 5
Chart audit worksheet, 196f
Chemers, Martin, 24
Civil rights protection, 253
Clinical nurses, 66
Clinical nurse specialist, 74
in magnet hospitals, 40
performance responsibilities for in middle
management, 84
role of, 67-68
Coach skill, 213
Coalitions, 4
Coercive power, 5, 6, 13
Collaboration, 180, 176-177
Collective bargaining, 50
College of Nurse-Midwifery, 71
Collyer, Margaret, on conflict resolution, 169
Commission on Graduates of Foreign Nursing
Schools (CGFNS), 63, 73
Common law, 239-240, 254
Common practice, 239-240
Communication
barriers to effective, 157-161, 166
physical, 157-158
social-psychologic, 158-159
and commonality of experiences, 156f
definition of, 151-152
downward, 162
effective, 166
flow control of, 163
goal of, 152
guidelines for effective, 153-157
horizontal, 162

Communication—cont'd
importance of, 152-153
informal, 161-162, 167
and information management, 164-166, 167
interpersonal, 152, 166
load, 163
management functions and, 162
model of, 153-157, 166
to motivate staff members, 152-153
need for clear and concise, 144-147
nurse-to-nurse, 145
organizational, 152
assessment of, 163-164
process of, 151-167
semantics and, 159-161
structure of in organizational chart, 130
supportive climate for, 166
types of, 152
upward, 162
Communication assessment questionnaire, 164f
Communication channels, 163
Communicator effectiveness, 163-164
Community health
costing out of services of, 188
growing complexity of, 97-98
need for expansion of services in, 68-69
nursing leadership in, 69
Community health nurse, 68-69, 74
Community health nursing, 40, 56
Community hospital mergers, 37, 55
Competition/power, 174-175, 180
Complexity, 107-110
sources of, 108f
Compromise, 175-176, 180
Computerized informational systems, 128
Computers
and future, 165-166
in information management, 164-166, 167
introducing nurses to, 164
nurse utilization of, 164-165
for self-learning programs, 234
Conceptual skill, 212
Conflict, 169
attitudes toward, 170
consequences of, 172-173, 180
definition of, 179
between health organizations, 171, 179
within health organizations, 171-172, 179
within individual, 170-171, 179
ineffective responses to, 173
with informal leadership, 3
kinds of, 170-172
management/staff, 171-172
methods of resolution of, 180
resolution model for, 176f
resolution of, 169-180

Conflict resolution styles, 173-177, 180
Consideration, 19
Consultive leadership, 22-23
Contracts, 249-250, 255
   analysis of, 49*f*
   breach of, 250
Control, 9
   basic steps in process of, 191*f*, 206
   and budgets, 184-189
   connotations of, 183
   nursing services system of, 189-192
   performance review session in, 203-204
   of problem employee, 204-206, 208
   process of, 183-184
   span of, 163
      factors influencing, 126-127
      narrow and wide, 127*f*
   of task analysis and quality, 192-202
   third-party, 183
Controlling leadership style, 21
Control process, 122
   results of, 121
Cooperation, lack of, 172
Coordination, interdepartmental, 130-131
Cost
   controls for, 183
   as issue in primary care nursing, 95
Costing out, 187-188, 206
Creighton, Helen, on proper documentation,
   245
Criminal law, 239
Criterion rating scale, 202
Critical care nurse (CCN), 67, 74
Culture
   in nursing management, 10-11
   and values, 11
Curtin, Leah, 66
   case management descriptions by, 100
   on clinical nurse specialist's role, 68
Cyclical staffing system, 88, 90*f*, 99

D

Davis, Keith
   on grapevine process, 161
   on leadership process, 2
Decentralized budgeting, 184
   model of, 187*f*
Decentralized organizational system, 45-46, 55-56
   advantages of, 46
   change in, 224-229
   disadvantages of, 46
   sample of organizational structure under, 47*f*
   significance of organizational charts in, 46-48
   in team nursing system, 93-94

Decision-making
   approaches to, 122
   complexity in, 107-110, 122
      source of, 108*f*
   emotional approach to, 112
   group, 52, 115-116, 122
   intangibles in, 108-109
   interdisciplinary input in, 109-110
   intuitive approach to, 111-112, 122
   long-term implications of, 109
   power and, 4
      for workers, 52
   pragmatic approach to, 112-115, 122
   process of, 107-116, 122
   risk and uncertainty in, 109
      strategy for under, 109*t*
   scientific approach to, 110-111, 122
   styles of, 110-115
   uncertainty in, 110
   value judgments in, 110
   variables in, 107-110, 122
Decoding, 155-156, 166
Defamation of character, 253
Defensiveness, 159
Delegation, 147-148
   barriers to, 128-129, 148
   effective, 148
   as foundation of organization, 131
   of roles and tasks, 135
   significance of process of, 128-129
Democratic leadership style, 32
Departmentalization, 50
Development, *see also* Training
   definition of, 211
   nurse populations in need of, 214-215
Developmental tasks, 218, 219
Diagnosis-related groups (DRGs), 38-39, 55
   in cost control, 183
Diagnostic skill, 212
Direction, 9
   challenges in, 128
   clear and concise, 144-147
   definition of, 125, 147
   versus dictatorship, 131
   formal, 144-147
   four types of, 129
   informal, 147
   in nursing systems, 148
   preparation for, 148
   responsibilities of, 129-149
Direction-giving conference, 148
   behavioral objectives for, 145-147
Directive leadership style, 21
Discipline policy, progressive, 205-206, 208
Documentation
   need for, 245

Documentation—cont'd
    for someone else, 246
Drucker, Peter, on MBO concept, 116

E

Education, 63-65
    continuing, 215
    for managerial skills, 213
Emergency
    explaining of procedures for, 144
    nurses' responsibility in, 248
Employees, control of, 204-206
Employment procedures, 80-82
Encoding, 154-155, 166
Environmental barriers, 157-158, 166
Equal Employment Opportunity Commission,
        performance appraisal guidelines of, 200
Ethical issues, 250-256
    and values, 11
Ethics committees, 250-251
Evaluation, 122
    results of, 121
Exchange, 3
Experience, of managerial skills, 211-214
Expert power, 5, 13
Expert witness, 247-248, 255
    qualifications of, 247
    responsibilities of, 247
Express contract, 249-250

F

Family nurse practitioners, 70
Fayol, Henri, on bureaucracy, 48
Feedback, 156-157, 166
    targeting of, 157
    timing of, 157
Fiedler, Fred, 24
    on situational leadership, 30-31
Fight or flight response, 179
Financial control system, 184
Follett, Mary Parker, 51
Follett studies, 51
Followers
    attitudes and needs of, 30
    characteristics and expectations of, 29-30
    knowledge, competency and level of, 29
Followership styles, 23-24
Foreign nurses, 73
Formal leadership, 3, 12
Frew, David, on leadership and followership styles,
        23-24
Full-time equivalent positions (FTEs), 185-186

Functional nursing, 91-92, 99
    direction in, 148
    identifying responsibility and accountability in,
        131-133

G

Geriatric nurse practitioners, 70
Goals, 122
    achievement of, 10, 206
        by MBO, 119
    differences in, 172
    of management levels, 117-118t
    versus objectives, 116
Good Samaritan laws, 249, 255
Government-owned health agencies, 35-36
Grapevine, 167
    utilization of, 161-162
"Great man" theory, 17
Group
    cohesiveness of, 223
    development of, 222
    member roles in, 222-223
    norms of, 235
        and conformity in, 222
    status in, 222
Group decision making, 52, 115-117, 122
    power of, 115-116
Group dynamics, in training and development
        programs, 221-223
Grove, Andres, on delegation, 128

H

Hawthorne studies, 51
Health care, values and assumptions underlying, 11
Health care agencies, see Health care institutions;
        specific institutions
Health Care Financing Administration (HCFA), 38
Health care institutions, 35
    conflict between and within, 170-172, 179
    examples of, 36-37t
    goals of, 35
    government-owned, 35-36
    proprietary, 36
    purpose of, 55
    types of, 35-36, 55
    values of, 10-11
    voluntary, 36
Health care reimbursement systems, 37-39
Health maintenance organizations, 55
    establishment of, 68
    nursing case management in, 97
    payment system of, 39

Health Nurse Specialist, 40-41
Herrick, Kathleen, on information management, 165
Hersey and Blanchard's situational leadership, 24, 29*t*
Hierarchy, 44
HMO model, 98
HMOs, *see* Health maintenance organizations
Holistic approach, 129
Home health care agencies, 56
Home health care nurse/visiting nurse, 69-70, 74
Home health care/visiting nurse services
    organization of, 42, 56
    origin of, 41
    services provided by, 41-42
Hospital personnel contracts, organizational structure and, 49*f*
Hospitals
    costing out services of, 187-189
    history of, 35
    magnet, 39-40, 55
    types of organization in, 35-36
    typical organizational chart of, 44-45
Human needs, Maslow's hierarchy of, 9, 52, 53*f*
Human relations approach, 50-51
    advantages of, 52
    compared with bureaucratic approach, 54*t*
    limitations of, 52-54
    view of conflict from, 179
Human relations movement, 56
Human skill, 212
Hygienic care, assignment of, 131-132

I

Impersonality, 50
Implied contract, 250
Incidental requests, protocol for, 143-144
Influence
    action of, 3-4
    communication and, 153
    definition of, 3, 12-13
    managerial, 4
    tactics, 3-4
Informal communication, 161, 167
    process of, 161
    utilization of, 161-162
Informal leadership, 3, 12
Information
    accessibility of, 163
    management, 164, 167
        computers and future of, 165-166
        nurse utilization of computers in, 164-165
Information-processing styles, 107
Information sender/receiver, 153, 166

Ingratiation, 3
Initiating structure, 19
Insincerity, 159
Institute of Medicine public health study, 69
Insurance-based model, 98
Insurance companies, and case management systems, 98
Interpersonal communication, 152, 166
Interpersonal relationships, 9-11, 13
    in management role, 11
Interpretation, meaning, 166
Intrapersonal conflict, 170-171
Intuition, 111-112

J

JCAHO, 55
    accreditation by, 42-43
    quality assurance mandate of, 195
Job descriptions, 83, 98
Job satisfaction, and positive communication, 167
Judgment, suspension of, 160

K

Kennedy, John F., on consumer rights, 250

L

Labor, division of
    in bureaucratic management, 50
    vertical, 51
Laissez-faire managers, 21-22
Law
    definition of, 239, 254
    importance of to nurse, 238-239
    in practice of nursing, 239-240
Lawsuits, 248-249
    avoidance of, 245, 255
    common causes of against nurses, 243
Leader(s)
    availability of to staff members, 143
    characteristics of, 17-18
    common traits of successful, 18*f*
    conflict and, 173
    definition of, 12
    effective, 2-3
    names of, 2
    nurse as, 6
    similarities and differences between managers and, 6, 7*f*, *see also* Manager(s)
Leader-follower relationships, 30

Leadership, *see also* Management
  definition of, 2
  dynamics of, 3f, 12
  informal and formal, 3
  lack of preparation for, 1-2
  process of, 2-3
  styles of, *see* Leadership styles
Leadership and Followership Style test, 23, 24, 25-28t
Leadership skills, needed for nursing practice, 212f
Leadership styles, 16
  authoritarian, 20-21
  comparison of, 23-24
  and conflict resolution, 174f, 180
  democratic, participative, or consultive, 22-23
  flexibility of managers to use, 31
  permissive, ultraliberal, or laissez- faire, 21-22
  theory of, 18-20
  types of, 31-32
  and work situation, 30-31
Learned behavior, 20
Learner
  adult as, 220-221
  receptiveness of, 217
Learning
  factors influencing capacity for, 217-219
  patterns of, 219-220, 235
  process of, 217-221, 235
  and stage of life, 218, 235
Learning curve, 220f
Legal issues, 238-243, 254-255
Legitimate power, 5, 6, 13
Length of stay (LOS), in cost control, 183
Liability, 239
  for short-staffing situations, 244
Licensed practical nurses (LPNs), 74-75
  role of, 72
  supply of, 63
Licensed vocational nurses (LVNs), 72, 74-75
Licensure, 61-62, 73, 240, 254
  foreign, 63
  mandatory, 240
  renewal of, 240
  requirements for, 240
Likert, Rensis, 52
Likert studies, 52
Lincoln, Abraham, 17
Listening, 160
  with eyes, 161
  between lines, 160-161
  skills of, 166-167
LPN/LVN programs, 72, 75
  graduates from, 63
  technical, 72
Lumbertson, Elanor, on team nursing, 93
Lundborg, Louis, on qualities of leaders, 17

M

Magnet hospitals, 39-40, 55
Malpractice, 254
  definition of, 239
Malpractice insurance, 244-247, 255
  employer coverage in, 244
  nurse coverage in, 244
  and proper documentation, 245
  statue of limitations in, 244
  transcribing order in, 245-246
Management, *see also* Leadership
  behavioral science approach to, 9
  and communication, 162
  comparison of with leadership, 6, 7f
  definitions of, 6
  human relations approach to, 50-54
  interdependent relationships in role of, 11
  lack of preparation for, 1-2
  nurse in, 6
  organizational structure and functions of, 7-8
  process of, 6-7, 13
    in nursing, 8-9
  by situation, 24-28
  span of, 44, 126-128, 147
Management by objectives (MBO), 122
  guidelines for, 116-117
  introduction of, 199
  in nursing management, 117-119
  process of, 116
Management control process, 147
Management skills, 234
  acquisition of, 213-214
  needed by staff nurses, 211-213
Management style, 32, *see also* Leadership styles
  and conflict resolution, 169-170
Manager(s)
  authoritarian, 21
  barriers to delegation by, 128-129
  decision-making process of, 110-111
  definition of, 12
  effective, 2-3
  flexibility of to use leadership styles, 31
  leadership style and expectations of, 28-29
  levels and types of, 8, 13
  nurse as, 6
  planning function of, 104-107, 121
  in planning process, 121-122
  preparation of budget by, 187-189
  role of in quality control, 207
  sample behaviors of, 19f
  similarities and differences between leaders and, 6, 7f, *see also* Leader(s)
Managerial Grid, 19-20, 31
Managerial influence, 4, 13

Manthey, Marie
  LPN/LVN program and, 72
  professional mind-set, 178-179
Maslow, Abraham, 52
Maslow's theory, 9, 52, 53f
Master of science in nursing (MSN), 73
Matrix organizational structure, 45-48, 52
  advantages and disadvantages of, 46
  organizational structure using, 48f
May-Hawthorne studies, 51
Mayo, Elton, 51
McCullough, Sandra, on information management, 165
McGregor, Douglas
  on autocratic attitudes, 20-21
  human relations studies of, 51
  Theory Y personality of, 116
Medical Practice Act, 193
Mentor relationships, 214
Mentor skill, 213
Merger, process of, 38t, 55
Merging organizations, 37
Merit appointments, 50
Message, 153-154, 166
  clarity of, 163
  interpretation of, 159
Mission, 10-11
Mistakes, honest, 246
Modular nursing, 96, 99
  direction in, 148
  identifying responsibility and accountability in, 138
Monitoring systems, in case management, 138-142
Motivation
  through communication, 152-153
  Follett's concept of, 51
  and satisfaction and productivity, 9-10
Mouton, Jane, Managerial Grid of, 19-20

N

National Association of Pediatric Nurse Associates and Practitioners, 70
National League for Nursing, on patients' rights, 250
Needs
  of followers, 30
  of managers, 28-29
  of patient/client, 130
Nightingale, Florence
  characteristics of, 17
  as leader, 2
Noise, 158
Nonprofit agencies, *see* Voluntary health agencies

Nornhold, Patricia, on computers in health care, 165
North Eastern model, 98
Nurse(s)
  community health, 68-69
  community health/public health, 69
  contracts for, 249-250, 255
  critical care, 67
  employment procedures for, 80-82
  expectations of, 61t
  foreign, 63, 73
  graduating seniors' priorities of, 79
  guidelines for suits against, 248-249
  home health care/visiting, 69-70
  as leader and manager, 2-3, 6
  liability of for short-staffing situations, 244
  licensure of, 61-63, 240, 254
  malpractice insurance for, 244-247
  number of, 73
  occupational health, 71
  operating room, 68
  recruitment of, 80
  responsibilities of, 98-99
    in emergency, 248
  role of, 61
    variety of, 67-73
  salaries for, 79-80, 98
  school, 71
  self-protection and risk management for, 243-244
  shortage of, 62-63, 78-79
  staff, 67
  supply of, 62-63, 78-79, 98
  as teachers, 217, 235
  turnover of, 79, 98
  as witness, 247-248, 255
Nurse assistant (NA), 75
  need for, 72-73
Nurse case manager, 66, 71-72, 74
Nurse clinician, role of, 67-68
Nurse examiners board, 254
  disciplinary procedures of, 242-243
  membership of, 242
  responsibilities of, 242
Nurse internship, 230-232
Nurse licensure, 61-62, 240, 254
  foreign, 63
Nurse manager(s)
  communication of to motivate staff members, 152-153
  effective, 2-3
  merger and, 37
  responsibilities of, 8t
    for performance appraisal, 196
  role of, 61
  time spent in communication, 152
  types of communication by, 152

Nurse midwife, 70-71, 74
Nurse-patient ratio, 132-133
Nurse Practice Act, 193
  advanced or expanded nursing practice under,
    241-242
  composition and control in, 240-241
  control under one board, 241
Nurse practitioner (NP), 74
  role of, 70
Nurse registry, 98
Nurse specialists, 66
Nurse Training Act, 67-68
Nursing, *see also* Nursing practice
  community health, 40
  as decision-making process, 1
  leadership and management in, 1-13
  technical and professional levels of, 73
Nursing assignments, 148
Nursing behaviors, performance of, 232t
Nursing care delivery systems, 78, 88, 99-100, *see
    also* Nursing practice
  advantages and disadvantages of different types,
    96t
  functional nursing, 91-92
  modular nursing, 96
  need for effective contemporary, 88-91
  nursing case management, 96-98
  planning for, 119-121
  primary nursing, 94-96
  team nursing, 92-94
  total care nursing, 91
Nursing care hours (NCH), in cost control, 183
Nursing care plans, 122
  in direction giving, 130
Nursing case management, 99
  delivery system in, 96-98
  models of, 98, 100
  organizational structure of, 97
  origin of, 96
  preparation for, 100
Nursing education, 63-65
  programs in U.S., 64t
  upswing in enrollment in, 65
Nursing homes, costing out of services of, 188
Nursing law, 239
Nursing leadership, *see also* Leadership
  in community health nursing, 69
  definition of, 2
Nursing management, *see also* Management
  behavioral science approach to, 9-11, 13
  definition of, 6
  framework for, 12f, 13
  interrelationships in, 13
  in magnet hospitals, 40
  process of, 8-9
  seven roles in, 62t

Nursing personnel, *see also* Nurse(s)
  assistive, 72
  induction and orientation of, 82
  need for variety and development of, 143
  number of needed to staff unit, 85t
  responsibility for selection of, 81-82
  roles of, 60-75
Nursing practice
  arenas of, 66
  changes in environment of, 66-67
  ethical dilemmas in, 253-254, 256
  expanding scope of, 74
  law in, 239-240
  legal issues in, 254
  risk management in, 243-244
  roles of, 60-61
  technical versus professional, 65-66
Nursing schools
  enrollment in, 65
  number and types of, 63-65
Nursing services
  costing out of, 187-189, 206
  mission, 10-11
Nursing services control system, 189
  corrective action in, 192
  establishing methods for measuring performance
    in, 191
  establishing standards for measuring performance
    in, 189-191
  measuring performance in, 191-192
  well-designed, 183-184, 206

O

Objectives, 122
  formulation of, 129-130
  versus goals, 116
  of management levels, 117-118t
Obstetric-gynecologic nurse practitioners, 70
Occupational health nurse (OHN), 71, 74
Ohio State leadership studies, 18-19, 31
Omnibus Budget Reconciliation Act (OBRA), 39,
    55, 188
Openness, 159
Operating budget, 185
Operating room nurse (ORN), 68, 74
Organization, 9
  definition of, 43
  descriptions of power in, 5-6
  formal vs. informal, 56
  objectives of, 6-7
  strength of, 43
Organizational chart, 44
  significance of in different organizational forms,
    46-48

Organizational chart—cont'd
  of typical hospital, 44-45
Organizational communication, 152
  assessment of, 163-164
  components of, 163f
  forms of, 167
Organizational conflict, 179
  consequences of, 180
  sources of, 171-172
Organizational design, 48-54, 56
  bureaucratic vs. human relations approaches in, 54t
Organizational structure
  of accreditation, 42-43
  adoption of appropriate form of, 54
  centralization, decentralization, and matrix, 45-48
  in community health nursing, 40
  and community hospital mergers, 37
  decentralized, 47f
  definition of, 7, 43-45
  designs of, 48-50
  formal and informal, 35
  forms of, 55-56
  and goal achievement, 10
  of health care institutions and hospitals, 35-36
  health care reimbursement systems and, 37-39
  in home health care/visiting nurse services, 41-42
  and hospital personnel contracts, 49f
  and interrelationships in, 13
  in magnet hospitals, 39-40
  and management functions, 7-8
  in nursing case management system, 97f
  public health, 40-41
  in team nursing, 93
Orientation program, 229-230
Outcome standards and criteria, 194

P

Participative leadership, 22-23, 32
Participatory management approach, 50-54
Participatory organizational structure, 45
Passive behavior, 178, 179t, 180
Patient's Bill of Rights, 250, 252, 255
Patient care
  assessment of priority of, 133-135
  plan for, 120f
  safe, continuous, 142-143
Patient care assignments, 133-136
  in primary care, 136-138
  sample sheet for, 137f
Patient classification systems, 85-86, 185
  by computer, 86

Patient classification systems—cont'd
  disadvantages of, 86
Patients
  assignment of, 133-136, 137f
    worksheet for, 148
  needs of
    determination of, 148
    first priority to, 130
  rights of, 250, 255
Payment systems, see Reimbursement systems
Pediatric nurse practitioners, 70
Peer review, 194-195
Performance
  establishment of standards of, 189-191
  and leadership style, 32
  evaluation of, 9
  measurement of, 191-192
    methods of, 207
Performance appraisal, 195-196, 207
  checklist for, 201-202
  components of effects system, 200-201
  criterion rating scale for, 202
  formal, 201
  history of, 196, 199-200
  informal, 201
  methods for measuring of, 201-202
  nurse manager's role in, 196
  Supreme Court and, 199-200
Performance goals, 52
Performance responsibilities, 83, 98-99
  for clinical nurse specialist, 84
  for primary care nurses, 83-84
Performance review session, 207-208
  process of, 203-204
  purpose of, 203
Permissive leadership style, 21-22, 31-32
Personal goals, achievement of, 51
Personal health services, 40
Personality traits, 31
  focus on, 17
Personal power, achievement of, 32
Personnel, nursing, 60-75
Personnel budget, 185
  case managers and economic control in, 186
  classification system in, 185
  full-time equivalent positions in, 185-186
Personnel review session, 203-204, 207-208
Philosophy, 10-11
Physical support systems, 128, 147
Physicians orders
  in person or over phone, 246
  questionable, 246
  transcription of, 245-246
Plan
  evaluation or controlling of, 121, 122
  implementation of, 119-121

Planning
    continuous process of, 105f
    definition of, 104, 121
    by lower-level managers, 105-107
    by middle-level managers, 105
    nursing care, 119-121
    process of, 8-9, 121
    reasons for, 106, 121
    scope of, 104-107, 121
        for nurse managers, 107f
    by top-level managers, 105
Power, 13
    and authority, 4-6
    basis of, 5-6
    communication and, 153
    and competition, 174-175
    definition of, 4
    effects of on behavior, 4-5
    effects of on decisions, 4
    effects of on situations, 5
    forms of, 13
    partial or informal relationships, 45
    relationships with authority and ability, 5f
    types of, 5-6
Power position, 30-31
Preceptor, 214
    matching of, 214
Preceptor workshop, 232-233
Preferred Provider Organizations (PPOs), 39, 55
    nursing case management in, 97
Primary care nurse, typical performance
        responsiblities for, 83-84
Primary nursing, 94-95, 99
    advantages and disadvantages of, 95-96
    direction in, 148
    identifying responsibility and accountability in,
        136-138
    lines of authority in, 95
Problem, identification of, 112-114
Problem employee, control of, 204-206, 208
Problem solving, pragmatic approach to, 112-115
Productivity
    and change, 224
    and leadership characteristics, 51
Professional case management, 99
Professional certification, 66
Professional nurse case manager (PNCM), 71-72,
        74
    role and responsibilities of, 97
Professional Standards Review Organizations,
        193
Progressive discipline policy, 205-206, 208
Proprietary health agencies, 35
    examples of, 37f
Prospective Payment System (PPS), 38-39, 55, 74
    and community health nursing, 74

Prospective Payment System (PPS)—cont'd
    implementation of, 68-69
Psychological testing, 17
Public health nurse (PHN), 69, 74
Public health nursing, 40
Public Health Nursing, Director of, 40
Public health services, 40, 56
    organizational structure of, 40-41
Public law, 239

Q

Quality assurance, 127-128
    evolution of, 193
    guidelines for, 197-199f
    problem-focused program of, 195
Quality control, 147-149, 192-195, 206-207
    accountability for, 207
    in primary nursing, 95
Quality of working life, 224

R

Rationality, 3, 4
Records, falsification of, 246-247
Recruitment strategies, 80
Referent power, 5-6, 13
Registered nurses (RNs)
    in magnet hospitals, 40
    number of, 73
    scope of practice of, 66-73
    work priorities of, 79
Registry nurses, 81
Reimbursement systems, 37-39, 55
    adaptations to, 39
Relationships, interpersonal, 9-11
Reports
    need for clarity in, 144
    taping of, 144-145
Resources, for self-learning programs, 233-234
Responsibility
    guidelines for implementation of, 129-149
    identification of, 131-142
Retrospective payment systems, 38, 55
Reward power, 5, 6, 13
Risk management, 243-244, 254
Rogers, Martha, 67
Role
    ambiguity, 217
    characteristics of, 61, 73
    clarification of, in training and development
        programs, 215-221
    conception of, 217
    congruence, 217

Role—cont'd
    expectation of, 216-217
    significant factors in, 215-217

S

Salaries, 98
    for experienced nurses, 79-80
    for new graduates, 80
Sanctions, 3
Scheduling, 86, 99
    in advance, 87-88
    centralized versus decentralized, 86-87, 99
    cyclical, 88, 90f, 99
    traditional, 99
Schmidt, Warren, 24
School nurse, 71, 74
Scope of practice, 239
Self, wise and systematic use of, 16
Self-learning programs, 233-234, 235
Selye, Hans, on stress, 171, 179
Semantics, 159-161, 166
Sender/receiver (communications), 153, 166
Sensory overload, 159-160
Shaw, Malcolm, on performance, 84
Shift reports, 144-145
Simon, Herbert, on manager's decision process, 110
Situational leadership, 24-31
Skilled/intermediate care facilities, costing out of services of, 188-189
Skills
    needed by staff nurse, 211-213
    ways to acquire, 213-214
Smoothing behavior, 175, 180
Social factors, values and, 11
Social man concept, 51
Social-psychological barriers, 158-159, 166
Social Security Act
    Amendments of, 39
        mandating Professional Standards Review Organizations by, 193
    Title XVIII of, 41
Solutions
    evaluation of results of, 114-115
    generation of alternative, 114
    implementation of, 114
    selection of, 114
Sovereign immunity doctrine, 249, 255
Specialization, in bureaucratic management, 50
Staff
    mix of, 86
    training and development of, 210-235
Staff development programs, 229-234, 235
Staffing patterns, methods of, 89t

Staffing process, 78
    criteria important to, 83-84
    data collection in, 84-85
    employment procedures in, 80-82
    patient classification systems in, 85-86
    and performance, 98
    recruiting in, 98
    responsibilities and, 98-99
    scheduling in, 86-88
    staff mix in, 86
Staffing systems, 99
Staff nurse, 67, 74
    management skills needed by, 211-213
    training and development of, 215
Staff orientation program, 229-230
Standards, 194
State-based medical model, 98
Statutory law, 239
Statute of limitations, 244, 255
Stogdill, R., on leadership characteristics, 17
Stressors, 171
Stress responses, 171, 179
Structures, formal and informal, 35
Support services
    coordination and efficiency among, 130-131
    physical, 128, 147
System overload, 158

T

Tannenbaum, Robert, 24
Task accomplishment, 30
Task analysis, 192, 206
    quality control and, 192-195
Taylor, Frederick, on bureaucracy, 48
Teaching process, 217-219, 235
Team building, 223, 235
Team nursing, 92-93, 99
    advantages and disadvantages of, 93-94
    behavioral objectives in, 133-136
    direction in, 148
    identifying responsibility and accountability in, 133-136
    lines of authority in, 94f
Technical skills, 211-212
Theory Y, 51
    personality of, 116
Third-party control, impact of on nursing, 183, 206
Toffler, Alvin, on information management, 164
Tort law, 239, 254
Total care nursing, 91, 99
Training
    definition of, 211
    function of, 211

Training—cont'd
    importance of, 210-211
    of new employee, 215
    of new graduates, 214-215
    nurse populations in need of, 214-215
    of staff nurses, 215
Training programs
    group dynamics in, 221-223
    role clarification in, 215-221
Trait theory, 17
Transmitting (communication), 155, 166
Tri Council, 73
Trust, 143
    barriers to, 158
    lack of, 158-159, 166

U

Ultraliberal leadership style, 21-22
Unionization, 50
Union-management relations, 50
Upward appeal, 4

V

Value judgments, 110
Values, 11
    in American culture, 11
    differences in, 172
    identification of, 193
    in nursing management, 10-11

Verbal communication, 159-160, *see also*
        Communication
' .siting nurse, 69-70, 74
    services of, 41-42
    societies of, 41, 70
Visiting nurse associations (VNAs), 70
Voluntary health agencies, 36, 55
    examples of, 37*t*

W

Wadia, Maneck, on management, 9.
Wagner Act, 50
Walking rounds, nurse-to-nurse communication
        during, 145
Weber, Max, on bureaucracy, 48, 50
Wills, nurse's responsibility for, 251-253, 255-256
Witness, expert, 247-248, 255
Workers, *see also* Nursing personnel; Staff
    decision-making power of, 52
    factors influencing number of, 126-127
    human relations and, 50-51
    knowledge, competency, and level of, 29
Work group
    definition of, 222
    and organization goals, 235
    purpose of, 222
    size and mix of, 126-128
Work interdependence, 172
Work priorities, 79
Work situation, 30-31